W9-BEZ-765

Observation and Participation in Early Childhood Settings

 A Practicum Guide

SECOND EDITION

Jean Billman
Winona State University

Janice Sherman
Winona State University

Allyn and Bacon

Boston   New York   San Francisco
Mexico City   Montreal   Toronto   London   Madrid   Munich   Paris
Hong Kong   Singapore   Tokyo   Cape Town   Sydney

Editor-in-Chief, Education: Paul A. Smith
Series Editor: Traci Mueller
Editorial Assistant: Erica Tromblay
Marketing Manager: Elizabeth Fogarty
Editorial Production Administrator: Anna Socrates
Editorial Production Service: Matrix Productions
Text Design/Electronic Composition: Denise Hoffman
Composition and Prepress Buyer: Linda Cox
Manufacturing Buyer: Chris Marson
Cover Administrator: Kristina Mose-Libon

For related titles and support materials, visit our online catalog at
www.ablongman.com.

Copyright © 2003, 1996 Pearson Education, Inc.

All rights reserved. No part of the material protected by this copyright notice may
be reproduced or utilized in any form or by any means, electronic or mechanical,
including photocopying, recording, or by any information storage and retrieval
system, without written permission from the copyright owner.

To obtain permission(s) to use material from this work, please submit a written
request to Allyn and Bacon, Permissions Department, 75 Arlington Street, Boston, MA
02116 or fax your request to 617-848-7320.

Between the time Website information is gathered and then published, it is not
unusual for some sites to have closed. Also, the transcription of URLs can result in
unintended typographical errors. The publisher would appreciate notification where
these errors occur so that they may be corrected in subsequent editions.

Library of Congress Cataloging-in-Publication Data

Billman, Jean.
    Observation and participation in early childhood settings : a practicum guide /
Jean Billman, Janice Sherman. — 2nd ed.
        p. cm.
    Includes bibliographical references and index.
    ISBN 0–205–37555–3
        1. Early childhood education. 2. Early childhood teachers—Training of.
    3. Observation (Educational method) 4. Child development. I. Sherman,
Janice A. II. Title.
    LB1139.23.B552 2003
    372.21—dc21

                                                                    2002020545

Printed in the United States of America

10 9 8 7 6 5 4 3 2 1   08 07 06 04 03 02

To our children and grandchildren,
from whom we continue to learn

Contents

Preface   xv

◆ **Chapter 1**
**The Role of Observation and Participation
in Early Childhood Education**   **1**

Observing Young Children   1

What Is Observation?   1

Purposes of Observation   4

Observation and Children's Privacy   7

How to Do Observations in Early Childhood Settings   7

Observation as a Major Part of the Assessment Process   9

Participation in Early Childhood Settings   10

The Need for Field Experience as a Part of Early Childhood
Teacher Education   10

Tips for Practicum Students and Student Teachers   11

Summary   13

References   14

◆ **Chapter 2**
**Methods for Recording Observations
of Young Children's Behavior**   **15**

Keeping a Reflective Diary/Journal/Log   16

ACTIVITY 2.1   Keeping a Reflective Diary   20

Audio Recording   20

Videotaping   21

ACTIVITY 2.2   Videotaping   22

Anecdotal Records   22

Sociometric Techniques   24

Event Sampling   25

ACTIVITY 2.3   Event Sampling   28

Running Record   28

ACTIVITY 2.4   Running Record   32

Rating Scales   32

Checklists   **34**

    ACTIVITY 2.5   Making a Checklist   36

Case Studies   **37**

Child Studies   **39**

Portfolios   **42**

    ACTIVITY 2.6   Choosing an Observation Method   45

Summary   **46**

References   **46**

◆ **Chapter 3**
Caring for Infants and Observing Them
in Home and Group-Care Settings   **49**

The Prenatal Experience   **50**

    ACTIVITY 3.1   Maternal Behaviors that Affect
                Prenatal Development   51

    ACTIVITY 3.2   Paternal Behaviors that Affect
                Prenatal Development   52

    ACTIVITY 3.3   Fetal Monitoring Procedures   52

The Birthing Experience   **52**

    ACTIVITY 3.4   Prepared Childbirth Methods   53

    ACTIVITY 3.5   Alternative Childbirth and Care Arrangements   54

The Newborn   **54**

    ACTIVITY 3.6   Assessing a Newborn (Part 1)   54

    ACTIVITY 3.7   Assessing a Newborn (Part 2)   54

At-Risk Infants   **56**

    ACTIVITY 3.8   Neonatal Intensive Care Units (NICU)   58

Development of Infants   **58**

   Physical Development   58

   Brain Development   59

   Cognitive Development   60

   Language Development   61

   Socioemotional Development   62

    ACTIVITY 3.9   Observation of an Infant under One Year   62

Out-of-Home Care   **63**

   The Controversy over Infant Care   64

    ACTIVITY 3.10   Pros and Cons of Infant Day Care   64

   Caring for Infants from Birth to Sixteen Months   65

The Physical and Social Environment of Infant Programs   65

    ACTIVITY 3.11   Evaluate the Environment in an Infant Program   66

    ACTIVITY 3.12   Design an Environment for Infant Care   67

    ACTIVITY 3.13   Keeping a Journal about Infants   67

Common Health Problems of Infants and Toddlers   67

Infants and Toddlers with Special Needs   68

Cultural Differences in Infant and Toddler Programs   69

Staff Development for Infant Caregivers   70

    ACTIVITY 3.14   Inservice Training   70

Summary   71

References   72

◆ **Chapter 4**
Exploring the World of Toddlers   75

Toddler Development   75

Physical Development—Gross Motor   76

Physical Development—Fine Motor   76

Cognitive Development   76

Language Development   77

Socioemotional Development   78

Toddler Play   80

Preparation of Teachers for Toddlers   81

Helping Toddlers Learn Appropriate Behaviors   82

Parent-Teacher Relations in Toddler Programs   83

    ACTIVITY 4.1   Critiquing a Parenting Book   84

Observing Toddlers in Home and Child-Care Settings   84

Observing a Toddler at Home   84

    ACTIVITY 4.2   Observations in the Toddler's Home   85

    ACTIVITY 4.3   Toddler Play Materials   86

    ACTIVITY 4.4   Toddlers' Fears   87

Observing a Toddler in a Family Day-Care Home   87

    ACTIVITY 4.5   Toddlers' Interaction with Others in Family
                 Day-Care Home   87

Observing a Toddler in a Child-Care Setting   88

    ACTIVITY 4.6   Design a Toddler Playground   90

    ACTIVITY 4.7   Observe a Toddler's Physical Development   91

    ACTIVITY 4.8   Observe Sensorimotor Intelligence   91

    ACTIVITY 4.9   Observe Pretend Play in Older Toddlers   93

    ACTIVITY 4.10   Analyze Toddlers' Language Development   94

ACTIVITY 4.11   Toddlers' Need for Autonomy   95

ACTIVITY 4.12   Toddlers' Social Development   95

ACTIVITY 4.13   Comparison of Toddler Care Arrangements   95

Summary   96

References   96

◆ **Chapter 5**
**Interacting with Preschool Children
in Group Settings   99**

Development of Preschool Children   100

Motor Development   100

ACTIVITY 5.1   Preschoolers' Large Motor Skills   101

ACTIVITY 5.2   Children's Free Play   103

ACTIVITY 5.3   Preschoolers' Small Motor Development   105

Health and Safety   105

Intellectual Development   106

ACTIVITY 5.4   Preschoolers' Intellectual Development   107

ACTIVITY 5.5   Recognitive Memory in Preschool Children   107

ACTIVITY 5.6   Counting Skills and One-to-One Correspondence
in Preschool Children   108

ACTIVITY 5.7   Design Two Learning Environments for
Preschool Children   108

ACTIVITY 5.8   Plan a Week-Long Unit for a Half-Day
Preschool Session   108

ACTIVITY 5.9   Carry Out and Evaluate Your Unit Plan
(Student Teachers and Advanced Students)   110

Language Learning   110

ACTIVITY 5.10   Preschoolers' Listening Skills   111

ACTIVITY 5.11   Preschoolers' Verbal Interactions   111

ACTIVITY 5.12   Tell a Story to a Group of Children   112

Social Development   112

ACTIVITY 5.13   Observe How Children's Temperamental
Characteristics Shape Their Social
Environment   115

ACTIVITY 5.14   Teaching Social Skills   115

Emotional Development   116

ACTIVITY 5.15   Evaluate a Child's Stress Level   116

ACTIVITY 5.16   Provide Emotional Support for an Individual Child
(Advanced Students or Student Teachers)   117

Creative Expression   118

ACTIVITY 5.17   The Expression of Creativity and Individuality through Art   119

The Teacher's Role in Guiding Preschoolers' Play   120

ACTIVITY 5.18   The Teacher's Role in Play   121

Guiding Preschoolers' Behavior   122

ACTIVITY 5.19   Teachers' Guidance of Children's Behavior   123

Multicultural Education   123

ACTIVITY 5.20   Art Center   124

ACTIVITY 5.21   Plan a Multicultural Movement or Music Activity   124

ACTIVITY 5.22   The Availability of Multicultural Children's Literature   124

Children with Special Needs   125

ACTIVITY 5.23   A Case Study of a Child with Special Needs   125

ACTIVITY 5.24   Observing an IFSE or IEP Meeting   125

Transition to Kindergarten   126

ACTIVITY 5.25   Transition-to-Kindergarten Activities   126

Staff Development   126

ACTIVITY 5.26   Plan an Inservice Workshop or Classroom Presentation   126

ACTIVITY 5.27   Develop an Annotated List of Videos on Preschool Development and Education   127

Summary   127

References   128

◆ **Chapter 6**
Living and Learning with Kindergarten Children   131

What Is Kindergarten?   131

Developmental Characteristics of Kindergarten Children   132

Physical Development   132

Observing the Physical Development of the Kindergarten Child   137

ACTIVITY 6.1   Measurement of Self   137

ACTIVITY 6.2   Classroom Survey of "Lost Teeth"   137

ACTIVITY 6.3   Checklist of Gross Motor Skills   137

ACTIVITY 6.4   Analyze Children's Responses to a Story   138

ACTIVITY 6.5   Small Motor Activities in the Kindergarten Classroom   138

ACTIVITY 6.6   Children's Paper Folding and Cutting Skills   138

ACTIVITY 6.7   Children's Psychomotor Needs   138

Cognitive Development   138

Literacy Development in Kindergarten   140

    Reading   *141*

    Writing   *141*

    ACTIVITY 6.8   Reading or Writing Assessment   145

    ACTIVITY 6.9   Design a Cognitive Development Inventory   145

    ACTIVITY 6.10   The DIAL–III   145

    ACTIVITY 6.11   Kindergarten Screening   145

    ACTIVITY 6.12   Interview with a Teacher   149

    ACTIVITY 6.13   Group Report Card   149

    ACTIVITY 6.14   Classroom Organization   149

    Social and Emotional Development of the Kindergarten Child   *150*

    Atypical Development   *152*

    ACTIVITY 6.15   Observing Social and Emotional Development of the Kindergarten Child   153

    ACTIVITY 6.16   Gender Roles   154

    ACTIVITY 6.17   Gender Observation   154

The History of Kindergarten   154

A Portrait of Kindergarten Children   155

    Academic Skills   *155*

    Health and Behavior   *155*

Differences in Kindergarten Children   156

    Age-Related Differences in School Readiness   *156*

    Sex-Related Differences   *157*

    Family Background   *157*

Types of Kindergarten Programs   157

Variations in Kindergarten   158

    Length of Day: Half-Day, Full-Day, or Full-Day, Alternate-Day Scheduling   *158*

    Entry Age   *159*

    Kindergarten Retention   *160*

    Teacher Education Requirements   *160*

    ACTIVITY 6.18   Length of Kindergarten Day   162

    ACTIVITY 6.19   Others' Views on Kindergarten Schedules   162

    ACTIVITY 6.20   Observation of Length of Class Day   162

    ACTIVITY 6.21   Entry Age for Kindergarten   163

    ACTIVITY 6.22   Interviewing Teachers   163

    ACTIVITY 6.23   Observation in a Kindergarten Intervention Classroom   164

    ACTIVITY 6.24   Education of Kindergarten Teachers   164

Summary   **165**

References   **165**

◆ Chapter 7
Work and Play in the Primary Grades   167

What Are the Primary Grades?   167

Developmental Characteristics of the Six- to Eight-Year-Old   168

Physical Development   *168*

*Observing the Physical Development of Children
in the Primary Grades*   *169*

ACTIVITY 7.1   Measuring Growth   169

ACTIVITY 7.2   Fine Motor Activities   170

ACTIVITY 7.3   Writing Tools   170

ACTIVITY 7.4   Gross Motor Activities   170

ACTIVITY 7.5   Physical Education   170

ACTIVITY 7.6   Art Activity   171

ACTIVITY 7.7   Vision Center   171

ACTIVITY 7.8   Vision Problems   171

ACTIVITY 7.9   Health and Safety Curriculum   171

Cognitive Development   *171*

Work and Play in the Primary Classroom   *176*

Technology and Cognitive Development in the Primary Grades   *186*

*Observing Cognitive Development through Work and Play
in the Primary Grades*   *189*

ACTIVITY 7.10   Your Own Primary Classroom   189

ACTIVITY 7.11   Piagetian Conservation and
Classification Tasks   191

ACTIVITY 7.12   Cognition   192

ACTIVITY 7.13   Teacher's Plan Book   192

ACTIVITY 7.14   Learning Centers   192

ACTIVITY 7.15   Choices in the Classroom   193

ACTIVITY 7.16   Work versus Play   193

ACTIVITY 7.17   Developmentally Appropriate Software and
Websites   193

Social and Emotional Development in the Primary Grades   *193*

*Observing Psychosocial Development through Work and Play
in the Primary Grades*   *197*

ACTIVITY 7.18   Children's Self-Recognition   197

ACTIVITY 7.19   Children's Fears   197

ACTIVITY 7.20   Sociometric Technique   197

ACTIVITY 7.21   Friendships   198

ACTIVITY 7.22   Multi-age Classroom Observance   198

ACTIVITY 7.23   Paley's Rule   198

ACTIVITY 7.24   Development in Literature   198

ACTIVITY 7.25   Developmental Needs   199

ACTIVITY 7.26   Event Sampling   199

ACTIVITY 7.27   Teaching Tolerance   199

Atypical Development   203

ACTIVITY 7.28   ADD or ADHD Observations   204

Summary   205

References   205

Videos about the Primary Grades   206

◆ Chapter 8
Working with Families of Young Children   207

Understanding Diversity in Families   207

Parental Involvement in Education   209

Parents as Nurturers   209

Parents as Participants in Adult Relationships   210

Parents as Individuals   210

Parents as Workers   210

Parents as Consumers   210

Parents as Community Members   211

Parents as Educators   211

Parent/Family Education   211

Family Literacy Programs   214

ACTIVITY 8.1   Parent Education Activities   215

ACTIVITY 8.2   Minnesota Early Childhood Family Initiatives   215

ACTIVITY 8.3   Parent Education   216

ACTIVITY 8.4   Family Education Activities   216

ACTIVITY 8.5   Parent Education Meeting Plan   216

ACTIVITY 8.6   Family Literacy Websites   216

Home Visits   216

ACTIVITY 8.7   Role-Playing a Home Visit   218

ACTIVITY 8.8   Making Home Visits (Student Teachers and Advanced Students)   218

ACTIVITY 8.9   Home Visit (Student Teacher or Advanced Student)   219

Parent Involvement/Volunteers   219

Parental Support of the Program   219

ACTIVITY 8.10   Activities for Volunteers   223

ACTIVITY 8.11   Parent Involvement Survey   223

ACTIVITY 8.12   Volunteer Guidelines   223

ACTIVITY 8.13   Volunteer Observation   224

Home–School Communication   224

Oral Communication   224

Written Communication   226

ACTIVITY 8.14   Role-Play Parental Interaction   228

ACTIVITY 8.15   Role-Play a Parent Conference   228

ACTIVITY 8.16   Role-Play a Conflict   228

ACTIVITY 8.17   Parents' Bulletin Board   229

ACTIVITY 8.18   Create a Newsletter   229

ACTIVITY 8.19   Activity Calendar   229

Parent Meetings/Orientations/Open Houses   229

ACTIVITY 8.20   Initial Contact with Parents   230

ACTIVITY 8.21   Parental Evaluation of the Program   230

ACTIVITY 8.22   Plan the First Family Meeting   230

ACTIVITY 8.23   Plan a Kindergarten Orientation   231

ACTIVITY 8.24   Parental Thank You   231

Summary   231

References   231

◆ **Chapter 9**
Curriculum and the Young Child   233

What Is Curriculum?   233

Early Childhood Curriculum Models   234

Froebel's Kindergarten Gifts and Occupations   235

ACTIVITY 9.1   Froebelian Occupations and Gifts   235

The Montessori Method   235

ACTIVITY 9.2   Montessori Classroom   238

The Bank Street Approach/Developmental–Interactionist Model   238

ACTIVITY 9.3   Bank Street Website   240

The Direct Instruction Approach   240

The Cognitively Oriented High Scope Approach   243

ACTIVITY 9.4   High Scope Website   244

Early Childhood Curriculum in a New Millennium   244

Literacy Development in a New Millennium   245

ACTIVITY 9.5   Integrated Curriculum Unit   254

Transformational Curriculum   255

The Project Approach   256

ACTIVITY 9.6   Reggio Emilia Websites   261

Emergent Curriculum   261

ACTIVITY 9.7   Observe Two Classrooms   263

Multiethnic, Multicultural, Anti-bias Curriculum   263

ACTIVITY 9.8   Classroom Practices Inventory   266

Curriculum for and about Young Children with Special Needs   275

ACTIVITY 9.9   Special Needs Observation   277

Decisions, Decisions, Decisions!   277

Summary   278

References   278

◆ **Appendix A**
   **A Time-Sampling Technique for Evaluating
   Infant/Toddler Programs   281**

◆ **Appendix B**
   Playground Improvement Rating Scale   289

◆ **Appendix C**
   **Ways to Increase Positive Social Interaction
   among Children   293**

◆ **Appendix D**
   Websites Related to Early Childhood Education   297

   Index   299

Preface

Young children from birth through age eight are cared for and educated in diverse early childhood programs. This book is written to give undergraduate and graduate students experience in using effective methods for observing and documenting young children's development. Understanding how each child in a group setting is developing is essential to planning a curriculum that meets each one's needs.

This guide is designed to direct students' participation with children of different age groups in a variety of early childhood settings. By carrying out the activities outlined in each chapter students will interact with children at the same time that they are learning more about development. Students will have many opportunities to use the information gained to plan curriculum activities and actually try them out.

This book is intended to accompany a comprehensive program for the training of early childhood teachers. It is assumed that students will already have had or are simultaneously enrolled in a survey course in lifespan development and learning. The first two chapters might be taught in an introductory course in early childhood education in which observation and participation methods are included. Those who will be licensed to teach children from birth through the primary grades will be taking courses that detail more closely growth and development in the early childhood years. Chapters 3 to 7 could be used separately or in some combination with courses on infant, toddler, preschool, kindergarten, and primary development and education. Ideally, about one-fourth of the credit for each course would be based on observation and participation assignments. Chapter 8 addresses relationships with parents and families and could accompany a course on home/school relations or socialization of the young child. Chapter 9 is concerned with the way developmental knowledge is translated into an appropriate curriculum for children and could be part of any course that is concerned with early childhood methods and curriculum.

We have provided a variety of activities using different observational methods in the last seven chapters. This is designed to give students and instructors a choice of assignments that can be based on each individual student's own background and experiences with young children. The activities are designed to make students fully analyze and reflect on what they are seeing and experiencing.

Please bear in mind, however, that this is not a textbook on development, observation methods, or curriculum. Rather, it is a practical way to apply what students are learning about young children. By interacting with real children in authentic early childhood settings, students will gain the experience and confidence to help them make the decisions that can affect what is happening with a given child or group of children on an everyday basis. We realize that career teachers are always learning more about children and constantly revising the ways they facilitate children's development and learning.

Successful use of this observation and participation guide also depends on the placement of students in groups or classes where children are cared for and taught by exemplary teachers. Students should also be supervised by university/college personnel knowledgeable in developmentally appropriate practices for young children. They need mentors who can guide and direct their early teaching attempts without smothering their creativity and risk-taking abilities. Students should be allowed to experiment to find out what works with certain children and what doesn't. For many students, theories of child development and pedagogy are meaningless unless they can see how they are manifested in practice.

In this second edition, we have tried to provide updated information that reflects the latest research and trends in the field of early childhood education. Of special note are incorporation of information on brain research, literacy development and longitudinal research on kindergarten children. Many activities have been updated and new ones have been included, some of which require students to use the Internet to do research on a variety of topics related to early childhood education. We hope that you and your students find this revised edition useful.

Acknowledgments

The help of many people has made this book possible. Our graduate assistants, Cai Xinsheng and Jill Grunewald, provided much technical help for the first edition. They took photographs, obtained copyright permissions, did library searches, and proofed copy. Cindy Landwehr also provided technical support for the first edition. Emily Dohlman, student worker, provided research and clerical support for the second edition. Without her help, the completion of this second edition would not have been possible.

Gail Midthune, special education teacher for the Winona, Minnesota, Public Schools, gave us access to information about the Individualized Family Service Plan. Pat Temple, Alice Kerr, Linda Rouhoff, Julie Stenejhem, and Kim Firstbrook, teachers in the Rochester, Minnesota schools, provided access to their classrooms for photographs and materials.

Terry Migrala took photographs at the Camden County Community College Child Care Center, made possible by Janet Brown and her staff. Sue Rislove and Molli Kook at the Winona State University Nursery School and Barb Nagel at the WSU Child Care Center also made photographing in their programs possible. Special thanks to all children and parents for their cooperation.

M. Leah Timberlake, Highland Community College of Illinois; Linda Estes, St. Charles County Community College of Missouri; and Joy Faini Saab, West Virginia University reviewed the text and made helpful suggestions. Toni Campbell, San Jose State University; Vivian N. Harper, San Joaquin Delta College; and Diane Lawler-Prince, Arkansas State University reviewed the first edition of this book.

We also thank our families and colleagues at Winona State University for their encouragement and support.

Chapter 1

The Role of Observation and Participation in Early Childhood Education

In this chapter you will read information and choose from a menu of activities to help you learn more about:

◆ The role of observation in learning about children
◆ The purpose(s) of observation
◆ Privacy and confidentiality issues related to observing
◆ Observation as a part of the assessment process
◆ The need for field experiences as a part of early childhood education
◆ Tips for practicum students in early childhood settings.

Observing Young Children

What Is Observation?

Observation is a system or plan for looking at behavior. Hills (1992) has outlined some current observational practices that teachers use. Many of these methods have their roots in the history of early childhood education. The child study movement developed in the first few decades of the twentieth century, growing out of a social reform effort intended to improve the health and welfare of children. Several large universities were given government grants to conduct research on young children's behavior. The results of the work being done by researchers at these Child Study Institutes and in other university settings receiving government funding still inform the field of early childhood education today.

In the 1960s and 1970s another influx of money grew out of President L. B. Johnson's "war on poverty." The idea was to start with this country's youngest citizens in order to help those living in poverty lead more productive lives. Grants were awarded to psychologists at universities to design and direct Head Start Programs intended to give preschoolers living in low-income communities the skills they would need to be successful when they reached school age. The "planned variation" models of ten different prekindergarten programs later received Follow-Through funds to see if the gains made in preschool would be continued in the primary years. All the programs were analyzed and the results (Lazar, Darlington,Murray, Royce, and Snipper 1982) strongly suggested that children who received instruction did significantly better in school and on other social measures than did the controls who received no special programs. In 1999 Head Start received a federal appropriation of $4.7 billion to again set up rigorous research studies headed by renowned researchers to demonstrate the effectiveness of their programs on a nationwide basis (http.//www.acf.dhhs.gov/programs/hsreac/home.htm.)

In the 1980s and 1990s an increasing number of researchers used qualitative methods outside laboratories—such as observation of children in their homes, child care centers, or school and community settings—to collect raw descriptive data on an individual child or children, and then sorted, interpreted, and quantified the data to ferret out trends and make hypotheses about children.

Teachers have also used formal and informal observations for years to assess children's behavior in the classroom in unobtrusive ways. They employ both commercial observation instruments and teacher-made ones in order to find out how young children are developing and learning. All experienced teachers have several different ways to observe children. For example, caregivers in child care centers must do a quick health check each day to see if each child is well enough to be in a group setting. Teachers in a primary classroom must make a determination of when the class is ready to move on to the next lesson. They must also possess an array of observational and recording skills to make an assessment of each child's developmental profile.

Effective planning for the group is based on the teacher's general knowledge of the principles of child development and specific knowledge of each child's physical, emotional, social, and intellectual functioning. The child's cultural and family background and individual talents and interests also inform classroom practice.

The great advantage of observation over other forms of assessment of young children is that it is nonintrusive. It does not interrupt children's play or other activities—indeed, it can often be done without children even being aware that someone is watching what they are doing.

Early childhood education students and teachers need to learn effective ways to look at, listen to, and document what children are doing and saying. Students will be trying to corroborate what has been learned in child development courses with what they see in individual children. They may be following a particular child over a period of several weeks or months in order to see how development proceeds. Experienced teachers will also need a plan for observing the children in the group or classroom. They need to know children's ability and developmental levels so they can plan an appropriate curriculum, devise teaching strategies and appropriate interaction, be able to communicate children's progress to parents, and refer children they identify as needing further assessment or special services.

Because formal assessment of children younger than five using standardized instruments is expensive, difficult because the children often cannot articulate their own answers, and often inaccurate (Shepard, Kagan, and Wurtz 1998), it is vitally important to their well-being that we become accomplished observers so that we can determine that each child is developing and learning at optimal levels.

Teachers and physicians are in unique positions to examine each child. Often they are the first professionals outside the family that see a child on a regular basis. Medical personnel make certain that children get their immunizations, and chart their growth and weight gains. They also see that any abnormalities are corrected or that children's health needs are supplied. Vision and hearing checks are routinely done as part of medical check-ups. If a child care provider or teacher notices a problem, he or she should have a referral process set up and know of community resources that can provide the services required. Many free or low-cost programs exist to serve low-income families.

Observation is a plan for looking at children for which you must consider the following:

1. *Who* will be observed? Will you be looking at the whole group, a small group, or at individual children?

2. *What* behavior(s) will you observe? Do you want to target particular responses children make? For instance, you might want to know how often certain children initiate interaction with peers or how often they respond to another's suggestions in a dramatic play setting?

3. *How* will you observe the behavior(s)? What method will you use for observing? Are some methods more appropriate for certain kinds of behaviors than others?

4. *Where* will you observe? Will you observe in the home, the classroom, on the playground, or at the shopping mall? Will you use an observation booth, a balcony, or station yourself at the back of the room?

5. *When* and *for how long* will you observe? Are there certain times of the day that might work better for some observations? Will you try to get samples of behavior from several different times of the day? Will the observations be based on one occurrence or several? Will they last for two minutes or ten minutes? Will they be spaced over several days, weeks, or months?

6. *How* will you document your observations? Will you keep a page in a loose-leaf notebook for each child? Will you make a chart, a videotape, a case study, or use some other way of documenting your observations?

7. *How* will you use the information that you have obtained? Will you share the data you have gathered with parents, the principal, other teachers, curriculum specialists? What form will this sharing take? How will it be used in making changes within the classroom, in shaping the curriculum?

Purposes of Observation

Even the most experienced teachers of young children need to step back occasionally to gather information about the children in their care. By watching them and recording their behaviors, teachers can find out how children move, what they think, and how they feel (Lay-Dopyera & Dopyera 1993). By observing and discovering a child's abilities and interests they can begin to make an educational plan for each individual child as well as for the group (Hendrick 1990). Teachers can use the information gathered to see if children are meeting the education goals they have set or if they are making progress toward them. Williams and Fromberg (1992, 269) have noted that "in the enduring search for ways of understanding and fostering children's development and learning, the most significant recent shift has been toward viewing the teacher as a participant observer-researcher." "Teachers continually observe children's spontaneous play and interaction with the physical environment and with other children to learn about their interests, abilities, and developmental progress. On the basis of this information, teachers plan experiences that enhance children's learning and development" (Bredekamp & Copple 1997, 17).

In addition to monitoring children's progress, both preservice and inservice teachers need a way to monitor their own performances. If they experience problems at some particular time of the day or when they are trying to get across a concept that children have difficulty understanding, they need to be able to consider what *they* might be doing that is contributing to the misunderstanding; by examining their own actions they may be able to identify ways to solve the confusion. And if they try something that proves effective, they will want to make note of that for use in the future.

Teachers also need to have a general picture of how each group of children is operating. Each classroom has its own personality. A global assessment

◆ *A student teacher in a kindergarten class leads the whole group in discussing the morning letter.*

of the group's abilities can often help the teacher make modifications to curriculum plans. For example, one kindergarten class may need the experience of walking with a partner on short visits to the park before being ready for a longer trip to the science museum, while another group may be ready for a field trip without such practice.

 The purposes of observation are listed here:

1. *Teachers need to identify children's interests.* Often, knowing what an individual child or a certain group of children like and respond to can help the teacher *and children* plan educational experiences that take advantage of their preferences. This could lead to webbing (finding connections or relationships between concepts) as a means of planning curricula with children (Workman & Anziano 1993). For example, if one group is very interested in bees, they might plan a walk to find bees gathering honey, choose books and songs about bees, invite a beekeeper to show how he or she dresses to extract honey from a hive, or plan a snack that uses honey as a sweetener. Individual children or a small group may be interested in a particular topic, such as earth-moving equipment. A teacher could set up an activity center with toy bulldozers, dump trucks, and backhoes in the block corner. The children who wanted to could use that equipment, and other children who were not initially interested might join in.

2. *Teachers need to chart the developmental level of each child.* This means that a child must be seen from several different angles. Observation is one way to make an informal assessment of each child's functioning in several different developmental domains. The teacher will want to know about the cognitive, physical, social, and emotional development of each child and whether it can be considered within the normal range for that particular age group.

3. *Having developmental knowledge of each child will assist the teacher in planning an appropriate curriculum based on individual needs.* A child may be advanced in cognitive development but lack social skills. The teacher could intervene with this child to help him or her adjust to the group. Another child may be physically adept, but have difficulty containing emotional outbursts. The teacher may be able to structure some physical ways that the child can learn to express feelings kinesthestically through movement or dance. Children may be at different developmental levels in different domains. Knowing this lets the teacher individualize instruction and caregiving.

4. *Teachers need to do periodic observations to find out how children are progressing.* In order to document changes in the child's or children's behavior, some systematic schedule of observations is necessary. For example, a teacher of toddlers may be working to lessen the amount of hitting in the room. Doing an event tally in a proscribed time period will help determine if, in fact, the children hit fewer times after learning some other ways to ask for what they want.

5. *Observation can help early childhood teachers appraise their own teaching practices and design appropriate staff development.* Teachers and students need to be aware of what *they* are doing. They might want to find out how often they interact with certain children, how a discipline technique works with different children, or how much attention children pay when a certain story is read to them. They might also want to examine their facial expressions and body language. They could listen to their speech patterns to see how often they use positive and negative language. Videotaping themselves and reviewing the tapes can be very revealing to novice teachers. Further, teachers and program administrators can use these analyses of staff strengths and weaknesses to design professional development that will meet the needs of those who work with young children.

6. *Observation can give practitioners a general overview of the program and, at the same time, help them analyze specific classroom management problems.* Group cohesiveness, how well the group takes directions, and how helpful members are with each other are important determinants in how the group is "working." The general developmental levels of all the children often determine the curriculum and the social-emotional climate of the group.

7. *Written observations on individual children can be added to other information to be shared with study teams, parents, and administrators.* Having many examples of observations taken at different times, in various circumstances, and using different methods has the potential to give a well-rounded picture of each child's development.

◆ *Observing a child's play can tell the teacher how well educational goals are being met.*

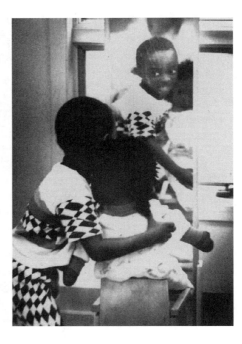

Observation and Children's Privacy

Protecting the confidentiality of the children is a paramount concern in all observations. Children have the right to privacy. In any reporting to parents, only their child should be discussed. The identity of children and groups of children should similarly be protected in discussing what has been observed to administrators and other school personnel. Names and identifying characteristics should be omitted from written materials unless they are specifically called for. Students and teachers should be very careful about discussing children in the teachers' lounge or to friends and relatives. Such casual discussion is a breach of confidentiality.

For some of the observations in later chapters we will suggest you may need signed parental permission. Your instructor may also need to submit a proposal to the Human Subjects or another committee on your campus before you can proceed. If you are unsure about the ethical considerations involved in a particular exercise, clarify any questions you have with your instructor.

How to Do Observations in Early Childhood Settings

When observers enter any environment, just by being there they change what might otherwise go on. Fortunately, most children adapt fairly quickly to having someone watching them. If that person is someone they have gotten to know, they rapidly revert to their typical behaviors and ignore the onlooker. Being unobtrusive when observing is something to strive for.

When observing in a classroom or child care center, make certain that the school or center has signed permission from parents allowing students from your college or university to observe their child (children.) Often schools and centers have blanket permission forms that parents sign when their child enters the program. If not, prepare a permission form telling who you are, whom you represent, why you are doing the observation, and what uses will be made of the observations. You will need to assure parents of confidentiality and let them know that the name of their child will not be used in any written reports you make. Leave room for parents to write in the name and age of their child, and a place for their signature and the date. A typical form is seen in Example 1.1.

Some suggestions about how to make the time worthwhile and accomplish what is needed during observations are helpful to the student or beginning teacher (Benjamin 1994). Every aspect of the observation should be planned in advance. Knowing a number of different observational methods and having clear goals in mind are the starting points. Discussing with the staff what they want to find out about each child or group of children and setting priorities about what kind of information is sought will help the observer plan and schedule observation time. If, for instance, the teacher wants to know something about how each child uses the time during a certain period of the day in order to share that information with parents at conference

◆ **EXAMPLE 1.1**
   Permission Form

Dear Parents,

My name is _____ and I am observing your child as

part of an early childhood education course at _____ University. Our

instructor,_____, has taken this assignment through

the university Human Subjects Committee.

Our class is learning about how preschool children behave in group settings. Your

child's identity will be protected. At no time during our class discussions or in my

written report will your child's name be used.

Please sign this form if you are willing to let me observe your child.

   Student's Name _____

- -

I give my permission for my child to be observed by an early childhood education

student, _____, at _____ University.

I understand that my child's privacy will be protected and that no identifying

information will be included in the written work of any student.

   Child's Name _____

   Birthdate _____

   Parent's Signature _____

   Date _____

time, observations would need to be done several weeks before the conferences actually take place. A rotation system of when each child would be observed would have to be worked out.

Planning might also include selecting and procuring any equipment
such as tape recorders, checklists, and notebooks that might be needed. Benjamin (1994, 17) suggested that observers "might stock a small suitcase with
sand timers (one-, three-, and five-minute), a stopwatch, a watch with a second hand, a kitchen timer, a tally or grocery counter, a clipboard, and extra
consumable supplies (batteries, notepads, graph paper, pens and pencils). If
the budget allows, include a camera, film, a small tape recorder, and extra
tapes. A video camera is also invaluable, although it is expensive and subject
to eliciting atypical behavior from children unless it has been part of their

experience well before the actual observation begins. Keep equipment and supplies in a predictable place and separate from other classroom materials. This simple step helps teachers locate everything easily and also helps them remember to replace items after use and to restock as needed. A suitcase is a good choice because it is portable and easily stored in a closet when not in use."

When observing in the home or in a family day care setting always make preparations ahead of time. Contact the parent or provider by phone to set up the day and time. Make certain you have signed parental permission. (See Example 1.1.) Carry all the materials you will need to do the observation with you. When you arrive keep your comments to parents, provider, or children brief. Situating yourself out of the line of traffic but with a clear view of what the child or children are doing, set up an observation station with all the necessary paraphernalia. Keeping a low profile, avoiding eye contact, and saying to children when they ask you what you are doing, "This is work I am doing for a class," are ways a student can keep from disrupting the group. A teacher may need to say to students demanding attention, "I need time right now to watch children to see what they are doing. I'll be able to help you when I'm finished here."

Students and teachers should keep records of their observations. These can either be written down or spoken directly into a handheld tape recorder for later transcription.

The children can be shown ways to record their own behavior. Even preschool children can learn to document participation in a certain task by depositing their name tags or markers in a designated bin. For example, if a kindergarten teacher wants to know who has completed an assigned task at one of the activity centers, he or she can ask each child to check his or her own name off the class list placed there, making it easy to see who has yet to finish.

Observation as a Major Part of the Assessment Process

As the use of standardized instruments such as intelligence, readiness, developmental screening, and achievement tests are increasingly being seen as inappropriate for young children, other ways of assessing them are being sought. Teacher observations and the portfolio method are deemed less intrusive and more comprehensive than one-shot group tests with children under eight.

The Southern Association of Children Under Six (SACUS 1990) has released a position statement on developmentally appropriate assessment. Its members believe that assessment should be valid (related to the goals and objectives of a program), encompass the whole child, involve repeated observations, be continuous over time, and use a variety of methods.

After extensive study the National Association for the Education of Young Children (NAEYC 1991a) identified 18 principles to guide assessment procedures for young children. They felt very strongly that assessment should be an integral part of every program, benefit children, be used to adjust curriculum and instruction, and never be used to exclude, segregate, or retain children. Identifying children with special needs so as to ensure that they receive the services they require was seen as another legitimate purpose of assessment. NAEYC also endorsed the use of assessment to evaluate the worth of the program.

Teacher observations and the portfolio process are recognized by these early childhood organizations as appropriate ways to document the work each child has done based on a variety of assessment measures.

Participation in Early Childhood Settings

The Need for Field Experience as a Part of Early Childhood Teacher Education

Being a part of children's programs is an essential component of the preparation of early childhood teachers. Programs for children from birth to age eight take place in many diverse settings. The delivery of services can vary from private homes, child care centers, and public and private schools to programs geared for special populations. The length of the program day, the ages of children served, the ability levels of the children, the sponsorship, and the preparation of the teaching staff can all be quite different from program to program. Participation with young children also means assuming all the mundane caregiving routines such as handwashing, changing diapers, and feeding for infants and toddlers, or collecting milk money, passing out supplies, and listening to readers for primary children.

The NAEYC, the agency that has set the guidelines for accreditation of teacher education programs in early childhood education, has outlined two types of field experiences that undergraduate preservice teachers will need (1991b, 19–20). The first type involves field work with varying degrees of participation in connection with coursework. This should be done in multiple settings with children from birth through age eight and should include interaction with families of different cultural and socioeconomic backgrounds. The second type is labeled "student teaching/practica," and is intended to be the culmination of the undergraduate program. Candidates assume major responsibility for the full range of teaching duties in an early childhood setting. Every effort is made to use exemplary early childhood settings as placements for student teachers who are supervised regularly by onsite personnel as well as college faculty. According to the guidelines, student teaching/practica consists of a minimum of 150 clock hours spent in at least two different settings (totaling 300 clock hours), serving children of two different age groups. One setting must serve infants and toddlers (birth to three-year-olds) or preprimary age children (three-year-olds through kindergartners). The other setting will be in a primary classroom. Seminar meetings accompany student teaching to provide an opportunity for analysis, evaluation, and discussion of field experiences. Student teaching includes supervised experience in working with parents and with interdisciplinary teams of professionals where appropriate.

Graduate students working toward a master's or specialist's degree also need to have opportunities to apply knowledge gained through coursework in early childhood settings. This can be done in their own classroom or through a supervised field assignment. Their applications will be more complex and in-depth and might include action research, curriculum projects, field study projects, or observed clinical practice.

While not all teacher education programs seek accreditation from the National Council for the Accreditation of Teacher Education (NCATE), their guidelines, as outlined by NAEYC (1991b), help to ensure that teachers will have the knowledge, skills, and experience needed to understand young children, design programs for them, and make the hundreds of educational decisions that teachers are confronted with every day in meeting the needs of any group of young children. The exercises included in the rest of this book are intended to give undergraduate teachers-in-training and more experienced teachers guided opportunities to interact with children of different age levels and abilities in a variety of early childhood settings. They are devised to cover a wide spectrum of circumstances under which care and education are offered to young children in groups. Instructors and students are urged to choose those exercises that best fit their needs and the needs of the various programs in which they find themselves. The book is meant to be a practicum guide for several individual courses as well as for student teaching.

Tips for Practicum Students and Student Teachers

While each college or university will have guidelines for practicum students and student teachers, the suggestions given here could also prove useful.

1. Always arrive on time or even early. Stay as long as the teacher or later. Often these are the only times you will have to discuss children, make curriculum decisions, and get feedback on how you are doing. If you must be absent, offer to make up the time somehow. Work out a plan with the classroom teacher and university supervisor. Excessive absenteeism may be grounds for dismissal.

2. Be sure you are covered by liability insurance. This is usually available for a small fee through student membership in professional teacher organizations such as the National Education Association (NEA) or the American Federation of Teachers (AFT). You may be covered by a "rider" on a homeowner's policy or other private insurance. At no time should a student "substitute" for the regular teacher. You should be under the supervision of the classroom teacher at all times. While the teacher may leave the room for short periods, you are not qualified to take over that teacher's role. If the teacher must be absent, a qualified substitute should be in the classroom with you.

3. You are considered a teacher when you are practicing in centers and schools. Teachers are professionals, so wear appropriate clothing. Take

your cues from the other teachers. Clothing should be neat and clean. Skimpy blouses, shirts, shorts, or dresses are not appropriate. Be sensitive about wearing clothing with slogans that might project an unprofessional image.

4. While each school district must follow the code of ethics that their state government has adopted, the early childhood profession also has a Code of Ethics that was adopted in 1989 and amended in 1997. The text of the NAEYC Code of Ethical Conduct that applies to teachers of young children is found on the web at http://www.naeyc.org/about/position/pseth98.htm. Please read and discuss this code, which governs the professional behavior of each early childhood practitioner with children, parents, colleagues, and the community, before you go out to observe children.

5. Become familiar with the school's philosophy and rules. If there is a handbook, ask for a copy. If you don't know, ask for clarification of how certain problems are to be handled.

6. Make a name tag for yourself with your name and your college or university affiliation—for example, "Sandy Siegal, Student Teacher, Anderson College." This helps the teachers, children, and parents know who you are. You could also prepare a set of name tags for the children in your group or class. Infants and toddlers are less likely to tear them off if they are safety-pinned to the back of their clothing. Older children will enjoy having a souvenir to take home after you have learned all their names.

7. Get down to the child's level whenever possible. With very young children, this may mean sitting on the floor. Sit with children as often as possible, particularly during snacks or mealtime. This is a good time to hold conversations and find out more about each one. Kneel or sit when helping them on with coats, shoes, or boots.

8. Encourage children to do as much for themselves as they can. Help only when needed or when the task of putting away the blocks, for instance, is rather overwhelming.

9. Handle the discipline with the children near you. If there is a problem you are unsure about say, "Let's ask the teacher."

10. Take time to listen to children. The younger the child, the more difficulty they may have in finding the words to express what they want to say. Wait. When you are talking, keep your voice moderated. Instead of yelling to a child on the playground, go to the child and speak in a normal tone.

11. Handle toileting in a matter-of-fact way. Young children may be so busy that they forget to go to the bathroom. Simply say, "It's time to go to the bathroom now" when they show signs of needing to go. If accidents occur, know where extra clothing is stored and remain calm. Make sure that children wash hands after using the bathroom.

12. While touching and holding are appropriate with very young children, they may not be desirable in kindergarten and primary grades, where the teacher-to-child ratio is larger. Be sensitive to the appropriate uses of touch and holding in all situations.

13. Be prepared to supervise outdoor as well as indoor activities. Dress for the weather.

14. Although it is natural to find some children more appealing than others, try not to play favorites. Respond to children by attending to their needs, not your own.

15. Anticipate what needs to be done. Don't always wait for the teacher to ask you to do something. Volunteer to carry out needed tasks outside of school time. Assist the teacher with routine tasks such as copying, making bulletin boards, grading, or reporting grades. However, if these are the *only* tasks you are asked to do, discuss it with the teacher or your university supervisor—you want to do *all* the tasks that a regular teacher does.

15. As much as possible, focus on how the children are doing rather than on your own performance. Get to know the children well so that you can relax and be yourself. In the end, the teacher's abilities are measured by the outcomes for the children. Teachers are accountable for helping children grow and develop and reach their own potential.

16. Comply with any medical regulations. Some states or individual schools require proof of freedom from infectious disease before you can be a part of the group.

Summary

Observation is a systematic way of viewing children to find out as much as possible about how they are developing. One of the major purposes of observation is to help teachers make appropriate educational decisions based on a knowledge of each child's intellectual, physical, social, and emotional functioning and their cultural and family background and individual interests. They also need to document what they see so they can share the information with parents, administrators, and other members of the educational team. Observation can be coupled with other means of assessment to give a comprehensive picture of each child's capabilities. It is the way students and teachers get to know the children in a particular group.

Observation is part of the participation process. Participation in early childhood settings also means "being there" for children, relating to them on a warm, personal level, and beginning to make educational decisions with the guidance of classroom and university supervisors. Students and teachers can use what they have learned through observation to help them decide how each child can be integrated into the group setting, which individual and group goals should be set, how the group should be managed, which teaching practices are appropriate with different ages, how and when to involve parents, and what curriculum content children should be learning.

REFERENCES

Benjamin, A. C. (1994). Observations in early childhood classrooms: Advice from the field. *Young Children, 49*(6), 14–20.

Bredekamp, S., and C. Copple (Eds.) (1997). *Developmentally appropriate practice in early childhood programs* (rev. ed.). Washington, DC: National Association for the Education of Young Children.

Hendrick, J. (1990). *Total learning: Developmental curriculum for the young child.* Columbus, OH: Merrill.

Hills, T. (1992). Reaching potentials through appropriate assessment. In S. Bredekamp and T. Rosegrant, Eds., *Reaching potentials: Appropriate curriculum and assessment for young children.* Washington, DC: National Association for the Education of Young Children.

Lay-Dopyera, M., and J. Dopyera (1993). *Becoming a teacher of young children* (5th ed.). New York: McGraw-Hill.

Lazar, I., R. Darlington, H. Murray, U. Royce, and A. Snipper (1982). Lasting effects of early education: A report from the Consortium for Longitudinal Studies. *Monographs of the Society for Research in Child Development, 47*(2,3).

Minnesota Board of Teaching (1978). *Official state code of ethics.* St. Paul, MN.

National Association for the Education of Young Children (1991a). Guidelines for appropriate curriculum content and assessment in programs serving children ages 3 through 8. *Young Children, 46*(3), 21–38.

National Association for the Education of Young Children (1991b). *Early childhood teacher education guidelines: Basic and advanced.* Washington, DC: NAEYC.

National Association for the Education of Young Children (1996). Guidelines for preparation of early childhood professionals, 1996. Pub. No. #212.

National Association for the Education of Young Children (1997). *Code of ethical conduct.* Washington, DC: NAEYC. http://www.naeyc.org/about/position/pseth98.htm

Shepard, L. A., S. L. Kagan, and E. Wurtz (1998). Goal 1 Early Childhood Assessments Resource Group recommendations. *Young Children, 53*(3), 52–54.

Southern Association on Children Under Six (1990). Developmentally appropriate assessment. Little Rock, AR.

Williams, L. R., and D. P. Fromberg (1992). *Encyclopedia of early childhood education.* New York: Garland.

Workman, S., and M. C. Anziano (1993). Curriculum webs: Weaving connections from children to teachers. *Young Children, 48*(2), 4–9.

Chapter 2

Methods for Recording Observations of Young Children's Behavior

In this chapter you will read information and choose from a menu of activities to help you learn more about:

◆ A variety of methods for making observations of young children

◆ Advantages and disadvantages of each observation method

◆ How to choose the appropriate observation technique.

This chapter will describe some effective methods for observing children's behavior to get important information about their underlying development. These methods often can be more effective than formal testing because both the nature of young children and the inadequacies of instruments available make routine testing questionable for children under age eight. Observations done by a skillful early childhood teacher can, however, provide insights that are useful for planning strategies to meet each child's needs.

However, watching children is not enough. If we don't have some ways to record what we are seeing, it can be difficult to remember and analyze what we have observed and to decide how our observations can be used to benefit the child. We need to have a variety of methods to document our observations. The only way to become truly familiar with these different strategies is through the experience of actually using them. We will consider the advantages and disadvantages of each method and offer suggestions for appropriate uses of each method. Later chapters will include exercises that will suggest methods most appropriate for observing children of certain ages. The bulk of the methods can be used to document developmental issues; some can also be helpful in analyzing classroom practices and environments. An effort has been made to include examples of each.

Keeping a Reflective Diary/Journal/Log

Students and teachers can keep a journal about children's development. They can choose to focus on the behavior of one child or on the whole group. A child's ability to do a fine motor task, such as completing a wooden puzzle, might be the target of one observation. Another might concentrate on the child's emotional outburst on seeing her father at pick-up time. The reactions of a group of infants when a stranger enters their room or the degrees of participation in a kindergarten class's singing at circle time are some examples of more global observations. Almost anything about children that captures the interest or is of concern to the teacher or student can be the topic of a journal entry.

Focusing on what certain children are doing helps students learn more about child development in general and about each child in particular. The following entry (Example 2.1) is taken from the journal of a student who was spending two mornings a week with a group of eight infants in a campus child care center. Over several weeks she was able to document the changes she saw in these children. (We have selected some of her observations on just one child.) Although the entries on this child were very brief, they do allow the student, her university supervisor, and the other teachers to learn more about the child and her development.

Journal writing also has other uses for the practicum student or student teacher. For instance, it is a flexible way for a student or teacher to record what he or she is experiencing in an early childhood setting. After each day or session the teacher or student writes down in narrative form reflections about certain aspects of the program. Each entry can range from a mere recitation of the schedule for the morning or day to personal feelings about how he or she handled a discipline problem. Journal entries can focus on several different aspects of the program. One day the student or teacher might describe the physical setting; another day, the emotional climate. For example, one might assess what areas of the room are most used by the children in the group by taking a head count of the number of children in each learning center during a five-minute period. One could listen to the phrasing of directives by caregivers to toddlers to see if they use positive statements or a series of *don'ts*.

Keeping a journal allows teachers and students a great deal of latitude: They can decide what to look for and how to record what they have experienced. They can reflect on their own reactions to what they have seen and done that day. They can examine a problem or situation more "in depth" or look more closely at a given child to see what is causing him or her to behave in a certain way.

A journal is also a good way for students to communicate with their supervisors. It gives the supervisor who cannot visit every day a chance to learn what the student is experiencing and how he or she is feeling about the assignment. What the student writes in the journal is read only by the supervisor and is kept confidential. Some supervisors choose to accept whatever the student has written, acknowledging only that he or she has read it by a distinctive mark. Other supervisors may suggest aspects of the program that the student should explore further. Still others may ask questions or make observations in the margins that will prompt students to think critically about what they have experienced.

◆ **EXAMPLE 2.1**
A Journal Account

March 16. When I first got there, I gave K. (nine-month-old female) her bottle and she fell asleep between my legs, so I had to be careful and put her in the playpen and still have her sleep. She did open her eyes, but I just rubbed her stomach and she fell back to sleep . . . She hadn't eaten any breakfast and they (the other teachers) thought that she was either cutting some teeth or was sick.

March 23. K. had a fall today on the slide. She climbs up the steps, then sits on the top, but when she slides down, she loses control. She hit her head and got a rug burn. (The other teachers) told me that she's a daredevil. She keeps on climbing up the slide even though she has fallen down a couple of times.

April 1. Today when I got there I set up the water table. They were all so excited. It was amazing to see them get excited about just water. It's not just water to them; it's something new and different. They must all like to take baths. They even screamed when I was pouring the water in. They had a good time splashing in the water. Sometimes they would get carried away and splash each other in the face . . . K. would get so excited that she would scream and, boy, does she have a scream. (The teacher) says that she likes to hear her own voice.

April 20. K. was aggressive today. She hit C. and made her cry . . . Today we played some music while they were playing. It seems to calm them down. Today, though, they were all aggressive. They have a soft, cushiony tunnel that they like to play with. Both E. and K. were trying to get into it at the same time. They were wrestling each other, laughing most of the time; but then the hitting and hair pulling started.

April 27. K. was my buddy today for a while. She wanted me to help her go up and down the slide. I must have done it about five times. She is having problems with her teeth so she wanted (the teacher) to give her her bottle today, not me.

May 6. K.'s mom came in worried because she saw blood on K.'s car seat. R. told her she had a paper cut when she came in. (Her mom) took K. with her for an hour before she had class.

May 11. Today was such a nice day out that we decided to take the infants for a walk after we had snack and changed diapers . . . K. fell asleep in the back of the wagon. Her head was leaned way back and everyone would look at her as we were walking through campus. We just told everyone that she had a bad night. Our walk lasted about forty minutes.

May 13. K. is going all day without a bottle now. She will be one on the 24th of May. Her mom told us that she thought it would take her longer to get K. off the bottle. To get her to sleep, we usually just rock her.

Journal Writing

*Advantages**

1. Students have a wide choice of topics and can focus on those of interest to them.

2. They can write about their own feelings and experiences, which are an important part of the learning process. The way one experiences what goes on in a particular setting will be different from how others saw or felt it.

3. The actual writing does not need to be done on site. Notes may be taken during the session. These can be expanded later into the word processor or into a notebook.

4. Keeping a journal helps students clarify what is happening in the group or classroom by forcing them to synthesize the information they are receiving and make choices about what they put into writing.

5. The journal can help the university supervisor know what the student is experiencing. Often the supervisor sees the student only a few times each quarter or semester. The journal provides a starting point for discussing what the student is getting out of the practicum or student teaching.

Disadvantages

1. Writing in a journal several times a week is time consuming.

2. The information students choose to record may not be very useful for planning a curriculum.

3. Some students may have a difficult time understanding the usefulness of reflecting on their own practice. It may require a skillful supervisor to help them interpret what they are seeing.

4. Observations are subjective. Students who have not worked much with young children may misinterpret what they are seeing.

When to Use

Journal writing can be done any time and anywhere.

* The format of using advantages, disadvantages, and when to use was suggested in a presentation by L. Fader (1992), *Understanding children: Observation is the key*. NAEYC Conference, New Orleans, LA.

Zeichner and Liston (1985) divided supervisors' comments into four categories: (1) factual—supervisor is concerned with what occurred in a teaching situation or with what will occur in the future; (2) prudential—comments revolve around suggestions of what to do or evaluations of what has been accomplished; (3) justificatory—supervisor focuses on the reasons employed when answering the adequacy questions of the form. Why do this rather than that?; and (4) critical—supervisor assesses the adequacy of justifications offered for pedagogical activities and examines the values and assumptions embedded in the content of the curriculum and instructional practices. Supervisors may require that journal entries be turned in or mailed to them on a weekly basis. Others will read the journal two or three times in a quarter/semester.

Rhoten (1991) reported that journals were used at one university by student teachers to record their negotiations with the cooperating teachers. Before they went out into the schools, the student teachers planned "developmentally appropriate" practices that they were to try to implement in their primary grade placements. In their journals students reflected on their own successes or failures in shaping the curriculum. Some students' journals reflected low autonomy. They eliminated their plans because the teacher scheduled the day, leaving no time to include what the students had proposed. Middle levels of autonomy were achieved when student teachers were able to "add" their activities to the regular schedule. Students who rated themselves as attaining high levels of autonomy integrated their developmentally appropriate ideas into the ongoing curriculum on a regular basis.

Reflecting on their own practices, inservice teachers can analyze and modify their curriculum. Williams (1989) asked teachers in a master's practicum to reflect on their ongoing classroom behavior with young children. The instructors' written comments in their journals were seen as instrumental in getting teachers to change or refine their practices.

Journal writing is also a good way to practice writing skills. Students benefit by having to find new ways to express what they are feeling and experiencing. Students who enjoy writing often find keeping a journal therapeutic and look forward to sitting down and sifting through their thoughts for the most salient episodes of the day to commit to paper.

 Some tips on writing a journal entry:

1. Always write in the date and time of the observation.

2. Decide ahead of time what aspects of the program will be the focus of each entry. You cannot write about everything you observe each time, so you need to be selective.

3. In order to protect the identity of each child use initials or pseudonyms in your journal.

4. Write in your journal each time you observe. It is amazing how quickly your impressions and ideas can fade if they are not written down immediately. If you are in a program five days a week, you may decide to write in your journal only twice a week. Allow yourself at least a half hour to write each entry.

◆ **ACTIVITY**
2.1

Keeping a Reflective Diary

In a loose-leaf notebook, start a journal of your experiences in the early childhood setting where you have your practicum or student teaching assignment. Concentrate on what the children are doing. You might start by focusing on one or two children who seem to be having difficulty adjusting to the group or classroom setting. Write in your journal each day you observe or participate.

Teachers with their own classroom may choose a time or place for journaling once or twice a week. If you have a computer in your classroom, that might make your recording easier. Find a time and place that works for you. Use this journal as a time to reflect on your own teaching practices as well as recording observations of children. "How else could I have handled that?," "How should I follow up or extend this activity or lesson?," "Why did that activity fail to elicit the children's interest?," "What do I believe about how children learn?" are all appropriate questions to examine.

Audio Recording

If students and teachers want to learn more about young children's language skills, they can use a tape recorder to get samples of children's verbal abilities. Students and teachers may also want to see how they use questions to elicit children's responses or may want to examine strategies they use to keep

---

 Audio Recording

Advantages

1. Tape recorders are easy to operate. Children can learn to use them.
2. Tape recorders are portable and can be moved around easily.
3. They can be listened to repeatedly by different people in order to analyze the material collected.
4. Children can listen to themselves and evaluate their own performances.

Disadvantages

1. Some children (and adults) are reluctant to talk in the presence of a tape recorder.
2. Listening to and transcribing audiotapes can be an arduous task, especially if not done soon after the observations.

When to Use

1. Audio recording can be used any time language samples are needed.
2. Verbal interactions between the teacher and child or between children can be recorded and analyzed.

conversations going. They may wish to listen in on child–child or child–teacher verbal exchanges to see where misunderstandings occur. Recorders can be placed strategically around the room. Audiotapes are inexpensive to use: Teachers can play the tapes repeatedly in order to understand what is being said and can then record over tapes they have finished analyzing. While some young children are inhibited from speaking by the presence of a tape recorder, most really like to listen to themselves.

Another use of audio recording may be to document and analyze children's progress in reading. Primary grade teachers may ask for a cassette to be provided for each child. Periodic recordings of the child's reading progress can be used as a conferencing tool with parents. The tapes can be kept by parents at the end of the year or sent on to the next teacher for an ongoing record.

A busy teacher may find it easier to carry around a small tape recorder and speak her observations into it than to take the time to write them down.

Videotaping

Videotaping is an obvious educational tool in providing instruction, but it is also one of the most accurate ways to observe and record interaction in the group or classroom. Not only is there a visual moving picture, noises and spoken words are included as well. A video recorder can be set up on a tripod and placed in an unobtrusive spot. Children soon become used to its being there.

A videotape has numerous uses: A short video of each child playing or working with others can be included in the child's portfolio for review by parents, allowing the parent to see the child in a group context. Teachers can review tapes to get information on many different aspects of a child's development. At one point, they may want to examine the tapes to look at chil-

 Videotaping

Advantages

1. Videotaping gives a visual and auditory record of what really happened.
2. Teachers and students can review the tapes numerous times, often focusing on different aspects of the situation.

Disadvantages

1. The equipment is expensive and, except in the case of very small video recorders, heavy. Not all schools or programs have the equipment.
2. It takes time to review and analyze the tapes.

When to Use

1. Videotaping can be used any time to get a general picture of the classroom environment.
2. It can be used for specific purposes with a particular child or group of children.

dren's physical abilities. At another time, they may look at the same tape to find out how long children persevere in a certain task. Recording children at different times during the year can give a very accurate longitudinal profile.

Teachers or students can also see how *they* relate to children and examine their own speech and gestures. This method is especially helpful to student teachers. They can arrange to have themselves taped and then review and analyze what they have seen. Some university supervisors may also review the tape or require that students submit a short written summary of what they have discovered about their own behavior from watching themselves on videotape.

◆ **ACTIVITY**
2.2

Videotaping

If the program or school has videotaping equipment, see if you can use it to record your own performance or to document the behavior of a particular child in the classroom. Bring in your own blank tape. You could have another student operate the camera or just set it up somewhere in the classroom and let it run. If you are focusing on a child, be certain that you have written permission from the parents stating how the tape will be used. Make a 30-minute tape.

Tapes are only as good as the analysis you make of them. Review the tape at least twice. Take brief notes as you view it the second time.

If you are taping yourself, write down what you were doing well. Then review the tape and write down behaviors that should be modified. It can make you conscious of gestures and body language you might want to change. Are you constantly repeating yourself or using the same words to respond to every child? Try turning off the volume and focusing only on your actions or gestures. Identity any that you think need to be improved. These are behaviors you can work on.

If you are focusing on a particular child, again review the tapes at least twice. Write down what you saw the child doing well and where that child may need teacher guidance to change an inappropriate behavior.

Anecdotal Records

An anecdote is a brief account of an important developmental event. Anecdotes tell stories. Stories are inherently interesting, and all cultures use them to communicate information. Feelings, as well as facts, can be revealed. Anecdotes recorded over time and representing all developmental areas can give a comprehensive picture of a child's development and become the basis for planning instruction.

Writing an anecdote about children at play or work can be illustrative of their levels of development in several domains. A story of an individual child and how he or she tackles a task can reveal much about his or her intellectual functioning. An anecdote that chronicles what a pair of children is doing and saying in a dramatic play episode can reveal much about each child's social

◆ *Anecdotes of dramatic play provide information about children's social and language skills.*

and language skills. Describing what happens when the classroom is overcrowded or a fire drill takes place can show strengths and weaknesses in the program.

Anecdotes have a beginning, a middle, and an end. Generally, the setting is described first. This may include the physical setting, time of day, and number of children involved. It may be helpful to have the names, genders, ages, and socioeconomic statuses of the children involved. Events are then recorded in the sequence in which they occur. At the end conclusions are drawn. An anecdote is presented in Example 2.2.

◆ EXAMPLE 2.2
An Anecdotal Account

C. W., a five-year-old boy, was playing in the housekeeping corner with two younger girls. He had lined up all the dolls and stuffed animals. Each time one of the other children reached for one, he would authoritatively yell, "That's mine." The other children would go back to playing with the dishes and play food. They tried several times to take one of the dolls or animals. Ms. K. overheard the struggle finally and came over and whispered to C. W., "You're one of the oldest children in the group and you know how to share the toys. I'm counting on you to show the others how to share." C. W.'s behavior changed immediately. He handed some of the dolls and animals to the girls and they prepared meals together and fed the babies until clean-up time.

The teacher inferred from this abrupt change in behavior that C. W. had a good understanding of what kind of behaviors were expected of him, but had momentarily forgotten. Her clearly stated reminder helped C. W. exhibit more mature behavior. Ms. K. could follow this incident up at group time by discussing the need for "sharing with our friends at preschool" or use a storybook to reinforce cooperation.

Anecdotal Records

Advantages

1. They are quick and easy to do. They require only pencil and paper.
2. They can be used to focus on significant behaviors in different developmental domains.
3. They can include information about the context of the behavior and give a richer picture of the child than some other methods.
4. Stories are appealing to most audiences.
5. They can be done without separating self from ongoing classroom activities.
6. They can focus on both typical and atypical behavior—understanding a child's unusual way of coping in the classroom is as important as understanding his or her usual reactions.

Disadvantages

1. Anecdotes are not a complete picture of the behavior. An anecdote may focus on a unique incident and not be a representative sample of the child's behavior.
2. Bias is possible in writing anecdotes because the observer chooses what to record.

When to Use

1. Anecdotes can be used almost any time you are observing children: You simply tell a story about what you see.
2. They may be valuable for recording the context of a situation in which a child does something usual and again when he or she displays ways of interacting different from his or her typical behavior.

Roberta Shreve (1993) has suggested using sticky notes to record anecdotal observations, as they can later be transferred to a page in the child's folder or portfolio. She also recommends that every observation be followed by a statement indicating the developmental significance of what was observed and the implications for teaching or planning.

Sociometric Techniques

Beginning in the early childhood years children spend increasingly less time with family members and more time with peers. Therefore, it is essential to optimal development that children learn appropriate social skills that enable

Sociometric Techniques

Advantages	**Disadvantages**
1. Sociometric techniques can be used to help teachers understand the dynamics of a particular group of children.	1. Young children's social preferences are often ephemeral—they change from day to day.
2. Teachers can use the information to identify children who may need help learning appropriate social skills.	2. Teacher interventions may need to be long-term before some children are fully accepted into the group. Children who are neglected or rejected often have well-established patterns of interacting and are not temperamentally disposed to changing them.

When to Use

1. When the class is not working together.
2. When some of the children in the group are being rejected or neglected.

them to interact effectively with peers. Sociometric techniques have been developed to enable teachers to assess the social interactions of children in group settings. These techniques, often referred to as sociograms, allow teachers to classify children as being *popular*, *rejected*, or *neglected* with their peers (Cole & Koeppel 1990; Dodge *et al.* 1986).

Sociometric techniques may be employed by systematic observations of children in group settings to see who plays together and who plays alone. Other effective sociometric techniques involve direct interviewing or surveying of children by asking them to identify members of the group they would like to work or play with and those they would prefer not to work or play with. Teachers are then able to sort children into the three categories. They can use this information to form work and play groups that enable rejected or neglected children to observe the social skills of popular children. They can also plan lessons and interventions for these children to help them acquire the appropriate social skills that they will need for success in school and life.

Event Sampling

Often it is necessary to have a very specific focus for observing. You may need to zero in on a particular recurring problem. Essa (1990) has suggested that conscious observation can yield valuable information and provide the basis for more exact handling of problem behaviors. For example, if the children in the toddler room are becoming irritable before lunch and several are falling asleep at the table, it may be beneficial to document how often this happens over the period of a week or ten days. You could think of several alternative ways to solve this problem. You might decide to ask the director and kitchen staff to serve lunch to the toddlers a half-hour before the preschool group. You would observe the toddlers' behavior for several days after you have instituted the new lunch time to see if that makes a difference.

Some teachers and students may choose to do a random sample of children. They may observe what one child is doing for fifteen seconds, record for thirty seconds, and then go on to the next child on the list. The behaviors can be coded to make recording simpler. For example, any time a child is smiling, it can be recorded as *S*. When the child is taking something in another child's possession, a *T* can be marked. The behaviors to be recorded are defined beforehand and tallied later. This way the behaviors of a large number of children can be recorded in a relatively short time. Children who show a large number of inappropriate behaviors over several days or weeks can be targeted for more detailed observations.

The next step would be to focus on a particular child's behavior. If three-year-old Franny is showing many instances of nonparticipation and wanders around the room never really engaging with others, she may need the teacher's attention. For instance, she may need some help in making decisions about what she wants to do, or something that is happening at home may be bothering her. Finding out what the problem is and determining possible solutions may help her to function better.

Another child, Nicole, a kindergartner, seems to be unpopular with the other children. The teacher may observe her to see how she tries to enter groups. If she is pushy and always demands that she get her own way, she may need to learn some negotiating skills. If the others reject her because she is overweight, they may need some help recognizing their biases. These observations will serve to pinpoint the causes of inappropriate behavior. The observations could be a prelude to teaching children more adaptable social skills or intervening in some other way.

A form could be developed that might include the following components:

1. Targeted behavior
2. Causes of misbehavior
   a. Antecedent events
   b. Consequences of behavior
   c. Interpretation of information from observations
3. Behaviors to be encouraged
4. Strategies to be used in intervening
5. Follow-up—Later observations to see if the problem is solved

Example 2.3 shows how this form could be used when a child's behavior is not what he or she usually displays or is inappropriate to classroom expectations.

◆ **EXAMPLE 2.3**
   Event Sampling

Group observed _____   Child's age _____

Date and time _____   Observer _____

Target Behavior

The first graders in Ms. W's class report that Simon, usually well-behaved in the class-room, has been hitting children on the playground. (Ms. W observes the group in outdoor play during recess. Usually an aide supervises this.)

Time	Antecedent Behavior	Behavior	Consequences
9:45	Several of the other boys in the class tease Simon about his inability to catch them when they are playing tag. Simon has a slight physical disability attributable to mild cerebral palsy that makes it difficult for him to run.	Simon reacts by lashing out with his fists.	Children get hurt when Simon hits. Simon is angry and hurt by the teasing. The other children are not finding ways to include Simon.

Preferred Behavior

Simon should be a part of the group games without being teased and without losing his temper and hitting. The other children will be aware of the need to include all who want to play in their games.

Interpretation

Simon gets very frustrated by their taunts. The other children do not understand the effect their behavior has on Simon.

Interventions to be Made

The teacher can talk to all the children involved and see if they can find a solution to the problem. She might tell them about the difficulty Simon has because of his disability. She could also suggest some other games they could play that would not require speed. Simon can be coached in ways to express his displeasure by verbalizing his anger.

Follow Up

The teacher or aide can observe the outdoor play of the group for the next several days to see if the situation is remedied.

Event Sampling

Advantages	**Disadvantages**

Advantages

1. This method can uncover causes and effects of behavior.
2. Results of observations can be used to plan appropriate interventions at individual child's developmental level.

Disadvantages

1. Results cannot be generalized to another child or group of children.
2. Event sampling requires time and skill to code behaviors and record incidents.
3. It is not always easy to establish the causes of behaviors.

When to Use

1. Event sampling can be used to explore causes and effects of behaviors.
2. Event sampling can be used when a child behaves in ways that are atypical for him or her or when a child shows repeated inappropriate behavior.
3. When the schedule seems inappropriate for a group of children, event sampling may help identify the problem.

◆ **ACTIVITY**

2.3

Event Sampling

Using the format given in Example 2.3, make up a blank sheet with the same categories. Observe children on a playground, in the park, at a mall, at a restaurant or some other public place. When you see an instance where a child is doing something that would usually be labeled misbehavior by adults, make suggestions about how an adult could intervene. If there were adults in the area, tell what they actually did or said.

Running Record

A quick way to study the behavior of one or two children is through the use of the "running record" method (Hills 1992). She defines a running record as a "sequential record over a given time, recorded while the behavior is occurring: used to document what children are doing in the particular situation (with a focus on social or pre-academic activity); used for teachers' planning for individuals and groups." A student or teacher who can sit on the sidelines and follow a particular child or children can learn much about what each child does, with whom he or she interacts, and what interests the child. In the running record method behavior is recorded at regular, preset intervals.

 Running Record

Advantages	Disadvantages
1. Teachers can observe behaviors in a natural setting.	1. Running record takes time and training to do.
2. They can serve as a basis for further assessment or to validate other assessment measures.	2. When engaged in running record, the students and teachers cannot interact with children.
3. They can be fairly objective.	3. Observers may miss some important information when recording their observations because behaviors are not seen in context.
4. Teachers can use them to observe interactions between children.	
5. They can be used with more than one child at a time.	4. Observers can overestimate the frequency of occurrence of certain behaviors based on a small sample of time.
6. Teachers can document small changes in behavior.	
7. They can be used to develop learning experiences for particular children.	

When to Use

Running record should be used when teachers are concerned about the behavior of a particular child or small group of children.

Ten minutes is probably too long an interval; two minutes may be too short. Three to five minutes is more workable. That gives the observer a minute to observe and two or three minutes to record.

One easy way to manage the running record with one child is to make a chart with the time units listed on the left. The middle column is used to record, as objectively as possible, the behaviors the child exhibits. A third column can be added to give the observer a place to write comments or inferences about the behaviors observed. The teacher or student then examines the running record observations and writes a paragraph about the educational implications for this child or children—that is, what follow-up or intervention the teacher should plan as a result of what was discovered through this method.

The following observation (Example 2.4) took place during free-play time in a preschool. Two children were observed alternately: L., a boy, is four-and-a-half years old. M., who just turned five, is a girl. The teacher suspects M. might have fetal alcohol syndrome. Both have been in this group about four weeks.

◆ **EXAMPLE 2.4**
Running Record Method

Time	Observation	Comments
9:00	L. tells the teacher he didn't have time for lunch. She ignores or doesn't hear him. He gets a drink from the fountain and moves over to talk to some boys just entering.	He probably means breakfast.
9:04	L. is painting at the easel—first with his left hand, then with his right, then with both at one time. He stops to watch children at the art table. He tells the teacher, "I'm done," when she walks by.	His handedness isn't set yet. He takes advantage of teacher's nearness.
9:09	L. is sponge-painting at the art table. He stops to watch children moving by the table. He takes his painting to the windowsill to dry.	He does a lot of watching of other children
9:12	L. is sitting in boat with two other boys. He's fishing with a large magnet on a string. The other boys leave. He continues to rock the boat. The boys come back. They stop the boat completely so a boy with difficulty walking can climb in.	He is adept at hooking fish. He can play on his own. They were considerate of child with handicap.
9:16	L. is still in boat watching other boys building with cardboard blocks. He goes to sit at the piano and plays softly.	L. seems to pay attention to what other children are doing.
9:19	L. and M. are still at piano. L. roars at her and she runs away. He goes over to watch boys building with blocks. He then goes over to sink and asks teacher, "Why did you put it (key to towel dispenser) up there?" When the teacher goes to answer the phone, he takes a wooden puzzle and sits down to put it together.	L. moves around a lot, but always seems to be engaged.
9:26	L. is still at puzzle table with peg board. He puts in a few pegs, takes them out, and leaves the table. He sits down at namecard table with teacher who is encouraging children to try writing their names. He recognizes the first letter of his name when the teacher shows him several on tagboard. He makes several letter-like marks on his paper.	L. seems pleased with his efforts to write his name.
9:32	L. takes name to mailbox. A girl comes to tell teacher that L. can't find his mailbox. The teacher comes to help him.	L. seems adept at getting help from others.
8:52	M. and another girl walk over to the dramatic play area, a fruit and vegetable market. They seat the large doll at the table. M. opens a grocery bag and begins to fill it with dishes.	M. and girl play with the same toys, but do not speak to each other.
9:02	M. moves to table where teacher is putting out markers. Then she and other girl go back to market. She pets a stuffed tiger. She looks at self in mirror and follows her friend.	The teacher later tells me that tiger is her favorite toy. So far, she has not spoken.
9:08	M. stands behind another child at art table watching the children there. She puts her tiger down and walks to the block area and watches 3 children in the rocking boat.	She doesn't seem able to enter any scene.

Time	Observation	Comments
9:10	M. is by herself at the piano. She experiments with the pedals and plays a few notes. She runs over to children in boat, yells, "Ow, ow." When they pay no attention, she gets a drum. She plays it and says, "Too loud, too loud."	The other children ignore her bids for attention.
9:15	M. is still trying out different rhythm instruments one at a time.	She's experimenting with different sounds.
9:17	M. goes to boat and swings the magnet ineffectively trying to catch fish. She rushes back to piano and pushes pedals for L. with her hands.	She doesn't seem to know how the fishing game works. She's trying to see what the pedals do.
9:23	M. is sitting in boat with big doll and another girl. Again, she waves magnet at fish without picking any up. She leaves boat, sits near it to watch boys building. She talks to self and slaps her head.	There is no interaction with others.
9:28	M. is at sponge-painting table. She completes her painting very quickly, takes off apron, washes her hands, and gets a drink. The student reminds her to take her painting to windowsill. She goes to block structure and sits in the middle. M. ignores teacher's invitation to come to name-writing table.	When given directions, M. follows them, but still doesn't seem really involved.
9:33	M. was able to recognize her namecard. She is scribbling on her paper with markers.	I was surprised to see that she recognized her name. Her scribbling seems immature.

Implications

L. seems to be adjusting well to this group setting. He is able to make decisions about what he will do. He can work alone or with others. He asks for help when he needs it. He completes the tasks he starts. He follows adult directions well.

M.'s language development seems slow for her age. I did hear her say, "Too loud." It sounded like an admonition to herself. She did not talk to the other children or adults. She went from one part of the room to another without really getting involved in anything except the experimenting with sounds. Could there possibly be a hearing problem?

Perhaps a teacher could show her how the magnet fishing game works and set up a center with magnets for her to try out. A teacher might also help her enter into play situations with the other children.

M. may need special services.

◆ **ACTIVITY**
2.4

Running Record

Arrange to observe a child between two and six in an early childhood setting, preferably when the children have some choice about where they will work or play. Ask the teacher to suggest a student you could observe. Keep a running account of that child's actions and verbalizations (if you can hear them) for about forty-five minutes. Be sure to leave a column for your comments. When you are finished, write up a summary of your assessment of that child's adjustment to the group based on what you observed in this short time. Remember to change the name of the child and not to discuss what you observed outside of class.

Rating Scales

Several different designs of rating scales are used with young children. One kind requires that the informed observer determine where a child's behavior fits on a 3- to 7-point scale. Generally, a Likert scale has several points that

 ### Rating Scales

Advantages

1. Rating scales are easy to use. They require less time than most other methods.
2. They can be used to compare the behaviors of several children.
3. Students and teachers can use them to assess many different areas of the program or many different child behaviors at one time.

Disadvantages

1. They may be biased because the rater is asked to make judgments.
2. They are not very accurate. Sometimes none of the categories fit the behaviors observed.
3. There is a need to carefully define what different ratings mean to maintain consistency among raters.

When to Use

1. Rating scales should be used when teachers want to know, in general, how well or how often a behavior takes place.
2. When assessing many different aspects of a program or several child behaviors, rating scales are appropriate.
3. They are useful in making overall assessments for diagnosing individual needs.
4. They can be used to chart a child's growth over time.

vary along a continuum from "almost always" to "almost never" or from "very quickly" to "very slowly" or other polar descriptors. They require that the rater make judgments as to where to score the child on each item. They also require that some criterion of inter-rater reliability be established. This means that there is reasonable assurance that two people rating the same child at the same time on the same behaviors will agree a certain percentage of the time. Galle (1993) suggested videotaping examples of targeted behaviors and using these as training tools to establish a satisfactory rate of inter-rater reliability. An acceptable rate must be decided on by the observers. Generally, an agreement rate of 85 percent or better is considered very good. In situations were it may be difficult to differentiate targeted behaviors, 70 percent or better may be the rate set.

Another scale uses written categories of behavior and asks the observer to choose the category most similar to the child's behavior. This type of scale can be used to measure how well or how often a child exhibits certain pre-stated behaviors. An example of a rating scale designed to rate individual pre-school children's performance is the *Child Observation Record* (1992), published by High/Scope Educational Research Foundation. Example 2.5 is a sample of this type of rating scale.

Of special help to early childhood professionals are rating scales that consider the program environment. They assess the physical arrangement of the room, the effectiveness of health care routines, the learning and social environment for the children, and the provisions for meeting adult needs. Harms and Clifford (1980, 1989) and Harms, Cryer, and Clifford (1990) have developed instruments to examine the strengths and weaknesses in programs for young children. Shimoni, MacLean, and MacWilliam (1990) have developed an infant/toddler program evaluation instrument based on the work of Belsky and Walker (1980). See Appendix A.

The NAEYC accreditation process involves ratings by teachers, administrators, and parents. Hildebrand (1993, 43–44) has outlined the steps that must be taken to complete that process.

◆ **EXAMPLE 2.5**
Sample Item from a Rating Scale Using Categories of Behavior

Temporal Sequencing
1. Child does none of the following
2. Child plans/anticipates future sequence of events (e.g., next activity in the daily routine)
3. Child describes/represents past events
4. Child represents the order/sequence of events in own activities (e.g., drawings, dramatic play, series of construction)
5. Child is aware that clocks and calendars mark the passage of time

Checklists

Checklists are an easy way to gather specific information on a group or whole classroom of young children when the behaviors can be easily observed. Good checklists have clearly defined items—the child either has the ability or does not. For example, it would be fairly simple to observe a small group of four-year-olds at the collage table and check which on the list were able to cut along a straight line with scissors. You could talk to children individually to see who could identify colors or count to ten. Checklists can be completed in a natural context without putting the child in a "testing" situation. When you are finished with a checklist of skills to be mastered, it would be easy to see at a glance who needed more time or experience to learn certain skills.

 Checklists

Advantages

1. Checklists are easy to use. Usually the behavior or condition is either present or it is not.
2. They can be helpful in planning for individual needs. The teacher can tell at a glance who does or does not possess a certain skill or has had a specific experience.
3. The teacher can record more than one child at a time.
4. The checklist can often be done without the child being aware that he or she is being observed.
5. The checklist usually specifies in detail which behaviors are to be observed.
6. Teachers can make their own checklists to fit their curricula.

Disadvantages

1. Teachers may use checklists that are not appropriate for the developmental level of the children.
2. Teachers may follow a checklist too rigidly.
3. The checklist may dictate the curriculum: Teachers who want children to do well may teach according to the checklist, but some children may not yet be ready to learn certain skills.
4. Quality and context of behaviors are compromised with checklists.

When to Use

1. When teachers want to know who has or has not completed a certain task or learned a clearly defined skill, checklists are a way to assess many children within a short time.
2. Checklists are used to identify children who need remediation to master specific tasks.

If observing a larger group, the names of several children could be placed on the chart. A small set of particular behaviors could be given code letters or numbers. The group could be observed for a certain time interval and if any of the target behaviors are exhibited by members of the group, they could be recorded next to the child's name. Gordon and Browne (1993, 192) give an example in which seven children were observed at five-minute intervals to see if they showed Parallel, Associative, or Cooperative play (Example 2.6). These terms were clearly defined so observers could distinguish them from one another. No other behaviors were recorded.

While there are several checklists commercially available, teachers can themselves identify the behaviors they want to target and make their own checklists. A "Kindergarten Checklist" from the Hattiesburg, Mississippi, Public School District (Grace & Shores 1992, 44) can be marked *S* for "satisfactory," *I* for "needs improvement," or / (slash mark) for "has not been taught in the curriculum at this time." It includes fifty-eight items under social/emotional, verbal, cognitive, linguistic, visual perception, and prenumber and number concepts. An example from the visual perception section is "Demonstrates ability to complete puzzles with more than ten pieces." The child is either able to do it and receives an *S*, has attempted to do it and been unsuccessful and gets an *I*, or, if there are no ten-piece puzzles in the room or if this child has made no attempts to put one together, he or she gets a /. In Activity 2.5 you and your classmates or teaching colleagues can make your own checklists.

◆ **EXAMPLE 2.6**
   A Checklist

Type of Play Behavior Exhibited

P = parallel
A = associative
C = cooperative

Child's Name	9:00 P A C	9:05 P A C	9:10 P A C	9:15 P A C
1. Stephanie	— — —	— — —	— — —	— — —
2. Ricky	— — —	— — —	— — —	— — —
3. Samantha	— — —	— — —	— — —	— — —
4. Natalie	— — —	— — —	— — —	— — —
5. Rashad	— — —	— — —	— — —	— — —
6. Michael	— — —	— — —	— — —	— — —
7. Noah	— — —	— — —	— — —	— — —

◆ **ACTIVITY**
2.5

Making a Checklist

Whatever the age-group you are targeting, with a classmate or colleague make a checklist that any early childhood teacher should be able to fill out after working with the group for a few weeks. Some possible items for different age groups are given. You will think of more as you work with children at different developmental levels.

- Infants
  Sleep habits
  Diaper changes
  Eating habits
  Social behaviors
  Developmental milestones (rolling over, sitting)

- Toddlers
  Language skills (uses gestures to make needs known, one-word utterances)
  Motor skills (walks by self, holds crayon, etc.)
  Social behaviors (watches others, plays near, but not with, others)

- Preschoolers
  Motor skills (galloping, climbing)
  Play preferences (plays with others, shares toys)
  Cognitive abilities (counting, recognizes colors, etc.)
  Social behaviors in the group setting (can enter into group, participates in group activities)

- Kindergarten children
  Fine motor skills (cutting, writing name)
  Cognitive abilities (letter/number recognition, sequencing)
  Communication skills (listening, retelling stories)
  Social skills (shows concern for others, engages in cooperative/dramatic play)

- Primary children
  Motor skills (printing, folding, skipping)
  Social skills (group games, follows rules)
  Cognitive skills (letter/sound association, writing skills)
  Communication skills (active listening, makes eye contact)

After you have made your checklist, ask others to look at it and give you their reactions. Would it be feasible to rate a child using your instrument? Revise if you need to. Try out your checklist in the classroom. Evaluate your results. Did you learn anything valuable about the children you rated? What might you suggest as intervention for those children who showed lacks or problems in certain areas?

Case Studies

A case study is an in-depth look at an individual child. It is often based on both observations of and interviews with the child (Berger 1994). Often these interviews and observations take place within a short timeframe. Ideally more than one observation is made while the child is engaged in various types of activities to provide a comprehensive view of the child's development. Lay-Dopyera and Dopyera (1993) provide questions to guide observation of children's physical and motor development, affective and social development, and cognitive and intellectual development. For example, they ask about a child's ability to seriate: "On what basis does the child appropriately order objects or events? How many?" Efforts to acquire background information about the child by interviewing parents, teachers, and other significant adults who know the child and by examining available documentation such as medical or educational records, baby books, or pictures enrich the portrait of the child.

The case study method is often employed when teachers or agencies are working with children who may have special needs or are at-risk. Indeed, a case study may be required by state or federal agencies to supplement observations and interviews of the child and formal screening instruments (Examples 2.7 and 2.8) or standardized diagnostic tests in order to obtain such funding. (While many early childhood education professionals consider the use of standardized testing inappropriate as a general assessment tool for young children, it is sometimes necessary to use such instruments on individual children to determine their eligibility for special services. Spodek and Saracho (1994, 47–100) suggest methods of screening and assessing young children to identify their educational needs. They also provide a brief list of available screening and assessment instruments for young children and note the age range and a general description of each instrument.)

Case studies are usually summarized in written form to identify the child's strengths, needs, and recommendations for continued development. McAfee and Leong (1994) suggested that gathering information about a child

◆ **EXAMPLE 2.7**
Screening Instruments Teachers Might Use

ABC Inventory (1965). Muskegon, MI: Research Concepts.
Comprehensive Identification Process (1970). Bensenville, IL: Scholastic Testing Service.
Cooperative Preschool Inventory (1970). Princeton, NJ: Educational Testing Service.
Denver Developmental Screening Test (1970). Denver, CO: Ladoca Project and Publishing, Inc.
Developmental Indicators for the Assessment of Learning (1975). Highland Park, IL: DIAL, Inc.
Metropolitan Readiness Test (1976). Atlanta, GA: Psychological Corp.

From Spodek & Saracho 1994, 242. Used with permission of Allyn & Bacon.

◆ **EXAMPLE 2.8**
Assessment Instruments for Young Children

Instrument	Age Level	Purpose
Caldwell Preschool Inventory	3–6 years	Assessing abilities in a variety of areas
Denver II	2 weeks–6 years	Diagnosing developmental delays in adaptive, motor, language, and personal-social areas
Engleman's Basic Concept Inventory	preschool and kindergarten	Assessing basic concepts and awareness of patterns, using repetition and completion of statements
Cassell Developmental Schedules	4 weeks–6 years	Diagnosing the maturity of the young child's adaptive, motor, language, and personal-social development
Illinois Test of Psycholinguistic Abilities	2–10 years	Assessing auditory, visual, verbal, and memory abilities
Metropolitan Readiness Tests	kindergarten and first grade	Assessing educational abilities such as listening, matching, and copying, as well as understanding the alphabet, numbers, word meanings, and totals (drawing a person is optional)
Peabody Picture Vocabulary Test	2 1/2–18 years	Assessing vocabulary, matching a word to one of four pictures
Stanford-Binet Intelligence Scale	2 years and older	Assessing individual intelligence
Wechsler Preschool and Primary Scale of Intelligence	4–6 years	Assessing intelligence in fourteen areas of verbal and perceptual performance

Taken from Spodek & Saracho 1994, 243. Used with permission of Allyn & Bacon.

through "windows" of multiple *sources* (child, peers, family, teachers, written records), *methods* (observations, interviews, work samples), and *settings* (outdoors, indoors, school, home) results in a more complete and comprehensive picture of the child. Lay-Dopyera and Dopyera (1993) suggested that observers produce a descriptive narrative of a child's behavior by recording the time, setting, and as much detail as possible. They felt that professionals must distinguish in writing descriptive narratives between *reporting*, *inferring*, and *evaluating*. Reporting is describing actual behaviors of the child, while inferring goes a step beyond what is seen as you try to guess or infer the underlying goals, causes, or feelings related to the behavior. Evaluating involves making a judgment as to whether the behavior observed is appropriate/inappropriate, mature/immature, or positive/negative.

Case Study

Advantages	*Disadvantages*
1. It focuses on the strengths and needs of one child.	1. Case studies involve a number of people and a commitment of time. It is often difficult to schedule a meeting time so everyone can be included.
2. Case studies use a variety of sources, methods, and settings.	2. Results are individual and do not apply to other children.
3. A case study produces a multifaceted picture of one child.	
4. A case study is useful in planning a comprehensive intervention program for a particular child.	
5. Case studies may meet the requirements for special educational services.	

When to Use

Case studies are a longitudinal, detailed study of one child. They can be very helpful in examining the long-term care and education for any child, but especially for children with disabilities.

The case study may form the basis for writing an Individualized Family Service Plan (IFSP), to provide special services for children from birth through age five, or an Individualized Education Program (IEP), for children (three to twenty-one years) needing special education services (Cohen & Spenciner 1994). The IFSP documents required for special services are completed by teams consisting of the child's parents or guardians, early childhood teacher, and other specialists such as the speech therapist, social worker, physical therapist, and so forth, depending on the needs of the child or family (Mc-Gonigel *et al.* 1991, Bennett *et al.* 1990). A multidisciplinary team that includes the parents is also responsible for writing an IEP, which must include specific assessment information.

Child Studies

G. Stanley Hall, Arnold Gesell, and Lawrence Frank were key people in the early child study movement of the late 1800s and early 1900s (McAfee & Leong 1994). In order to learn more about "developmental norms" in the growth and development of children, these pioneers established child study centers at universities and developed surveys and questionnaires for children and parents. Norms tell us what behaviors to expect from *most*, but not all, children of a given age or developmental period. The child study methods

Child Studies

Advantages

1. Research can be used to establish developmental norms.
2. Having normative data means that teachers and others who work with young children can predict behavior that is likely to occur.
3. Research results can often be generalized to larger populations.
4. Results can often be used to design educational plans for a group of children.

Disadvantages

1. Research is often costly in time and resources.
2. Specialized training in research methods and statistics is needed to carry out and report findings.
3. Research generally focuses on groups of children rather than on individuals.
4. Some research on children's development does not have clear educational implications.

When to Use

1. Students and teachers can use the child study method to find out more about how young children develop.
2. Child studies can be done in the classroom to test the effectiveness of a particular method or practice.
3. Reading child study research and summaries can give practitioners ideas about how to shape their curricula.

currently employed by students of child development enable us to examine developmental change of children as they grow older.

Berns (1994) defined three methods for analyzing developmental change, including *longitudinal study*, *cross-sectional study*, and *sequential study*. Study of the developmental changes in a group of people over an extended period of time in one or more areas of development is known as a longitudinal study. The study of the Perry Preschool Project, for example, followed a group of children from their preschool years through their twenties in order to determine the long-term effects of early education. This kind of research takes many years to complete and has several inherent problems, such as the attrition of subjects, personnel changes, the effects of repeated testing, the use of obsolete instruments, and finding adequate funding.

A cross-sectional study includes groups of subjects of different ages in order to learn about the changes in one or several areas of development. For example, one might observe and/or interview groups of five-year-olds, ten-year-olds, and fifteen-year-olds to gain a perspective on how morals and gender roles develop and change. This method of child study involves a smaller amount of time, but it still has weaknesses. Finding a representative sample and avoiding "cohort effects" are two concerns of those who do this kind of research.

Sequential study combines longitudinal and cross-sectional methods with the study of several samples of children at different ages over a certain time period. Children in a sequential study are observed, tested, or interviewed over several years in order to determine the changes that result over time for different groups of children.

Experimental research designs randomly assign children to experimental or control groups. Quasi-experimental studies carefully match groups of children on many different variables such as age, sex, socioeconomic status, and family background. They can thus control some of the inherent problems in long-term studies.

The results of child study research are reported in educational and psychological journals. Some of those that focus on young children are listed in Table 2.1. These studies can be very helpful to early childhood educators.

◆ **TABLE 2.1** *A Partial List of Journals of Child Study Research Available in Most College or University Libraries*

American Educational Research Journal	Gifted Child Quarterly*
American Journal of Education	Harvard Educational Review
American Journal of Orthopsychiatry*	Infant Behavior and Development*
Child Abuse and Neglect	Journal of Abnormal Child Psychology*
Child and Youth Care Forum	Journal of Applied Behavior Analysis
Child Care Information Exchange†	Journal of Child Language*
Child Development*	Journal of Child Psychology and Psychiatry
Child Study Journal*	and Allied Disciplines*
Childhood Education†	Journal of Counseling Psychology
Children Today†	Journal of Educational Psychology
Day Care and Early Education†	Journal of Experimental Education
Developmental Psychology*	Journal of Home Economics
Early Childhood Education Journal	Journal of Marriage and the Family
Early Childhood Research Quarterly*	Journal of Research in Childhood Education*
Early Childhood Teacher	Journal of School Psychology
Early Childhood Today	Journal of Special Education
Early Education and Development*	Journal of Teacher Education
Education and Treatment of Children	Merrill-Palmer Quarterly*
Education Digest	Minnesota Symposia on Child Development*
Educational and Psychological Measurement	Phi Delta Kappan†
Educational Research	Psychoanalytic Study of the Child (yearbook)
Educational Theory	Psychology in the Schools
Elementary School Journal	Review of Educational Research
ERIC/EECE Newsletter†	Theory into Practice†
Exceptional Child*	Topics in Early Childhood Special Education
The Exceptional Parent	Young Children†

* = research most pertinent to teachers of young children

† = summaries of theory and research meant for teachers

They may be summarized in child development textbooks or in journals meant for practitioners. However, students and teachers should be aware of the wealth of information about young children available through reading the actual research articles themselves. Sometimes the educational implications of the studies noted are mentioned near the end of the article.

Portfolios

Many teachers have tried multiple ways of observing and evaluating children and found the portfolio an effective way to collect data on each child (Meisels & Steele 1991; Paulson *et al.* 1991; Grace & Shores 1992). It is especially valuable when reporting to parents about the child's progress. Grace and Shores (1992) found that the portfolio provided a basis for discussion at the parent–teacher conference.

Teachers and children can meet to select work samples such as drawings, photos of constructions, tape recordings of the child reading or telling a story, or writing samples to include in the portfolio. Teachers can also include test scores and their own recorded observations, checklists, rating scale, or other examples of systematic observations. All work will be dated to allow adults to follow the child's developmental progress in certain skills areas. Engel (1990) called this "keeping track" and emphasized that teachers should follow a child's successes rather than his or her failures. Children as early as preschool can help prepare their own portfolios by choosing which materials they want to present to their parents. The materials in each child's portfolio are much more tangible and concrete than abstract standardized test scores. After the child's portfolio is put together, the teacher writes a summary of the child's work for that time period.

Meisels and his associates at the University of Michigan (Harrington, Meisels, McMahon, Dichtelmiller, and Jablon 1997) have developed a performance assessment system, called the Work Sampling System, that is used in preschool through fifth grade. This is a plan for ongoing assessment three times per year. The system is complex and requires teachers and caregivers to develop skills for focusing and recording their observations of children.

Teachers usually receive two days of training before they are ready to implement the assessment plan. The trainers suggest that teachers start with only one or two domains the first year they use the instrument. There are developmental guidelines for each age group and children are assessed on several components in seven different domains: personal and social development, language and literacy, mathematical thinking, scientific thinking, social studies, the arts, and physical development. (See Example 2.9.)

Portfolios allow parents to ask questions or give information directly related to their child's work. When King (1991) used portfolios in a kindergarten classroom, the parents commented that they gave them tangible and visual proof of their children's achievements that far surpassed the experience of seeing a letter grade on a report card.

The Work Sampling System Summary Report

CHILD_____ AGE/GRADE _____

TEACHER _____ DATE _____

SCHOOL _____

ATTENDANCE: DAYS TARDY_____ DAYS ABSENT _____

FALL ☐
WINTER ☐
YEAR-END ☐

GENERAL COMMENTS: Give reasons for "Needs Development" and/or note special strengths and talents in each domain. Also give explanation if progress is other than expected. Describe plans for supporting child's growth.

WHITE – FAMILY   YELLOW – OFFICE   PINK – TEACHER

PROGRESS
- Other than Expected
- As Expected

PERFORMANCE

PORTFOLIO
- Needs Development
- As Expected

CHECKLIST
- Needs Development
- As Expected

DOMAINS & COMPONENTS

I Personal & Social Development
Self Concept
Self Control
Approach to learning
Interaction with others
Conflict resolution

II Language & Literacy
Listening
Speaking
Literature & reading
Writing
Spelling (1–3)

III Mathematical Thinking
Approach to mathematical thinking
Patterns and relationships
Number concept & operations
Geometry & spatial relations
Measurement
Probability & statistics (K–5)

IV Scientific Thinking
Observing
Questioning & predicting
Explaining & forming conclusions (K–5)

V Social Studies
Human similarities & differences
Human interdependence
Rights & responsibilities
People & where they live
People & the past (1–3)

VI The Arts
Expression & representation
Artistic appreciation

VII Physical Development
Gross motor development
Fine motor development
Personal health & safety

©1996 Rebus Planning Associates, Inc.

SEE REVERSE FOR HOW TO READ THE SUMMARY REPORT

© 2001 Rebus Inc. a Pearson Education, Inc. Company

◆ *Samples of a child's written work and drawings can become part of his portfolio.*

Cohen (1999) sees many benefits in using the portfolio method. 1)It provides a record of the child's changing development over time. 2)You can use the information gained to design instruction. 3)Children can use the process to understand their own strengths and needs and can see their own development by looking at their samples. 4)It provides a very effective tool for communication between children, parents, and teachers.

She suggests that before beginning the portfolio process you go through the following steps:

1. Involve the children. Tell them you will be collecting some of their work. Get their suggestions about what to put in and how to organize it. Let them ask questions.
2. Decide what you will use to organize and contain children's work. She suggests accordion folders or shopping bags that can hold video and audio tapes as well as art and work samples.
3. Also figure out where you will store these materials. They need to be within easy reach of the children and adults. She suggests putting them in different areas of the room so when it is time to get portfolios the children won't all be crowding into one space.
4. Try to make your assessment as comprehensive as possible. Because some areas such as physical, language, and social-emotional development don't lend themselves to concrete products, use different methods to show progress. For example, you could take pictures of the child/children actually building a block structure, write up an anecdotal account of two children resolving a conflict, or take a video of a class discussion session.

Portfolios

Advantages

1. Portfolios give a comprehensive picture of the child's abilities in many different areas of the curriculum.
2. Children can be involved in selecting materials to be included.
3. They are very useful to teachers for sharing information with parents or administrators.

Disadvantages

1. Portfolios require much advance planning and organization and require the teacher and children to set priorities about what is to be included.
2. They may tend to focus only on paper-and-pencil accomplishments. Musical and athletic abilities, for example, may be difficult to document.

When to Use

1. Portfolios develop over a period of several weeks or months. Samples to be included can be gathered at almost any time.
2. When parents or others need evidence they can respond to, portfolios are appropriate.

Many university teacher education programs require that each student prepare his or her own portfolio before beginning student teaching. The student can use the portfolio to present what he or she has done to the classroom supervisors and with some revision it can be presented to future employers. The portfolio would hold representative materials from courses taken, photos of the student working with children, writing samples, test scores, and any other material the student wants to share. The organization of the portfolio would also give others an indication of the student's abilities.

(Note: Preservice and practicing teachers may want to prepare their own professional portfolio. The National Board of Professional Teaching Standards (2000) has guidelines for putting together such a portfolio if your university or school district doesn't already have a system developed. Besides being an excellent way for teachers to examine their own practice, the portfolio can be used to explain your qualifications to parents, administrators, and hiring committees.)

◆ **ACTIVITY 2.6**

Choosing an Observation Method

Students and Practicing Teachers: Decide what method or instrument described in this chapter would work best for observing and assessing children in the following situations. Often, more than one will be appropriate. In each case, describe why you chose this method and how you will set up the process.

1. The infant seems to lag behind other children in reaching developmental milestones. At four months he doesn't turn over and he still has trouble lifting his head from a supine position.
2. Alissa, a two-year-old, is biting other children when she doesn't get what she wants. What method will you use for documenting this before sharing this information with other staff and parents?
3. Two four-year-old girls are playing together in the housekeeping corner. They tell another girl that she can't play with them. How will you record this incident?
4. You want to find out which children going to kindergarten next fall still need help with cutting, writing their name, counting objects, etc. What method would you employ?
5. You want to include kindergartners in your class in their own assessment process. You want something concrete you can share with parents and administrators. What method would you choose? How would you structure the time when you share the results with parents?
6. A first-grader is having a difficult time completing his work. He seems to spend most of his time watching what others are doing. When it comes time to start a new activity he is still involved in finishing the first task.

Summary

Early childhood preservice and inservice teachers have a variety of observational methods they can use to learn more about individual children and groups of children. They can, with practice, become very efficient observers. Using the methods outlined, they will be better able to determine children's backgrounds and interests and to assess children's physical, social, emotional, and intellectual abilities.

REFERENCES

Belsky, J., and A. Walker (1980). *Infant-toddler center spot observation system.* Unpublished manuscript, Pennsylvania State University, Department of Human Development and Family Studies, University Park, PA.

Bennett, T., B. V. Lingerfelt, and D. E. Nelson (1990). *Developing individualized family support plans: A training manual.* Cambridge, MA: Brookline Books.

Berger, K. S. (1994). *The developing person through the life span*. New York, NY: Worth Publishers.

Berns, R. M. (1994). *Topical child development*. Albany, NY: Delmar.

Childhood observation record (1992). Ypsilanti, MI: High/Scope Press.

Cohen, L. (1999). The power of portfolios. *Early Childhood Today,* February, 22–29.

Cohen, L. G., and L. J. Spenciner (1994). *Assessment of young children*. White Plains, NY: Longman Publishing Group.

Cole, J. D., and G. K. Koeppel (1990). Adapting intervention to the problems of aggressive and disruptive rejected children. In S. R. Asher and J. D. Cole, Eds., *Peer rejection in childhood*. New York: Cambridge University Press.

Dodge, K. A., G. S. Petit, C. L. McClaskey, and M. M. Brown (1986). Social competence in children. *Monographs of the Society for Research in Child Development, 55*, 1646–1650.

Engel, B. (1990). An approach to assessment in early literacy. In C. Kamii, Ed., *Achievement testing in the early grades: The games grown-ups play*. Washington, DC: National Association for the Education of Young Children.

Essa, E. (1990). *Practical guide to solving preschool behavior problems*. Albany, NY: Delmar.

Galle, L. (1993). Contribution during session, *Observation and Participation in Early Childhood Settings*, presented at the Midwest NAEYC Conference, Indianapolis, IN.

Gordon, A. M., and K. W. Browne (1993). *Beginnings and beyond*: Foundations in early childhood education. Albany, NY: Delmar.

Grace, C., and E. F. Shores (1992). *The portfolio and its use: Developmentally appropriate assessment of young children*. Little Rock, AK: Southern Association of Children Under Six.

Harms, T., and R. M. Clifford (1980). *The early childhood environment rating scale*. New York: Teachers College Press.

Harms, T., and R. M. Clifford (1989). *Family day care rating scale*. New York: Teachers College Press.

Harms, T., D. Cryer, and R. M. Clifford (1990). *Infant/toddler environment rating scale*. New York: Teachers College Press.

Harrington, H. L., S. J. Meisels, P. McMahon, M. L. Dichtelmiller, and J. R. Jablon (1997). *Observing, documenting, and assessing learning: The work sampling system handbook for teacher educators*. Ann Arbor, MI: Rebus Inc.

Hildebrand, V. (1993). *Management of child development centers*. New York: Macmillan.

Hills, T. (1992). Reaching potentials through appropriate assessment. In S. Bredekamp and T. Rosegrant, Eds., *Reaching potentials: Appropriate curriculum and assessment for young children*. Washington, DC: National Association for the Education of Young Children.

King, M. J. (1991). A portfolio approach to assessment in a developmentally appropriate kindergarten. A Practicum Report presented to the Ed.D. program in Early and Middle Childhood in Partial Fulfillment of the Requirements for the Degree of Doctor of Education, Nova University. ERIC ED 338329.

Lay-Dopyera, M., and J. Dopyera (1993). *Becoming a teacher of young children*. (5th ed.). New York: McGraw-Hill.

McAfee, O., and D. Leong (1994). *Assessing and guiding young children's development and learning*. Boston, MA: Allyn & Bacon.

McGonigle, M. J., R. K. Kaufmann, and B. H. Johnson (1991). *Guidelines and recommended practices for the individualized family service plan* (2nd ed.). Bethesda. MD: Association for the Care of Children's Health.

Meisels, S., and D. Steele (1991). The early childhood portfolio collection process. Center for Human Growth and Development. Ann Arbor, MI: University of Michigan.

National Board of Professional Teaching Standards (2000). *Standards*. Retrieved January 20, 2000, from the World Wide Web: http://www.nbpts. org/nbpts/standards/five-props.html/

Paulson, F. L., P. R. Paulson, and C.A. Meyer (1991). What makes a portfolio a portfolio? *Educational Leadership, 48*, 60–63.

Rhoten, L. 1991. The role of student journals in reflective early childhood teacher education. *Journal of Early Childhood Teacher Education, 12*(1), 15–16.

Shimoni, R., D. MacLean, and C. MacWilliam (1990). Issues in infant/toddler care: Evaluating programs. *Day Care and Early Education*, 42–46.

Shreve, R. (1993). Contribution at session, *Observation and Participation in Early Childhood Settings*, presented by J. Billman and J. Sherman, Midwest AEYC Conference, Indianapolis, IN.

Spodek, B., and O. N. Saracho (1994). *Right from the start: Teaching children ages three to eight*. Boston, MA: Allyn & Bacon.

Williams, L. R. (1989). Some reflections on reflection: Comments in inservice teachers' journals as vehicles for refinement of practice. *Journal of Early Childhood Teacher Education, 10*(3), 13–17.

Zeichner, K., and D. Liston (1985). Varieties of discourse in supervisory conferences. *Teaching and Teacher Education, 1*, 155–174.

◆ Chapter 3

Caring for Infants and Observing Them in Home and Group-Care Settings

In this chapter you will read information and choose from a menu of activities to help you learn more about:

◆ Factors that influence prenatal development and the newborn experience

◆ Stages of development during the first eighteen months of life

◆ Ways to observe infants in home or center-based care

◆ Ways to evaluate the quality of care in infant programs.

Record numbers of infants and toddlers are now being cared for outside their homes. Because both parents are in the workforce and the United States has very limited parental leave (only companies that employ more than fifty employees need give six weeks of *unpaid* leave) babies only a few days or weeks old are being placed in care facilities outside the home. However, the care of this youngest group is more often mediocre or poor than for any other age group (Cost, Quality, and Child Outcomes Study Team 1995.)

Yet the babies in this youngest group of children already have a history. Each one experienced a different environment *in utero* and during the birthing process and early neonatal period. The observation and participation activities in this chapter are designed to help preservice and inservice teachers gain a better understanding of the issues and trends in infant programming and acquaint them with practices that foster each child's optimum development. The activities in this chapter and the next should be integrated into a course (or courses) that focuses on development and programming for children in the first three years of life.

The Prenatal Experience

Much of the makeup of the child and eventually the adult is determined at conception and during the prenatal period. An understanding of the basic principles of genetics and prenatal development is helpful to early childhood educators, who need to see how the infant is influenced by the genes inherited from both parents and how the in utero environment has helped to determine who that child is.

Genetic abnormalities can cause life-altering defects. Down syndrome, the most common genetic abnormality, causes altered physical and mental development. Some genetic disorders such as Tay-Sachs or Lesch-Nyhan syndrome result in early death. Others, such as hemophilia, sickle cell anemia, thalassemias, cystic fibrosis, diabetes, and epilepsy are treatable, but have recurrent severe episodes. Some genetic conditions, namely cretinism, disorders of the sex chromosomes, and phenylketonuria (PKU), can be ameliorated with treatment. Training and education can help those who are born with congenital blindness, deafness, or some of the many forms of mental retardation or childhood psychosis. The mapping of the genetic code, an international bio-technological endeavor, is nearing completion and there is reason to hope that this information will provide researchers with the tools needed for finding ways to prevent or lessen the impact of these genetic anomalies.

After the first two weeks of fertilization (period of the zygote), the blastocyst is implanted in the wall of the uterus and becomes known as the embryo. This period is when tissues are differentiating rapidly and organs are beginning to form. Example 3.1 shows the development during this period. It is during this embyonic stage that the uterine environment has major implications for the baby. The list of drugs and maternal factors that have been proven or are virtually certain to be harmful (teratogens) is very long. Each chemical, substance, or condition affects the infant from eighteen to sixty days after conception in different ways (Moore & Persaud 1993, Diav-Citrine & Ornoy 2000.) The latter citation has an article on the Internet that lists some of the medicines and substances and maternal diseases known to cause permanent malformations or impair normal brain functioning during this period. They stress that, as a rule, these drugs should not be taken during pregnancy. However, they may be necessary to treat maternal diseases; and uncontrolled disease may be more harmful to the developing fetus than the administered drug.

Other parental factors such as genetic disorders, poor diet, smoking, stress can also affect the fetus throughout gestation. Outside forces such as pollution, exposure to toxic substances on the job, radiation, and poverty conditions also take their toll on the unborn.

The ninth week of pregnancy marks the beginning of the fetal period. The fetus moves and grows and the organs continue to develop. The fetus reaches the "age of viability" sometime between twenty-two and twenty-six weeks of gestational age and has a good chance of surviving outside the womb. In the last weeks of pregnancy the brain continues to grow and the fetus puts on a fatty layer and lengthens. During the last couple of weeks the fetus receives antibodies from the mother that temporarily prevent some common communicable diseases such as measles and mumps.

◆ **EXAMPLE 3.1**
Sensitive Periods in Prenatal Development

During this time the normal development of certain organs and structures is subject to disturbance by teratogens.

Three weeks	Heart and central nervous system are forming. Central nervous system sensitive until birth and after. Sensitive period for heart lasts until eighth week.
Four to five weeks	Eye and arm and leg buds are formed. Eye formation is sensitive throughout pregnancy and still developing after birth. Upper limbs sensitive until end of fifth week; lower limbs until middle of sixth week.
Sixth week	Teeth, palate, and ears begin formation. Teeth formation not complete until after birth; palate formation until sixteenth week. Ear formation is not complete until twenty-one weeks.
Seventh week	The external genitals begin forming and are sensitive.

Early childhood teachers must realize that many of the conditions they see in the infants and young children they care for and teach were present before birth. Activities 3.1 to 3.3 will help you understand some important before-birth factors.

◆ **ACTIVITY**

3.1

Maternal Behaviors that Affect Prenatal Development

Choose one of the following maternal behaviors known to affect prenatal development. Make a short presentation to your classmates on how the developing fetus is influenced by this behavior during pregnancy. Find at least two research studies that contribute to your understanding on this topic.

1. Consuming more than two ounces of alcohol a day on a regular basis
2. Taking aspirin or other nonprescription drugs
3. Smoking cigarettes or marijuana
4. Mother's exposure to radiation
5. Using illicit drugs such as cocaine or heroin
6. Ingesting caffeine products
7. Mother's nutrition
8. Maternal age
9. Maternal stress
10. The rh factor
11. Maternal diabetes

◆ **ACTIVITY**

3.2

Paternal Behaviors that Affect Prenatal Development

Which behaviors of the father are believed to influence prenatal development? Report to the class.

◆ **ACTIVITY**

3.3

Fetal Monitoring Procedures

Fetal monitoring is frequently used in hospitals to track the progress of labor and delivery. The use of electronic equipment is still a controversial subject with both benefits and drawbacks. Choose one of the following, describe why and how it is used, and list its benefits and risks.

1. Ultrasound
2. Amniocentesis
3. Blood and urine tests
4. Chorionic villus sampling
5. Fetoscopy

The Birthing Experience

Nearly all American babies are born in hospitals or birthing centers. Birthing practices can vary from one hospital to the next (Snow 1998). However, most obstetricians and midwives emphasize the importance of regular prenatal care. Most centers or hospitals have childbirth preparation classes that involve both parents or the mother and a coach. Fathers are now routinely present for the birth.

Parents are usually free to choose a method of delivery and determine if and when pain relief will be given. The effects of different types of drugs on the infant are complex. Rosenblith (1992, 159–165) has summarized the advantages and disadvantages of the most commonly used drugs.

Most babies (96 percent) are born headfirst (Snow 1998). The other 3 to 4 percent are in the breech position—these births are more difficult. When the baby can't be turned, it is surgically removed through a cesarean section. There has been a rapid increase in the number of cesarean deliveries in the past 25 years; they now number almost a quarter of all births. Physicians, afraid of malpractice suits, use this method if there are *any* indications of maternal or fetal stress. Sometimes labor is induced by medication if the baby is overdue, or if the mother lives far from the hospital or birthing center, has diabetes or other complications, or simply if it is more convenient for the parents or doctor.

The stages of childbirth generally follow the timetable given in Table 3.1. Activities 3.4 and 3.5 will familiarize you with some birthing practices.

◆ **TABLE 3.1**   *The Stages of Childbirth*

Pre-Labor

During the last weeks of pregnancy the mother can experience false labor. The contractions of the uterus are brief and unpredictable. About two weeks before delivery the baby's head drops down into the uterus, called lightening. Soon before birth the mother releases a mucous plug that often produces a bloody discharge (Berk 1994). Sometimes the amniotic sac breaks, releasing a watery discharge, before contractions are felt.

Stage One: Dilation and Effacement of the Cervix

This is the longest stage of labor and may last twelve to fourteen hours for a first birth and four to six with later births. During this stage the cervix, which has already softened during the final weeks, begins to widen and thin. Uterine contractions become regular, increasing in both frequency and forcefulness. In the final part of this first stage the contractions may come every two or three minutes and last sixty seconds, heralding transition. This occurs when the cervix is fully dilated and effaced.

Stage Two: Delivery of the Baby

This stage lasts from twenty minutes to an hour. The baby's head crowns (fills the vaginal opening). The mother pushes with the contractions, forcing the baby down and out. Unless the doctor has performed an episiotomy, a small incision that increases the size of the vaginal opening, there may be some tearing of tissue—either way, stitches may later be necessary to repair the vaginal wall. The doctor or nurse catches the baby and holds him or her upside down to drain fluids from the nose and mouth or uses suction to clear the air passages. The baby is placed on the mother's abdomen and when the blood in the umbilical cord stops pulsing, the cord is clamped and cut.

Stage Three: Birth of the Placenta

During this stage, which usually lasts five to ten minutes, the placenta is expelled by the last few contractions and pushes.

Aftercare

During this time the mother and infant are checked at frequent intervals. The infant is assessed using the APGAR scale for heart rate, respiration, reflex irritability, muscle tone, and skin color. The mother is monitored for excessive bleeding. In most hospitals this is a quiet time for infants and parents to be together. The baby is generally awake in the first hour after birth.

◆ **ACTIVITY**

3.4

Prepared Childbirth Methods

Discuss the different methods of prepared childbirth training. Which method is most used by doctors and midwives in your community?

1. Read method
2. Lamaze method
3. Bradley method
4. Hypnosis
5. Leboyer method

◆ **ACTIVITY**
3.5

Alternative Childbirth and Care Arrangements

Choose two of the following alternatives in childbirth and hospital care and tell your group about the advantages and disadvantages of each.

1. Rooming-in
2. Home delivery
3. Midwives
4. Birthing centers

The Newborn

The newborn must make adjustments to temperature changes, breathing, nursing or sucking from a bottle, and eliminating body wastes. First-time parents also have enormous adjustments to make to a drastic change in lifestyle. They must make special efforts to become acquainted with their infant and start the bonding process. Early childhood educators will also want to learn as much as they can about the capabilities of babies in the first few weeks of life. Activities 3.6 and 3.7 will help.

◆ **ACTIVITY**
3.6

Assessing a Newborn (Part 1)

Arrange a visit to the maternity ward of your local hospital or birthing clinic. An alternative would be to have a newborn, parents, and pediatrician or nurse practitioner visit the class. Ask the pediatrician to do a neonatal assessment of the newborn using either a standard instrument such as the *Brazelton Neonatal Assessment Scale*, the *Dubowitz Assessment of Gestational Age*, the *Graham-Rosenblith Tests*, or the doctor's own assessment of the baby's reflexes, muscle tone, posture, and motor development. Be familiar with the reflexes that are normally present at birth so you can also assess the baby's status. Viewing the video *Infant Reflexes in Human Motor Development* beforehand would be helpful.

◆ **ACTIVITY**
3.7

Assessing a Newborn (Part 2)

Visit the home of a family with a baby who is no more than three weeks old or arrange to have the newborn and parents visit the class. Observe and record the types of behavior listed below. Be aware of the baby's state—it is easier to assess a baby who is in an actively or inactively alert state than one who is drowsy, sleeping, or crying.

1. *Cries.* See if you can identify the different cries during the visit or ask the parents if they can tell yet what different cries mean.
   - Rhythmic—regular pattern (often associated with hunger)
   - Mad—rhythmic but energetic
   - Pain—a shriek followed by a few seconds of silence as the breath is recovered, followed by extremely energetic crying
   - Fake—sobs that do not seem to be stimulated by any particular condition, except perhaps the desire to arouse a response from others

2. *Responses to faces and voices.* Place your face close to the baby's face and stick out your tongue. Wait seven seconds to see if the baby imitates your behavior. Try opening and closing your mouth and blinking your eyes. Observe the newborn closely to see if he or she makes any effort to imitate your actions. If you can't get a reaction, ask the mother or father to try.

3. *Smiles.* See if the newborn smiles. Notice what state the infant is in—active alert, inactive alert, drowsy, and so forth. If the baby is in the drowsy state, make a humming or whistling sound, then wait ten seconds. The newborn may respond with a smile. See if the baby smiles for his or her parents.

4. *Interactional synchrony.* Talk to the baby in a rhythmical way (reciting nursery rhymes with emphasis on the rhythm works well.) Observe the baby to see if he or she makes head and body movements in time with your voice. Ask a parent to try if you have no success.

5. *Reactions to mother's voice and face.* Have the mother (or father) and a stranger stand where the baby cannot see either. As the two take turns talking to the baby, observe the infant to see if the mother's voice arouses a greater response than the stranger's. Carry out the same procedure within the baby's line of vision and see how long the baby focuses on each face.

6. *Reciprocal shaping.* Observe the relationship between the newborn and the parents. Does the baby seem to shape the behavior of the parents? For example, does the baby vocalize and try to get the mother or father's attention, then stop when he or she is picked up?

7. *Do an informal survey of the infant's reflexive behavior.* The following suggestions will help.
   - The sucking reflex can be measured by watching how the baby nurses or sucks on the nipple. If the baby does not exhibit this while you are there, try inserting a (clean) finger into the baby's mouth.
   - The rooting reflex can be seen when the baby turns his or her head when touched on either side of the mouth as if to take the nipple. This is replaced by voluntary movements by three or four months.
   - The palmar grasp can be elicited by placing a finger in the palm of the baby's hand. The baby will close his or her fingers and hold on tight. This reflex usually disappears by five months.

- The eye blink occurs when a hand is waved in front of the infant's face. The infant's pupils will also adjust to bright lights by narrowing and to dim lights by widening. This reflex continues throughout life.
- The Babinski reflex is measured by stroking the sole of the baby's foot from heel to toe. If this reflex is well established, the baby will spread the little toes and lift the big one. This reflex should disappear by six months.
- The Moro or startle reflex is a reaction to a loud noise or to the baby's being dropped a few inches, in which the baby extends his or her limbs and digits and then draws them back. This disappears at about four months.
- The stepping reflex occurs when the infants show walking behavior when they are held upright and their feet are touching a firm surface. This disappears after two or three months.
- The tonic neck reflex is elicited by turning and holding the baby's head to one side. They extend the arm and leg on that side and bend the arm and leg on the opposite side into a fencing position. This also disappears by four months.

In some babies these reflexes will be weak or nonexistent. In babies who have cerebral palsy or who have received some trauma to the brain, these reflexes do not disappear and will interfere with voluntary motor development.

8. Talk to parents about what you are doing as you assess their child. Emphasize all the abilities their baby possesses.

At-Risk Infants

SIDS (Sudden Infant Death Syndrome) is the leading cause of unexpected death in infants one to twelve months old in the United States. While its cause is unknown, several factors are associated with increased risk of SIDS. These are 1) placing a baby on the stomach (prone position) to sleep; 2) being exposed to tobacco smoke during pregnancy and after birth; 3) using soft surfaces and/or objects that could obstruct breathing in baby's sleep area; 4) not breast-feeding an infant. (The A, B, C's of Safe and Healthy Child Care, 2000.)

Caregivers in child-care settings can reduce the risk of SIDS by placing infants on their backs for sleep, providing a smoke-free environment, avoiding soft objects in the sleep area, and supporting mothers' breast-feeding.

Babies who are born prematurely or "small for gestational age" often must have special postnatal care. The neonatal intensive care unit has made many advances in the past two decades. As a result, babies born very early or of very low birthweight have good chances for survival today. Most of these infants will have some developmental delays in the first few months or years.

However, most of them catch up to their age mates by the time they are four or five years old. A small percentage of them, however, have learning difficulties that may require special services when they reach school age.

Babies born addicted to drugs or infected with the AIDS virus are also considered at risk. They are often abandoned by their mothers in hospitals. Finding ways to deal with their care is a problem for overtaxed health agencies and their staffs.

When children with prenatal drug exposure enter an early childhood setting, they make demands of the caregiving/teaching staff. While most of these children are of normal intelligence, they may not have formed a secure attachment to their parents, may require more comforting, be emotionally unstable, have poor language development, be aggressive, or have other difficulties (Conen & Taharally 1992). Teachers and caregivers need to develop skills in meeting these children's needs and coping with their demands. Administrative supports are necessary for keeping group size small and assessing special education services.

Children born HIV-infected will also need the services of multidisciplinary teams (Jessee *et al.* 1993). Everyone involved with them will need to practice universal precautions of wearing gloves and scrupulous handwashing whenever coming into contact with any bodily fluids. AIDS-infected children must also be protected from any infectious diseases. Support groups and information sessions for parents and teachers can help them deal with the problems of these children.

The Jewish Family and Children's Service Agency of Boston has developed general guidelines for staff in dealing with HIV/AIDS in early childhood centers and specific guidelines for issues of confidentiality and disclosure (Black 1999.) Black also lists other agencies that are resources for families with HIV/AIDS. Staff are urged to use universal precautions as set out by the Canadian Child Care Federation:

1. Wash your hands for thirty seconds after contact with blood and other body fluid contaminated with blood.
2. Cover cuts or scratches with a bandage until healed.
3. Use disposable absorbent material such as paper towels to stop bleeding.
4. Wear disposable latex gloves when you encounter large amounts of blood, especially if you have open cuts or chapped skin. Wash your hands as soon as you remove your gloves.
5. Immediately clean up blood-soiled surfaces and disinfect with a fresh solution of one part bleach and nine parts water.
6. Discard blood-stained material in a sealed plastic bag and place in a lined garbage container.
7. Put blood-stained laundry in sealed plastic bags. Machine wash separately in hot soapy water.

Staff are asked not to delay emergency action because they can't apply universal precautions. The risk of transmission of blood-borne diseases is too small to justify endangering a child.

◆ **ACTIVITY**
3.8

Neonatal Intensive Care Units (NICU)

If you live in a community with a NICU, invite a nurse or nurse practitioner to visit your classroom to talk about how parents are currently involved in the care of their infant and how they are prepared to care for the infant at home. Ask about the long-term prognosis for these infants. Get information on how the hospital deals with drug-addicted or HIV-infected babies.

Development of Infants

Early childhood education students and teachers need to understand the normal course of development in the early months and years. They also need an awareness of the many factors that influence that development. The child's genetic makeup, the way parents interact with the child, the socioeconomic status of the family, the child's and the parents' temperaments, gender, race, past illnesses, and disabilities are some of the factors that influence how each child will develop and grow. The following is a very brief summary of some of the highlights of infant development.

Physical Development

The most rapid period of growth in humans happens before birth. The second most rapid time is during the first year. The baby goes from an average birthweight of seven and a half pounds to triple that weight by his or her first birthday. In the first twelve months the baby adds nine or ten inches to his or her birth length, which is usually between nineteen and twenty-one inches. Infants whose head circumference is either extremely small or extremely large are at risk for handicapping conditions.

Brain growth is very rapid both before birth and immediately after. The brain at birth is twenty-five percent of its adult weight. By six months of age it reaches fifty percent and by age two it is seventy-five percent of its adult weight. This is the primary reason that adequate nutrition is crucial in the first few months and years. Babies who do not get enough protein cannot manufacture the normal amount of brain cells. At birth the baby's movements are controlled by the brain stem and the cerebellum. By three months most of these functions become voluntarily controlled by the cortical areas of the brain, particularly those of the hands, arms, and upper trunk. The primary sensory areas of vision, hearing, touch, taste, and smell are mature by age two. Some areas of the brain and nervous system are still myelinating and developing axons and dendrites until puberty and beyond (Rosenblith 1992).

The work of researchers in the 1930s (Bayley 1935; Gesell 1934; Shirley 1931) established norms for motor behavior and development. They showed that development tends to proceed *cephalocaudally*, that is, from the head

◆ *Infants need many sensorimotor opportunities to explore materials and textures.*

downward. The baby can control the head and arms before it can sit or stand. It also goes *proximodistally* from the trunk outward. For example, arm control precedes hand control, which comes before finger control.

It is useful for early childhood students to consult the motor milestones on the *Bayley Motor Scales* (1969) to obtain a fairly accurate idea of when most babies acquire certain skills. In this revision of the scales, babies attained skills earlier than did babies tested in the 1930s, thus showing a secular trend (long-term changes in population developmental norms over time). In some cultures babies are given more practice and coaching in motor development than in others, which may account for the fact that infants in some ethnic groups seem to develop faster than those in others. A combination of genetics and experience seems to influence the age of onset of certain motor skills.

A baby's ability to use his or her hands is perfected during the first ten months (Bayley 1969). From two to seven months babies begin to reach for and grasp objects using the outer part of the hand. By seven months (range, five to nine months) they have complete thumb opposition. Between six and ten months they are able to transfer an object from one hand to the other at the midline. They become increasingly proficient in securing small objects. Most can use the whole hand to scoop up an object by seven months. By nine months they can use a neat pincer grasp—the forefinger and thumb in opposition—to pick up tiny objects.

Brain Development

New research into brain development in the human infant has confirmed what most early childhood professionals have long known. The infant is learning from the moment of birth and, indeed, prenatally (Hopson 1998). Through interaction with parents and caregivers the synapses (connections between brain cells) of the infant brain are made and strengthened. This interaction happens, not through any specific stimulation rituals, but through the everyday holding, talking to, feeding, diapering, and singing to an infant that caring adults do (Begley 1997; Newberger 1997.)

Babies who receive little stimulation will have fewer synapses and their brains will have made fewer connections. Stress from emotional or physical trauma (Gunna *et al.,* 1996) can also retard the growth of synapses. The closer the ties between the infant and parent and/or caregivers, the lower the level of certain stress hormones such as cortisol found in the baby's blood.

It is also very important that the infant form a close attachment with parents and caregivers. These early bonds in some ways protect the child from later adversities. The kind of attachment infants form to the primary caregivers at age one predict teacher ratings, behavior problems, and quality of relationships with peers in preschool (Hofer 1995, Shore 1997.)

Certain areas of the brain, such as visual and language learning centers, seem to have "optimum periods." If the visual centers are not stimulated during the first two years, babies will be unable to see. Likewise, if babies do not hear spoken language during their early years, they will not be able to learn to speak a language later.

The brain of the infant during the early months after birth is changing at a more rapid pace than it ever will again (Zero to Three 1997.) The infant brain increases in size thirty-five percent by year one. By age three the brain is fifty percent of adult size and by six is nearly adult size (http://www.zerotothree.org/brainworks/pediatricians.html). The early learning that is taking place will prepare the infant and growing child for later learning and interaction. Caring adults will make sure the infants get the right kind and amount of stimulation to develop their brain capacity to the fullest.

Cognitive Development

Piaget (1952, 1954) completely revolutionized the way we understand cognitive development. Through careful observation he found height, weight, and sensory and motor development to be important measures of cognitive ability during the first year. Piaget (1952, 1954), through careful observation of his own three children in Switzerland in the 1920s, brought to child psychology a new understanding of how infants seek to comprehend the world by using their senses and motor skills. His interactionist theory of the acquisition of sensorimotor intelligence has formed the backbone for all subsequent study of infant cognition. He found that infants and young children were constantly testing their ideas of how the world works. Piaget's theories have been the subject of a huge body of research in the last fifty years and have held up well with some revisions.

Gopnik, Meltzolf, and Kuhl (199, 156–162) have what they call a "theory theory." They think that "Children and scientists are the best learners in the world, and they both seem to operate in very similar, even identical ways, ways that are unlike even our best computers. They never start from scratch: instead, they modify and change what they already know to gain new knowledge. But they are also never permanently dogmatic—the things they know (or think they know) are always open to further revision." This is completely consistent with Piaget's theories. These authors also believe that babies are driven to learn about the world and that they take intense pleasure when they come up with an idea that makes sense out of the phenomena that surrounds them.

While most neo-Piagetians agree with most of his work, they feel that learning is much more gradual than Piaget's Stage Theory makes clear. However, they do find that all infants and young children worldwide seem to go through a remarkably similar sequence in developing their intellectual abilities. Piaget's Stages of Sensori-Motor Cognitive Development are used here merely to designate the general ages of infants when they go through certain steps in the process of discovery.

At birth and during the first four months the infant's actions revolve around his or her own body. During the first month (Stage one) infants have only the reflexes and abilities they were born with (sucking, grasping, seeing, hearing). From one to four months (Stage two) these reflexes, for the most part, fade out or become adapted and voluntary. Bodily actions such as kicking, arm movements, and sucking are increasingly controlled by the infant.

During Stage three (four to eight months) infants become more aware of objects and people in their environment. They will try to make interesting sights remain or to continue actions that they find enjoyable. They seem to take great pleasure in manipulating objects. In Stage four (eight to twelve months) babies are able to combine and coordinate schemes. Their behavior becomes more goal-directed and purposeful. They also gain the ability to predict and anticipate events. For example, a ten-month-old may start to cry when he sees his mother put on her coat, knowing that this is the usual prelude to her leaving him.

During the first six months of the second year (Stage five) babies begin actively exploring and experimenting. They use trial-and-error methods to find out just what will happen and seek new methods to reach their goals. By the latter half of the second year (Stage six) they are using mental combinations to actually think about what they are doing. This new ability to use mental images and processes enables them to remember what happened in the past and to anticipate future events, which gives them the power to solve problems mentally that they could only do motorically before.

Language Development

All children go through the same sequence at about the same time in developing early language skills. As newborns they signal distress by crying and making facial grimaces. By two months they coo to attract the attention of others, fuss when irritable, and cry when they need help. Between three and six months they develop a wider repertoire of vowel sounds, gurgles, and growls. During the early months of life a baby learns the intonation and rhythm of the language of their caregiver. Therefore the babbling and gurgling of a Japanese infant will sound different from that of an infant born in an English-speaking environment. By about six months they use both vowel and consonant sounds in combination. They repeat the same syllable over and over to become babblers. By ten months they can comprehend certain words and say a word or two that can be understood by those closest to them.

They also use several gestures meaningfully. At that age, deaf babies express their first signs. By twelve months most babies utter at least one recognizable word. From twelve to eighteen months their vocabulary grows to fifty words. Babies learn very early the turn-taking nature of communication (Rutter & Durkin 1987).

Socioemotional Development

Human infants are social beings. The face and eyes of another person face-to-face with them are particularly salient for their visual and manual exploration (Palmer 1989). The interaction between adults and infants is reciprocal. Even newborns exhibit *interactional synchrony*, that is, they respond with gestures and bodily movements when someone is talking or playing with them. Babies usually have social smiles by about forty-six weeks gestational age. Babies born at term usually smile by six weeks of age. Babies born six weeks prematurely typically smile at about twelve weeks. These smiles reward the parent, who then continues the interaction. Babies are rewarded when a parent imitates their sounds or gestures. These mutually reinforcing behaviors are the basis of parent–child interactions. Babies will turn away or disconnect when they need a rest or the exchange becomes more than they can handle. The sensitive adult recognizes these signals from the baby and adjusts his or her own behavior.

Attachment theory (Ainsworth 1972, 1973, 1974; Sroufe 1979; Sroufe & Waters 1977) describes the nature of the infant's love relationship with another person (usually his or her mother) and also looks at the quality of the patterns of interactions that took place between the two. About seventy percent of all American infants seem *securely attached*. They seek the company of the mother, show positive behaviors when reunited with her, and use the mother as a secure base from which to explore their environment. *Resistant* infants (about ten percent) are happy to see their mothers after separation, but also display angry, resistant behaviors such as kicking and hitting. *Avoidant* infants (twenty percent), on being reunited with their mothers, avoid and ignore them or combine approaching and withdrawing behaviors.

Although much of the research on interaction focused on the mother as primary caregiver, some recent studies (MacDonald & Parke 1986; Pollack & Grossman 1985) showed that although fathers interact differently (usually more physically and playfully than mothers), they are quite capable of meeting the care needs of their infants.

Assess the development of an infant under twelve months using the guidelines in Activity 3.9.

◆ **ACTIVITY**

3.9

Observation of an Infant under One Year

Do an observation in the home of an infant younger than twelve months using the following guidelines:

1. Note the baby's name, birthdate, age in weeks, position in the family, whether the baby was full-term or premature, weight and height at birth, any complications during pregnancy or delivery, and type of pain relief used during delivery. Also note any illnesses since birth, any traumas or other "life events" such as moving, parents separating, and so forth.

2. Observe the child for ten minutes when he or she is awake and alert. What physical actions does the child do during this time? Does the infant meet the normal milestones for gross motor skills (Frankenburg *et at.* 1981). For instance, can the baby lift his or her head and shoulders when prone by four months, roll over by four to five months, creep on all fours by eight to ten months, stand holding onto a stable object by six to ten months, stand momentarily alone by ten to thirteen months, take first steps by twelve to fourteen months? It is important to remember that genetics and caregiving practices can account for much of the variation in the acquisition of motor skills (Berger 1994). If there are delays that cause you concern, consult with your instructor.

3. Make note of any sounds or words the infant makes. What stage is he or she at: cooing, babbling, repeats "da-da," "ma-ma," says one word? What sounds does the infant make?

4. Using a running record method, observe the infant's interaction with the mother or father for ten minutes. Who initiates the activity? What kind of interactions take place? How long do they last?

5. Using Piaget's stages of sensorimotor development, write a paragraph showing what stage this infant is in. Use explicit examples of the child's behavior to substantiate your choice of stage.

6. What other information did you learn about the infant by talking to the parents?

7. How does the infant relate to siblings, if there are any?

8. Give your assessment of this child's general development based on what you have observed.

Out-of-Home Care

Caring for infants in group settings is fast becoming an accepted and necessary part of our culture. In the past two decades the number of children under one-and-a-half years being cared for by someone other than a parent has increased dramatically. Mothers of very young children are the fastest-growing segment of the labor force. As mothers have returned ever-earlier to work in the office, hospital ward, or corporate headquarters, they have had to rely on others to care for their children.

However, the care of this youngest group is more often mediocre or poor than for any other age group (Cost, Quality, and Child Outcomes Study Team 1995). A study being conducted by the National Council of Child Health and Human Development (2000) at several sites throughout the country found that, unlike European countries that offer mothers a year of maternity leave, businesses in the United States offer only six weeks and only to businesses that employ more than fifty employees. This study has found that infants and toddlers cared for in groups of three or fewer children received more sensitive and appropriate caregiving.

Infant and toddler care has generally been of inconsistent quality, costly, and in short supply. Many families have had to reconcile themselves to placing their infants with untrained caregivers in less-than-ideal settings. Families who were fortunate enough to find trained caregivers offering quality programs often found they were unable to afford the expense.

Experts in the field of early childhood agree about what is developmentally appropriate practice for infants and toddlers (Bredekamp & Copple 1997, Zero to Three 1997). Please read and study the NAEYC pages pertaining to Infant and Toddler Care (55–94) to become aware of what constitutes good caregiving for children under three.

The Controversy over Infant Care

Reports on day care of infants less than eighteen months old (Barglow 1987; Belsky & Rovine 1988; Schwartz 1983; Howes *et al.* 1998) indicate that nearly half the infants whose mothers are employed outside the home full time are insecurely attached as assessed by the *Ainsworth Strange Situation Test*. Other researchers (Benn 1986; Clarke-Stewart 1988) have refuted these results. Still others (Howes 1988; Howes *et al.* 1998) have argued that it is the quality of the substitute care that is the best predictor of later social and emotional competence in preschool. Those seen to be at highest risk for insecure attachment are "boys who are rated as difficult and/or fussy and whose mother had strong career orientations, worked full-time, and expressed less anxiety about being separated from their infants" (Fogel 1991, 334). Group care of infants and toddlers is seen to be of poorest quality in low-income and minority neighborhoods (Phillips *et al.* 1994.) Regardless of the controversy and parents' concern for the well-being of their infants, children younger than three years make up an ever-increasing proportion of children in group care.

◆ **ACTIVITY**

3.10

Pros and Cons of Infant Day Care

Study the issues involved in the controversy over the effects of infant care on the mother–child attachment behaviors and later effects on preschool behavior. Find at least one research study on each side of the issue. (Divide your group in half and have a debate, one side in favor of infant day care, the other against).

Caring for Infants from Birth to Sixteen Months

State regulations regarding group care of infants vary as to how old babies must be before they can be placed in group care. However, many families depend on the combined salaries of both parents and cannot afford to have one take a long leave without pay before or after their child is born. In the past, a six-week leave without pay was considered ample. (The results of the new parental leave policy passed by the Clinton administration are still to be seen. Only companies with over fifty people on the payroll are required to provide twelve weeks of unpaid leave. That means that ninety-five percent of the nation's businesses are not affected by this bill.) As a result, many child-care facilities accept infants at six weeks. Family day care providers may take children even younger.

Placing their infant in a family day care home is an option for some families. The caregiver typically has four to six children besides her own. States usually restrict the number of infants that can be placed in a single setting. In Minnesota, for example, only two children under two years old, may be cared for at a time. Because of the extra care infants take, it is difficult to find providers who are willing to take infants or toddlers under two.

In center care infant programs states regulate the group size. Generally, the group can have no more than eight or nine infants and there must be one caregiver for every four infants.

In infant programs the caregiving is the curriculum (Castle 1991; Gonzalez-Mena & Eyer 1993; Watson *et al.* 1999). The relationship the baby has with the caregiver is of primary importance. Some problem-solving experiences are initiated by the baby, some by the caregiver. That means that all domains of the infant's development are affected by the quality of the caregiver–infant interaction. What happens when the caregivers feed babies, talk to them, change their clothes, wash their hands and faces, change their diapers, or hold them close influences each baby's physical, social, emotional, intellectual, and language development. The baby's actions and reactions also shape the dynamics of the interchange. In an attempt to evaluate infant-toddler programs Shimoni *et al.* (1990) developed an instrument based on the *Infant and Toddler Spot Observation Scale* (by Belsky and Walker, Penn State University) that considers both the positive and negative aspects of the interaction between babies and their caregivers (see Appendix A).

The Physical and Social Environment of Infant Programs

Much thought and preparation must go into designing the environment for infants. Greenman (1988) has looked at what babies "do" and "need" as a preparation for setting up room arrangements. He pointed out, however, that a rich, safe environment is not enough to guarantee a good program for babies. Providing the environment is still secondary to "the more funda-

◆ *Caring for infants in group settings is a rapidly increasing phenomenon. The training and experience of caregivers are of primary importance in the quality of infant programs.*

mental concern: the critical nature of the adult–child relationship" (Greenman 1988, 50).

Activities 3.11 through 3.13 are designed to provide insights and practice in understanding what babies' developmental abilities are and what kind of settings they require.

◆ **ACTIVITY**
3.11

Evaluate the Environment in an Infant Program

Make arrangements to participate in the infant room of a child-care program in your community.

1. Spend at least two hours interacting with the babies. Sit on the floor or in some other way make yourself accessible to babies. Ask about the procedures that are used in feeding and diapering. Take part in those activities if appropriate.

2. During a second visit, observe the infant room and complete the Infant/Toddler Environment Rating Scale (Harms *et al.* 1990), available from Teachers College Press, P.O. Box 939, Wolfeboro, NH 03894-0939. Present your findings to other class members. If possible, compare your ratings with those of other classmates.

3. Advanced students. Use the Shimoni *et al.* instrument (see Appendix A) to observe and evaluate the infant–caregiver interaction. Describe how the information could be used to improve the program.

◆ **ACTIVITY**

3.12

Design an Environment for Infant Care

Design an infant room for eight infants under sixteen months. You will want to have separate areas for diapering, feeding, sleeping, and playing. Consult Greenman (1988) and Dodge *et al.* (1991, Chapter 3) to find out what infants need before you begin.

◆ **ACTIVITY**

3.13

Keeping a Journal about Infants

If you work as an infant caregiver or have the opportunity to spend at least five weeks as a volunteer or aide in an infant program, you can focus on one or two children in your journal. Document their emerging physical skills, their changing vocalizations, their likes and dislikes, their feeding behaviors, and their interest in the world around them. Studying two children of nearly the same age will help you to make comparisons. Talk to parents or make home visits to learn more about how each child is being raised. Do you notice any differences in the ways mothers and fathers interact with their babies? Are there cultural or generational differences that might make the parents' interactions different from those of the caregiver?

Common Health Problems of Infants and Toddlers

Infants in group settings are especially vulnerable to infectious disease. Because of their immature immune systems, they are especially prone to such diseases as infectious diarrhea, hepatitis A, haemophilus Influenzae type B (Hib), and other infectious illnesses (Kendall & Moukaddem 1992.) Their parents and caregivers are also at risk for these illnesses. Caregivers must do all they can to maintain a sanitary and disease-free environment. The American Adademy of Pediatrics (1996) has set standards of care. Local and state health guidelines for center and home care are to be carefully followed. Exclusion of sick children, sanitizing of toys and furnishings, group-limiting strategies, and procedures for handwashing and diapering are some of the health precautions that must be addressed in making policies and training staff for protecting all children's health. Warrick and Helling (1997) have provided feeding and diapering procedures that protect each baby's health and provide an ideal time for infant–caregiver interaction.

Some signs and symptoms that could indicate severe illness in infants are listed below.

- unusual lack of movement
- crying
- coughing

- different breathing or wheezing
- uncontrolled diarrhea
- vomiting
- rash
- sores in the mouth
- red conjunctivitis
- head lice

Infants, toddlers, or older children should be excluded from the home/center unless there is an isolated "sick room" with a trained nursing staff using the following guidelines:

- until twenty-four hours after starting antibiotics for strep throat
- until six days after onset of rash or until sores are dried and crusted from chicken pox
- until five days after being placed on antibiotics with influenza homophilus pertussis
- until nine days after onset of swollen glands with mumps
- until one week after onset of illness or as directed by health official when immune serum globulin has been administered to all other children and staff
- until six days after onset of rash from measles and rubella

At the first sign of any of these illnesses the infant or child should be isolated from the rest of the group until picked up by a parent or other adult responsible for the child. (Watson, Watson, and Wilson, 1999.)

Kendall and Moukaddem (1992) also point out that parents and caregivers, and pregnant women in particular, are also vulnerable to infectious diseases. Using universal precautions—"performing a task as if all the recipients of the service were infected, even in the absence of signs or symptoms of illness"—is the best preventive measure (Organization for Safety & Asepsis Procedures 2000.)

Infants and Toddlers with Special Needs

Increasingly, infants with special needs are being cared for in group settings. As well as the infants considered at risk, more and more parents are choosing family day care homes and infant-toddler center care for their very young children with physical and mental disabilities. Both parents of these infants and professionals are concerned that caregivers may not have the training to maximize the development of infants with special needs. Other parents are afraid that the rest of the group may not get the attention they need. While most of the research has focused on preschool-aged children with mild disabilities, there is evidence that special needs infants and toddlers benefit from being with normally developing children their own age. They tend to develop the same intellectual and social skills as others in the same group. Normally developing infants and toddlers show no ill effects from exposure to those with special needs and teachers and parents come to have more positive attitudes toward them as a result of their inclusion (Shimoni *et al.*, 1992).

Certain conditions are necessary to make the integration of special needs infants and toddlers in group care work. A support system must be available. Parents must choose to send their child to the family day care home or center program. Each child must have a case manager who coordinates the work of the professional team. This team may consist of psychologists who evaluate intellectual functioning; physiotherapists, who plan activities to promote the child's motor development; occupational therapists who help the caregivers teach daily-living skills such as eating, dressing, and toilet training; audiologists and speech pathologists who are concerned with language development; and the early childhood educator who implements the learning program. Cases where the infant or toddler has a severe disability such as blindness or cerebral palsy may require extra staff. Parents must be involved and approve the plan. Caregivers' acceptance of the fact that children with disabling conditions are much like other babies is critical in making integration work in a infant or toddler program.

Cultural Differences in Infant and Toddler Programs

Cultural differences between the parents and the caregivers must be taken into account. It is easy for caregivers to respect parents' wishes for their children when their child-rearing ideas coincide. Many of the theories and research on infant care in this country are based on studies of white, middle-class infants—it is important to keep that in mind. Even our theoretical understanding of what is good for a child may be biased.

In the United States cultural and ethnic minorities are growing at a faster rate than the Caucasian race, which has historically been in the majority. Within a few decades there will be more of a mix of several ethnic and racial groups with no one group having a clear majority. We are just beginning to understand the implications of the various differences in child-rearing values and practices among cultural and ethnic groups (Garcia Coll *et al.* 1995). Further, each individual family has its own ideas on how infants are to be treated, how and why they exhibit certain behaviors, and how adults should interact with them.

As Shimoni *et al.* (1992) have pointed out, it is very difficult to reach agreement about what constitutes "quality care" for infants and toddlers, but some agreement about how to handle issues such as health and nutrition, safety, child development and the learning environment, interactions and relationships, group size and ratios, coordination of home and programs, and management of child care services are essential in a quality program.

Those providing care need to be sensitive and respectful of parents' cultural practices and values. They may require training in communicating with parents about their ideas and wishes. Books about multicultural issues in child care (Gonzalez-Mena 1993, Neugebauer 1992, and York 1991) can provide caregivers with strategies to help families and children appreciate and celebrate their heritage.

Generational and gender gaps are also real (Gonzalez-Mena & Eyer 1993). Older caregivers may have different ideas than young parents. A father's methods of caring for the baby are seldom the same as the mother's. Male caregivers also respond to infants differently than females do.

Staff Development for Infant Caregivers

While it is fairly easy to make changes in the room arrangement and the furnishings, working with the staff is more complex and requires different skills. As the early childhood education experts on the staff, the director and the head teacher of the infant group will have some input into the hiring of new staff members. They will also be involved in working with the staff to help them plan and find continuing education about infant development and their role as caregivers.

Often the infant caregivers will have different training needs and different learning styles. Finding out as much as you can about what information they need and the learning modalities that best suit each one is the first step in planning an effective inservice program. Training sessions that include a variety of teaching methods will reach a broader audience. Some learn best through demonstration; others through the written or spoken word. Videos are useful, particularly if followed by discussion. Monitoring each trainee's progress after the sessions will be an important aspect of any training program. Some caregivers may need help incorporating what they have learned into the daily program. Activity 3.14 offers suggestions for topics and methods to use in inservice sessions.

◆ **ACTIVITY**
3.14

Inservice Training

(The advanced student may use this exercise to prepare material that could actually be used for training purposes.)

Prepare an inservice training session for the staff in an infant room or for other students in your class. Make an outline emphasizing the most important points you want to cover and offer a one-page handout to accompany your session. Plan to involve the staff and class as much as possible. Using props, pictures, posters, or other visual aids can enhance your presentation. If you are working in an infant program, survey the staff to see what kinds of concerns they have or what they would like to learn more about.

Here are some suggestions for topics:

1. Toys and games for infants under sixteen months
2. Parent–caregiver communication
3. Sensory activities for infants to hear, see, taste, touch, and smell
4. Health and safety in group care
   - Childproofing the environment
   - Written policies outlining immunizations, health procedures, accidents, emergency measures
   - Permission forms, administering and recording medications
   - Preventing the spread of infections (including diapering and hand-washing procedures)
   - Procedures to follow in case of fire, tornado, hurricane, or other disaster
5. What to look for and how to report when abuse or neglect of an infant is suspected
6. Talking to babies (facilitating language development)—this might include sharing books, rhymes, and songs with babies
7. Sleeping arrangements and sleep disturbances
8. Attachment and separation issues
9. Cultural/ethnic issues in infant caregiving
10. Promoting peer play with older infants
11. Setting up a feeding program with infants—show how feeding methods and needs will change as infants get older and discuss the needs of nursing mothers and their babies.

What other topics would you add?

Summary

Infants now make up a rapidly increasing portion of young children being cared for in early childhood settings in this country and other parts of the world where mothers of very young children are entering the labor force. Understanding their physical, mental, and emotional capacities and needs is an essential first step in designing programs that promote their growth and ever-changing developmental needs. Students and caregivers need many methods to assess each infant's developmental milestones appropriately. Only then can environments be set up and activities planned that fulfill the requirements of each baby for nurturing, stimulation, and care.

REFERENCES

The A, B, C's of Safe and Healthy Child Care. Washington, D. C.: U. S. Department of Health and Human Services. Retrieved January, 10, 2000, from the World Wide Web. http:www.cdc.gov.ncidod/hip/abc/facts40.htm

Ainsworth, M. D. S. (1972). Attachment and dependency: A comparison. In J. L. Gewirtz, Ed., *Attachment and dependency.* Washington, DC: Winston.

Ainsworth, M. D. S. (1973). The development of infant–mother attachment. In B. M. Caldwell & H. N. Ricciuti, Eds., *Review of child development research,* Vol. 3, 1–94. Chicago: University of Chicago Press.

Ainsworth, M. D. S. (1974). Infant–mother attachment and social development: Socialization as a product of reciprocal responsiveness to signals. In M. Edwards, Ed., *The integration of the child into the social world.* Cambridge: Cambridge University Press.

American Academy of Pediatrics (1996). *Caring for our children: National health and safety performance standards.* Washington, DC: American Public Health Association.

Barglow, P. (1987). Effect of maternal absence due to employment on the quality of infant–mother attachment in a low-risk sample. *Child Development, 58,* 945–954.

Bayley, N. (1935). The development of motor abilities during the first three years. *Monographs of the Society for Research in Child Development, 1.*

Bayley, N. (1969). *Manual for the Bayley Scales of Infant Development.* New York: Psychological Corporation.

Begley, S. (1997). How to build a baby's brain. *Newsweek,* Spring/Summer, 28–32.

Belsky, J., and M. J. Rovine (1988). Nonmaternal care in the first year of life and the security of infant–parent attachment. *Child Development, 59,* 157–167.

Benn, R. K. (1986). Factors promoting secure attachment relationships between employed mothers and their sons. *Child Development, 57,* 1224–1231.

Berger, K. S. (1994). *The developing person through the life span* (3rd ed.). New York, NY: Worth Publishers.

Berk, L. E. (1994). *Child development* (3rd ed.). Boston: Allyn & Bacon.

Black, S. M. (1999). HIV/AIDS in early childhood centers: The ethical dilemma of confidentiality versus disclosure. *Young Children. 54,*(2), 39–45.

Bredekamp, S., and C. Copple (Eds.) (1997). *Developmentally appropriate practice in early childhood programs* (rev. ed.). Washington, DC: National Association for the Education of Young Children.

Castle, K. (1991). *The infant and toddler handbook: Invitations of optimum early development.* Atlanta, GA: Humanics Limited.

Clarke-Stewart, K. A. (1988). The "effects of infant daycare reconsidered" reconsidered: Risks for parents, children, and researchers. *Early Childhood Research Quarterly, 3,* 293–318.

Clay, M. (2000). *Running records for classroom teachers.* Woburn, MA: Heineman.

Cohen, S. and C. Taharally (1992). Getting ready for young children with prenatal drug exposure. *Childhood Education, 69*(1), 5–9.

Cost, Quality, and Child Outcomes Study Team. (1995). Cost, quality and child outcomes in child care centers, executive summary. Denver: Economics Department, University of Colorado at Denver.

Diav-Citrine, O., and A. Ornoy (2000). Adverse environment and prevention of early pregnancy disorders. *Early Pregnancy: Biology and Medicine, IV*(1), 5–18. http://www.earlypregnancy.org/EPMB/EPMB%20IV/Vol.%20Num%201/EPBM1287.htm

Dodge, D. T., A. L. Dombro, and D. G. Koralek (1991). *Caring for infants and toddlers,* Vol. 1. Washington, DC: Teaching Strategies, Inc.

Frankenburg, W. K., A. Grandel, W. Sciarillo, and D. Burgess (1981). The newly abbreviated and revised Denver Developmental Screening Test. *Journal of Pediatrics, 99,* 995–999.

Garcia Coll, C., E. Meyer, and L. Brillon (1995). Ethnic and minority parenting. In M. Bornstein (Ed.), *Handbook of parenting* (Vol 2.) (pp. 189–210). Mahwah, NJ: Erlbaum.

Gesell, A. (1934). *The atlas of infant behavior* Vols. 1 and 2. New Haven, CT: Yale University Press.

Gonzalez-Mena, J. (1993). *Multicultural issues in child care.* Mountain View, CA: Mayfield Publishing Company.

Gonzalez-Mena, J., and D. W. Eyer (1993). *Infants, toddlers, and caregivers* (3rd ed.). Mountain View, CA: Mayfield.

Gopnik, A., A. N. Meltzoff, and P. K. Kuhl (1999). *The scientist in the crib: Minds, brains, and how children learn.* New York: William Morrow and Company.

Greenman, J. (1988). *Caring spaces, learning places: Children's environments that work.* Redmond, WA: Exchange Press.

Gunnar, M. R. , L. Brodersen, K. Krueger, and R. Rigatuso (1996). Dampening of behavioral and adrenocortical reactivity during early infancy. Normative changes and individual differences. *Child Development, 67*(3), 877–889.

Harms, T., D. Cryer, and R. M. Clifford (1990), *Infant/toddler environment rating scale.* New York: Teachers College Press.

Hofer, M. A. (1995). Hidden regulators: Implications for a new understanding of attachment, separation, and loss. In S. Goldberg, R. Muir and J. Keer (Eds.), *Attachment theory: Social development and clinical perspectives.* Hillsdale, NJ: The Analytic Press.

Hopson, J. L. (1998). Fetal psychology. *Psychology Today,* September–October, 44–48.

Howes, C. (1988). Relations between early child care and schooling. *Developmental Psychology, 2,* 53–57.

Howes, C., D. E. Hamilton, and L. C. Phillipsen (1998). Stability and continuity of child–caregiver and child–peer relationships. *Child Development, 69*(2), 418–426.

Jessee, P. O., M. C. Nagy, and D. Poteet-Johnson (1993). Children with AIDS. *Childhood Education, 70*(1), 10–14.

Kendall, E. D., and Moukaddem, V E. (1992). Who's vulnerable in infant child care centers? *Young Children, 47*(5), 72–78.

MacDonald, K., and R. D. Parke (1986). Parent–child physical play: The effect of sex and age of children and parents. *Sex Roles, 15,* 367–378.

Moore, K. L. (1993). *Before we are born* (4th ed.). Philadelphia: Saunders.

Moore, K. and Persaud, T. (1993). *The developing human: Clinically oriented embryology* (5th ed.). Philadelphia: Saunders.

National Council of Child Health and Human Development. (1998). *Study measures quality of infant care.*

Neugebauer, B. (Ed.) (1992). *Alike and different: Exploring our humanity with young children* (rev. ed.). Redmond, WA: Exchange Press.

Newberger, J. J. (1997). New brain development research—a wonderful window of opportunity to build public support for early childhood education! *Young Children, 53*(4), 4–9.

Organization for Safety & Asepsis Procedures, http://www.osap.org/o-what.htm, retrieved February 2000.

Palmer, C. F. (1989). The discriminating nature of infants' exploratory actions. *Developmental Psychology, 25,* 885–893.

Phillips, D., K. McCartney, and S. Scarr (1987). Child-care quality and children's social development. *Developmental Psychology, 23,* 537–543.

Phillips, D. A., M. Voran, E. Kisker, C. Howes, and M. Whitebook (1994). Child care for children in poverty: Opportunity or inequity? *Child Development, 65,* 474–492.

Piaget, J. (1952). *The origins of intelligence in children.* New York: International Universities Press.

Piaget, J. (1954). *The construction of reality in the child.* New York: Ballantine Books.

Pollack, W. S., and F. K. Grossman (1985). Parent–child interaction. In L. L'Abate, Ed., *The handbook of family psychology and therapy,* Vol. l. Homewood, IL: Dorsey Press.

Rosenblith, J. F. (1992). *In the beginning: Development from conception to age two* (2nd ed.). Newbury Park, CA: Sage.

Rutter, D. R., and K. Durkin (1987). Turn-taking in mother–infant interaction: An examination of vocalization and gaze. *Developmental Psychology, 23,* 54–61.

Schwartz, P. (1983). Length of daycare attendance and attachment behavior in eighteen-month-old infants. *Child Development, 54,* 1073–1078.

Shimoni, R., J. Baxter, and J. Kugelmass (1992). *Every child is special: Quality group care for infants and toddlers.* Don Mills, Ontario: Addison-Wesley.

Shimoni, R., D. MacLean, and C. MacWilliam (1990). Issues in Infant/Toddler Care: Evaluating Programs. *Day Care and Early Education, 17*(3), 42–46.

Shirley, M. M. (1931). *The first two years: A study of twenty-five babies* Vol. 1: *Postural and locomotor development.* Minneapolis: University of Minnesota Press.

Shore, R. (1997). *Rethinking the brain: New insights into early development*. New York: Families and Work Institute.

Snow, C. W. (1998). *Infant development* (2nd ed.). Upper Saddle River, NJ: Prentice-Hall.

Sroufe, L. A. (1979). Socioemotional development. In J. D. Osofsky, Ed., *Handbook of infant development*. New York: John Wiley, 462–516.

Sroufe, L. A., and E. Waters (1977). Attachment as an organizational construct. *Child Development, 48*, 1184–1199.

Vaughn, B. E., F. L. Grove, and B. Egeland (1980). The relationship between out-of-home care and the quality of infant-mother attachment in an economically disadvantaged population. *Child Development, 51*, 1203–1214.

Warrick, J., and M. K. Helling (1997). Meeting basic needs: Health and safety practices in feeding and diapering infants. *Early Childhood Education Journal, 24*(3), 195–199.

Watson, L. D., M. A. Watson, and L. C. Wilson (1999). *Infants and toddlers: Curriculum and teaching* (4th ed.). Albany, NY: Delmar.

Wisconsin Fetal Alcohol Surveillance System. Retrieved from the World Wide Web January 20, 2000. http://www.wisc.edu/fasscreening/index.htm

York, S. (1991). *Roots and wings: Affirming culture in early childhood programs*. St. Paul, MN: Redleaf Press.

Zero to Three: National Center for Infants, Toddlers, and Families. (1997). *Caring for infants and toddlers in groups: Developmentally appropriate practice*. Arlington, VA.

Chapter 4

Exploring the World of Toddlers

In this chapter you will read information and choose from a menu of activities to help you learn more about:

◆ The developmental characteristics of children from eighteen to thirty-six months

◆ Methods for observing toddlers in homes or child-care settings

◆ Activities to do with toddlers

◆ Activities to allow you to assess specific areas of toddler development.

Who are toddlers and what are their behavioral characteristics? What are the developmental sequences that children between the ages of one and three normally go through in coordinating their movements, learning concepts and language, expressing their feelings, and relating to the important people in their lives both at home and in group care settings? What competencies do caregivers who work with children between those ages need?

Toddler Development

Many articles on infant-toddler development are accessible on the Web through the National Network for Child Care at http://www.nncc.org/InfantToddler/inftod.page.html. These articles are updated on a regular basis. You may want to use some of these articles to complement your textbook reading.

Physical Development—Gross Motor

Toddlers are changing all the time. By about one year they are standing erect and learning to walk with a wide-stance toddling locomotion. Learning new skills requires being able to balance in an upright position and having enough strength and coordination to perform these new motor tasks. With continuous practice they soon move from unsteady, tentative steps to more coordinated walking, running, and stair climbing. They are learning to control their bodies in space.

When toddlers start walking on their own, they need constant supervision since they have not yet learned what safety hazards they need to avoid. By eighteen months they can fill and empty containers; push and pull objects; climb on furniture and rocks; crawl in, under, and over things; and chase a ball. They can bend, twist, swing their arms, and rock to and fro to music.

Most two-year-olds can run without support, jump down from a small height with both feet, throw and kick a ball, make delayed attempts to catch thrown objects, and go up and down a slide endlessly without tiring.

Physical Development—Fine Motor

By the time they are one year old, children have mastered the basics of hand–eye coordination. By four months, babies reach for objects held in front of them, but generally make no contact. By five months they make contact and can hold a rattle or object shaped to fit their small hands. By seven months they can pick up a cube using a hand or palmar grasp. At nine months they can use their forefinger and palm to pick up objects. By twelve months they have coordinated their pincer grasp using the thumb and forefinger (Snow 1998). By sixteen to eighteen months toddlers can pick up, hold, and transfer objects; take out and put back pieces of puzzles; grasp and hold spoons, forks, large crayons, or markers; twist and turn bottle tops, busy boards, and steering wheels; and open and shut drawers, hinged objects, and boxes. They are still exploring the physical properties of objects through active manipulation, so they need safe toys and household items to examine. Materials such as sand, mud, and water and accompanying utensils are exciting tools for feeling, moving, experimenting, and even tasting.

Cognitive Development

Young toddlers (twelve to twenty-four months) realize that objects and persons continue to exist even when they are not immediately present (Piaget 1954). By that age they have become increasingly able to learn through trial and error. Between eighteen and twenty-four months they are capable of holding mental images, which allows them to think about events beyond the "here and now." They understand the causes of some physical phenomena and can defer imitation and use one object to represent another (Piaget

1962). For instance, a doll becomes a real child for them. They have the beginnings of symbolic behavior and can pretend.

By two years most children have entered Piaget's early preoperational stage (Piaget & Inhelder 1969). This stage is characterized by Piaget as what the child before age seven is generally unable to do. They cannot conserve—that is, they do not understand that physical attributes such as mass and weight remain the same even if appearance changes. They are bound by their perception and how things look to them. They are unable to follow the transformations that objects go through. Another characteristic of their thinking is centration—they concentrate on only one aspect of a situation. When faced with two rows of the same number of coins, for example, they are likely to say that the row with more space between the coins has more than the closely spaced row. They also cannot reverse operations. They do not understand that they can add objects to an array and then take the same number away to have the same number as when they started.

Toddlers still rely on motor action and learning through their senses, but they are able now to use their thought processes in place of sensorimotor activity. They have an increased memory of past events, and begin to plan and predict what will happen in the future.

Language Development

Language develops rapidly in the second and third years of life. At 12 months infants can understand many words and may be able to say 1 or more intelligible words. Often they use gestures to signal their wants and needs. By 18 months their speaking vocabulary has increased and they are beginning to make 2-word utterances. The average 2-year-old knows and can say about 270

◆ *Language develops rapidly between ages two and three. A pretend phone conversation makes use of these emerging skills.*

words, a 3-year-old knows about 900 words. A 2-year-old's mean sentence length is 1.8 words; a 3-year-old's, 3.4 words. Some sounds are more difficult than others for toddlers to say, but by 3 years of age 75 percent of their speech should be intelligible to adults (Patterson *et al.* 1991).

Hart and Risley (1995) did a study with toddlers between twelve and twenty-four months and found that their vocabularies were made up almost entirely of words that were also in their parents' vocabulary. Large amounts of diverse speech, responsiveness to child utterances, encouragement of autonomy, and talk about relations between things and events were the main factors in promoting toddlers' speech production.

Caregivers who describe to a child what is happening in the immediate surroundings, answer inquiring gestures or questions as much as possible, label objects and the child's own actions, listen to and extend the child's first attempts at words are establishing an environment in which language can develop rapidly. Reading to a child and discussing the pictures and story with him/her on an everyday basis can increase a child's vocabulary and interest in the printed word.

Socioemotional Development

Central to toddlers' emotional development is their growing awareness of themselves as separate entities. Self-concept is seen as following certain development stages (Stipek *et al.* 1990). In the earliest stage toddlers develop physical self-recognition. Next, they make neutral and valuative references to themselves. They use their own name or "me" in their descriptions and refer to themselves as, for example, "big girl" or "good boy." In the third stage, which begins in the latter half of the second year and is fairly well developed by age three, children are capable of evaluating their own behavior and knowing when standards of conduct have been violated (Lamb 1989).

At one year infants and toddlers are still looking to adults to gauge their reactions to help them determine their own emotional responses. This "social referencing" enables them to imitate the expressions of others and gives them some clues as to what their own reactions should be. However, their emotions are still volatile and subject to physiological and external conditions. Hunger, fatigue, time of day, slight frustrations, and even low barometric pressure can trigger emotional outbursts. Temper tantrums appear to peak about the middle of the second year.

With their increasing ability to evoke symbolic mental images in the latter half of the second year (sleep disturbances at this age may be from dreams), toddlers begin to show fear. Toddlers can now express their fears with limited words (Dunn *et al.* 1987). Many toddlers also use a transitional object, such as a favorite toy or blanket, to cope with stress when separated for short periods from parents or caregivers.

Self-awareness is also expanding—toddlers now recognize themselves in the mirror. They express joy by smiles and laughter in the presence of others, but not when they are alone (Jones & Raag 1989). They show anger, defiance, and negativism toward adults who try to limit their growing sense of autonomy (Fogel 1991).

Erikson (1950) labels the toddler stage as one of autonomy versus shame and doubt. Toddlers must exert their developing powers in the face of the imposed restrictions of adults. Failure to achieve a certain level of independence, according to Erikson, would leave the child fearful and unsure. "In thus asserting themselves, which is a very healthy and positive development, children need assurance that they can do so without alienating those persons to whom they have primary attachments. This can constitute a serious conflict, since toddlers are still very small and helpless and in need of the goodwill of caregivers" (Lay-Dopyera & Dopyera 1993, 102).

Carter (1993) reports that teachers often ask how to get toddlers to *stop* doing certain behaviors—frequently the very behaviors that will give the toddler more autonomy. Carter asked teachers to chart the toddlers' efforts toward autonomy on a large sheet of paper on the wall. For example, "Randy climbed up on the cupboard to reach the car he wanted" or "DeeDee took off her shoes and socks when we went outside." Opposite each description they were to write ways in which they facilitated or could support each toddler's efforts. Besides making the teachers more aware and sensitive to each toddler's needs, it also demonstrated to parents and visitors that the staff was engaged in observing and planning.

Other people are important to toddlers. By twelve months of age most infants have established some kind of attachment to their parents. The quality of this attachment can be measured (Ainsworth *et al.* 1971; Sroufe 1979; Waters 1983). While their strongest attachments are to their parents and siblings, toddlers are increasingly interested in others outside their immediate family circle; stranger anxiety is generally less acute after the first birthday. Toddlers in group settings can and do form close relationships with particular caregivers and peers. Cryer (1992) felt that child-care centers should abandon the practice of moving toddlers when they reach a certain age away from the caregiver and environment they have known as infants. She suggested that

◆ *This student and toddler have clearly established a close relationship. He feels safe enough to fall asleep in her arms.*

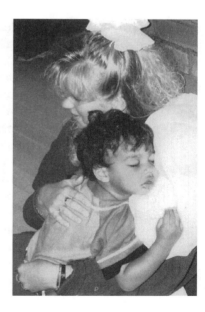

infant caregivers continue to be the child's primary caregiver until the child is ready to enter the preschool group. This would provide continuity and avoid the trauma of loss that separation from a loved one can create for both the infant and the caregiver.

Toddlers are developing new strategies for interacting with adults and other children. Eckerman and her associates (Eckerman & Didow 1989; Eckerman *et al.* 1989; Eckerman & Stein 1990) have been studying toddlers' changing social responses to both adults and same-age peers. They find that these responses changed from nonverbal imitation at the age of twelve months to being increasingly mediated by language as they grew older. Imitation progressed through different stages also. If imitated by either adult or peer, toddlers were more likely to repeat an action. These imitations later developed into "do as I do" games. As toddlers became older (over two years) they responded to an adult's programmed play overtures with language that described their own activities. They also gave adults verbal directions and let them know when it was time to change activities or roles.

The caregiver's relationship to individual toddlers is related to that child's attachment to his or her mother. "In general, teachers were more sensitive to and involved with children in the secure category and least sensitive and involved with children in the avoidant category" (Howes & Hamilton 1992, 864).

The influence of the mother–child attachment also carries over into toddlers' interactions with peers. Those who are securely attached are more effective in their social behaviors with peers (Jacobson *et al.* 1986). Toddlers are capable of real friendship (Vandell & Mueller 1980; Press & Greenspan 1985)—toddler friends seek each other's company, share toys, and like to participate in activities together.

Toddler Play

For toddlers as for older children, play is a necessary part of existence. "Play provides children with unparalleled opportunities for integrating their personalities, because when children play, all the selves are used simultaneously" (Hendrick 1994, 40). Toddlers are exercising their bodies, using their fine motor skills, problem solving, expressing their feelings and sense of self, and practicing their emerging language in play interaction. Leavitt and Eheart stressed that play is the central activity of childhood. They felt that caregivers could best support toddler play by providing an environment that "invites toddlers to explore and manipulate materials, with opportunities for making choices, for being challenged, and for succeeding" (1985, 18). Caregivers must also be responsive to each child's individual ways of playing, supporting and expanding the scope of play while always allowing the toddler to take the lead.

Toddlers no longer play with just one object at a time as infants do. They start combining objects; for example, putting large beads into a cup. They also begin to understand the functions of objects. They know that a ball

◆ *Toddlers are discovering who they are and what they can do through play.*

is to throw and a spoon is used to eat. But they can also use one object to represent another: A narrow block can be a telephone. Some toddlers as young as eighteen months already show a preference for gender-appropriate toys.

Play with adults is very beneficial for young toddlers, because adults usually structure the play so toddlers are maximally aroused and are encouraged to explore and learn (Hughes 1991). When given the opportunity to play with peers, most toddlers increase their ability to engage in complementary and reciprocal play (Howes 1988).

Preparation of Teachers for Toddlers

Most toddler "educarers," a term used by Weiser (1991) and others to indicate the dual nature of the teaching and caregiving role, receive very little training for working with toddlers and two-year-olds. Most early childhood education programs concentrate on children younger than one year or older than three. Yet toddlerhood is a unique stage in a child's life and toddlers have some characteristics that require a special kind of caregiving. The *energy and strength* needed to keep up with, physically lift and carry one- to three-year-olds, and handle the seemingly endless caregiving routines; the *patience* to wait for a dawdling two-year-old and to repeat the same stories over and over again; the *emotional stability* to accept the colossal messes and constant demands of toddlers; the *vigilance* to be constantly aware of safety and supervision needs; the *intellectual ability* to plan a program that challenges and interests toddlers without treating them as "immature preschoolers not quite ready to do educational activities" (Gonzalez-Mena & Eyer 1993, 27)—all these require toddler teachers who really enjoy and want to be with this age group. Clyde

(1990) points out some of the problems toddler caregivers in daylong programs face. These include society's undervaluing of the child caregiver role, the ambiguity surrounding the caregiver and parent relationship, the need to balance the needs of the individual child with those of the group, the repetitive, tedious tasks that must be performed; problems involved in the physical and emotional climate of the workplace, lack of a support system, and personality variables such as a need for approval or a demand for perfection. All of these factors interfere with job satisfaction. She suggests that increasing teacher knowledge of toddler development and of the importance of the environment in fostering all aspects of development can help alleviate some of the stress and burn-out many toddler teachers feel.

As with infants, the relationship between the toddlers and their caregivers is of paramount importance. Gonzalez-Mena and Eyer (1993, 9–23) set forth the following principles to guide those who work with infants and toddlers:

 Principles of Caregiving

1. Involve infants and toddlers in things that concern them.

2. Invest in quality time.

3. Learn each child's unique ways of communicating and teach them yours.

4. Invest in time and energy to build a total person.

5. Respect infants and toddlers as worthy people.

6. Be honest about your feelings.

7. Model the behavior you want to teach.

8. Recognize problems as learning opportunities and let infants and toddlers try to solve their own.

9. Build security by teaching trust.

10. Be concerned about the quality of development in each stage.

Helping Toddlers Learn Appropriate Behaviors

Some of the behaviors that toddlers engage in can be problematic for both parents and caregivers. It helps to remind yourself that toddlers have an insatiable desire to explore. This is how they learn about the physical world. By the time they are walking on their own, they are into everything. While there is no substitute for constant supervision, parent and caregivers can "child-proof" the home or playroom to prevent problems. Putting plastic plugs in wall sockets, removing plants that might be potentially poisonous if ingested, clearing away objects that could be broken, padding sharp corners, checking to see that all small objects are gone from the area will make the area safer for a curious toddler. Plastic bowls, pots and pans, cardboard boxes, and other household items are delightful playthings to very young children. Pull toys and push toys exercise new walkers' growing abilities.

Both parents and caregivers must strive to help a toddler develop a healthy sense of self-esteem and a growing awareness of others and their needs. A strategy that Nixon (1999) sees as effective in negotiating with toddlers is being aware of each child's methods of communication. Some have words; others pull hair or shout to get attention. Recognize your own emotions and model correct and respectful behavior for the child. Validate the toddlers' feelings by expressing in words how you think they are feeling. Address the behavior, not the child, by saying, for example, "Biting hurts Jessica. If you are angry with her, please tell her." Offer real choices. For example, "Do you want to eat lunch now?" may not be a choice, but "Do you want cheese or meat on your sandwich?" lets the child decide. This helps them feel some control over what happens to them. Give a warning before transitions occur. They are more likely to get ready because they can now predict what will happen next. Keep rules to a minimum and explain them often. Be consistent with follow-up consequences. Allow children to work out their own problems, but be ready to intervene if necessary. Acknowledge each child's efforts and triumphs.

Tantrums seem to peak in toddlerhood. They become frustrated when they can't do something they want to do. They don't have the verbal skills that later will help them explain what is wrong. There are several strategies that the adult can use when a child under three is out of control. The adult should remain calm, hold the child until he/she is quiet enough to talk, ignore attention-getting behavior, or help the child untangle a frustrating problem that caused the upset. Tantrums do seem to abate as the child gets older, so parents and caregivers need to get through this volatile period with as much patience as they can muster.

The National Network for Child Care has a website (http://www/nncc. org/) that gives parents and caregivers some suggestions for handling difficult behaviors such as biting, hitting, refusing to share, etc. There are many books on child-rearing on the shelves of every bookstore and library. In Activity 4.1 you will get an opportunity to review some of these books with your classmates.

Parent–Teacher Relations in Toddler Programs

As with infant teachers, toddler caregivers must be in constant communication with parents. They need to work together to make individual plans for feeding, toilet training, napping, comforting, and guiding the behavior of each child. This requires daily written and verbal exchanges between the child's main caregiver and the parents about the child's abilities and needs. It also means listening to the parents' concerns and ideas. When problems arise between the caregiver and parents due to differences in age, gender, culture, social class, or childrearing practices, every effort must be made to overcome them. Establishing rapport between the parent and caregiver is essential to the child's well-being. There is no room for competition or misunderstandings. Caregivers must be supportive of the parent and vice versa if the relationship is to thrive and the child is to do well in both the home and group setting. Chapter 8 gives a fuller discussion of teacher–parent communication.

◆ **ACTIVITY**

4.1

Critiquing a Parenting Book

Go to the public library, drug store, or bookstore and get an "advice to parents" book written within the last ten years that focuses on families with young children from birth to five. Read the book and write a short critique.

A critique is different from a review in that it looks at what is good and bad in the book. You might answer some of the following questions:

- Who is the audience for this book? Is it middle-class parents, teens, other professionals, or other researchers? What is the reading level?
- What did you think this book did well?
- What topics did you think this book didn't cover adequately?
- Would you recommend this book to parents and caregivers of toddlers? Why or why not?

Observing Toddlers in Home and Child-Care Settings

In order to understand more about toddlers, students must observe them in three different types of settings: at home, in a family day care home, and in a child-care center.

Observing a Toddler at Home

At home toddlers may be cared for by parents, other relatives, sitters, or nannies. They may or may not have siblings, since the average number of children in an American family is now fewer than two. Many toddlers are also in family day care homes or in child-care centers.

Nixon (1999, 60) said, "Every interaction, every connection will be perceived by each child differently, so it is important to consider individual children and where they are coming from, as well as their developmental stages. Often, this is best learned through observation and processing with other adults."

Toddlers' behavior also varies depending on how tired they are, how they're feeling physically, and whether they are in a familiar setting or new to a child-care home/program. Many people think that even the barometric pressure has a bearing on children's behavior. Maybe there's a reason that rainy days are usually difficult ones both at home and in a group setting.

Activity 4.2 should help you to recognize the developmental abilities of toddlers and give you some insights into toddler–parent interactions, while Activity 4.3 will acquaint you with play materials toddlers find most engaging. To complete Activity 4.4 you will need to talk to parents about their toddler's fears.

◆ **ACTIVITY**
4.2

Observations in the Toddler's Home

For this exercise you will need to have a copy of the *Denver II* manual, test forms, training video, and test kit. The test materials are available from Denver Developmental Materials, Inc., P. O. Box 6919, Denver, CO 80206-0919 (303-355-4729.) The *Denver II* (Frankenburg & Dodds 1992) is one of the most widely used screening tests for children from birth through age five and is used to give an "organized impression of the overall development and to alert the user to potential developmental difficulties" (test manual, 2). The test items are arranged in categories of gross motor, language, fine motor/adaptive, and personal/social development and along a continuum of normed behaviors present at different ages. Feeney and Bernthal (1995) found it an effective tool in predicting the need for formal assessment in language development and articulation.*

The *Denver II* is a screening instrument that examines several different developmental domains. Validity studies show that the test correctly identifies children with abnormalities 92 percent of the time, and early childhood students can learn much about the course of normal development by administering this screening tool. It can be given in thirty to forty minutes and is fairly easy to score and interpret. It was developed to screen infants and toddlers for gross developmental delays and is *not* an IQ test. It is made up of 105 items in the areas of personal-social, fine motor-adaptive, language, and gross motor. Depending on the child's age, however, only twenty to twenty-five of the items would be used with one child. An example of personal-social behavior in a child aged ten to fourteen months is "indicates wants without crying." A child older than nineteen months is expected to "wash and dry hands."

You will need to participate in a supervised training session, read the manual carefully, and practice giving and scoring the test with another student before administering it to a child.

Administer the *Denver II* to a toddler between twelve and thirty months old. Arrange to give the test in the child's home and plan to be there at least ninety minutes. Spend fifteen to twenty minutes talking to the parents and child informally before starting the testing. If siblings are present, have them help you with the test or give them something to play with. Explain to the parents that you will be testing the child with some activities that he or she will already know how to do, but that you will also be giving him or her activities at which you would not expect him or her to be successful. In talking with parents after the test, emphasize what the child *can* do rather than what he or she can't do.

*Because the *Denver II* is often administered by nurses, you may be able to borrow the materials from the university nursing department or from your local health department.

In the unlikely event that you find that the child has two or more areas in which he or she has developmental deficits, try not to alarm the parents. Tell them you will have your instructor contact them about readministering the test or referring the child for further testing.

After giving and scoring the test write a two-page summary. Include the circumstances under which the test was given (who was present, how the toddler responded, how the parents reacted, what distractions there were). Briefly summarize the toddler's abilities in each of the four sections and describe any problem areas you saw. Include any other information you learned about the child during your observations or from talking with parents. Describe how the toddler interacted with any siblings who were present.

◆ **ACTIVITY**
4.3

Toddler Play Materials

As a class project, develop a list of favorite toddler play materials, with each student observing one toddler. Observe the play materials available to the toddler at home and note which toys the child seems to play with most. Talk to the parents about the toddler's favorite objects. At a local store make a list of ten manipulative toys and educational materials that would be appropriate for toddlers. What commonly available household items could you find that might accomplish the same goals as these purchased toys? Compare your list with those of other classmates to come up with fifteen items that appear to be favored by most toddlers.

Toys available for purchase	Price	Household items with similar use
_____	_____	_____
_____	_____	_____
_____	_____	_____
_____	_____	_____
_____	_____	_____
_____	_____	_____
_____	_____	_____
_____	_____	_____
_____	_____	_____
_____	_____	_____
_____	_____	_____

Materials in home that are favorite toddler playthings.

_____

_____

_____

_____

_____

_____

_____

_____

_____

_____

_____

_____

◆ **ACTIVITY**

4.4

Toddlers' Fears

Find out from parents what fears their toddlers have. Talk to an older toddler's parents to find out what frightens him or her and how he or she copes with these fears. Find a children's story that deals with one of these fears and identify the coping strategies used by character(s) in the book. Compare with your classmates' observations and make one list of common stressors or fears and another of the coping mechanisms toddlers use.

Observing a Toddler in a Family Day-Care Home

Many toddlers are also in family day-care homes. You will need to arrange a visit to a day care home to observe a toddler for Activity 4.5.

◆ **ACTIVITY**

4.5

Toddler's Interaction with Others in Family Day-Care Home

Your instructor will make arrangements with family child-care providers that will allow you and your classmates to visit and observe toddlers between the ages of sixteen and thirty-six months.

As a class or in small groups, you will need to develop two documents. First, develop a permission form that the child-care provider will ask parents to sign. These forms would allow you to observe, videotape, or make a running record of their child's interactions with others. You would want to include a simple explanation of what your purposes are. Also include a statement that assures parents of confidentiality of the written work you would do for class.

Next, develop a coding system for interaction behaviors you would expect to see when observing a child this age with others. (For example, G = Gives objects to another child, T = Takes object from child, VA = verbalizes to adult, VC = verbalizes to a child, etc.) You may find the need to introduce more categories into observations once you actually watch a toddler's early attempts at social behaviors with other children either older, younger, or the same age. Because most toddlers are not very skilled at socializing with others at this age, some will exhibit very few sharing behaviors and be content just to be near others or to watch. Having a videotape would be ideal because you will get to see who initiates the action and measure how long it lasts and what the outcomes are. Some children may exhibit strong anti-social behaviors as well. Be prepared to step in or help the toddlers sort out their conflicts as they arise.

When you have the name of the provider and permission to observe a toddler, call the provider and work out a time you could come to observe. Try to go when children are free to play as they wish or have several choices of activities available to them and routines such as meals and naps are at a minimum.

If possible, videotape twenty minutes of play focusing on one toddler and his or her companions. If you cannot get the equipment or permission to videotape, use a running record along with your coding system to get the details of the interactions.

If you still need more information, you may ask the care provider if you could telephone after the children have left to ask more information on the child's normal behavior with others. Have a list of questions prepared in advance so you cover everything you need to know.

Observing a Toddler in a Child-Care Setting

Before continuing with this chapter read pages 81 to 94 of *Developmentally Appropriate Practice in Early Childhood Programs* (Bredekamp & Copple 1997) to get a brief overview of the recommendations for caring for toddlers in group programs. Neither an infant program nor a preschool program fits the developmental needs of children from about sixteen to eighteen months up to three years. They need programming that is specific to their stage of development.

When you, as a student, are observing in a toddler program you will want to be aware of what makes a high-quality child-care program for toddlers. The *Infant/Toddler Environment Rating Scale* (Harms, Cryer, & Clifford

1990) assesses programs for children up to thirty months of age. If you have that instrument available to you, you may want to read through it before you visit an infant or toddler program. The instrument can be used to rate seven categories:

Furnishings and Display for Children
Personal Care Routines
Listening and Talking
Learning Activities
Interaction
Program Structure
Adult Needs

As part of a large national study of child-care centers Cryer and Phillipsen (1997) summarized what they found as the strengths and weaknesses of programs for infants and toddlers.

- They found that positive methods of discipline were used and realistic expectations set. The children were adequately supervised and problems such as hitting or biting were stopped. However, toddlers' positive peer–peer interactions were rarely reinforced.
- Even though health policies were in place, the prescribed procedures were not adequately followed for diapering, toileting, personal grooming, and meals and snacks. Handwashing for adults and children, as necessary for protecting the health of this vulnerable age group, was often missing.
- While caregivers used some social talking with children, they didn't make much effort to respond to children's attempts to communicate; nor did they expand on children's use of language.
- Adults were warm to children during routine activities and responded with sympathy when appropriate. However, children were rarely assigned a primary caregiver to encourage stronger bonds with one caring adult.
- Parent–caregiver communication was strong and there was a cooperative spirit among staff.
- Toys, books, and sand and water (for older toddlers) were not adequate and there was little evidence of ethnic or racial materials.

If you are a visitor to any children's program, you will want to keep your observations of either the overall program or of a single child confidential and share only as a part of your class discussion or written assignments. If you are a caregiver in the program, you may or may not feel that you can share your observations with the staff that works with toddlers.

As well as looking at the programmatic categories, toddler programs need to make spatial arrangements for one- and two-year-olds. Because their bodies are changing and their physical abilities are developing at a rapid pace, toddlers require indoor and outdoor environments that meet their particular needs. Greenman (1988, 53) confronts some of the issues involved in planning space for toddlers:

> *How do you develop an environment that allows collecting, hauling, dumping, and painting (with the requisite tasting of the paint and experimenting with the logical primary canvas, themselves)? How do you allow the necessary robust, explosive, and occasionally clumsy motor learning with a group of amoral beings who are largely oblivious to the safety of others—a group, however, that often hums with a current of collective energy. In a group setting, how do you accommodate to and support the wonderful assertion of "No!" and still accomplish anything in a reasonable time frame? Finally, how do you muster up the time, let alone the patience and sensitivity, to help each child through the agony and ecstasy of toilet training? Perhaps mission impossible may understate the situation.*

Sebastian (1990) and Wynn *et al.* (1991) have positive approaches to meeting toddlers' developmental needs for a safe, responsive environment by outlining factors that must be considered when planning indoor space that is stimulating, orderly, and emotionally warm without being overly restrictive. Sebastian feels toddlers' needs for safety, warmth, stimulating learning experiences, and support for their developing social skills require adults who are creative and resourceful. She points out that noise level, ease in changing the environment, careful arrangement of the space, and the toddlers' need for order, a separate sleeping area, and a pleasant toilet area all should be considered when planning an indoor area for toddlers. An entrance planned with parents in mind and a place for the staff to relax are also important to the overall plan. Wynn *et al.* find that the rearrangement of the room to provide open vistas and the removal of distracting items such as unnecessary shelving and bulletin boards seems to promote greater peer interaction.

Often teachers and program planners give much thought to the indoor space and expect toddlers to share the same outdoor playground as older children. Toddlers, however, benefit when the outdoor space is also designed to fit their needs. Activities 4.6 through 4.13 are designed to give you a better awareness of the developmental issues that influence group care of toddlers.

◆ **ACTIVITY**

4.6

Design a Toddler Playground

Design an outdoor playground exclusively for toddlers from twelve to thirty-six months. Take into consideration the following goals advocated by Stewart (1989) concerning playground design for this age group:

1. The outdoor space should be integrated with the indoor curriculum.
2. Children should have a choice of appropriate activities.
3. The activities available should promote the child's own creativity.
4. The space should provide stimulation for children to explore and expand their experiences.
5. The playground should also contribute to the child's total development.

The space you are designing is thirty by sixty feet and has building walls on two sides. One wall has a door into the building. The other perimeters have a five-foot-high chain link fence with one latched gate. There are two small trees in this area.

As part of this assignment you will want to consult Lovell and Harms's *Playground Improvement Rating Scale* (1985) and Wortham and Wortham's (1989) article on design for outdoor play areas for the very young (see Appendix B).

◆ **ACTIVITY**

4.7

Observe a Toddler's Physical Development

Follow a toddler on a playground or in the gym for twenty minutes. Attempt to imitate all of his or her motor actions. At another time follow this procedure with a toddler of the same age, but the opposite sex. Write about your experiences. What motor skills were being practiced? Did you feel there were sex differences in activity level? Did girls engage in physical activities that were different from those of boys?

◆ **ACTIVITY**

4.8

Observe Sensorimotor Intelligence

You will perform this activity with two toddlers between twelve and twenty-four months, one at a time. For this observation it would be ideal to have the toddler sitting on the lap of a caregiver or parent. The area you are in should be away from the group and free of distractions. Use the following Piagetian tasks to assess each toddler's grasp of the object concept.

1. Arrange three washcloths or other small pieces of fabric in front of the child. After selecting an attractive toy that is small enough to fit in the palm of your hand and showing it to the child, hide the toy under the first cloth. Does the child search for the toy or lose interest as soon as it is covered? If the toddler tries to uncover the toy, that means that he or she realizes the toy is still present even though it is not in view. This represents Piaget's Stage IV of sensorimotor intelligence.

2. If the toddler searches for and finds the toy two or three times under the first piece of fabric, place the toy under the second piece. Where does the child look first? If the child continues to look under the first piece, he or she is still in Stage IV. If the child can follow visual displacements from the first piece of fabric to the second, he or she is in Stage V. Next try placing the toy under all three pieces of fabric in succession to determine if the child will look in the last place where he or she saw the toy placed.

3. If the child is successful at task 2, hide the toy in a small box and move it first under the first cloth, then under the second, and finally under the third. Where does the child look for the object? If he or she can follow invisible displacements, the child has attained Piaget's Stage VI.

Analyze in detail how each child performed on these tasks. Compare your results with those of your classmates. Can you find an age range for the stages at which toddlers are able to accomplish these tasks?

Child #1   Sex _____ M _____ F   Age in months _____

Circumstances under which tasks were given.

_____

_____

_____

_____

What Piagetian stage best matches this child's performance?

_____

What did the child do to show that he or she is at that stage?

_____

_____

_____

_____

Child #2   Sex _____ M _____ F   Age in months _____

Circumstances under which tasks were given.

_____

_____

_____

_____

What Piagetian stage best matches this child's performance?

_____

What did the child do to show that he or she is at that stage?

_____

_____

_____

_____

How do the ages and stages of the children you tested compare with those other students observed?

_____

_____

_____

_____

_____

◆ **ACTIVITY**

4.9

Observe Pretend Play in Older Toddlers

During the second half of their second year toddlers see mental images that allow one object to represent another. This is when the child begins to engage in pretend play. Pretend play for toddlers happens any time they act as if an object or an event is real with the clear knowledge that it is not. For example, they may appear to drink out of a cup that is empty to emulate dad at the breakfast table. Or they may put on a woman's shoes and be mom getting ready to go shopping. They may be playing alone or with other children. Children this age are often engaged in parallel play; that is, they may seem to be playing together, but each child is really playing out his or her own script. Observe in a toddler room over a period of weeks. Write down an anecdotal account for two or three children under age two who are making the transition to pretend play.

Anecdote #1

How many children were involved? _____

Name	Age	Sex
_____	_____	_____
_____	_____	_____
_____	_____	_____
_____	_____	_____

Who initiated the play, or how did it get started?

_____

_____

What roles did the children assume?

_____

_____

What happened?

_____

_____

_____

Anecdote #2

How many children were involved? _____

Name	Age	Sex
_____	_____	_____
_____	_____	_____
_____	_____	_____
_____	_____	_____

Who initiated the play, or how did it get started?

_____

_____

What roles did the children assume?

_____

_____

What happened?

_____

_____

_____

ITY

)

Analyze Toddlers' Language Development

Choose three children in each of the following age groups: twelve to fourteen months, eighteen to twenty months, and twenty-four to twenty-six months. In your journal, write a list of the sounds, words, or sentences each says. How does each one use language? To whom does each address words? How do they use gestures to communicate? Do you feel their language development is slow, normal, or advanced? Give reasons for your assessment. Observe these same children, if possible, a month later. How has each child's language development changed since the last time?

◆ **ACTIVITY**

4.11

Toddlers' Need for Autonomy

Write an anecdotal account of an incident you observed in which a child was trying to exert his or her autonomy. Did the caregiver in a group setting thwart or facilitate this attempt to "do it myself"? What kinds of verbal and nonverbal communication did the caregiver use? What else might the caregiver have done? Discuss some ways to protect toddlers' safety without saying "no" all the time.

◆ **ACTIVITY**

4.12

Toddlers' Social Development

From your observations in a toddler room, or from a discussion with the teachers, identify a child who does not seem to relate well to caregivers or other children. Arrange to spend fifteen to twenty minutes alone with this child. Have some toys available and try to match your actions and emotional tone to that of the child. Remember that imitation is often the first step in forming a relationship. If you have the opportunity, try to have these one-on-one sessions with this child several times over a period of weeks. Keep a daily log of your experiences with this child. Do you see any improvement in the way this child relates to you? Is there a carryover in the way this child relates to peers and caregivers?

Toddlers who have developmental delays, sensory deficiencies, or physical disabilities are being included in regular group care whenever possible. See the section in Chapter 3 "Infants and Toddlers with Special Needs" for a fuller explanation. Activities 5.23 and 5.24 in Chapter 5 can be adapted to use with toddlers. They will involve you in writing a case study of an atypically developing child and in attending meetings to set up an Individualized Family Service Plan for a child with special needs. In Activity 8.9 in Chapter 8 you will accompany the special educator when she or he visits the home of a toddler with disabilities.

After you and your classmates have observed toddlers in a home setting, a family day-care home situation, and in a child-care center, you will want to discuss what you see as the relative merits of each for the optimal development of toddlers. Activity 4.13 will help you document your impressions.

◆ **ACTIVITY**

4.13

Comparison of Toddler Care Arrangements

In your classroom, discuss what you learned about the various care arrangements that parents make for their toddlers. Make a chart on the board and list the advantages and disadvantages you saw in the three different settings—home care with parents or in-home caregiver, family day-care home, or toddler group in a child-care center. As a class did you find that some arrangements were better for toddlers than others or did all have some good points and drawbacks?

Summary

Young children between the ages of one and three years are undergoing dynamic changes in every part of their development. Toddlers' ability to walk opens up a whole new world for them to explore and manipulate motorically. Their intellectual abilities are also changing. They are moving from exclusively sensorimotor ways of knowing as they begin to use mental images to think beyond the immediate situation and start to use schemas in new combinations. Their changing language skills enable them to communicate with others more effectively. As they move from their home into toddler programs, their social world is also growing. They no longer relate only to parents, but now have peers and caregivers who help to extend their concepts of the social world. Their increasing self-awareness prompts them to test the limits that surround them. They need to discover how they can affect their environment.

Toddlers' parents and caregivers must meet their exhausting demands with humor and understanding. Giving toddlers as much freedom as they can handle while being constantly aware of all their developmental needs is a necessary challenge.

REFERENCES

Ainsworth, M., and S. Bell (1970). Attachment, exploration, and separation: Illustrated by the behavior of one-year-olds in a strange situation. *Child Development, 41*, 49–67.

Ainsworth, M., S. Bell, and D. Stayton (1971). Individual differences in strange situation behavior of one-year-olds. In H. R. Schaffer, Ed., *The origins of human social relations.* London: Academic Press.

Bredekamp, S., and C. Copple (1997). *Developmentally appropriate practice in early childhood programs* (rev. ed.). Washington, DC: National Association for the Education of Young Children.

Cadman, D., L. Chambers, S. Walter, W. Feldman, K. Smith, and R. Ferguson (1984). The usefulness of the *Denver Developmental Screening Test* to predict kindergarten problems in a general community population. *American Journal of Public Health, 74*(10), 1093–1096.

Carter, M. (1993). Building self-esteem: Training teachers of infants and toddlers. *Child Care Information Exchange, 92*, 59–60.

Clyde, M. (1990). Staff burnout—the ultimate reward? In A. Stonehouse, Ed., *Trusting toddlers: Planning for one- to three-year-olds in child care centers.* St. Paul, MN: Toys 'n Things Press.

Cryer, D. (1992). Improving the quality of life for infants and toddlers in day care. Presented at the National Association for the Education of Young Children, New Orleans.

Cryer, D. and L. Phillipsen (1997). Quality details: A close-up look at child care program strengths and weaknesses. *Young Children, 52*(2), 51–61.

Dunn, J., I. Bretherton, and P. Munn (1987). Conversations about feeling states between mothers and their young children. *Developmental Psychology, 23*, 132–139.

Eckerman, C., and S. M. Didow (1989). Toddlers' social coordinations: Changing responses to another's invitation to play. *Developmental Psychology, 25*(5), 794–804.

Eckerman, C., C. C. Davis, and S. M. Didow (1989). Toddlers' emerging ways of achieving social coordinations with a peer. *Child Development, 60*(2), 440–453.

Eckerman, C., and M. R. Stein (1990). How imitation begets imitation and toddlers' generation of games. *Developmental Psychology, 26*(3), 370–378.

Erikson, E. H. (1950). *Childhood and society.* New York: Norton.

Feeney, J. and J. Bernthal (1995). The efficiency of the Revised *Denver Developmental Screening Test* as a language screening tool. *Language, Speech, and Hearing in Schools, 27*(4), 330–332.

Fogel, A. (1991). *Infancy: Infant, family, and society.* St. Paul, MN: West.

Frankenburg, W. K., and J. A. Dodds (1992). *Denver II.* Denver, CO: University of Colorado Press.

Gonzalez-Mena, J., and D. W. Eyer (1993). *Infants, toddlers, and caregivers* (3rd ed.). Mountain View, CA: Mayfield.

Greenman, J. (1988). *Caring spaces, learning places: Children's environments that work.* Redmond, WA: Exchange Press.

Harms, T., D. Cryer, and R. Clifford (1990). *The infant and toddler environmental rating scale.* New York: Teachers College.

Hart, B., and T. Risley (1995). *Meaningful differences in the everyday experience of young American children.* Baltimore: Brookes.

Hendrick, J. (1994). *Total learning: Developmental curriculum for the young child.* New York: Merrill.

Hofferth, S. L., and A. Brayfield (1991). *Child care in the United States: 1990.* Paper presented at the biennial meeting of the Society for Research in Child Development, Seattle, WA.

Hofferth, S. L., and D. A. Phillips (1987). Child care in the United States, 1970–1995. *Journal of Marriage and the Family, 49,* 559–571.

Holdgrafer, G. E., and C. J. Dunst (1989). Use of low structured observation for assessing communicative intents in young children. Presented at the biennial meeting of the Society for Research in Child Development, Kansas City, MO. ERIC ED 312046.

Howes, C. (1988). Peer interaction of young children. *Monographs of the Society for Research in Child Development, 53* (Serial No. 17).

Howes, C., and C. E. Hamilton (1992). Children's relationships with caregivers: Mothers and child care teachers. *Child Development, 63*(4), 859–866.

Hughes, F. P. (1991). *Children, play, and development.* Boston: Allyn & Bacon.

Jacobson, J., R. Tianen, D. Wille, and D. Aytck (1986). Infant–mother attachments and early peer relations: The assessment of behavior in an interactive context. In E. Mueller and C. Cooper, Eds., *Process and outcome in peer relations.* New York: Academic Press.

Jones, S. S., and T. Raag (1989). Smile production in older infants: The importance of a social recipient for the facial signal. *Child Development, 60,* 811–818.

Lamb, S. (1989). The emergence of morality in the second year of life. Presentation given at the biennial meeting for the Society for Research in Child Development, Kansas City, MO.

Lay-Dopyera, M., and J. Dopyera (1993). *Becoming a teacher of young children* (5th ed.). New York, NY: McGraw-Hill.

Leavitt, R. L., and B. K. Eheart (1985). *Toddler day care: A guide to responsive caregiving.* Lexington, MA: D. C. Heath and Company.

Lovell, P., and T. Harms (1985). Playground improvement rating scale. *Young Children, 40*(3), 7–8

National Network for Child Care, http://www.nncc. org/, material retrieved February 2000.

Nixon, P. D. (1999). Caregivers' corner: Negotiating with toddlers. *Young Children, 54*(3), 60–61.

Patterson, K., M. Schmidt, and R. Welling (1991). Language as a pre-literacy skill. Presentation at the ACEI Annual Study Conference, San Diego, CA.

Piaget, J. (1954). *The construction of reality in the child.* New York: Basic Books.

Piaget, J. (1962). *Play, dreams, and imitation in childhood.* New York: Norton.

Piaget, J., and B. Inhelder (1969). *The psychology of the child.* New York: Basic Books.

Press, B., and S. Greenspan (1985). Ned and Dan: The development of a toddler friendship. *Children Today, 14,* 24–29.

Sebastian, P. (1990). Toddler environments: Planning to meet the needs. In A. Stonehouse, Ed., *Trusting toddlers.* St. Paul: Toys 'n Things Press.

Snow, C. W. (1998). *Infant development.* Englewood Cliffs, NJ: Prentice Hall.

Sroufe, L. A. (1979). Socioemotional development. In J. Osofsky, Ed., *Handbook of infant development.* New York: Wiley.

Stewart, R. L. (1989). Improving learning environment for infant/toddler and preschool children through planning a developmentally oriented playground. ERIC ED 316323.

Stipek, D. J., J. H. Gralinski, and C. B. Kopp (1990). Self-concept development in the toddler years. *Developmental Psychology, 26*(2), 972–977.

Vandell, D., and E. Mueller (1980). Peer play and friendships during the first two years. In H. Foot, A. Chapman, and J. Smith, Eds., *Friendship and social relations in children*. New York: Wiley.

Waters, E. (1983). The stability of individual differences in infant attachment: Comments on the Thompson, Lamb, and Estes contributions. *Child Development*, *56*, 516–520.

Weiser, M. (1991). *Infant/toddler care and education* (2nd ed.). New York: Merrill.

Wortham, S. C., and M. R. Wortham (1989). Infant/toddler development and play: Designing creative play environments. *Childhood Education*, *65*(5), 295–299.

Wynn, R. L., D. Belcher, and B. Havens (1991). Facilitating toddler interaction through interior environmental design in a child care setting. Paper presented at the biennial meeting of the Society for Research in Child Development, Seattle, WA.

Chapter 5

Interacting with Preschool Children in Group Settings

In this chapter you will read information and choose from a menu of activities to help you learn more about:

◆ Developmental characteristics of preschool children aged three to five
◆ Activities to do with preschoolers that will allow you to observe and assess development in specific areas
◆ How teachers can incorporate multicultural education, children with special needs, and transition to kindergarten into their planning
◆ The teacher's role in guiding the play of preschoolers
◆ Staff development for preschool teachers.

Children from age two-and-a-half until kindergarten age are rapidly changing and growing. They are developing in all domains—motorically, mentally, socially, and emotionally. They are discovering which movements their bodies can make while they are becoming linguistically more fluent and learning the meanings of words. They are curious about how things work and discover new phenomena every day. They want to be with other children and have playmates and they are being exposed to new and different experiences, materials, and people. While this chapter is divided into studying these compartmentalized developmental aspects of children, it is important to remember that children are whole people.

According to the Women's Bureau of the U.S. Department of Labor (2000) the trend of children being cared for by father or other family member while mothers work is continuing. In 1997, 43 percent received care from a relative other than the mother. In-home baby-sitters or family day-care homes cared for 21 percent. The percentage in organized child-care facilities was 29. Mothers took their children to the workplace in 6 percent of cases.

The fastest increase in care arrangements in the last thirty years has been in child-care centers. While trying to remove families from the welfare rolls has been a goal for states, there has been a concomitant demand for more government-subsidized child care. During the 1990s the federal government increased the funding for such programs as Head Start and Even Start. Even so, these programs do not reach all the children that are eligible to receive them. Half-day programs and nursery schools are available in most communities, but parents often need care for more hours than these programs can accommodate.

The job market affects the number of trained employees that are available to work in child-care programs. Because the wages, working conditions, and benefits are often more attractive in other businesses, child-care facilities have a high employee turnover rate. The problems involved in recruiting and retaining trained child-care workers is reaching crisis proportions in many parts of the country.

Whatever the program designed for preschoolers, the curriculum that teachers and caregivers plan needs to be responsive to each child's developmental needs, what the cultural and family background can contribute, and the strategies that community members and policymakers can use to promote children's development in each developmental domain. Caring for and educating young children must be done in the context of the social milieu of which each child is already a vital participant.

(*The Minnesota Early Childhood Indicators of Progress* which lists how typically developing four-year-olds can show progress is used throughout this chapter. Copies of this document are available for $4.00 each, or less if ordered in quantities, from Minnesota Department of Children, Families & Learning, 1500 W. Hwy 36, Roseville, MN 55113-4266. The publication is also available on http: //cfl.state.mn.us/ecfi.)

Development of Preschool Children

Motor Development

Preschool children are becoming better able to control their body movements as they develop their hand–eye coordination and large-muscle skills. Movement is necessary for learning basic motor skills and also affects cognitive and social-emotional development (Hester 1992). However, many preschoolers do not get the amount of exercise they need to keep them physically fit (Taras 1992). A preschool curriculum must include physical activity and creative movement so young children can become more confident of what they can do with their bodies.

◆ *A well-planned outdoor environment allows preschool children to develop both large and small motor abilities.*

A child of preschool age—from three to five—should be able to run with coordination, jump off the floor with both feet, and hop three to six times on one foot (most children cannot gallop or skip skillfully until they are six). Throwing is done with stationary feet and forearm extension. Three-year-olds turn their heads away when catching and/or use a basket catch involving the whole body. By age five, they are able to use their hands to catch a small object such as a ball or beanbag (Hendrick 1994). Activities 5.1 to 5.3 will help you assess a preschooler's large and small motor development.

Preschoolers are also increasing in strength and flexibility, and need exercise to help make these gains. They need objects to push and pull. They can use a variety of equipment for climbing, jumping, crawling through, crawling under or over, for swinging on, sliding down, or balancing on. They can ride all kinds of wheeled vehicles. They are finding out all the different ways their bodies can move and be in space. While they should be free to explore in an indoor gym or a well-equipped playground, they are also ready for short sessions playing a cooperative game or activity, following directions, or practicing an age-appropriate skill. These games and skills can be used again and again. They need practice to perfect their new abilities. They are also learning to work with others to achieve a goal. Games should emphasize cooperation, not competition.

◆ **ACTIVITY**

5.1

Preschoolers' Large Motor Skills

For this exercise you will observe the physical skills of two preschoolers who differ in age by one year. To carry out these activities go to a gym, large room, or hallway. You will need a rope, a ball that is four to seven inches in diameter, a bean bag, masking tape (in a straight line on the floor) or a low balance beam, a chair or something to crawl under, a mat for somersaults, and a set of stairs. Set up an obstacle course and observe children using it.

Begin by demonstrating the first three activities and ask the children to do as you do. Then direct the children through the obstacle course. Use a checkmark to indicate each child's degree of skill. If the children have no opportunity to demonstrate the skill, set up a situation so they can or else mark it NA (not applicable).

Motor Development Checklist

	Child 1	*Child 2*
1. Stretch arms high over head		
Can do it	_____	_____
Has difficulty doing it	_____	_____
2. Twist at the waist		
Can do it	_____	_____
Has difficulty doing it	_____	_____
3. Bend over and touch toes		
Can do it	_____	_____
Has difficulty doing it	_____	_____
4. Walking downstairs		
One foot after the other	_____	_____
Two feet on each step	_____	_____
Needs to hold railing or adult's hand	_____	_____
Walks down without holding anything	_____	_____
5. Walking upstairs		
One foot after the other	_____	_____
Two feet on each step	_____	_____
Needs to hold railing or adult's hand	_____	_____
Walks up without holding anything	_____	_____
6. Running between two points		
Runs with ease	_____	_____
Has difficulty running	_____	_____
Comments:		
7. Balance		
Walks on tape or beam with ease	_____	_____
Goes off once or twice	_____	_____
Has difficulty balancing	_____	_____
8. Catching and throwing a ball		
Catches ball on bounce _____ out of ten times.		
Can throw ball back	_____	_____
Has difficulty throwing ball back	_____	_____

9. Catching and throwing a bean bag
    Catches a bean bag thrown six feet   _____   _____
    Catches a bean bag thrown three feet   _____   _____
    Has difficulty catching   _____   _____
    Can throw back six feet   _____   _____
    Can throw back three feet   _____   _____
    Has difficulty throwing back   _____   _____

10. Jumping
    Can jump over rope on floor   _____   _____
    Can jump over rope five inches off floor   _____   _____
    Can jump over rope ten inches off floor   _____   _____

11. Can broad jump from starting line   _____   _____
    Two feet together   _____   _____
    One foot ahead of the other   _____   _____

12. Hopping for distance of ten feet
    Can hop on both feet   _____   _____
    Can hop on one foot   _____   _____
    Has difficulty hopping   _____   _____

13. Crawling under chair
    Can crawl under chair with ease   _____   _____
    Has difficulty crawling under chair   _____   _____

14. Somersault
    Can turn somersault   _____   _____
    Has difficulty turning somersault   _____   _____
    Cannot turn somersault   _____   _____

15. Galloping
    Can gallop with one foot ahead   _____   _____
    Has difficulty galloping   _____   _____

16. Skipping
    Can skip   _____   _____
    Has difficulty skipping   _____   _____
    Cannot skip yet   _____   _____

Write a concluding paragraph making a comparison of the two children's physical development.

◆ **ACTIVITY**
5.2

Children's Free Play

Observe children's free play in the gym or on the playground for a minimum of two twenty-minute periods. The first day see how many different types of motor activities you can identify (for example, hopping, sliding, climbing, or running). On the second day, plan an activity that will promote the children's physical development. Follow the activity plan outlined below or one your instructor recommends.

Any of the following activities would engage children in movement:

- have children play a circle game such as Ring-around-the Rosie, Little Sally Ann, Farmer in the Dell, Punchinello, Here We Go Round the Mulberry Bush
- have them pretend to walk, slither, gallop, jump, etc. as if they were certain animals.
- have them act out a familiar story without using words.
- ask the children to move quickly-slowly, lightly-strongly, high-low or in a combination such as moving slowly, strongly, low or lightly, quickly, high
- do movement exercises by imitating the movements *you* make such as swinging arms, nodding head, moving with a partner touching elbows
- move with an object (bean bags, streamer, ball, scarf)

Submit your plan to the classroom teacher at least one week before you intend to try it. Solicit input from the teacher on ways to make this activity work with this group of children. You do not have to do the activity with the whole group. Try it with individual children or a small group. The activity may be teacher-led or set up as part of a center in which children can explore on their own.

The following activity plan can be used to help you prepare for any learning experience you devise for young children.

A. **Name of activity:**

B. **Developmental goals for children to achieve:** Explain how this activity will benefit children intellectually, physically, emotionally, and socially, or how it will strengthen their multicultural awareness.

C. **Equipment and materials needed:** First check to see what is available in the classroom. What materials might be available from the physical education department or elsewhere in the school? What will you need to supply?
   - **Advance preparation:** What will you need to do to get this activity ready for the children?
   - **Suggested procedure:** What steps will you go through in introducing this activity to a child, small group, or large group of children? Could children demonstrate for each other how to carry out this activity?
   - **Evaluation:** Tell what this experience was like for most of the children. Did some succeed? Did some have difficulty doing it? Was it too easy for most, too hard? How would you change this activity if you were to do it again? How might you build on this activity in future planning?

◆ **ACTIVITY**
5.3

Preschoolers' Small Motor Development

Preschoolers' hand–eye coordination is still developing. The preschool situation sets up new demands and opportunities for young children to learn new small motor skills. Teachers ask children to put their names on their pictures or cut on the line. Observe what kinds of small motor activities take place in the preschool classroom. Set up a group activity for four to six children using the plan designed in Activity 5.2 that will foster children's learning a new skill requiring hand–eye coordination. Make it an activity that most children could do on their own. Suggestions for small movement activities (some of these are adapted from Maria Montessori's Practical Life exercises) you could set up for preschoolers include:

- Use an eye-dropper to transfer liquids from one container to another
- Cut pieces of apple or banana with a table knife
- Spread peanut butter on crackers
- Sew with large plastic needles on burlap
- Pour liquids from one small container to another
- Pick up cotton balls with large tweezers
- Cut paper using child-size scissors. (Have beginners snip the edges to make a fringe. As they get more proficient they can cut along a straight line and then proceed to curved lines before trying more complex patterns.)
- Use markers or crayons to make a drawing

Because most preschoolers get little practice in these skills at home, try to limit adult intervention. Encourage the children to help each other. Evaluate your lesson noting each child's ability in handling these tools. Make a list of those who need more practice or more instruction.

Health and Safety

Teachers and family members can do a lot to prevent health and safety problems in young children. They can make sure that young children receive adequate food, exercise, and rest. Parents can take them for routine medical and dental check-ups. Vision, hearing, and developmental screenings should be done on a regular basis. Both parents and teachers can foster self-care routines such as handwashing, teeth brushing, toileting, etc. that can get the child off to a healthy start. Child caregivers can ensure that licensing regulations concerning sanitation and prevention are strictly performed by all staff members. They can help children and families be aware of basic health and safety rules and report any signs of abuse or neglect. They can model health and safety activities for children and parents.

There are many opportunities that community members and policymakers can use to promote children's physical development. Providing parks and sponsoring recreation and health programs including immunization clinics, providing health education and nutrition programs for families of young children, developing safety education and prevention programs, and intervention when health and safety needs are not being met are all important goals. Providing universal health programs for all young children, making sure that nutrition programs are available to eligible children, and promoting policies and providing funding to help families meet basic needs are goals that elected representatives can accomplish (MNDCFL 2000.)

Intellectual Development

Children come to preschool ready to learn. They are trying to make sense of the world. The components of intellectual development are the same for everyone. Mathematical and logical thinking, scientific thinking and problem solving, and social systems understanding are part of each person's cognitive make-up. Young children are curious, exploring, eager to acquire knowledge, and use increasingly complex ways to organize and use information.

Recent research on the young child's brain has shown us the remarkable abilities of children to take in and process information. Young children are better able to learn during the early years than they will be at any other time of their lives. At age three preschoolers have twice the brain activity they will have as adults. The number of synapses at three holds steady until the child is about ten and then decreases until late adolescence (Shore 1997).

Children's brain development is not fixed at birth. The early experiences a child has and the genetic endowment each has at birth interact in complex ways to shape the child's intellect. The emotional milieu, the care received, the adequacy of the diet, and the stimulation given by parents and caregivers all have an impact on the development of the young child's brain. Both genetic make-up and the reactions a child has to his/her environment affect the child's ability to learn.

Much of the theoretical work on children's intellectual learning was done by Jean Piaget (1896–1980) and Lev Vygotsky (1896–1934). Piaget (1954) believed that young children create their own understanding of the world based on their own action with objects, their interactions with people, and their own reflections and thinking based on their experiences. He thought that their conceptions of the natural and social world were constantly forming and reforming as they gained maturity and experience. Vygotsky shared that view, but saw greater importance for language in learning. He also felt that adult–child interactions were of primary importance. Adults and older children "scaffold" new learning for children. They challenge younger children to go a little further than they would on their own by demonstrating or explaining the next steps to be taken.

Later theorists have found that learning processes develop more gradually than Piaget predicted. They have modified and refined the theories of Piaget and Vygotsky to reflect new research. Psychologists and educators are always trying to find out more about how children learn.

We know that children's ability to recall events improves dramatically with age. As they get older they also develop increasingly sophisticated strategies to help themselves remember.

The thinking of young children, however, is qualitatively different from the thinking of an adult. It is important for early childhood teachers to learn as much as possible about how children think and learn. Experts in the early childhood profession have found that preschoolers learn best when they are in programs that use "developmentally appropriate practice." Before going on to the exercises in the rest of this chapter, read pages 3 to 30 and pages 97 to 138 in *Developmentally Appropriate Practice in Early Childhood Programs,* Revised Edition (Bredekamp & Copple 1997.)

◆ **ACTIVITY**

5.4

Preschoolers' Intellectual Development

Choose two children who are at least one year apart in age. You might first devise a game to see if each child has an understanding of the word *more.* They should be able to identify a set of objects that actually has more items than another. Take each child away from the group. Accepting whatever answer the child gives, ask him or her to complete the following Piagetian tasks:

1. *Conservation of number.* Divide twelve pennies into two lines of equal length with pennies equidistant from each other. Show them to the child and ask "Are there the same number of pennies in each row?" Next, push the pennies in one row closer together. Then ask, "Now are there the same number of pennies in each row or does one have more?"

2. *Conservation of liquid.* Fill two glasses of the same size and shape with water and ask, "Does each glass have the same amount of water?" Now pour the water from one glass into another glass of a different shape (from tall and narrow to short and wide or vice versa). Ask, "Does each glass have the same amount of water or does one have more?"

3. *Conservation of mass.* Show each child two balls of clay that are about the same size. Ask, "Is there the same amount of clay in each ball?" Next roll one ball into a sausage shape. Then ask, "Now does each piece of clay have the same amount or does one have more?"

Record each child's responses. Later write up your conclusions from this experiment. Did age make a difference in these two children's reasoning? (*Note:* These same exercises could be tried with kindergarten and primary children. However, many children cannot complete these tasks successfully until they are seven years or older).

◆ **ACTIVITY**

5.5

Recognitive Memory in Preschool Children

Cut at least fifty pictures of familiar objects (toys, household items, clothes, vehicles) from magazines or catalogs. Mount them all on three-by-five cards. Show forty of them to a child. The next day shuffle all fifty cards together. Ask the same child to tell you which pictures he or she saw the day before and which are new. If possible, try this with more than one child. Write in your journal what you learned about the preschooler's recognitive memory.

◆ **ACTIVITY 5.6**

Counting Skills and One-to-One Correspondence in Preschool Children

Create a display of ten small objects. Ask the child to count them for you. Then ask the child to give you four objects, three objects. If the child is able to do this, bring out a second set of ten objects. Ask the child to pair these objects with those in the first set. For example, you could ask the child to put a spoon by every cup or a token by every small block. If the child is able to do this, he or she has achieved one-to-one correspondence. Try this with preschoolers of different ages remembering that many children will not be able to do this until they are older. Accept whatever answer they give.

◆ **ACTIVITY 5.7**

Design Two Learning Environments for Preschool Children

Draw two detailed floor plans for a preschool classroom. Put in all the permanent fixtures first (sinks, cupboards, immovable furniture, and so forth). Arrange the room into easily recognizable learning centers. Show (with lines and arrows) how the traffic will flow. Using the same fixtures and furniture, set up another room arrangement in which the traffic follows a different pattern. For example, the traffic could go around the outside walls instead of through the middle of the room.

◆ **ACTIVITY 5.8**

Plan a Week-Long Unit for a Half-Day Preschool Session

Work with a partner to plan a week-long unit for a half-day (two-and-a-half hours a day) program. Plan an integrated unit based on concepts that are relevant to young children's lives. Check your topic with your instructor before beginning and follow guidelines from your instructor or those given here.

1. Write a letter to parents giving them a rationale for including this unit in the preschool program. Tell them what you want children to learn from this unit and why it is relevant to them. Include a brief description of some of the activities you will undertake during this week that relate to the topic. Ask for the parents' input in some way (supplying materials, volunteering in the classroom, or offering their expertise). Although this should be the first page of the unit, it makes sense to do this last, after you have thought through what you want to accomplish with this unit.

2. Make a chart of the developmental domains. Consult your instructor or use those suggested by Hendrick (1994, 70–72): Physical/small motor and large motor, emotional/mental health, social, multicultural/nonsexist, creative, cognitive, language development, and

special activities for children with special needs. Show the activities you will have each day and state the developmental purpose of each. While you do not have to cover each domain every day, you will want to have activities that meet the children's developmental needs in each domain at least once or twice during your unit.

3. Make a general, flexible schedule that you will follow. Try to plan for at least one long work and play center time every day. Create a balance of child-directed and teacher-directed activities. During this time children should be helped to choose their own activities while being encouraged to participate in activities the teacher thinks would be beneficial for their development. Some refusals, however, should be respected.

4. Make a detailed daily schedule for each of the five days, showing where the activities you've planned will fit. Be specific. Write in names of songs, books, and so on. Note that not all activities need to fit into the theme. For example, the science experiment with lights and shadows need not relate to the rest of the unit on "what kinds of houses people live in."

5. Write detailed activity plans for two of the activities you have chosen.

6. Design two learning centers that will be specific to this unit. For example, if you are doing a unit on weather, you might have a dress-up corner with clothing that is representative of the seasons. At another center you might have charts where children could record the daily temperature, type of clouds they see, or signs of the season they have identified on a walk. Also name the other centers, such as block corner, art table, or dramatic play area, that will be available for children to explore during this unit.

7. Be prepared to tell how these plans could be adapted for older or younger children or for a child with a specific handicap such as hearing or vision impairment. Also be prepared to demonstrate how these plans could be used in a whole-day format.

Your classmates and your instructor will evaluate your unit plan using several criteria. These might include the following:

1. The activities are at the appropriate developmental level.
2. The schedule has a balance of child-directed and teacher-directed learning.
3. The topic and activities are relevant to children's lives.
4. Enough time is allotted for children to do the activities.
5. The plans are well-written and comprehensive enough that another teacher could use them.
6. It is evident that the partners have collaborated in making the plan.

◆ **ACTIVITY 5.9**

Carry Out and Evaluate Your Unit Plan (Student Teachers and Advanced Students)

Design a unit (as above), implement it in the classroom, and write a two-page evaluation. This evaluation will include the following considerations:

1. What changes did you have to make and why?
2. How was the plan adapted to accommodate children of different ability levels?
3. What feedback did you get from the children, parents, or other teachers concerning this unit?
4. What would you do differently the next time you teach this unit?

Language Learning

Conversations between teachers and children and children and children should be a big part of every day. By age three most of what children say should be intelligible to others. (They should be able to say M, N, NG, P, F, H, and W sounds. Four-year-olds should be able to say Y, K, B, D, G, and R sounds. By four-and-one-half they should have developed the S, SH, and CH sounds. Children of six or seven will be able to use the T, V, L, TH, Z, ZH, and J sounds. Patterson *et al.,* 1991.) Many of the problems preschoolers have with speech are developmental in nature and will disappear with increased experience and maturity. Teachers should encourage them to try making new sounds, ask them to repeat what they said if they have trouble understanding the child's utterances, and, as a last resort, interpret what they are trying to say for other children if they get frustrated in trying to make themselves understood.

Three- to five-year-olds need to have real-life experiences so they have something to talk about. Teachers provide common experiences for children through class projects, field trips, and talking about what is happening in current events relevant to the children that lead to discussion with and among children. Teachers model good speech. They see that children also have many opportunities to enhance their vocabulary through listening to others, being read to, and acting out stories. Teachers take time to respond to children's speaking and extend what children say. They ask questions that encourage children to elaborate on their ideas.

Teachers and caregivers can support young children's emerging literacy. Preschool children need to have a quiet area of the classroom set aside for reading, looking at books, and listening to stories. Reading to children every day should be considered an essential part of every preschool program. Children learn that reading has a purpose and they can recognize the shape of a story that has a beginning, a middle, and an end. They internalize the left-to-right progression of the written words on a page.

Children should also be encouraged in their first attempts at writing. Writing centers should be stocked with pencils, crayons, markers, chalk and small chalkboards, notebooks, and different sizes and textures of paper. If these supplies are readily available they will prompt children to attempt writing. Writing tools can also be put in other places in the classroom—in the block corner to make signs or in the dramatic play area to be order pads for restaurants. A typewriter with primary print or a computer with a simple word processing program can be placed near the writing center. Children can either dictate their stories to an adult or older child or experiment with their own attempts to write.

Depending on their age and ability this early writing goes through a predictable continuum and is closely associated with their growing ability in the use of oral language and their early attempts at reading (Whitmore and Goodman 1995.) Children first begin to distinguish between drawing and writing and make marks that begin to look letter-like. They may learn to write the first letter of their name and then use other familiar letters to hold places for meaning in written language. Then they learn that certain letters are related to certain sounds and that books and other written materials contain meaning that can be read. Their written language goes from invented spelling and becomes increasingly conventional in terms of the language system used. All these early attempts at writing and reading should be accepted. Combining their drawings with a written narrative helps parents and others know what the child is thinking. Gathering these early attempts at authorship into a journal works very well for older preschoolers.

◆ **ACTIVITY**

5.10

Preschoolers' Listening Skills

Plan two or three activities that would encourage three- or four-year-olds to be good listeners. Make them into a game the children would enjoy.

◆ **ACTIVITY**

5.11

Preschoolers' Verbal Interactions

Set up a situation in which you can have a conversation with one or two children. You might want to have some toys or props to prompt discussion. If possible, tape record the dialogue. Consider both verbal and nonverbal communication. Include the following in your analysis:

1. What was good about the communication and why?
2. What would you do differently if the interaction could be repeated and why?
3. What was the most important thing you learned about yourself and the way you talk to children?

◆ **ACTIVITY**
5.12

Tell a Story to a Group of Children

Discuss this activity with the teacher beforehand and choose a story you know well. Use props, a puppet, flannelboard pieces, or another visual aid to tell your story. Ask the teacher (or a classmate) to critique your storytelling techniques, answering the following questions:

1. Were you well prepared?
2. Did you know the story without reading it?
3. Were children attentive?
4. Did you include the children somehow in the storytelling?
5. Was the story developmentally appropriate for this group of children?
6. Were the props large enough so everyone could see them?

Social Development

Being in a group of preschool children means that children are developing in all domains in a social context (Vygotsky 1978). "We approach the social world of the classroom with the view that what happens there is teaching and learning, but this is only part of the story. What happens in classrooms is living" (McLean 1991, 175). The relationship between the teacher and child, the nature of the child–child interactions, the feeling of being part of the group that grows with familiarity—all these daily encounters affect how children see themselves. This self-concept, in part, influences how willing they are to try new activities, take risks, and learn new skills.

Children's social development encompasses learning skills to get along with others, their growing understanding of social roles and rules, their developing the attitudes needed to be responsible citizens, and their learning more about how people of the world, both now and in the past, live together. For preschool children this means concentrating on their immediate environments of home and classroom.

Children's early experiences with parents shape their social development. Growing up with nurturing adults can help children learn the skills they need to relate to peers (Staub 1971; Yarrow *et al.* 1973). Denham *et al.* (1991) show that positive mother–child interaction during infancy is predictive of children who show prosocial and nonaggressive social behavior, assertiveness, and a lack of sadness in preschool.

Social development is also influenced by the child's own characteristics. Some researchers (DeCarie 1965; Kohlberg 1964, 1969; Kohn & Rosman 1972) find a correlation between children's social abilities and their intellectual development. During the preschool period children's ability to understand social situations, take another's perspective, and learn ways to accommodate their behaviors appropriately to group norms is roughly parallel to their growing ability to understand the workings of the physical world.

The children's own characteristic ways of relating to the people, objects, and situations in their lives shape the preschool experience for them. Preschoolers' temperament or behavioral style has also been shown to influence classroom interactions (Billman & McDevitt 1980; Keogh & Burstein 1988).

Both academic experiences and personal-social behavior between peers and between child and adult are affected. While not all researchers agree on how to define and measure temperament (Hubert *et al.* 1982), there does seem to be some stability of individual differences across situations and over time. Keogh (1982) finds that temperament is particularly important in assessing the classroom interactions of children with handicaps.

Caregivers' expectations and their conception of the "ideal" temperament are also shaped by cultural values and experiences (De Vries & Sameroff 1984; Klein 1991; Super & Harkness 1981). In some cultures being quiet and undemanding are highly valued traits, whereas in other societies assertiveness and independence are seen as desirable. Children with different temperament patterns make different demands on parents and teachers. Children who are "easy" may be liked by teachers but may get little adult attention. Those who are "slow to warm up" may require careful preparation for transitions. "Difficult" children are often perceived as less able and more troublesome than they actually are (Gordon & Thomas 1967; Lerner *et al.* 1985).

The preschool group is the natural setting for observing how young children interact with peers. For some children without previous group care experience the preschool is their first opportunity to participate with age-mates as part of a group. Parents are often seeking a place where their child can learn socialization skills; their child may have no siblings or neighborhood playmates who are close in age. Children's peer relations are seen as a legitimate area of the preschool curriculum (McLean 1991). "Getting along with others" is a significant developmental hurdle for three- and four-year-olds (Moore 1981).

Preschool teachers employ many effective strategies for helping children get along with their age-mates. Hendrick (1994) recommended teaching children the social skills they can use to get what they want. For example, children can suggest alternatives to their friends: "I'll give you this ball if I can use that rope." They can ask permission: "May I use that cape when you are through?" They can be helped to think of other activities they can do while waiting for favorite play materials. Teachers need to be supportive when children are using some of these strategies for the first time. If the child isn't successful in negotiating, the teacher could help him or her think of other ways to accomplish these goals. "Maybe it would work if you . . ." or "Perhaps you could try . . ."

Some children are very adept at entering ongoing play situations. Others need to learn to ask "May I play with you?" or say "I'll be the baby." Teachers can help them find a prop to introduce into play. "Let's pretend that this is the doctor's book. I'm the nurse making the appointments." Teachers can supply the words and materials the first few times. Then they could ask, "What could you say to let Sarah and Jason know that you'd like to play with them?" Hendrick (1994, 268–269) also suggests many ways to increase positive social interaction among children (see Appendix C).

When a conflict arises, teachers can help the children think of solutions. They can ask, "What is the problem? What are some ways you can work this out?" As the children become better able to handle their own behaviors, teachers may opt not to intervene at all. They may let children find their own ways of resolving conflict. Some children may need to have teacher support in sticking up for their own rights: "Tell her you aren't finished with the wagon yet." "Tell him it hurts when he squeezes your hand."

Children who are aggressive or impulsive are often rejected by peers. Helping a child use language to express his or her angry feelings rather than hitting or grabbing to get what he or she wants can make a child more socially acceptable to others.

Some children are also rejecting of others, excluding those who try to join in their play. This may be simply because they are overwhelmed by all the activity in the room and are trying to control their little piece of it. Adcock and Segal (1983, 8) compare a preschool classroom during free play to a frontier boom town.

> *A lot of the inhabitants are still unsettled, and it is hard to tell what might happen next. Someone may strike it rich by finding just the right plaything or by stumbling onto a really fun activity. If they do, it is a certainty that there will be a rush of other folks trying to get a share of the good fortune. First claims are hard to hold, because claim jumping is a common practice. And the legal system does not provide much protection. It usually is not around when you need it, and the justice that is meted out is pretty crude. Better to carry your own weapons and enforce the law yourself.*

You Can't Say You Can't Play (Paley 1992), describes some strategies to help children become more inclusive and willing to share. Children can be asked to make decisions about the fairness of whatever rule they try to make. They can be asked how they felt when other children excluded them. Writing down what they say and sharing everyone's views with the group can help them decide "Is it fair? Will it work?"

Other children who rarely interact with others or appear socially isolated (Bullock 1993) can be paired with a younger child (Furman *et al.* 1979). This often leads to opportunities to learn interaction skills with a child whose social maturity more closely resembles their own.

Teachers must also recognize that children in group settings may occasionally want to spend time working or playing on their own or may just need a few minutes of privacy (Readdick 1993). Setting up places where children can retreat or be alone is particularly important in all-day programs.

Teachers can help foster friendships among children. Pairing children to perform certain tasks, suggesting to parents that they invite another child to their home for a play afternoon, or setting up carpooling groups all help children form closer bonds with their peers. Mealtime or snacktime can also be seen as chances for a small number of children to learn more about each other and feel a part of the group. An adult who sits and converses with the children promotes pleasant and happy interchanges between them. Large group time can also be used to talk about problems between children and find ways to get along better. These discussions should be brief and not focus on past misdeeds or the actions of individual children (Hendrick 1994).

Preschool children are still struggling to understand their own sexual identity. They already know that they are a "girl" or a "boy." However, they are not sure that they couldn't change sexes. If a boy plays with dolls, is he a girl? If a girl plays with blocks and cars and likes to kick a ball, will she turn into a boy? Many four- and five-year-old girls go through a period when they will wear nothing but dresses in an effort to establish their femininity even though they don't see parents and teachers dressed that way.

Children's self-esteem is shaped by the important people in their lives. They often feel unworthy and incompetent because they have been belittled by adults and siblings. Those with low self-esteem are more likely to engage in inappropriate behavior as they grow older. Encouraging children's efforts, setting expectations they can meet or exceed, giving them responsibilities, giving appropriate praise, and showing how much you value and care about them gives them some new ways to feel and think about themselves.

◆ **ACTIVITY**
5.13

Observe How Children's Temperamental Characteristics Shape Their Social Environment

In an effort to understand how the child's temperament influences the social environment, ask the teacher to identify a child who is "difficult" and one who is "easy." At the preschool level having a "difficult" temperament may be defined as a child whose behavior is arrhythmic or unpredictable, withdrawn, negative in mood, intense, and who adapts to new situations slowly. An "easy" child exhibits behavior that is adaptable, rhythmic, positive in mood, calm, and approachable (Thomas & Chess 1977).

Observe each child for at least an hour in both fairly unstructured free play time and in teacher-directed activities. Pay attention to each child's interaction with peers and teachers. Are there cultural factors or standards of behavior that may be influencing his or her interaction? Write a summary stating how you feel each child's temperament affects his or her interactions with others in the two different classroom situations. If possible, interview the parents of each child and ask the following questions:

1. In general, how well does this child get along with siblings?
2. How does this child relate to other children in the neighborhood?
3. Would you say this child is easier or more difficult to raise than other children of the same age? In what ways?
4. What adaptations do you, as a parent, have to make for this child?

◆ **ACTIVITY**
5.14

Teaching Social Skills

Teachers employ many strategies for helping children learn social skills. Identify instances you have observed in the classroom in which teachers used the following methods to help children learn to get along:

1. Helped a child enter into an ongoing play situation.
2. Helped a child assert his or her own wants or rights.
3. Helped children find a solution to a conflict.
4. Helped foster children's friendship.
5. Used either small or large group time to talk about or reinforce social skills.
6. Helped a child get along with peers.

Emotional Development

Young children have feelings, but they often are unable to recognize them. However, adults can help them find words to describe what their emotions are (Faber & Mazlish 1980; Ginott 1969). Teachers can say, "You're feeling sad that your mommy had to go on a trip"; "You're angry that you didn't get a turn on the slide." The child will then either acknowledge that statement or correct it. The child begins to realize that he or she has a right to these feelings and that they can be labeled and understood by him- or herself and others.

Many young children live in stressful home situations. Parents who are dealing with crises such as separation or divorce, illness, care of an elderly parent, financial problems, job-related stress, or other problems often do not have the time, know-how, or energy to exercise good parenting skills. For children who are living in less-than-ideal conditions the preschool or child-care center can be a sanctuary. Having a predictable routine to follow and caring adults can help a child cope with everyday living.

Children can be helped to express their feelings verbally. Expressive experiences in creative art, music, or movement or relaxing activities such as sand and water play can also help to soothe and calm children. Or they can use dramatic play to act out their concerns (Frieman 1993). Being the parent or superhero for a change helps them feel some control over their world.

Adults need to share their feelings with children. Children need to see how parents and teachers handle their own emotions. "It is especially helpful for your children to know that they are not the cause of your edginess" (Reckinger 1990).

Cadiz (1994) offered three suggestions for implementing preventive measures to support constructive coping: (1) using circle time to assess the level of stress in the group; (2) helping children focus on socially appropriate ways to meet goals or find solutions; and (3) helping children form action plans so they can feel more in control of what they do each day.

◆ **ACTIVITY**

5.15

Evaluate a Child's Stress Level

Elkind (1988) adapted a "life event scale" for children that was designed to measure some of the life-changing incidents that can affect a young child. These events are weighted—the more traumatic experiences carry a higher rating. By adding up the events that a child has gone through in the last six to twelve months you can quickly gauge the magnitude of the stress he or she might be feeling.

Select a young child you know who is undergoing difficulties and use the stress test in Table 5.1 to rate him or her. Children with a score of 300 or higher are susceptible to serious changes in health and behavior.

Being careful to avoid any identifying information, discuss the children with high scores with classmates. Do not discuss a child whose anonymity you cannot protect. What strategies could the teacher and parents use to help each child cope with his or her situation?

◆ **TABLE 5.1** *Elkind's Stress Test for Children*

Stress	Points	Child's Score	Stress	Points	Child's Score
Parent dies	100		Older brother or sister leaves home	29	
Parents divorce	73		Trouble with grandparent	29	
Parents separate	65		Outstanding personal achievement	28	
Parent travels as part of job	63				
Personal illness or injury	53		Move to another city	26	
Parent remarries	50		Move to another part of town	26	
Parent fired from job	47		Receiving or losing a pet	25	
Parents reconcile	45		Change in personal habits	24	
Mother goes to work	45		Trouble with teacher	24	
Change in health of a family member	44		Change in hours with baby sitter or at day care	20	
Mother becomes pregnant	40		Move to a new house	20	
School difficulties	39		Change to a new school	20	
Birth of a sibling	39		Change in play habits	19	
School readjustment (new teacher or class)	39		Vacations with family	19	
Change in family's financial condition	38		Change in friends	18	
Injury or illness of a close friend	37		Attend a summer camp	17	
Starts a new (or changes) an extra-curricular activity (music lesson, Brownies, and so forth)	36		Change in sleeping habits	16	
			Change in number of family get-togethers	15	
Change in number of fights with siblings	35		Change in eating habits	15	
Threat of violence at school	31		Change in amount of TV viewing	13	
Theft of personal possessions	30		Birthday party	12	
Change in responsibilities at home	29		Punished for not "telling the truth"	11	

The Stress Test for Children is taken from *The hurried child, Growing up too fast too soon.* Revised Edition (pp. 163–165), ©1988 by David Elkind. Reprinted by permission of Addison-Wesley Publishing Company, Inc.

◆ **ACTIVITY 5.16**

Provide Emotional Support for an Individual Child (Advanced Students or Student Teachers)

View the video *Floor Time: Tuning in to Each Child.* This is based on the work of Stanley Greenspan (1992), who works with infants and young children with emotional and developmental problems.

After you have observed in the preschool for several weeks, talk with the teacher about a child who is having emotional problems. With the teacher's permission, spend some one-on-one time with the child in a place away from the group. Bring some play materials and follow the child's lead. Practice "active listening" by reflecting back to the child what he or she says and by keeping questions to a minimum. Use some of the techniques suggested by the video. What did you learn about the child? What did you learn about yourself? How did this one-on-one time change your relationship with the child? What plans have you and the teacher made to follow up these sessions? Write about your experiences in your journal.

Creative Expression

Creativity is a form of problem-solving in which there is no one correct response or conclusion. While creativity requires adaptibility and flexibility of thought, it is not the same as intelligence. "Just as all children are not equally intelligent, not all children are equally creative" (Moran 1998.)

Besides the need for space, materials, and adult encouragement Edwards and Springate (1995) suggest that children also need "unhurried" time to gain some proficiency in handling different media and seeing their works to completion. They suggest that the "project approach" (see Chapter 9) is an ideal way to help children communicate and document their creativity.

The easel, paints, scissors, construction paper, crayons, clay, blocks, and workbench have long been the staples available to children in most preschool programs. Music, movement, and drama are also all part of the curriculum. How creative children are, however, is largely determined by teachers (Edwards & Nabors 1993). In general, teachers must strive toward becoming more creative themselves (Shirrmacher 1993).

◆ *Children can express their feelings through paintings and drawings that are uniquely their own.*

Sometimes teachers introduce too many different art media for young children ever to gain mastery of one or two art forms. Children need repeated opportunities to use the same materials over and over so they can become familiar with the properties of each medium and how it can be used to create an art object. Limiting the art materials to easel painting and clay, at least at the beginning of the school year, may have some merit.

Some children seek other ways to express their creativity. They prefer to build with blocks, manipulate puzzles and small objects, or move to music or in other, more physical ways. Accept that doing art projects is not the only way to be creative and plan other activities that will draw their interest.

The focus of art for young children must be on the process. How children use the materials, how they express their own feelings and abilities, how they make something that is uniquely theirs are all at the center of the "artistic endeavor" for preschool children. Teachers who can be encouraging and flexible and supply materials without interfering (unless asked) can help children achieve fluency and originality in ways that they find personally meaningful. Whether pasting scraps to a collage, dancing to slow music, or building a bridge from blocks, children are expressing who they are. Teachers, if they need to, can preserve art objects, videotape the dancing, or photograph the finished bridge to show mom and dad. However, the real art is in the way the child shapes the experience, not in the product.

Besides teachers and parents giving children opportunities to express themselves through art, music, and movement, the community can use several strategies to promote children's development in creativity and the arts by sponsoring community-based arts programs for children and families, providing resources to support children's participation in creative expression and the arts, and exhibiting art in public spaces in the community. Likewise, policymakers can develop policies that support creativity and art in school-based and community arts programs, provide support for programs for visiting artists and performers, and provide support for media-based arts programs. (MNDCFL 2000.)

◆ **ACTIVITY**

5.17

The Expression of Creativity and Individuality through Art

Arrange with the teacher to do a creative art project with the children. With a partner or small group of students plan an art activity that is open-ended (that is, that children can carry it out in any way they wish). One idea might be to have them make a collage. Gather a variety of materials—feathers, ribbons, scraps of shiny foil, fabric, scissors, glue, and papers of different sizes and textures. Set up a table where several children can work at one time. Be on hand to help if requested—to remove caps from glue, to assist with cutting, and so forth. Otherwise, encourage children to use the materials in any way they want.

Write about different ways the children used the materials. How long did each child spend at the art table? How did he or she feel about his or her own work? Were there some children who did not want to participate? What did you learn about young children's art from this activity?

The Teacher's Role in Guiding Preschoolers' Play

When children in several kindergartens were asked to define play, they said that it was something you did without a teacher being present (King 1986). Teacher-directed activities were all seen as work. The less the teacher was involved, the more the activity seemed to be play. It did not matter that teacher-led tasks could also be pleasurable. Having exciting, dynamic play in the preschool with a minimum of teacher involvement takes knowledge and planning.

Early childhood teachers need to have a good understanding of play. They should be familiar with the classical and modern theories of play, have an understanding of ways that children benefit and learn from play, and be able to articulate the developmental stages that children go through as they move from toddlerhood to kindergarten (Parten 1932). They also need to schedule a relatively long play period each day in order for children to develop higher-order play. Group dramatic play requires at least thirty minutes to initiate, plan, and carry out (Christie *et al.* 1988).

Play patterns seem to differ with the sex of the child. Preschool boys tend to participate more in large motor activities such as running, climbing, and playing ball. Girls engage in less active play that often involves turn-taking and fine motor skills such as board games, playing house, and drawing pictures. Both boys and girls, from a very early age, seem to prefer same-sex playmates. Attempts by teachers to diminish gender stereotypes generally have not proven successful (Paley 1984).

Integrating developmentally appropriate play into the classroom is a major part of what the preschool teacher does. A short book on play that would serve as a good introduction is *Play in the Lives of Children* (Rogers & Sawyers, 1988). The task for teachers is to provide for, encourage, and facilitate play without interfering in what the children are doing.

Wolfgang and Wolfgang (1992, 75–96) have found that teacher behavior during children's different types of play follows a continuum. They have named five steps or ways of intervening that go from the least intrusive to the most. In Step one, visually looking on, the teacher merely gives the children who are playing approving looks or nods. Step two includes nondirective statements that are neutral in value, such as "I see you're ready to set the table" or "You've used all the square blocks in your building," which encourage the children to reflect on what they are doing. Step three asks "What will happen next?" or "Is there a way to make your dog house bigger?" These questions encourage the children to think about and develop their play further. In Step four the adult makes directive statements. "You're the doctor and my baby is sick" or "Keep the sand in the bucket" serve to model play behavior for the children and the teacher is directly involved in the play. Sometimes this involvement lasts only a few seconds. Children who have difficulty sustaining any play with others may need more of the teacher's direct involvement. Step five, physical intervention, could mean helping a child into a dress-up costume, facilitating conflict resolution when one child has

◆ *Materials, such as this old camera, can be used in children's play.*

grabbed a toy from another, or taking on a role in the ongoing play scene. The amount of intervention will depend on the developmental level of the children involved. Children with disabilities, because of lack of experience, may need special help to enter into and participate in play episodes (Brown *et al.* 1993). The goal is to lessen adult involvement as children become better able to manage play on their own.

◆ **ACTIVITY 5.18**

The Teacher's Role in Play

Write about scenes of children's play you observe and how the teacher is or is not involved.

1. In what ways has the teacher provided for children's dramatic play? Are the play materials, space, and time allotted for play adequate? What props might prompt more play?
2. Give two examples of teacher behavior when children are playing. Which involvement step (according to Wolfgang and Wolfgang) does each represent?
3. Give an anecdotal account of two or three children engaging in dramatic play. What roles do they play? How long did the play last?
4. Are there some children who rarely or never engage in dramatic play? Pick one child. What do you think might help that child to play more? What interests does that child have?
5. Describe a situation in which you facilitated children's dramatic play.

Guiding Preschoolers' Behavior

Children in this preschool age range need adult guidance to help them find positive ways to interact with others. The goal of all guidance is to help children recognize and internalize appropriate behaviors. Then *they* can control how they act or respond in social situations. Obviously, learning how and when to behave is a long developmental process (Gilligan 1982; Kohlberg 1976). However, the skills for self-discipline are begun in these early years.

Kostelnik *et al.* (1993) outline authoritative teaching strategies that parents, teachers, and other adults can use to help young children learn to govern their own behaviors. Again, these strategies follow along a continuum from least to most intrusive. First, adults must build a positive relationship with each child and model desirable behavior. They must use positive attribution to help children see themselves as capable and cooperative. Making very specific remarks about what the child did well helps reinforce good behavior: "I noticed how well you shared your blocks with Danny."

Adults must avoid fostering competition among children. Setting up situations that require children to work together and teaching them how to ask for or offer help to each other can support their prosocial behavior. Kostelnik *et al.* (1993) suggest other teaching strategies that help children learn nonaggressive ways to realize their goals. Helping them to share resources, using stories to teach social skills, and using real-life situations to help them learn conflict-resolution methods will enable them to learn ways to compromise with others and still get their needs met. Another strategy is to make good use of the classroom materials and space arrangement and to have a flexible schedule that takes into consideration young children's developmental needs and attention spans.

Having children participate in making the rules for the group is another way to help children feel involved in the classroom. Having only a few rules that are stated positively, enforced consistently, and accompanied by reasons help children to know *how* to act.

Giving children positive feedback when they exhibit appropriate behavior reinforces them. An example would be to say "I'm pleased that you helped Alison up when she fell. That's being a good friend." A child who is interfering with others' play may be redirected: "Please come with me now, Sari, to feed the gerbils." Stopping their unsafe behavior when they don't comply with stated rules should be the first step to changing inappropriate interaction. Using "either/or" statements to explain the consequences of noncompliance and following through with those consequences shows children that adults are serious about what they say. A teacher might say to a child who purposely threw her coat on the floor, "You can either hang your coat on the hook yourself or I will help you." Kostelnik *et al.* find that when teachers use these strategies, "teachers' actions become predictable to children" (1993, 360). Hayes (1989), who observed both three- and five-year-olds in group settings, shows that teachers generally respond to rule violations using informational strategies or indirect approaches. However, with five-year-olds they do not use strategies designed to inhibit behavior. Children in both age groups were allowed to take partial responsibility for their own behavior control. A more comprehensive treatment of early childhood classroom guidance with three- to eight-year-olds is available in a study by Gartrell (1994).

Teachers need to involve parents when children exhibit behavior problems in the classroom. Parents and teachers can decide together what strategies would work best with each child. Once parents have been consulted, they can reinforce the same rules at home that are used at school. Children benefit when there is some consistency in enforcing rules among the adults in their lives.

◆ **ACTIVITY 5.19**

Teachers' Guidance of Children's Behavior

Observe in a preschool classroom. Look for ways teachers use guidance with the group and with individual children and describe what happens.

1. Find an example of a teacher modeling the desired behavior for the group.
2. How does a teacher acknowledge a child's positive attributes or give encouragement when a child has shown good behavior?
3. Show an example of the teacher encouraging children to work together instead of competing.
4. How does the classroom arrangement help children control their own behavior?
5. Give an example of how the teacher changes the environment to prevent behavior problems.
6. List five storybooks you could use to teach children prosocial behavior.
7. Write about an occasion when a teacher helped children resolve a conflict.
8. Give an example of a teacher (or child) stating a classroom rule to a child who was exhibiting inappropriate behavior. What happened?
9. Discuss a situation in which a teacher offered the child an either/or choice. What was the outcome?
10. Do you agree with the kind of discipline used in this group? What would you do differently?
11. Discuss a situation in which you had to give guidance to a child. How did you handle it? How do you feel about this experience? What else could you have done?

Multicultural Education

We are a nation of many different races, ethnic groups, ages, sexes, and abilities. This diversity should be reflected in the preschool classroom as well as in the larger society. Every child should have many opportunities to see his or her culture, language, and sex affirmed on a daily basis (Derman-Sparks 1989; Neugebauer 1992; York 1991).

Multicultural education is a "strategy to prevent and eliminate prejudice and racism in children" (York 1992, 11). It also helps children learn to live and work cooperatively with people different from themselves. The "anti-bias" curriculum (Derman-Sparks 1989) includes activities teachers can use to help children explore physical and cultural differences and similarities. It also teaches children to challenge stereotyping and discriminatory behavior. Even very young children know that some societal practices are unfair. They can learn constructive ways to take action.

It is imperative that multicultural activities be integrated into the curriculum throughout the school year. The "tourist" approach should be avoided. Activities 5.20 through 5.22 are designed to help you and the children to become aware of similarities and differences among people.

◆ **ACTIVITY**
5.20

Art Center

Set up an art center where children can explore the differences in skin tones among children in the class. In this center you could include skin-tone color paints and crayons (commercially available) and paper. Older preschoolers could draw a self-portrait using the color that best matches their skin color. Younger preschoolers could have paint samples (available from hardware stores) and be encouraged to find matches. Trying to match their skin color by searching through a collection of knee-high hosiery in different shades would be another way to talk about differences and similarities. These ideas are suggested by Derman-Sparks (1989) and York (1992).

◆ **ACTIVITY**
5.21

Plan a Multicultural Movement or Music Activity

To help children learn more about an American minority culture—African American, Asian American, Native American, or Latino American, for example—plan to teach a song, dance, or movement activity from that culture.

◆ **ACTIVITY**
5.22

The Availability of Multicultural Children's Literature

Visit a preschool classroom when the children are not there. Examine the children's books for gender and age biases, and racial stereotypes. See if images of people with handicapping conditions are included. Your instructor may assign you to do this activity as a whole class or in small groups. Together design a rating form to evaluate the books you find.

As an added step, prepare a list of twenty-five multicultural preschool children's books (as a group or class project). There are several bibliographies of preschool children's books that reflect people from different cultures, of different ages and sexes, or of different abilities. If possible, review the books on these lists. With classmates compile a list of twenty-five multicultural books that you would recommend for any preschool classroom. Include the name(s) of the author(s), the exact title, the name of the publisher and address, and a short synopsis (two or three sentences) of the story. If funds are available, assist the program in ordering at least some of the books from your list. Find a way to distribute your list to preschools and child care centers in your region.

Children with Special Needs

Inclusion of children with atypical development into the regular preschool program is common practice since the passage of Public Laws 94–142 and 99–457. School districts must find and evaluate children and serve them in integrated settings whenever possible. The importance of peers in helping young children develop social, language, and cognitive skills has been well documented (Spodek & Saracho 1994). Parents also must be involved in educational planning for their child. Each child needs to have a case worker who is responsible for coordinating services he or she receives.

The preschool teacher becomes a part of the team making the Individualized Family Service Plan (IFSP). The teacher should be present at any meeting where the parents and professionals serving that child are making decisions that the teacher will be implementing. His or her input will be especially valuable in planning the educational goals for each child. The teacher will also be responsible for making efforts to help the other children and parents in the class be accepting of the child with different needs and abilities. The teacher must also see that the child with disabilities is made a full participant in the activities of the classroom to the extent possible. Further discussion of planning the curriculum to include special needs children can be found in Chapter 9.

◆ **ACTIVITY**
5.23

A Case Study of a Child with Special Needs

Choose a child who has been identified as having a handicapping condition. Use several methods to observe this child. Based on at least five to seven weeks' observation of and interaction with this child, write a case study in which you *report* what you have observed; *infer* what you think are the child's underlying feelings, goals, or causes of behavior; and *evaluate* what the child's major strengths and needs are. Describe also how the child is participating with the other children in the classroom and any particular efforts the teachers make to foster his or her inclusion in the group. This information can be shared with the child's other teachers and parents or can be used as part of the child's IFSE or IEP.

◆ **ACTIVITY**
5.24

Observing an IFSE or IEP Meeting

Ask to observe a meeting at which educational plans are made for a preschool-aged child with special needs. Be certain you understand the process involved first either from coursework or experience. Consult books by Bennett *et al.* (1990) or by McGonigle *et al.* (1991) to get a clear picture of the rationale for each of the procedures involved. Identify the participants. What is the role of each? How are parents included? Did you feel that the professionals really knew what was happening with this child? What was the main focus of the plan that was made? What else might the team have added? If you have the opportunity to observe the child after the plans were made, how well were the plans implemented?

Transition to Kindergarten

Most school districts have some activities that help prepare preschool children for the coming entrance into kindergarten. This might include inviting preschool groups for a visit to the kindergarten classroom, a general health and development screening of all those seeking kindergarten enrollment, or special programs for children and parents. Five-year-olds generally attend these activities in the spring before kindergarten enrollment.

◆ **ACTIVITY**

5.25

Transition-to-Kindergarten Activities

Volunteer to help with kindergarten "readiness" activities. You may be able to plan and carry out learning activities with the children, assist in screening, or be involved with explaining the curriculum and policies to the parents. Find a way to document your experiences.

As an alternative, develop a rating scale (as a class project) that parents would use to assess their child's abilities. The purpose of this scale would be to give the kindergarten teacher as much information as possible about this child's development and experiences. Be sure you ask questions about all areas of development—physical, intellectual, social, and emotional. Some typical items might be "My child can amuse himself with toys for more than ten minutes at a time" or "My child dresses herself without much help from me." Answers could range from one (never) to five (always).

Staff Development

Teachers of preschool children are generally mandated by state licensing agencies to spend a certain number of hours or a certain percentage of their work time in inservice training. Not only does this give them the opportunity to find out the new thinking in the field, it also gives them a chance to meet with others to discuss topics that are of interest to them. The purpose of all staff development is to improve the program for children.

◆ **ACTIVITY**

5.26

Plan an Inservice Workshop or Classroom Presentation

(Advanced students may do this as part of a staff meeting or as a workshop at an early childhood conference, alone or with a partner).

Make up a list of topics (between ten and fifteen) you think preschool teachers/caregivers would find helpful to them. For example, you might include topics such as the following: setting up a parent volunteer program, sandbox science, common health problems of young children, or how to help a shy, withdrawn child. Distribute it to a group of teachers or fellow students to find out what they are most interested in learning more about. Select one of the two or three topics that got the most checks and plan a one to one-and-a-half hour workshop on that topic. Classroom presentations may be shorter—check with your instructor. Follow these guidelines:

1. Keep lectures to a minimum.

2. Involve your audience in hands-on experiences. As one way to get them involved, let them see what it's like for children to learn a new skill by having them try something they have never done before, such as leather-working, French braiding, cross-stitching, building something at the woodworking bench, and so forth. Try to find adult-level activities that parallel children's experiences.

3. Have them get together in small groups of four or five to discuss questions or ideas you have given them. Let someone from the group report to the larger group at the end.

4. Give them a handout that they can take with them. One of the follow-up discussion questions might be how they will implement what they have learned in this workshop in their classrooms.

5. Get feedback from participants about the workshop. Have an evaluation form prepared in advance. Review the evaluations, remembering that you cannot please everyone. Make some notes for yourself about how you will change it the next time.

6. If you work in the center where you did the workshop, do a follow-up to see how the workshop ideas and experiences are being implemented in the classrooms.

◆ **ACTIVITY**

5.27

Develop an Annotated List of Videos on Preschool Development and Education

Consult the media resource library of your college or university. As a class or group project, make a list of the holdings available at your school of videos about preschool development and education. Include the name of the company that made it, the distributor's name, the year, and a short paragraph that describes what is included, and any cost to outside programs to rent it. Also consult the catalogs of nearby large universities and indicate on your list their addresses and phone numbers. Your list should include at least twenty-five videos made within the last ten years. Arrange to distribute this list to preschool programs in your area.

Summary

Children from two-and-a-half to five years need developmentally appropriate experiences that coincide with their increasing abilities. They need experiences that will build on their growing physical strengths and dexterity; they seek challenges to their emerging mental and language capabilities. They want to be socially accepted and learn how to succeed in their increased involvement with peers. They are eager to understand and manage their own emotions and behaviors.

Teachers and teachers-in-training will use many different strategies and methods to observe these children's development, to learn more about each child's individual strengths and weaknesses. This knowledge will help them plan an appropriate curriculum and environment that will meet the developmental needs of each child.

REFERENCES

Adcock, D., and M. Segal (1983). *Making friends: Ways of encouraging social development in your children*. Englewood Cliffs, NJ: Prentice-Hall.

Atkinson, R. C., and R. M. Shiffrin (1968). Human memory: A proposed system and its control processes. In K. W. Spence and J. T. Spence Eds., *Advances in the psychology of learning and motivation* (Vol. 2, 90–195). New York: Academic Press.

Beck, L. E. (1994). *Child development* (3rd ed.). Boston: Allyn & Bacon.

Bennett, T., B. V. Lingerfelt, and D. E. Nelson (1990). *Developing individualized family support plans: A training manual*. Cambridge, MA: Brookline Books.

Billman, J., and S. C. McDevitt (1980). Convergence of parent and observer ratings of temperament with observations of peer interaction in nursery school. *Child Development, 51*(2), 395–400.

Bredekamp, S., Ed. (1987). *Developmentally appropriate practice in early childhood programs serving children from birth through age 8*. Washington, DC: NAEYC.

Bredekamp, S., and C. Copple (Eds.) (1997). *Developmentally appropriate practice in early childhood programs* (rev. ed.). Washington, DC: National Association for the Education of Young Children.

Brown, M. H., R. Althouse, and C. Anfin (1993). Guided dramatization: Fostering social development in children with disabilities. *Young Children, 48*(2), 68–71.

Bullock, J. (1993). Lonely children. *Young Children, 48*(6), 53–57.

Cadiz, S. M. (1994). Striving for mental health in the early childhood center setting. *Young Children, 49*(3), 84–86.

Case, R. (1978). Intellectual development from birth to adulthood: A neo-Piagetian approach. In R. S. Siegler, Ed., *Children's thinking: What develops*. Hillsdale, NJ: Erlbaum.

Case, R. (1985). *Intellectual development: A systematic reinterpretation*. New York: Academic Press.

Case, R. (1992). *The mind's staircase*. Hillsdale, NJ: Erlbaum.

Christie, J. F., E. P. Jonsen, and R. B. Peckover (1988). The effect of play period duration in children's play patterns. *Journal of Research in Childhood Education, 3*, 123–131.

Craik, F. I. M., and R. S. Lockhart (1972). Levels of processing: A framework for memory research. *Journal of Verbal Learning and Verbal Behavior, 11*, 671–684.

Decarie, T. G. (1965). *Intelligence and affectivity in early childhood*. New York: International Universities Press.

Denham, S., S. Renwick, and R. Holt (1991). Working and playing together: Prediction of preschool social-emotional competence from mother–child interaction. *Child Development, 62*(2), 242–249.

Derman-Sparks, L. (1989). *Anti-bias curriculum: Tools for empowering young children*. Washington, DC: NAEYC.

De Vries, M. W., and A. J. Sameroff (1984). Culture and temperament: Influences on infant temperament in three East African societies. *American Journal of Orthopsychiatry, 54*, 83–96.

Edwards, C. P., and K. W. Springate (1995). Encouraging creativity in early childhood classrooms. *ERIC Digest*. ericeece@uiuc.edu.

Edwards, L. C., and M. S. Nabors (1993). The creative arts process: What it is and what it is not. *Young Children, 48*(3), 77–81.

Elkind, D. (1988). *The hurried child: Growing up too fast too soon* (rev. ed.) New York: Addison-Wesley.

Faber, A., and E. Mazlish (1980). *How to talk so kids will listen and listen so kids will talk.* New York: Rawson Wade.

Fischer, K. W., and M. J. Farrar (1987). Generalizations about generalizations: How a theory of skill development explains both generality and specificity. *International Journal of Psychology, 22,* 643–677.

Fischer, K. W., and S. L. Pipp (1984). Processes of cognitive development: Optimal level and skill acquisition. In R. J. Sternberg, Ed., *Mechanisms of cognitive development.* New York: Freeman.

Frieman, B. B. (1993). Separation and divorce: Children want their teacher to know—. *Young Children, 48*(6), 58–63.

Furman, W., D. Rahe, and W. W. Hartup (1979). Rehabilitation of socially withdrawn preschool children through mixed-age and same-age socialization. *Child Development, 50*(4), 915–922.

Gartrell, D. (1994). *A guidance approach to discipline.* Albany, NY: Delmar.

Gelman, R., and R. Baillargeon (1983). A review of some Piagetian concepts. In J. H. Flavell and E. M. Markman, Eds., *Handbook of child psychology: Vol.3 Cognitive development* (4th ed., 167–230). New York: Wiley.

Gilligan, C. (1982). *In a different voice: Psychological theory and women's development.* Cambridge, MA: Harvard University Press.

Ginott, H. G. (1969). *Between parent and child.* New York: Avon.

Gordon, E. M., and A. Thomas (1967). Children's behavioral style and the teacher's appraisal of their intelligence. *Journal of School Psychology, 5,* 292–300.

Greeno, J. G. (1989). A perspective on thinking. *American Psychologist, 44,* 134–141.

Greenspan, S. (1992). *Infancy and early childhood: The practice of clinical assessment and intervention with emotional and developmental challenges.* Madison, CT: International Universities Press.

Hayes, K. H. (1989). Teachers' use of control techniques with preschool children. *Child Study Journal, 19*(1), 29–38.

Hendrick, J. (1994). *Total learning: Developmental curriculum for the young child* (4th ed.). New York: Merrill.

Hester, D. (1992). Movement and motor development in early childhood. In C. M. Hendricks, Ed., *Young children on the grow: Health, activity and Education in the preschool setting.* ERIC ED350303.

Hofferth, S. L. (1987). Child care in the United States, 1970–1995. *Journal of Marriage and the Family, 47,* 559–571.

Hubert, N. C., T. D. Wachs, P. Peters-Martin, and M. J. Gandour (1982). The study of early temperament: Measurement and conceptual issues. *Child Development, 53*(3), 571–600.

Keogh, B. K. (1982). Children's temperament and teachers' decisions. In R. Porter and G. M. Collins, Eds., *Temperament differences in infants and young children.* CIBA Foundation, Symposium 89, London: Pitman.

Keogh, B. K., and N. D. Burstein (1988). Relationship of temperament to preschoolers' interactions with peers and teachers. *Exceptional Children, 54*(5), 456–461.

King, N. (1986). Play and culture of childhood. In G. Fein and M. Rivkin, Eds., *The young child at play,* Washington, DC: NAEYC.

Klein, H. A. (1991). Temperament and childhood group care adjustment: A cross-cultural comparison. *Early Childhood Research Quarterly, 6,* 211–224.

Kohlberg, L. (1964). Development of moral character and moral ideology. In M. L. Hoffman and W. W. Hoffman, Eds., *Review of child development research* (Vol. 1). New York: Russell Sage Foundation.

Kohlberg, L. (1969). Stage and sequence: The cognitive-developmental approach to socialization. In D. A. Goslin, Ed., *Handbook of socialization theory and research* (pp. 347–481). Chicago: Rand McNally.

Kohlberg, L. (1976). Moral stages and moralization: The cognitive-developmental approach to socialization. In T. Lickona, Ed., *Moral development and behavior: Theory, research, and social issues* (pp. 31–52). New York: Holt.

Kohn M., and B. L. Rosman (1972). Relationship of preschool social-emotional functioning to later intellectual achievement. *Developmental Psychology, 6*(3), 445–452.

Kostelnik, M. J., A. K. Soderman, and A. P. Whirren (1993). *Developmentally appropriate programs in early childhood education.* New York: Merrill.

Lerner, J. V., R. M. Lerner, and S. Zabski (1985). Temperament and elementary school children's actual and rated academic performance: A test of a "goodness of fit" model. *The Journal of Child Psychology and Psychiatry, 26*(1), 125–136.

McGonigle, M. J., R. K. Kaufmann, and B. H. Johnson (1991). *Guidelines and recommended practices for the individualized family service plan* (2nd ed.). Bethesda, MD: Association for the Care of Children's Health.

McLean, S. V. (1991). *The human encounter: Teachers and children living together in preschools.* London: The Falmer Press.

Minnesota Department of Children, Families and Learning (MNDCFL)(2000). St. Paul, MN http://cfl.state.mnm.us/ecfi

Moore, S. (1981). The unique contribution of peers to socialization in early childhood. *Theory into Practice, 20*(2), 105–188.

Moran, J. D. (1998). Creativity in young children. *ERIC Digest,* ericae.net/ED306008.

Neugebauer, B. (1992). "Where do we begin?" Bring the world into your classroom. In B. Neugebauer, Ed., *Alike and different: Exploring our humanity with young children.* Washington, DC: NAEYC.

Paley, V. G. (1984). *Boys and girls: Superheroes in the doll corner.* Chicago: University of Chicago Press.

Paley, V. G. (1992). *You can't say you can't play.* Cambridge, MA: Harvard University Press.

Parten, M. B. (1932). Social participation among preschool children. *Journal of Abnormal Psychology, 27,* 243–269.

Patterson, K., M. Schmidt, and R. Welling (1991). *Language as a pre-literacy skill.* Presentation at the ACEI Annual Study Conference, San Diego, CA.

Piaget, J. (1954). *The construction of reality in the child.* New York: Free Press.

Readdick, C. A. (1993). Solitary pursuits: Supporting children's privacy needs in early childhood settings. *Young Children, 49*(1), 60–64.

Reckinger, N. (1990). Open to feelings. *First Teacher, 12*(2), 2.

Rogers, C. S., and J. K. Sawyers (1988). *Play in the lives of children.* Washington, DC: NAEYC.

Shirrmacher, R. (1993). *Art and creative development for young children* (2nd ed.). Albany, NY: Delmar.

Shore, R. (1997). *Rethinking the brain: New insights into early development.* New York: Families and Work Institute.

Spodek, B., and O. N. Saracho (1994). *Dealing with individual differences in the early childhood classroom.* New York: Longman.

Staub, E. (1971). A child in distress: The influence of nurturance and modeling on children's attempts to help. *Development Psychology, 5,* 124–132.

Super, C. M., and S. Harkness (1981). Figure, ground and gestalt: The cultural context of the active individual. In R. M. Lerner and H. A. Busch-Rossnagel, Eds., *Individuals as producers of their own development: A life-span perspective.* New York: Academic.

Taras, H. L. (1992). Physical activity of young children in relation to physical and mental health. In *Young children on the grow: Health, activity, and education in the preschool setting.* ERIC ED350303.

Thomas, A., and S. Chess (1977). *Temperament and development.* New York: Brunner/Mazel Publishers.

United States Department of Labor (2000). http://www.dol.gov/dol/wb/childcare/costats.htm

Vygotsky, L. (1978). *Mind in society: The development of higher psychological processes.* Cambridge, MA: Harvard University Press.

Whitmore, K. F., and Y. M. Goodman (1995). Transforming curriculum in language and literacy. In S. Bredekamp and T. Rosegrant, Eds., *Reaching potentials: Transforming early childhood curriculum and assessment* (Vol. 2) (pp. 145–166). Washington, DC: National Association for the Education of Young Children.

Wolfgang, C. H., and M. E. Wolfgang (1992). *School for young children: Developmentally appropriate practices.* Boston, MA: Allyn & Bacon.

Yarrow, M. R., P. M. Scott, and C. Z. Waxler (1973). Learning concern for others. *Developmental Psychology, 8,* 240–260.

York, S. (1991). *Roots and wings: Affirming culture in early childhood programs.* St. Paul, MN: The Redleaf Press.

York, S. (1992). *Developing roots and wings: A trainer's guide to affirming culture in early childhood programs.* St. Paul, MN: The Redleaf Press.

Chapter 6

Living and Learning with Kindergarten Children

In this chapter you will read information and choose from a menu of activities to help you learn about:

◆ Developmental characteristics of kindergarten children
◆ The role of literacy development in the kindergarten curriculum
◆ The history of kindergarten
◆ Factors that influence atypical development of children before they reach kindergarten
◆ Variations that impact kindergarten programs.

What Is Kindergarten?

Kindergarten education in the United States has traditionally been thought of as a child's first introduction to the educational experience (Kuschner 1989). However, a number of factors have contributed to a more seasoned or experienced kindergarten population today than was the case several decades ago. These factors include a larger number of families who are making use of preschool and day care programs because of work or other commitments outside of the home; an introduction of public school programs for children four years old or younger; and an expansion of early childhood special education programs and other early intervention programs for preschoolers. This change in the educational experiences of many kindergarten children can result in a mindset on the part of parents, teachers, and administrators that kindergarten education must be more challenging and academic because of the child's previous experiences. It is important to keep in mind that, while the experiences of kindergarten children have changed from those of several decades ago, the developmental characteristics of kindergarten children have remained the same.

Developmental Characteristics of Kindergarten Children

Physical Development

The average five-year-old weighs forty-one and a half pounds and is forty-one inches tall. By age six, the child has gained an average of four pounds and three inches (Berns 1994). Vision and perception have developed to the extent that the typical child is able to visually scan and focus on *large print* without difficulty. As children approach age six, many have lost the first of their "baby" (deciduous) teeth, which are being replaced by their permanent teeth.

Gross motor abilities and coordination have also increased by this time. The typical five-year-old can catch a bouncing ball, throws easily, is able to balance on either foot for ten seconds or more, can gallop and skip, rides a tricycle or wheeled toy with skillful steering and speed (some are riding bicycles), and can climb or descend a large ladder with alternating feet (Allen & Marotz 1994; Berns 1994). By age six, these abilities continue to increase and the child additionally develops the ability to walk backward heel to toe, increases jumping ability, and increases in running speed. By five to six years most children can jump over barriers, combine running with jumping, kick a ball with arms in synchronized motion, and throw a ball using a forward step (McAfee & Leong 1994). Most five-year-olds can catch a ball thrown from three feet using their hands rather than entrapment by their arms (Allen & Marotz 1994; McAfee & Leong 1994). By the time children enter kindergarten, they should be able to identify most body parts, clap a simple rhythm that is modeled for them, and engage in vigorous exercise for approximately ten to fifteen minutes without a need for rest (McAfee & Leong 1994).

Fine motor abilities are changing significantly as the child approaches the age for kindergarten enrollment. Most five-year-olds have established hand dominance and can copy designs including circles, triangles, squares, letters, and numbers; are able to fold papers to form rectangles, squares, and other shapes; can use scissors effectively to cut straight lines and simple shapes; and begin to represent people, animals, buildings, and so forth pictorially (Allen & Marotz 1994; Berns 1994). People in their drawings are often larger than buildings, but other proportions may be accurate (for example, trees are larger than buildings, flowers are smaller than buildings; McAfee & Leong 1994).

Table 6.1, developed by the Georgia Department of Education, outlines the developmental characteristics, needs, and resulting implications for classroom instruction for children between ages four and six in the areas of psychomotor (fine and gross motor), cognitive, and affective (social-emotional) development. Note that while children of this age are very active, they tire easily. Therefore it is important that teachers plan schedules for children that alternate active periods with quiet ones. In addition, because children's physical abilities differ significantly, there should be little if any competition stressed in active games.

◆ **TABLE 6.1**   *Developmental Characteristics of Children Ages 4–6*

Psychomotor Characteristics	*Psychomotor Needs*	*Implications for Instruction*
The child is . . .	*The child needs . . .*	*Adults should . . .*
Extremely active, easily fatigued; often shows fatigue by being cross or restless.	Physical activity, frequent rest periods; opportunities to use energy.	Plan individualized and group activities which alternate quiet and active periods; anticipate problems; plan for free play; plan for ample running games.
Restless: tires of doing any one activity for extended periods of time.	Activities requiring different levels of concentration and types of involvement.	Vary grouping patterns; implement planned schedule flexibility; prepare interesting, short "extras"; plan frequent play periods.
Developing small muscle control more slowly than large muscle coordination.	A variety of movement and manipulative experiences.	Provide individual and group activities involving large and small muscles; begin with exercises and rhythmic activities good for the whole body; limit time spent on activities requiring fine eye–hand coordination.
Physically flexible and resilient; skull bones remain soft.	Activities which are appropriate to developed skills of coordination.	Plan activities suited to the range of motor capabilities within the class; set clear limits to behavior in games and activities; provide class supervision.
Females are more skilled at motor tasks.	Motor tasks suited to personal skill level.	Plan for a variety of activities with different demands on coordination; avoid boy versus girl comparisons or competitions.
More interested in manipulation and movement than in product produced or ideas involved.	Opportunities for active participation.	Deemphasize relative quality of finished product; avoid comparisons; provide activities which do not always result in a product; don't insist on perseverance or completion of all activities; ask questions to extend the value of the activity.
Quite likely to be far-sighted; focusing on small objects is gradually becoming less difficult.	To avoid eye strain.	Plan activities requiring a minimum of close visual scrutiny (e.g., copying from chalkboard); eliminate very small objects if magnification is not provided; insist on books with slightly enlarged print.

(continued)

◆ **TABLE 6.1** *Developmental Characteristics of Children Ages 4–6 (continued)*

Affective Characteristics	*Affective Needs*	*Implications for Instruction*
The child is . . .	*The child needs . . .*	*Adults should . . .*
Demonstrating a decided preference handedness.	Practice in refining small muscle control.	Offer a variety of activities requiring the use of the small muscles for both the writing and nonpreferred hands; avoid insisting on handedness.
Capable of most self care.	Opportunities to demonstrate independence.	Plan activities to develop self care skills as needed; encourage the sharing of learned skills between peers; allow children to assume as much responsibility for themselves as possible; discuss the rules related to good health.
Self-contained; self-sufficient.	Experiences to support a growing sense of independence.	Appreciate each child's warm uninhibited nature and reciprocate in the same manner; provide sufficient encouragement, ample praise, warmth, and patience; plan for a variety of child-selected activities.
Eagerly exploring social relationships and all available activities.	Experiences to support personal interest and initiative.	Trust in children's desire to want to learn; plan ample child-selected activities; provide firm limits but freedom within limits.
Seeking attention of peers and adults; likes to be first.	Recognition; acceptance; status within group; positive satisfaction of needs.	Give affectionate attention to each child daily; provide individual help and attention as needed; provide sufficient activities so that each child can have a turn; use equitable techniques in daily routines (e.g., helper selected in alphabetical order); provide time for sharing experiences.
Expressing feelings openly; disagreements are of short duration.	Opportunities for successful peer interaction; security.	Encourage awareness of other children's feelings; state expectations and limits clearly; make limits reasonable; guide child to help maintain control as necessary; supervise closely as situations can deteriorate rapidly.

Affective Characteristics	*Affective Needs*	*Implications for Instruction*
The child is . . .	*The child needs . . .*	*Adults should . . .*
Imaginative.	Interaction with ideas and language of peers; experimentation with roles; help with irrational fears.	Provide simple props and time for imaginative play; allow children to face fears through observing others; provide verbal support; provide security in daily schedule by using simple, clear routines; draw distinction between reality and fantasy with stories, films, music, etc.

Cognitive Characteristics	*Cognitive Needs*	*Implications for Instruction*
The child is . . .	*The child needs . . .*	*Adults should . . .*
Becoming aware of personal sex role.	To avoid occupational stereotypes.	Make all activities available to both boys and girls; refer to people as persons (e.g., salesperson); discuss occupations as being open to both men and women.
Generally aware that others have rights; physical aggression may be used to settle disputes.	The attention of peers.	Encourage peer interaction and self-esteem by using positive reinforcement in the settling of quarrels; set clear limits to behavior; intervene only when necessary; redirect behavior; isolate to lessen stimulation as needed; accept child, not behavior.
Usually eager to conform to social expectations.	Adult approval.	Limit choices as necessary; provide supervision (continuous).
Likely to change friends rapidly; social groups are flexible.	Work and play in small group settings.	Provide many individual and small group activities; identify isolates (using e.g., the sociogram); aid children in making friends if necessary; reorganize play groups as necessary.
Often seeking immediate gratification; experiences difficulty in making too many decisions.	Reasonable opportunities for decision making.	Limit choices as necessary to allow assuming responsibility without undue pressure.
Organizing learning through sensory experiences; learns best through active participation.	Sensory input.	Provide concrete learning experiences which require active, direct participation.

(continued)

◆ **TABLE 6.1** *Developmental Characteristics of Children Ages 4–6 (continued)*

Cognitive Characteristics	Cognitive Needs	Implications for Instruction
The child is . . .	*The child needs . . .*	*Adults should . . .*
Continuing to acquire information, labels.	Opportunities to enrich repertoire of experiences and vocabulary.	Plan varied experiences and opportunities to explore environment, gain information, and share ideas with others; use stories, pictures, films, trips, TV, etc. to expand experiences; provide accurate labels for objects and experiences.
Thinking mainly in the present; thinking is limited to actual experiences.	Varieties of learning experiences.	Provide an environment rich in experiences to stimulate interest; base instruction and discussions on experiences.
Curious about environment; imaginative; inventive.	Information; opportunities to explore.	Plan time for self-directed activities; allow flexible use of materials.
Responsive, easily distracted.	Minimum interference when absorbed in learning tasks.	Plan large blocks of time which allow for absorption, completion of tasks; use centers to focus attention and limit stimuli.
Talkative.	Acceptance; practice in self-expression; opportunities to talk as well as listen.	Encourage the use of listening and speaking skills in total group, small group and individualized activities; support "sharings" with the full attention of adults to encourage good listening habits.
Interested in the present and immediate; interested in knowledge that is practical and accurate; asks questions that are purposeful and relevant.	Answers to questions.	Relate all experiences to what is already known; answer questions simply and discuss, then stimulate further thinking; reply "I don't know" when appropriate and help child find answers to questions.
Using varied sentence patterns; articulating clearly; possesses a vocabulary adequate to express thoughts.	Opportunities to elaborate language and refine verbal skills; to hear and use language in many ways.	Encourage verbal exchanges; model correct grammar and usage; help the child who has difficulty with self-expression.
Imitating adult behavior and interests (e.g., hobbies, books, reading.)	Exposure to a variety of models.	Encourage the participation of a number of different adults and older children in classroom.

Source: Georgia Department of Education, *Personalized Education K-4*

Study the other information this table provides regarding the psychomotor development of children at this age before completing Activities 6.1 through 6.7. Return to the table after reading the sections on cognitive development and social and emotional development and before completing the activities that follow those sections.

Observing the Physical Development of the Kindergarten Child

Complete some of the following tasks to validate the information about the physical development of the typical kindergarten child.

◆ **ACTIVITY 6.1**

Measurement of Self

Weigh and measure a group of kindergarten children (at least five of them). Calculate the average weight and height for this group. How does their average weight and height compare with that reported by Berns (1994)? This activity could be done as a part of an instructional unit on measurement or self-concept.

◆ **ACTIVITY 6.2**

Classroom Survey of "Lost Teeth"

Survey a class of kindergarten children to determine how many children in the class have lost one or more of their "baby" (deciduous) teeth (some teachers have posters and other material for this purpose). How many children have lost one tooth? More than one? What is the average number of teeth lost for this class? How many children have not lost any of their temporary teeth? Make a chart showing the correlation between date of birth, number of teeth lost and gender of the child (for example, F, 5/20/98, two teeth lost). Again, this could be part of a lesson or instructional unit on dental health. Consider a graphing activity that will enable children to visualize how many children have lost one tooth, five teeth, and so forth.

◆ **ACTIVITY 6.3**

Checklist of Gross Motor Skills

Observe a group of kindergartners as they participate in gross motor activities including skipping; galloping; climbing; running; walking backwards on a balance beam; and bouncing, catching, and throwing a ball. Develop a checklist to use as you complete your observation. Include the child's first name, date of birth (if available), gender, and a list of the gross motor tasks to be observed. After your observation, do an analysis of the information you have collected. Are there differences in gross motor abilities related to the age or gender of the children observed?

◆ **ACTIVITY**
6.4

Analyze Children's Responses to a Story

Read a story that includes illustrations of people, animals, and buildings to a group of kindergarten children. After reading the story, ask the children to draw pictures about the story. Analyze their drawings to see what elements and details from the story they include in their pictures.

◆ **ACTIVITY**
6.5

Small Motor Activities in the Kindergarten Classroom

Which activities that you observed in the kindergarten classroom involved small motor activity? What material or equipment was available for small motor development? Consider other materials in addition to crayons, pencils, scissors, and so forth. Did you observe a difference in the skill level of girls and boys in small motor development (writing, drawing, cutting)?

Have two kindergarten children copy shapes that you have previously drawn in boxes on sheets of paper. Include a circle, square, rectangle, triangle, cross, letters, and numerals. Also ask the children to write their names.

◆ **ACTIVITY**
6.6

Children's Paper Folding and Cutting Skills

Observe the fine motor development of kindergarten children by planning activities that require five- to six-year-olds to fold paper into squares, rectangles, or triangles. Also prepare cutting materials with straight lines, curved lines, circles, squares, and so on. Work with a small group of children so you may provide assistance if needed.

◆ **ACTIVITY**
6.7

Children's Psychomotor Needs

How did the classroom schedule reflect the psychomotor needs of the children? Were active and quiet periods alternated? Did the schedule allow for the need of young children to move frequently? Was there an emphasis on process or product in projects completed?

Cognitive Development

Piaget characterized the thinking of five- to six-year-olds as shifting from preoperational to concrete operational thought patterns (Berger 1994). This period of transition is marked by the use of intuitiveness, which often enables children to select the correct answer or response but remain unable to explain the reason they have reached that conclusion. "It is because it is" may be the sort of response a child gives when asked to explain his or her reasoning.

The use of symbolic thought (manipulating and using symbols in thinking) is demonstrated by most kindergarten children through their use of representational drawing and their attempts at writing their names, other words, and numerals (McAfee & Leong 1994). The making and interpretation of pictorial graphs with adult assistance is also within the capability of most kindergarten children.

The ability to sort and classify objects according to specific properties of the objects being sorted (color, shape, size, and so on) is usually completed by kindergarten children on the basis of one attribute or characteristic—color *or* shape *or* size. Some children will begin to consider classifications on the basis of two attributes (large circles, small circles, large squares, small squares, and so forth). Five-year-olds are able to seriate materials on the basis of height or size (smallest to tallest, largest to smallest, and so forth). Thus, it is important to provide children of this age with many collections of items that can be sorted in a variety of ways. The math curriculum in many kindergarten classrooms makes use of sets of manipulative items that children can use to acquire classification and other mathematical skills.

Mathematical knowledge acquired by most five-year-olds includes the following (Allen & Marotz 1994; McAfee & Leong 1994):

Count to twenty or higher
Recognize numerals 1 to 10 or more
Equate clock time to events of the day: "It is time for bed when the clock points to the eight"
Read clock time on the hour
Understand the purpose of a calendar
Understand yesterday, today, tomorrow, before, and after
Understand ordinal numbers: first, second, last
Recognize and name coins: dime, nickel, penny

The oral language development of most kindergarten children is quite advanced. Speech has been mastered by the five-year-old so that it is 90 to 100 percent intelligible (Allen & Marotz 1994; McAfee & Leong 1994). By age five children have a vocabulary of fifteen hundred words or more and exhibit the following characteristics related to language development:

Define words by function: "a car is to ride in"
Identify and name most colors
Recognize humor in simple jokes, try making up jokes and riddles
Produce sentences with an average of five to seven words
Use past tense regular verbs accurately: went, rode, ran, and so on
Use singular and plural forms of nouns accurately: car/cars, toy/toys
Name town/city where living, birthday, parents' names
Retell familiar stories centering on one character accurately and in proper sequence
Use "book talk" appropriately, including title, author, cover, beginning, middle, end

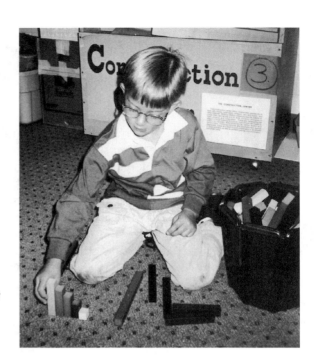

◆ *The abilities to sort, classify, and seriate materials develop when kindergarten children have access to sets of manipulative materials.*

Research over the past several decades has focused on how children acquire oral language, the effect of literacy environments in the home, the development of early reading, and the developmental stages of learning to write (Morrow 1993). This broad body of research embraces the concept of emergent literacy and helps us to better understand that becoming literate is a gradual process. It further helps us to recognize that most children are well on their way to becoming literate by the time they enter kindergarten. They have already become "book smart" if they have had sufficient exposure to literature at home and preschool. In other words, they know much about how books work—for example, that they have a front and back and that illustrations differ from print. In addition, prekindergarteners are very likely able to read environmental print such as a stop sign and favorite cereal box names, and can recognize their own name and those of family members and classmates. Many entering kindergarten already know how to print their names and a few other key words. The kindergarten teacher's nightmare used to be discovering that a child in his or her class could read. Now many teachers work hard at getting all kindergarten children in their classes to recognize themselves as readers and writers by implementation of emergent literacy strategies.

Literacy Development in Kindergarten

Work by the New Standards Literacy Committee has resulted in establishment of literacy standards for children in kindergarten through third grade (New Standards, Primary Literacy Committee 1999). Experts in the field of early childhood literacy including Lucy Calkins, Courtney Cazden, David Pearson, Gay Su Pinnell, Dorothy Strickland, and Elizabeth Sulzby were among the committee members who developed reading and writing standards for each grade level. The committee members came together with differing views of literacy instruction, but set aside their differences on how to organize literacy teaching and developed a set of guidelines that identifies what children need to know and be able to do in order to be successful in school and in life. The standards for reading and writing are organized under 3 broad categories including:

Reading

1. Print-Sound Code
2. Getting the Meaning
3. Reading Habits

Writing

1. Habits and Processes
2. Writing Purposes and Resulting Genres
3. Language Use and Conventions

Specifically by the end of kindergarten, the standards include

1. Print-Sound Code

Have knowledge of letters and their sounds

- By recognizing and naming most letters;
- By recognizing and saying the common sounds of most letters and writing a letter to go along with a spoken sound;
- By using knowledge of sounds and letters to write phonetically.

Acquire phonemic awareness (segmenting and blending sounds)

- By producing rhyming words and recognizing pairs of rhyming words;
- By isolating initial consonants in single-syllable words (/m/ is the first sound in man);
- By identifying the onset *(c)* and rime *(-at)* in single-syllable words such as **cat**, and beginning to fully separate the sounds (/c-/a-/t/) by saying each sound;
- By blending separately spoken sounds to make meaningful one-syllable words (when the teacher says /c-/at/, the child can say *cat;* when the teacher says /mmm-/ ahhh-/mmm/, the child can say *mom.*

Read words

- By using their knowledge of letter sounds, children are able to figure out a few simple, regularly spelled single-syllable words (consonant-vowel-consonant, such as man, dog, etc.)

- By reading simple texts containing familiar letter–sound correspondences and high-frequency words;
- By reading some words on their own, including about twenty simple, high-frequency words that are recognized by sight (when printed in a story they do not need to sound them out). It is important to note that this is a learning target, not a teaching target. Each child may know a different set of twenty words.

2. Getting the Meaning

Develop accuracy and fluency

- By reading Level B books they have not seen before, but which have been previewed for them (introduced to title, what it is about, and introduction of difficult or unfamiliar words). Children attend to each word in sequence and are able to read most correctly. (Level B books focus on a single idea, have high-frequency words that are used repeatedly throughout the text, etc.)
- By being given the opportunity to read emergently—in other words reread a favorite story, re-creating word and using fluent intonation and phrasing.

Use self-monitoring and self-correcting strategies

- To determine if they are looking at the correct page;
- To determine whether the word they are saying is the one they are pointing to;
- To recognize whether what they are reading makes sense;
- By asking questions or making statements about stories read aloud.

Comprehension

- By creating artwork or a written response that shows comprehension of a story read to them;
- By using knowledge from their own experience to make sense of and talk about the text;
- By making predictions based on illustrations or portions of stories.
- By retelling the story in their own words or re-enacting it, getting events in the correct sequence;
- By responding to simple questions about the book's content.

3. Reading Habits

Reading a lot

- By choosing reading as a way to enjoy free time and by asking for books to be read to them;
- By listening to one or two books read aloud each day in school and discussing the books with teacher guidance;
- By having one or two books read to them each day at home or in a day-care setting
- By rereading or reading along with two to four familiar books each day;

- By engaging with a range of genres (different types of literature, signs, labels, messages, etc.)
- By holding a book rightside up and turning the pages in the proper direction;
- By following the text with a finger, pointing to each word as it is read;
- By paying attention to what the words they read are saying.

Discussing books

- By giving reactions to books with supportive reasons;
- By listening carefully to each other;
- By asking each other to clarify things that they say;
- By using newly learned vocabulary;

Vocabulary

- By noticing unfamiliar words when they are read to or talked with and guessing what the words mean from the way that they are used;
- By talking about words and their meanings as they are encountered in books and conversation;
- By learning new words every day from conversations and books read aloud.

1. Writing Habits and Processes

- By writing daily;
- By generating content and topics for writing;
- By writing without resistance when given time, place, and materials;
- By using whatever means are at hand to communicate and make meaning (drawings, letter strings, scribbles, etc.)
- By making an effort to re-read their own writing and by listening and responding to the writing of others (laughing, asking questions, etc.).

2. Writing Purposes and Resulting Genres

Sharing events, telling stories: narrative writing

(Note kindergarten children may *tell* or *write* narratives)

- That contain a "story" of a single event or several events loosely tied together;
- That tell events as they move through time in chronological order;
- That include gestures, drawings, and/or intonations that enhance meaning;
- That incorporate storybook language ("Once upon a time . . .").

Informing others: report or informational writing

Kindergarten students delight in reporting to others and often make lists that tell "all about a particular topic (all about my brother, me, etc). By the end of the kindergarten year, students would be expected to:

- Gather and share information about a topic;
- Maintain a focus, stay on the topic;
- Exclude extraneous information when prompted.

Getting things done: functional writing

- By writing to tell someone what to do (giving directions, sending a message, etc.);
- By naming or labeling objects or places

Producing and responding to literature

- By re-enacting or retelling stories, poems, plays, songs;
- By creating their own stories, poems, plays, songs;
- By using literary forms and language (poetic language, repetition, etc.).

3. Language Use and Conventions

Style and syntax

- By producing their own writing that uses the syntax of oral language and is therefore easy to read aloud;
- By taking on the language of authors approximating the phrasing and rhythm of literary language.

Vocabulary and word choice

- By using words in their writing that they use in their own conversations (usually represented phonetically).

Taking on language of authors

- By using words from books read to them in their writing;
- By making choices about which words to use on the basis of whether they convey the meaning that they intend.

Spelling

- By independently writing text with words that an adult, knowledgeable about the content and about spelling development, can read;
- By being able to reread their own writing with a match between what they say and what they have written;
- By pausing voluntarily while writing to reread what they have written (tracking);
- By leaving space between words that they write;
- By demonstrating left to right and top to bottom directionality;
- By frequently representing words with the initial consonant sound.

Punctuation, capitalization and other conventions

- Children are not *expected* to show any regularity or awareness of punctuation and conventions (periods, capitals, commas, etc.).

The report card (see Figure 6.1 on pages 146–148) used by kindergarten teachers in schools in Rochester, Minnesota, reflects knowledge of the concept of emergent literacy and a whole language approach to instruction. In addition, it reflects several other important concepts, including a whole child approach to assessment by looking at aspects of social development as well as cognitive development and an acknowledgment of the continuity of development by use of continuums to indicate the child's level of development.

The cover sheet of this report card indicates to parents the importance of multiple means of assessing children's progress, including the use of checklists, portfolios, and so forth that each teacher might use to supplement the district-wide kindergarten report card.

◆ **ACTIVITY**

6.8

Reading or Writing Assessment

Work with a partner or small group to design activities to assess a kindergarten child's progress for <u>one</u> of the reading standards (print-sound code, getting the meaning, reading habits) **or** <u>one</u> of the writing standards (habits and processes, purposes and resulting genres, language use and conventions). Remember that the standards are expectations for children at the <u>end of the kindergarten year</u>. Try out your assessment on one or more kindergarten-aged children to see whether the child is making progress toward competency in the standard that you assessed.

◆ **ACTIVITY**

6.9

Design a Cognitive Development Inventory

Work with a partner or small group to design an inventory that will help you to determine the cognitive development of a five- or six-year-old as described earlier. Include activities such as counting objects (pennies), rote counting, use of ordinal numbers (first, second, third), the understanding of time concepts, color recognition activities, and so on. Make sure that you use manipulative and concrete materials as part of the activities that you design. Share your inventory with your instructor or classmates before trying it out with a child.

◆ **ACTIVITY**

6.10

The DIAL–III

Familiarize yourself with one of the commercial assessment kits that has been developed such as the DIAL-III (*Developmental Indicators for the Assessment of Learning-III*), which includes materials to assess motor, concept, and language development of children aged two to six years old (Mardell-Czundowski & Goldenberg, American Guidance Service, 1998). Use all or part of the instrument with a child who will attend kindergarten next fall.

◆ **ACTIVITY**

6.11

Kindergarten Screening

Make arrangements to observe or assist with a kindergarten screening in the local school district or your home school district. Write a brief (one to two pages) report describing the kindergarten screening process.

Rochester Public Schools
Rochester, Minnesota

Student Progress Report—Grade K

Student _____   Parent/Guardian Signature:

School _____   1st Quarter _____

Grade Level _____   2nd Quarter _____

Year _____   Teacher's Signature _____

Opening Comments to Parents/Guardians: The purpose of the student progress report is to indicate a child's performance at a specific time determined by a variety of ongoing assessments. These could include, but are not limited to: teacher observations, portfolios, formal testing, student self-evaluation, anecdotal comments, checklists, narratives, logs, journals, pre/post testing, tapes (audio/visual), and student/teacher interviews.

The student progress report is broken down into two categories: academic and personal/social. These areas allow students, parents/guardians, and teachers to look at the growth of the child while emphasizing student strengths and celebrating student accomplishment. Please discuss this progress report with your child.

Student Progress Report—Grade K

At the end of the reporting period, the appropriate symbol is placed on each continuum: 1=1st Quarter; 2 = 2nd Quarter; 4 = 4th Quarter; N = not observed/not evaluated. Conferences may replace this report as a means of sharing information with parents/guardians.

PERSONAL/SOCIAL GROWTH	Seldom Observed	Developing	Consistently Observed
1. Shows positive attitude toward learning			
2. Actively participates in learning			
3. Takes pride in a job well done			
4. Accepts challenges			
5. Is a self-directed learner			
6. Expresses feelings appropriately			
7. Displays self-control			
8. Cooperates with others			
9. Respects individual diversity			
10. Respects the rights and property of others			
11. Uses time wisely			
12. Is responsible for completing work			
13. Follows directions			
14. Follows rules			
15. Organizes materials			

ART

	Seldom Observed	Developing	Consistently Observed
1. Actively participates in activities			
2. Understands concepts introduced			

MUSIC

	Seldom Observed	Developing	Consistently Observed
1. Actively participates in activities			
2. Understands concepts introduced			

PERCEPTUAL MOTOR/PHYSICAL EDUCATION

	Seldom Observed	Developing	Consistently Observed
1. Actively participates in activities			
2. Understands concepts introduced			
3. Performs large and small motor skills			

PIC—HEALTH, SCIENCE, SOCIAL STUDIES

	Seldom Observed	Developing	Consistently Observed
1. Actively participates in activities			
2. Understands concepts introduced			
3. Communicates ideas			

MATH

	Seldom Observed	Developing	Consistently Observed
1. Explores/demonstrates problem solving using math concepts			
2. Recognizes/applies concepts of patterns and relationships			
3. Explores/demonstrates concepts of spatial sense (shapes/inside-outside)			
4. Explores/demonstrates number sense. (Counting sets, recognizing numerals, solves story problems)			

(continued)

LISTENING/SPEAKING	Seldom Observed	Developing	Consistently Observed
1. Expresses thoughts clearly			
2. Responds appropriately to what has been said			
3. Contributes to group discussions			

READING

Children become fluent readers by working through each stage at their own rate.

PRE-EMERGENT	EMERGENT
• Picture reads • Aware that print has meaning • Enjoys being read to	• Sees self as a reader (reads back stories written by teacher or self) • Is developing a sight word vocabulary (Reads signs, symbols, labels, and names; recognizes commonly used words) • Uses reading strategies • Identifies rhyming words • Hears beginning, ending, and middle sounds • Associates a sound with a letter
TRANSITIONAL	COMPETENT
• Uses reading strategies with independence • Continues to increase sight word vocabulary • Uses a variety of methods for comprehending • Is successful with a variety of reading materials	• Independently reads for meaning • Efficiently uses a variety of strategies and methods

WRITING

Children become fluent writers by working through each stage at their own rate.

STAGE 1	STAGE 2	STAGE 3
• Scribbles from left to right • Draws picture only	• Uses letters in drawings	• Uses beginning sounds only to communicate about drawing

STAGE 4	STAGE 5
iPLA SR (I play soccer) • Uses beginning, ending, and middle sounds to write words • Reads writing back to teacher • Uses invented spelling to write a sentence	*I. LoVe. skL* *SkL. is.* *GRAT.* • Writes recognizable words as well as uses sound spelling to write sentences • Writes from left to right • Is aware of spaces between words • Experiments with punctuation

Printed with permission Rochester Public Schools Rochester, Minnesota.

◆ **ACTIVITY**

6.12

Interview with a Teacher

Interview a kindergarten teacher to determine how he or she assesses the cognitive development of children in his or her class. Ask for examples of checklists, report cards, and so forth used by the teacher. Share them with your classmates.

◆ **ACTIVITY**

6.13

Group Report Card

With your instructor's approval, arrange for a kindergarten-aged child to attend your class. Design activities that will enable members of your class to fill out the report card designed by kindergarten teachers at Sunset Terrace School in Rochester, Minnesota (Figure 6.1). After the child has left, or during your next class meeting, break into small groups to compare how each class member in the group completed the report card for the same child. Where did you agree and disagree? Why?

◆ **ACTIVITY**

6.14

Classroom Organization

How is instruction organized in this classroom? Thematically (life on the farm, endangered animals)? Conceptually (shape, color, time, living and nonliving things)? By subject matter (reading, math, science)? Write a report about your observation using the format suggested below.

Guidelines for Observing in a Kindergarten Classroom

Write about the following aspects of each kindergarten classroom that you observe:

 The physical environment

1. How is the indoor space arranged? Make a floor plan of the space showing furniture placement. What equipment and materials are present and in what areas of the room are they placed? How and when are the materials used by children? What names do the teacher and children use to refer to the different areas of the room (book corner or library, doll corner or family living)? What do the names of the areas tell you? Are some areas used only by boys, only by girls, or by mixed-gender groups? Do some areas in the room serve multiple purposes at different times during the day?

2. What are the major activity areas in the outdoor space? Are different playing surfaces available? How are they used by children? What kind of equipment is available (both permanent and equipment brought outside by children or teachers)? Draw a bird's-eye view of the outdoor space showing major equipment and natural landmarks (trees, hills, rivers).

The social environment

1. What is the daily schedule? What names are given to different time blocks (snack time, outdoor play time)? What are children expected to do during these blocks of time? What do teachers do during these time blocks? For example, do teachers sit at tables and talk to children during snack time if it is served as a large group activity or does the teacher prepare for the next activity scheduled while children are having a snack?

2. What is the composition of the class? How many children are there? How many boys and girls? Are there children who are culturally diverse? Are children with special needs integrated or mainstreamed into the classroom for part or all of the day? How do teachers interact with these children? How do other children interact with these children?

3. In general, how do adults interact with children? What are adult expectations for children's behavior? How do these vary according to time periods throughout the day and according to activity areas? Does the teacher tend to stay in certain areas of the classroom or circulate to different areas of the classroom? When a child's behavior does not meet teacher expectations, how does the teacher respond?

4. How do children interact with each other? How do they work or play together? What do children do to solve problems?

5. How does the teacher interact with other teachers? With other staff members? With parents?

 Reflecting on your observations

(Be prepared to discuss this part of your paper in class).

1. Explain at least *three* things you learned from your observations of kindergartens that you did not know or think about kindergarten children and classrooms before.

2. List at least *three* questions you would like to have answered or concepts you would like to know more about.

Social and Emotional Development of the Kindergarten Child

As the child enters the arena of formal education, social and emotional development become interrelated. The emotional and social development of the kindergarten child can best be described as changing. Emotionally, the typical five- to six-year-old is positive and enthusiastic about most experiences and interactions. Children at this age have a positive regard for themselves and what they are able to do.

Erickson (1980) identifies the school years as the period when a child's personality and identity is shaped by the way he or she resolves the conflict or crisis of *industry versus inferiority*. As cognitive, physical, and social tasks become more important in the school setting, the child learns that his or her abilities are evaluated by adults while simultaneously learning to self-evaluate by comparing him- or herself to others, thereby influencing his or her self-concept or emotional being. When children have successful experiences and interactions, they resolve the crisis of this period of life with a feeling of competence and empowerment, or what Wasserman (1990) calls a strong sense that they are "can-do" or capable children. On the other hand, children who have early school experiences that are unsuccessful and negative will view themselves as inferior, incompetent, incapable, or, in Wasserman's words, as "can't do" children. The attitude toward work and achievement throughout the school years can be largely influenced by a child's early school experiences. Therefore, the primary goal of teachers in the early years should be to provide children with experiences and feedback that allow them to see themselves as capable and successful.

Play and Friendship in Kindergarten

As children move into the world of school, social relationships with peers become more important to them. Friendships and play among kindergarten children often have the following characteristics:

1. Friendships are often based on who is available to play and whether they are willing and interested in the same materials and activities. Playmates/groups are often flexible rather than constant (Selman & Selman 1979).
2. Play is often *associative* (it involves social interaction but no rules or plan for the play are apparent) or *cooperative* (it involves the sharing of materials and development of a plot, common purpose, or rules for the play activity) in nature (Parten 1932).
3. Children increasingly take on gender-specific roles (girls are the mothers, boys the fathers) and activities (girls in the art or housekeeping area, boys in the construction area) and segregate themselves into same-sex groups for play (Berger 1994; Paley 1984).
4. Conflicts are often short-term and may be resolved by giving in or leaving rather than by compromise. Children at this age can learn to compromise if given the appropriate guidance and suggestions.
5. Aggression becomes more verbal and less physical, resulting in teasing and boy-girl chases on the playground.

Paley (1993) stresses the importance of social development as children enter the world of school. In *You Can't Say You Can't Play* Paley describes what happens when she implements this new rule in her kindergarten class. In discussing the fairness of this rule with fifth graders at her school, Paley points to the comments of one student as affirmation of the importance of

◆ *The teacher has organized the learning environment so children can explore on their own or with others.*

teaching young children to treat each other fairly and with respect. After listening to the comments of her fifth-grade peers concerning the pros and cons of Paley's rule for kindergartners, a female student reached the conclusion that the rule was a good one to have since it was like wearing a seat belt—if you get used to wearing it when you are young, you do it automatically. Therefore, the fifth grader concluded, teaching kindergarten children to treat others fairly and with respect would develop a lifelong habit that would be beneficial.

Atypical Development

Ellen had been held out of kindergarten for a year by her parents. When she began kindergarten at age six, she spoke in three-word sentences and had difficulty relating with her peers, despite her advantages of age and physical development. Although this was her first year of teaching, it only took her teacher a few days of casual observation to know that a referral was in order. In another classroom, it was not discovered that Geraldine was a selective mute until November. A selective mute is a child who chooses not to talk in certain social situations or settings. Geraldine's selective mutism was overlooked because she competently—but silently—participated in classroom activities with the other children and because her teacher had not been taught that she should have a plan for observing and assessing each individual child in the classroom. Geraldine's selective mutism was discovered after the school principal suggested in a postobservation conference that the teacher was only calling on children who raised their hands. The next day the teacher planned an activity that required each child to respond. During this activity,

Geraldine refused to speak and the teacher realized she had not spoken at all in the classroom. Kindergarten teachers today routinely conduct assessments of the children in their classrooms at the beginning of the school year as well as periodically throughout the year.

Teachers who have had extensive education in child development coupled with observations of developing young children are more able to identify and make recommendations for special needs of kindergartners. Developmental alerts (Allen & Marotz 1994) or red flags are behaviors or characteristics that cause you to stop, look, and think about a possible developmental problem (McAfee & Leong 1994). Red flag guidelines include:

1. Look for patterns of behavior that seem atypical. A few in isolation may not signal atypical development.
2. Use your knowledge of normal growth and development as a guide and compare children who are six months older and six months younger with the child you have concerns about.
3. Remember that development is individual and is influenced by both biology and environment. Personality, family background, culture, and physical characteristics affect each child's development.
4. Use a checklist or other observational methods to keep track of the child's skills, development, and behavior (McAfee & Leong 1994).

◆ **ACTIVITY**

6.15

Observing Social and Emotional Development of the Kindergarten Child

Observe in a kindergarten classroom during a period that includes play or self-selected activity time and write a report addressing each of the following areas of social/emotional development:

Independence and Responsibility

What opportunities were given for children to choose activities? In what other ways were children encouraged to exhibit a sense of industry- to be independent and responsible and to view themselves as "can-do" or competent children?

Inferiority versus Competence

Were there any children you observed who might be developing a sense of inferiority rather than a sense of industry? Why do you think this is happening? What would you do in your own classroom to ensure that these children develop a sense of competence?

Play

What types of play materials did you observe children using? Did you see children display associative or cooperative play behavior?

Equal Opportunity

What strategies were used to ensure that all children were treated fairly and equally in the play setting? Was there a system in place to assure that all children had opportunities to participate in the play?

Teacher Guidance

What classroom guidance strategies did you observe? How were children encouraged to use self-control? What routines, procedures, and rules were in place? How were conflicts and problems resolved?

◆ **ACTIVITY**
6.16

Gender Roles

Note the types of activities and materials that are chosen by male and female children in the kindergarten. Do you notice particular activities or areas of the classroom that tend to draw groups of boys? Groups of girls? What steps could be taken to encourage children of the opposite sex to play in the other areas? What activities and materials seem to draw the interest of sex-integrated groups of children?

◆ **ACTIVITY**
6.17

Gender Observation

Pick one girl and one boy to observe during the free play time in the class. Chart the different activities and playmates each child interacts with during the entire play period.

The History of Kindergarten

Friedrich Froebel (1782–1852), the "father of kindergarten," originated kindergarten education in Germany in 1840. He viewed his classroom as a "garden of children," tiny seeds who needed nurturance to grow and blossom. His development of toys (known as *gifts*) and activities (called *occupations*) for children in his kindergarten is viewed as a landmark in recognizing the importance of play as a vehicle for children to learn (Watertown Historical Society 1988). His ideas were transplanted to the United States by Margarethe Meyer Schurz (1832–1876), who established a German-speaking kindergarten in Watertown, Wisconsin in 1856 (Watertown Historical Society 1990). Four years later, in 1860, Elizabeth Palmer Peabody established the first English-speaking kindergarten in Boston. Susan Blow is credited with starting the kindergarten movement in public schools when she volunteered to teach kindergarten in St. Louis, Missouri, in 1873.

A Portrait of Kindergarten Children

In 1998, the U. S. Department of Education launched a longitudinal study of 19,000 kindergarten children attending 940 public and private schools. Prior to this study, there was a lack of systematic information about what children know and can do at the time that they enter kindergarten. As a result of this study, measures of the knowledge, skills, health, and behavior of a large and nationally representative sample of kindergarten children in America are now available. There are plans to follow this sample of the Kindergarten Class of 1998–1999 through the fifth grade. Comprehensive documents related to the assessment tools and ongoing results of this study can be found at www. nces.ed.gov. Use the search word kindergarten to find documents related to this study. Key findings of the initial phase of the study are noted below.

Academic Skills

The Early Childhood Longitudinal Study-K (ECLS-K) assessments were designed for use at the beginning and end of kindergarten, into first grade and beyond. They were designed to measure early academic skills in three domains: reading, mathematics, and general knowledge (facts and understandings about nature, science, social studies, and citizenship). Assessors read questions to each child and exclusions or modifications were made in the assessments of children from families in which English was not the primary language used in the home. The typical U. S. child is five-and-a-half years old at the beginning of kindergarten and has the following knowledge, skills or understandings in the areas of reading, mathematics, and general knowledge when entering kindergarten:

- Most children know their letters (66%).
- Most children can count more than 10 objects, recognize some numerals, and identify basic shapes (94%).

Health and Behavior

- Most children are in very good to excellent health. Children were rated on a five-category scale of general health status ranging from excellent to poor. Fifty-one percent were rated in the highest category (excellent) and 83 percent were in at least very good health. No more than 3 percent were rated as being in "fair" or "poor" health. The average kindergarten boy is 3 feet, 9 inches tall and weighs 47 pounds, while the average girl is 1 inch shorter and weighs 1 pound less. More than 10 percent of children were found to have too much weight for their height (Rosner, Prineas, Loggie, and Daniels 1998).

- Some kindergarten children experience developmental difficulties. According to reports by parents, about 18 percent of kindergarten children show signs of hyperactivity, 13 percent are described as having difficulty in paying attention for lengths of time, and 11 percent have difficulty articulating words or in communicating with others. Relatively few have difficulties with vision (6%), hearing (3%), or coordination (4%).

- Most kindergarten children are reasonably well behaved. Parents and teachers, alike, report that most kindergarten children are able to get along with other children in a group setting. Only a few exhibit aggressive behavior.

- Most kindergarten children exhibit a positive attitude toward classroom tasks. The typical kindergarten child is eager to learn new things, pays attention in class, and is persistent in completing tasks according to assessments by teachers.

Differences in Kindergarten Children

Despite this optimistic picture of the typical kindergarten child, according to the findings from *America's Kindergartners* teachers do encounter a considerable range of skills from very advanced to skills that lag significantly behind (West, Denton, and Germino-Hausken 2000). Factors that help account for these variations in the knowledge, health, and behavior of children at school entry are discussed below.

Age-Related Differences in School Readiness

The ECLS-K findings support the idea that older students have advantages with respect to academics and self-regulating behaviors including the following:

- Older kindergartners are closer to being able to read;
- Older kindergartners are closer to being able to do arithmetic;
- Older kindergartners know more about nature, science, and human society;
- Older children have more advanced motor skills;
- Older children are more socially adept and less prone to problem behaviors;
- Older children are more persistent;
- Some developmental difficulties (coordination, speech) are more common among older kindergartners and may be the basis for parents choosing to delay their children's entrance to kindergarten by a year.

Sex-Related Differences

The ECLS-K showed that the variation in performance between kindergarten girls and boys was less for academic skills than for social skills. The variations are noted below:

- Girls and boys have similar skills, but girls are slightly ahead in reading;
- More boys experience developmental difficulties including speech and paying attention;
- Girls are more prosocial (comforting, helpful to others), and less prone to problem behavior;
- Girls have a more positive approach to structured learning activities as reported by teachers.

Family Background

According to the ECLS-K study, nearly half of all children entering kindergarten come from families with one or more of the following risk factors:

- Having a mother with less than a high school education;
- Living in low-income or welfare-dependent family;
- Living in a single-parent household;
- Having parents whose primary language is not English.

Children who have one or more of these risk factors are likely to live in large cities or belong to a racial-ethnic minority family. At the beginning of kindergarten, children coming from families with multiple risk factors

- Typically do not know their letters and cannot count to 20;
- Are more likely to be described as in fair or poor health ;
- Are less likely to be socially adept and more likely to be aggressive;
- Are less likely to have a positive approach to learning activities.

Types of Kindergarten Programs

For more than a century and a half, kindergarten education has experienced transplanting, growth, and blossoming. This growth and blossoming has led to great variation in kindergarten programs in the United States. Public school kindergarten programs have grown and are now offered in all fifty states. According to a 1987 survey (Robinson), only two states provide public kindergarten to fewer than half of their children. When law requires kindergarten programs to be provided, this is known as mandatory provision. However, parents still have the option of sending their children to kindergarten or waiting until they are eligible for first grade unless a state legislates compulsory kindergarten attendance. Robinson's survey also revealed that, beginning in 1988, six states were to have lowered their age of compulsory school attendance from six to five years.

Variations in Kindergarten

Kindergartens vary in many ways. Enter two kindergartens in the same school and you will probably note differences in room arrangement, curriculum, and teaching style, for starters. In this section we will briefly review a few of the major variations in kindergarten programs in the United States, including length of the kindergarten day, entry age requirements and screening for kindergarten, retention and transition classrooms, and education requirements for kindergarten teachers.

Length of Day: Half-Day, Full-Day, or Full-Day, Alternate-Day Scheduling

Research regarding the best length of day for kindergarten children is inconclusive (Peck *et al.* 1988). Some proponents of full-day programs argue that more time equals more learning opportunities. On the other hand, half-day program advocates maintain that quality is more important than quantity and that half-day kindergarten allows children a more gradual adjustment to the public school setting. While many children today enter kindergarten after several years' experience in full-day preschool or day care settings, the attitude that entrance into kindergarten is the real beginning of a child's educational journey persists (Kuschner 1989).

Supporters of full-day, alternate-day kindergarten schedules suggest that the best of both worlds is found when we allow children to experience a full-day experience on an every-other-day basis. There is even variation in the way schools schedule the full-day, alternate-day program. Some schools strictly follow an every-other-day schedule for kindergarten children, which means that a child may attend Monday, Wednesday, and Friday one week and Tuesday and Thursday the next. Other schools schedule groups of children to come on specific days each week (Monday and Wednesday only, for example).

While the most prevalent kindergarten schedules are half-days, full-days, or alternating full-days, one of the authors taught in a rural school in New Mexico that scheduled kindergarten for full days during the second half of the school year. Kindergarten started in January instead of September. This schedule was selected primarily because of the great distances involved in bussing some of the children from ranches in the school district. There were other advantages to the school district as well as to the children, parents, and teacher. Can you think of what some of those advantages might have been?

Activities at the end of this chapter will help you gain more insight into issues related to the length of the kindergarten day.

Entry Age

Margaret was four. Because her fifth birthday would be on December first, she was eligible to be in kindergarten that year. Robert, a student in the same kindergarten classroom, had turned five the previous November. However, his parents had elected to have him wait a year to enroll in kindergarten. When they started school, Robert was more than one calendar year older than Margaret.

The issue of kindergarten entry age is a national concern. As more mothers and fathers with young children have entered the workforce, many are eager to enroll their children in public schools as soon as possible. Others who are concerned that their child be successful in school or seek the advantage of advanced physical development for athletics may elect to hold their child out for a year.

In an effort to be consistent and fair, most U.S. schools select a date that determines when a child may begin kindergarten. Each state sets its own date for the entry age requirement. Common dates include turning age five by April 1 of the year prior to entering kindergarten; August 31, September 1, December 1 or the first day of the school year. Some professionals suggest that the lack of uniformity in kindergarten entry age in the United States causes problems for children who may move several times during their public school years. No matter what cutoff date is selected, there will always be the potential for 364 days' difference in chronological age (or more, as in the case of Robert and Margaret).

A synthesis of research indicates that younger kindergarten children are more apt to fail kindergarten as well as to have more difficulty throughout their school years (Peck *et al.* 1988). Some professionals advocate the use of readiness tests or other screening tools to determine when a child should begin kindergarten. Many schools have used such a procedure to allow children early entrance to kindergarten or to identify children who may be at risk and in need of special classroom placement. Criticisms of using such means to assess young children include the inaccuracy of test results; the fact that the rapid rate of development during this period of childhood makes spring decisions invalid and long-term interpretation difficult; the danger of early labeling of children who simply may need more time to develop; and the inappropriateness of using standardized tests to assess young children.

In New Zealand, where most schools are organized as ungraded continuous progress primary units, children begin school on the day of their fifth birthday or the school day closest after that date. Because children remain in the same classroom for several years, there are no traditional grade divisions and children progress through the primary curriculum at their own pace. They advance to the next level of schooling when they have completed certain competencies or levels of educational achievement. There seems to be a growing interest in the United States in reorganizing schools for children in grades kindergarten through two or three in this manner (American Association of School Administrators 1992; Katz *et al.* 1990). If such reorganization becomes widespread here, the issues of kindergarten entry age and kindergarten failure may be rethought on a national level. Many early childhood professionals advocate that schools must be ready for children rather than children being "ready" for school. Activities at the end of this chapter will help you to further consider issues related to entry age and school readiness.

Kindergarten Retention

The practice of kindergarten retention is considered by many experts both an ineffective means of producing long-term increases in academic ability and inappropriate and damaging to a child's self-esteem and attitude toward schooling. Such attitudes have been well documented by research in the last decade (Bredekamp & Shepard 1989; NAECSSDE 1987; Shepard 1989; Shepard & Smith 1989). In addition, there is growing consensus that special placement in early kindergarten intervention programs and transition classrooms is ineffective and inappropriate for many of the same reasons (Bredekamp 1990; Brewer 1990; Shepard 1989; Shepard & Smith 1989; Uphoff 1990).

Kindergarten intervention programs often target at-risk children through the kindergarten screening process and place these children in classrooms that are considered more developmentally appropriate with the assumption that the child will go on to the more academic kindergarten the following year. In a sense, these children are being labeled and retained before they ever start "regular" kindergarten. Transition or developmental grades between kindergarten and "regular" first grade have a similar effect. As teachers have become more knowledgeable about developmentally appropriate practice and adapting curricular practices to meet the needs of students, many school districts have phased out these "retention track" classrooms. For some school districts this has resulted in a move toward nongraded primary or multiage classrooms, where children can make continuous progress toward long-term goals.

Teacher Education Requirements

Just as entry age for kindergarten children varies from state to state, so do requirements for licensure of kindergarten teachers. In Minnesota, for example, kindergarten teachers must first be licensed for grades one through six and then take one to three additional courses and complete student teaching both at the kindergarten level and in an elementary classroom. In other states, however, a teacher must complete a minor in early childhood education to be qualified to teach at the kindergarten level. Some states, such as Pennsylvania and New York, have no additional requirements beyond an elementary teaching license for kindergarten. In 1992 Robinson surveyed all fifty states to determine the current status of licensure requirements for teachers of young children. Table 6.2 indicates which states have special educational requirements for teachers at the kindergarten and preschool levels (Robinson & Lyon 1994). In addition, the table provides information regarding the percentage of children in public kindergartens and private kindergartens and the percentage of classrooms with aides. It indicates a trend in licensing of early childhood teachers through grades three or four in some states.

◆ TABLE 6.2   *Early Childhood Education in the 50 States (1992)*

State	Percentage of Children in Public Kindergarten	Percentage of Children in Private Kindergarten	Specialized Training for Teachers of 5-Year-Olds*	Specialized Training for Teachers of 4-Year-Olds*	Percentage of Classrooms with Aides
Alabama	92	5	Yes (N–3rd)	Yes (N–3rd)	—
Alaska	75	20	No	No	Few
Arizona	—	—	No	No	Some
Arkansas	—	—	Yes[2]	No	Some
California	98	1	Yes[3]	Yes[4]	—
Colorado	—	—	Yes (3–8 yrs.)	Yes (3–8 yrs.)	—
Connecticut	—	—	EC for K	—	Some
Delaware	95	5	—	—	Few
Florida	60	30	Yes (Prim)	Yes (EC)	85–90
Georgia	—	—	Yes (K–5)	No	—
Hawaii	82	16	No	No	—
Idaho	95	5	Yes (3–8 yrs.)	Yes (3–8 yrs.)	3
Illinois	—	—	Yes (B–8 yrs.)	Yes (B–8 yrs.)	—
Indiana	81	10	Yes (Elem.)	No	Some
Iowa	98	—	Yes Pre-K–K	Yes (Pre-K–K)	Some
Kansas	—	—	Yes (Elem. K–9th)	Yes (EC)	—
Kentucky	—	—	Yes (K)	No	Some
Louisiana	—	—	Yes (K)	Yes (N)	—
Maine	95	—	No	No	20
Maryland	—	—	—	—	—
Massachusetts	85	10	Yes (N–3rd)	Yes (N–3rd)	35
Michigan	—	—	No	No	Some
Minnesota	88	12	Yes	Yes[5]	Some
Mississippi	—	—	Yes (K–3rd or K–8th)	No	100[6]
Missouri	—	—	Yes (B–3rd)	Yes (B–3rd)	Some
Montana	—	—	Yes (K–8th)	No	—
Nebraska	—	—	Yes (B–3rd)	Yes (B–3rd)	Some
Nevada	52	8	Yes (Elem.)	Yes (EC)	Most
New Hampshire	45	35	No	No	Some
New Jersey	85	—	No	No	Some
New Mexico	84	15	No	No	Most
New York	—	—	No	No	Varies
North Carolina	90	10	—	Yes (Pre-K)	100
North Dakota	88	10	Yes (K endorsement)	No	Some
Ohio	—	—	Yes (K–3rd, K–8th)	Yes (Pre-K)	Some
Oklahoma	—	—	Yes (EC)	Yes (Pre-K–3rd)	Few
Oregon	—	—	No	No	—
Pennsylvania	79	21	No	No	0
Rhode Island	49.7	50	Yes (Pre-K–2nd)	Yes (Pre-K–2nd)	Some
South Carolina[1]	87	14	Yes (K–4th)	Yes (K–4th)	100
South Dakota	75	15	Yes	Yes	Some
Tennessee	97	3	Yes	No	Some
Texas	75	20	Yes (Pre-K)	Yes	Some
Utah	90	5	Yes (EC)	Yes (EC)	Few
Vermont	90	10	Yes (EC or Elem.)	Yes (EC)	Some
Virginia	—	—	Yes (N–K)	Yes (N–K)	Some[7]
Washington	90	10	Yes (P–3rd or Elem.)	No	—
West Virginia	—	—	Yes (K–8th)	No	—
Wisconsin	83	16	Yes (Pre-K–3rd)	Yes (Pre-K–3rd)	Some
Wyoming	95	5	No	No	—

1. Total public and private adds to more than 100% because public K meets for only half-day.
2. Elementary 1–6 plus 15 hrs.
3. Teaching credential.
4. Children's center permit.
5. Any major plus 27 credits in EC for 4-year-olds; elementary certification plus one course, one practicum, and six weeks of student teaching for 5-year-olds.
6. Required by legislation.
7. Will provide if more than 25 students in class.

*B = birth; N = nursery; P = preschool; Pre-K = kindergarten; K = kindergarten; EC = early childhood certification; Prim. = primary certification (varies among states, usually encompasses K–3rd); Elem. = elementary certification (varies among states, usually encompasses grades 1–6).

Source: Early childhood offerings in 1992: Will we be ready for 2000? by Robinson & Lyon, *Kappan, 75*(10), 777. Reprinted with permission.

◆ **ACTIVITY**
6.18

Length of Kindergarten Day

With at least one other classmate, take the perspective of *one* of the following groups:

1. Kindergarten children
2. Parents of kindergarten children
3. Schools

Using the perspective of the group you selected, create a chart that lists the advantages and disadvantages for each of the three prevalent kindergarten schedules:

1. Half day
2. Full day
3. Full day, alternating days

When you have completed your chart compare it with other classmates who took the perspective of a group different from yours.

◆ **ACTIVITY**
6.19

Others' Views on Kindergarten Schedules

Select one of the groups listed below to survey regarding which kindergarten schedule they feel is preferable. Make sure you ask them to justify their choices. Survey at least five people from the category you select and share and compare your results with your classmates and instructor.

1. Parents of children who have already attended kindergarten
2. Parents of children currently enrolled in kindergarten
3. Parents with preschool age children
4. Single-parent families
5. Dual-career families
6. Kindergarten teachers
7. Primary grade teachers
8. Preschool teachers
9. School administrators
10. Grandparents

◆ **ACTIVITY**
6.20

Observation of Length of Class Day

Observe in a half-day kindergarten and in a full-day or full-day, alternating-day kindergarten. Try to observe for the entire time children are there. Write a report and include the following:

1. The schedule for both programs.
2. Similarities and differences in the programs.
    a. How is the curriculum organized? What subjects are included? Is there a theme or instructional integration?
    b. Do children have more time for play or self-directed learning when they are in school all day?
    c. What routines does the full-day program include that the half-day program does not?
    d. What differences do you observe in the attention, energy level, and so on, of children in the two different programs?
3. Talk with the teacher and ask the following:
    a. Does he or she prefer the half-day or full-day kindergarten length? Why? What advantages and disadvantages are there?
    b. If given a choice to change to the opposite schedule, would the teacher like to do so? Why?
    c. What is the reason that the school or district selected the present schedule? How long have they been using it? Are there any considerations being made to change the current schedule?

◆ **ACTIVITY 6.21**

Entry Age for Kindergarten

In small groups, discuss the following questions related to entry age for kindergarten and come to a consensus.

1. What is a reasonable date to set for the age requirement for kindergarten? Give your group's rationale for the date that is selected.
2. What other criteria could be used to establish kindergarten entry? Be creative. (Example: A child is old enough for kindergarten when he or she has sufficient balance to ride a two-wheeled bike without training wheels. What problems or issues may result from using this criterion?)
3. Six states now have compulsory school attendance for kindergarten while others simply mandate that kindergarten must be provided for those wanting to send their children. Should kindergarten be compulsory in more states? Why or why not?
4. There has recently been discussion about providing public school programs for four-year-olds. Should states lower the age for school entrance? Why or why not? What issues might result from passage of such legislation on a national level?

◆ **ACTIVITY 6.22**

Interviewing Teachers

Interview kindergarten teachers in two different school districts, if possible, regarding their retention practices. Some questions to ask might include: How often have they retained children in kindergarten during their careers?

Has there been a change in their philosophy or practice of retaining children in kindergarten since starting teaching? What criteria do they use in making the decision to retain a child in kindergarten? How much input do the parents have in making the decision? Who else is involved in making the decision? What is done to ensure that children do not suffer a loss of self-esteem or stigmatization by other children because of having "flunked" kindergarten? Share the information that you obtain during class. Be sure to inform teachers that their comments will remain anonymous.

◆ **ACTIVITY**

6.23

Observation in a Kindergarten Intervention Classroom

Arrange to observe in a kindergarten intervention classroom, developmental first, or transition classroom. How does this classroom seem different from a "regular" classroom? In what ways is it the same? How many children are in the classroom? How many boys? How many girls? What special educational programs or assistance are provided to assure that these children are successful? How would you feel about being a teacher in a transition classroom? Write a brief (one to two pages) report about your observation.

◆ **ACTIVITY**

6.24

Education of Kindergarten Teachers

Find out the licensing requirements for kindergarten teachers in your state and surrounding states, or states you are interested in teaching in. Request information that will help you to answer the following questions and others that you may have.

1. How many and what kinds of courses are required for kindergarten teachers that are different from teachers in grades one through six?
2. Is it necessary to student-teach at the kindergarten level to be licensed to teach kindergarten in the state?
3. Interview kindergarten teachers to see how they feel about the way they were prepared to teach kindergarten. Some of the questions that you might ask are:
   a. How well prepared did you feel to teach kindergarten through your teacher preparation program?
   b. How have you acquired additional knowledge and skills for teaching at the kindergarten level?
   c. Do you think you could have been better prepared for teaching kindergarten by your teacher preparation program? If so, how?
   d. What suggestions do you have for me, as a prospective kindergarten teacher, so I will feel well prepared and confident in teaching kindergarten?

Summary

Kindergarten practices blend the old with the new. Many materials and activities in today's kindergartens, such as blocks, paper weaving, and the singing of nursery rhymes, have their roots in the Froebelian kindergartens of the past. New information about how young children learn and appropriate curriculum methods have helped us to look at kindergarten policies and practices that are more sensitive to the kindergarten child and his or her developmental needs. All states provide public school kindergartens, though only a few have compulsory attendance.

REFERENCES

Allen, K. E., and L. Marotz (1994). *Developmental profiles: Pre-birth through eight.* Albany, NY: Delmar.

American Association of School Administrators. (1992). *The nongraded primary: Making schools fit children.* Arlington, VA: AASA.

Berger, K. S. (1994). *The developing person through the lifespan.* New York: Worth.

Berns, R. M. (1994). *Topical child development.* Albany, NY: Delmar.

Bredekamp, S. (1990). Extra year programs: A response to Brewer and Uphoff. *Young Children, 45*(6), 20–21.

Bredekamp, S., and L. Shepard (1989). How best to protect children from inappropriate school expectations, practices and policies. *Young Children, 44*(3), 14–23.

Brewer, J. A. (1990). Transitional programs: Boom or bane? *Young Children, 45*(6), 15–18.

Erickson, E. (1980). *Identity and the life cycle.* New York: Norton.

Goffin, S. G., and D. A. Stegelin, Eds. (1992). *Changing kindergartens: Four success stories.* Washington, DC: National Association for the Education of Young Children.

Katz, L. G., D. Evangelou and J. A. Hartman (1990). *The case for mixed-age grouping in early education,* Washington, DC: NAEYC.

Kuschner, D. (1989). Put your name on your painting, but . . . the blocks go back on the shelves. *Young Children, 45*(1), 49–56.

Mardell-Czudnowski, C., and D. S. Goldenberg (1998). *DIAL-III: Developmental indicators for the assessment of learning III.* Circle Pines, MN: American Guidance Service.

McAfee, O., and D. Leong (1994). *Assessing and guiding young children's development and learning.* Boston, MA: Allyn & Bacon.

Morrow, L. M. (1993). *Literacy development in the early years.* Boston, MA: Allyn & Bacon.

National Association of Early Childhood Specialists in State Departments of Education. (1988). *Unacceptable trends in kindergarten entrance and placement.* Lincoln, NE: NAECSSDE.

New Standards, Primary Literacy Committee (1999). Reading and Writing Grade by Grade. Washington, DC: National Center on Education and the Economy.

Paley, V. G. (1984). *Boys and girls: Superheroes in the doll corner.* Chicago: University of Chicago Press.

Paley, V. G. (1993). *You can't say you can't play.* Cambridge, MA: Harvard University Press.

Parten, M. B. (1932). Social participation among preschool children. *Journal of Abnormal Psychology, 27,* 243–269.

Peck, J. T., G. McCaig, and M. E. Sapp (1988). *Kindergarten policies: What is best for children?* Washington, DC: NAEYC.

Robinson, S. L. (1987). The state of kindergarten offerings in the United States. *Childhood Education, 64*(4), 23–28.

Robinson, S. L., and C. Lyon (1994). Early childhood offerings in 1992: Will we be ready for 2000? *Kappan, 75*(10), 775–778.

Rosner, B., R. Prineas, J. Loggie, and S. Daniels (1998). Percentiles for body mass index in U. S. children 5 to 17 years of age. *The Journal of Pediatrics, 103,* 211–222.

Selman, R. L., and A. P. Selman (1979). Children's ideas about friendship: A new theory. *Psychology Today*, 13, 71–80.

Shepard, L. A. (1989). A review of research on Kindergarten retention. In L. A. Shepard and M. L. Smith, Eds., *Flunking grades: Research and policies on retention* (pp. 64–78). Philadelphia, PA: Falmer Press.

Shepard, L. A., and M. L. Smith, Eds. (1989). *Flunking grades: Research policies on retention.* Philadelphia, PA: Falmer Press.

Shepard, L. A., and M. L. Smith (1989). Academic and emotional effects of Kindergarten retention in one school district. In L. A. Shepard and M. L. Smith, Eds., *Flunking grades: Research and policies on retention* (pp. 79–107). Philadelphia, PA: Falmer Press.

Siegel, D. F., and R. A. Hanson (1991). Kindergarten educational policies: Separating myth from reality. *Early Education and Development 2*(1), 5–31.

U.S. Department of Education, National Center for Education Statistics (2001). *Entering Kindergarten: A Portrait of American Children When They Begin School: Findings from the Condition of Education 2000.* Nicholas Zill and Jerry West NCES 2001-035, Washington, DC: U. S. Government Printing Office.

Uphoff, J. K. (1990). Extra-year programs: An argument for transitional programs during transitional times. *Young Children. 45*(6), 19–20.

Wasserman, S. (1990). *Serious players in the primary classroom.* New York: Teachers College Press.

Watertown Historical Society (1988). *Froebel's gifts.* Watertown, WI: Author.

Watertown Historical Society (1990). *Handi and Pussy go to kindergarten.* Watertown, WI: Author.

West, J., K. Denton, and E. Germino-Hausken (2000). *America's kindergartners: Findings from the Early Childhood Longitudinal Study, Kindergarten Class of 1998–99,* Fall 1998. Washington, DC: U. S. Department of Education, NCES (NCES-2000-070).

◆ Chapter 7

Work and Play in the Primary Grades

In this chapter you will read information and choose from a menu of activities to help you learn more about:

◆ Developmental characteristics and needs of primary-grade children

◆ Using multiple intelligence theory in primary-grade curriculum

◆ Engaging primary-grade children in self-directed learning

◆ Technology resources to enhance the cognitive and social development of primary-grade children.

What Are the Primary Grades?

The American Heritage Dictionary includes the following among their thirteen definitions of the adjective *primary:* occurring first in time or sequence; being first in degree, quality, or importance; and being a fundamental or basic part of an organized whole. All of these definitions apply to our understanding of primary grades.

Historically, grades one, two, and three have been viewed as the years of primary education in public school settings. During the early years of public schooling in the United States emphasis was placed on the "three *Rs*" (reading, writing, and arithmetic) during the primary years. These subjects were considered fundamental to life and later learning. After kindergartens were first introduced to U.S. public schools in 1873, the concept of primary education grew to include grades kindergarten through three, and teaching methods became more sensitive to the developmental levels of the young child. The organization of primary education today includes primary units in K through six settings, primary schools comprised of grades K through two or three, and nongraded, or multiage, schools or classrooms, where children are organized into early primary or later primary classrooms (American Association of

School Administrators 1992). Children in the primary grades need a school environment that provides for both work and play because they are at a developmental transition point.

Developmental Characteristics of the Six- to Eight-Year-Old

Physical Development

By the end of the early childhood period a child's rate of growth slows and steadies. Between ages six and eight, children gain about five pounds and two inches per year. By age eight the respective weights of boys and girls are fairly equal, at approximately fifty-five to sixty-one pounds (Black *et al.* 1992). At approximately forty-eight to fifty-one inches tall, eight-year-old boys remain slightly taller than girls of the same age, who average forty-six to forty-nine inches in height (Allen & Marotz 1994; Seifert & Hoffnung 1991). Increased endurance and coordination enable the six- to eight-year-old to enjoy many gross motor activities and games.

The tools needed for completing school tasks, such as cutting, pasting, writing, and drawing, require both large and fine motor development and coordination. Children who experience difficulty with these tasks should be provided both structured and unstructured opportunities to perform these activities as well as to use manipulative toys such as blocks and molding materials such as clay, sand, and mud (Charlesworth 1992). Research indicates that children who are at the beginning stages of writing and drawing find tools such as felt-tipped markers, chalk, and crayons easier to use and more appealing than pencils (Lamme 1979). In general, children tend to lessen the tenseness of their grip on writing tools as they approach age eight, which allows them to write more easily and at greater length. It should be noted, however, that because fine motor coordination is related to myelinization of the

◆ *Primary grade children need to have scheduled gym or outdoor times each day for physical health.*

central nervous system, there is great variation in fine motor coordination among children of this age. Therefore, the primary grade teacher should be patient with children who still have difficulty with neatness or completion of work involving fine motor coordination.

Because their eyes are continuing to change shape and size and because children, once in school, are using their eyes more to focus on writing and graphics, visual acuity may become a problem for primary grade children (Allyn & Marotz 1994). Routine eye checks at school can usually detect difficulties children are experiencing but may not have been aware of or mentioned. However, teachers should also watch for behaviors that indicate the child is having difficulty with vision, including eye-rubbing, complaining of burning or itching eyes, or blurred vision, sitting close to the board or other visual displays, and holding books closer or farther away than other children.

Overall health and physical/motor development contribute greatly to a child's potential for academic success during the early years of formal schooling. Because of this, schools and teachers need to provide opportunities and educational experiences that will allow children to experience optimal physical development. Ensuring that children have adequate nourishment during the school day, regular vision and health screenings, and daily opportunities for physical exercise are just some of the ways that teachers and schools provide for a child's physical needs. In addition, at this age it becomes increasingly more important for children to assume responsibility for their own physical well-being. Teachers can provide for this by:

1. Teaching units about proper nutrition, safety, dental care, and health practices;
2. Teaching children the importance of physical exercise through games and simple sports such as kickball and soccer;
3. Ensuring that there are opportunities for rest and relaxation during the school day; and
4. Providing children with self-protection information on bullying, staying at home alone, the effects of drugs and alcohol, and how to obtain help if lost, abused, or neglected.

Observing the Physical Development of Children in the Primary Grades

Complete some of the following tasks to validate information about the physical development of children in the primary grades.

◆ **ACTIVITY**

7.1

Measuring Growth

Plan an activity for children to work in pairs weighing and measuring each other. Provide them with a scale, tape measure, and sheet of paper to record the information. Make your own chart to record the same information, listing the weight and height of each boy on one half and of each girl on the other. Total and average the weight and height for each gender to determine if the information about similarity in weight but difference in height holds true. If possible, obtain the lifetime weight and height records for a few children to determine whether their rates of growth are congruent with the average for children during this period.

◆ **ACTIVITY**
7.2

Fine Motor Activities

Observe the classroom environment and keep track of what types of writing tools are available. In addition, note the types of writing tools children are instructed or permitted to use for written work. Are there materials and opportunities for children to engage in unstructured fine motor activities including use of clay, blocks, scissors, paint brushes, and so forth?

◆ **ACTIVITY**
7.3

Writing Tools

Conduct an experiment with some or all of the children in a first-grade classroom and a third-grade classroom. Ask them to write their names with four different writing tools including pencil, chalk, crayon, and marker (you may want to provide both fine-tipped and thick-tipped markers). Then ask the children to rank their preference for the writing tools. Analyze the results. Is there a difference according to age or gender?

◆ **ACTIVITY**
7.4

Gross Motor Activities

Survey the classroom schedule for the opportunities provided for gross motor activities on both a daily and a weekly basis. Are there daily outdoor play opportunities? What alternatives are provided in case of inclement weather? Observe the types of activities children engage in during outdoor play periods. Are there differences in activity levels of children that you observe? What kinds of things can you do to encourage children who are inactive to become more active?

◆ **ACTIVITY**
7.5

Physical Education

Observe a physical education class scheduled for a primary-grade class. What kinds of games and activities are provided? Note children who have difficulty with the activities and how that influences their level of participation in class.

◆ **ACTIVITY**

7.6

Art Activity

Observe a primary-grade art activity led by the classroom teacher or art teacher. Note the kinds of fine motor activities the children are asked to do. Watch for children who have difficulty with the activities. Look at the written class work of these children to determine if their difficulty with fine-motor skills in art correlates with written work completion.

◆ **ACTIVITY**

7.7

Vision Center

Set up a vision center as a self-directed learning area in the classroom. Provide eye charts, pointer, appointment book, smock, eyeglass frames with the lenses removed, mirror, tape line to assure uniform distance from the eye chart, and paper squares to cover the right and left eyes during examinations. (Be sure to instruct students in the importance of throwing away the paper square and using a clean one so that eye viruses such as conjunctivitis are not spread.) This could be a part of an instructional unit on health.

◆ **ACTIVITY**

7.8

Vision Problems

Systematically observe each child to detect any potential visual acuity difficulties. Observe how visual material is held and note any rubbing of eyes, or other symptoms discussed earlier. If you detect any possible problems, discuss your concerns with the classroom teacher.

◆ **ACTIVITY**

7.9

Health and Safety Curriculum

Examine the school curriculum for primary grades or interview the teachers to determine what skills are taught to children regarding taking responsibility for their own health, well-being, and personal safety.

Cognitive Development

Close your eyes and think about the room arrangement and learning experiences in your own first-, second-, and third-grade classrooms. How do those images compare with what you remember about your kindergarten and preschool classrooms? Were the desks arranged in rows in your first-grade classroom? Do you remember learning experiences consisting primarily of workbooks, worksheets, and other types of materials? Now consider what you have learned about the stages of cognitive development. Piaget believed that as children move from the stage of preoperational thinking to that of concrete operations, they still are in need of involvement with concrete materials and real-world experiences to move toward understanding information represented abstractly (Peterson & Felton-Collins 1986). As children in the concrete operations period interact with concrete materials, they develop many skills of conservation including the abilities to conserve number, length, mass, liquid, weight, and volume.

In addition, primary-grade children are becoming less egocentric and increasingly able to view situations from a variety of perspectives. This allows them to begin to classify objects on more than one attribute or characteristic. For example, a four-year-old child may be able to group shapes by one characteristic at a time (color *or* size *or* shape *or* composition). A seven- or eight-year-old will be more likely to group the shapes on multiple characteristics (color *and* size *and* shape *and* composition).

More contemporary research and theories about cognitive development and intelligence have also contributed to our understanding of how to provide appropriate learning experiences for children in the primary grades. Robert Sternberg (1986) suggests a triarchic model of intelligence that consists of *componential intelligence,* defined as the units of knowledge or information that we acquire; *experiential intelligence,* which focuses on experience and influences our ability to be creative and insightful; and *contextual intelligence,* which enables us to deal with the practical aspects of life, including how to get along with people, change a spark plug, or solve other problems that we find ourselves dealing with. Therefore, as primary-grade children are growing older, have more experiences behind them, and are widening their circles of human interaction, they are naturally increasing in componential, experiential, and contextual intelligence. To be meaningful and advance cognitive development, the curriculum in the primary grades should provide children with opportunities to develop their componential intelligence (information), experiential intelligence (additional experience with their environment), and contextual intelligence (learning applied to real-life experiences).

In 1983, Dr. Howard Gardner and a team of Harvard researchers postulated that there are many forms of intelligence. In Gardner's book, *Frames of Mind: The Theory of Multiple Intelligences*, he identified seven "ways of knowing" based on his observations of people around the world and from many different cultures. In order to qualify as an intelligence, an ability must pass the test of eight criteria. More recently, Gardner identified an eighth intelligence and speculates that there may be many more yet to be found and tested. The eight intelligences, which Gardner has identified, are briefly described below and illustrated in Figure 7.1.

1. *Logical/Mathematical intelligence* involves the ability to solve problems using abstract symbols including numbers and geometric shapes and to apply scientific thinking and deductive reasoning such as seeing the connections between various pieces of information. Albert Einstein and Marie Curie are examples of people with outstanding logical/mathematical intelligence.

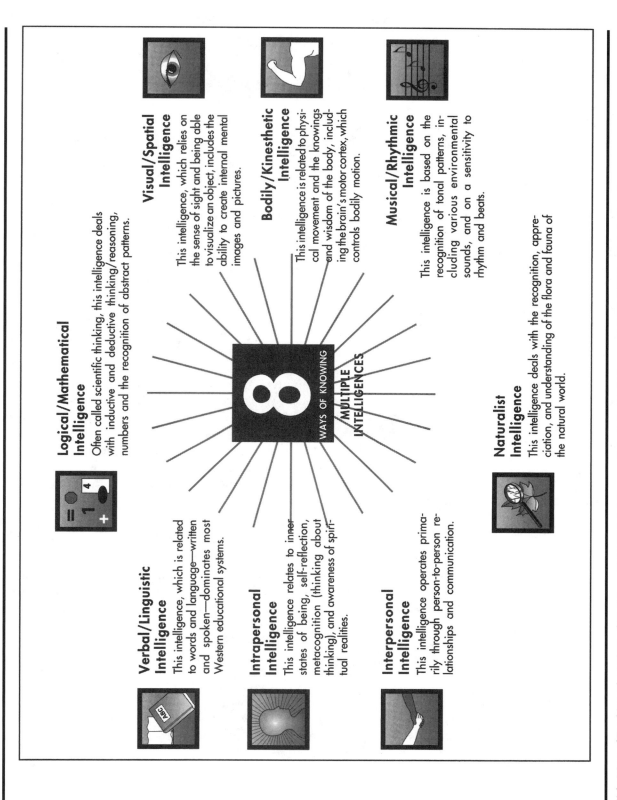

From *Eight Ways of Teaching: The Artistry of Teaching with Multiple Intelligences*, 3rd ed., by David Lazear. © 1991, 1999 by Skylight Training and Publishing, Inc. Reprinted by permission of Skylight Professional Development, www.skylightedu.com or (800) 348-4474.

2. *Verbal/Linguistic intelligence* is related to the effective use of words in writing and/or speech. The prolific writing of James Michener and the moving speeches of Rev. Martin Luther King, Jr. are products of exceptional verbal/linguistic intelligence.

3. *Visual/Spatial intelligence* involves strength in the visual arts including drawing, painting, architecture, mapping skills, and games such as chess, all of which require the ability to see things from different angles and perspectives. The architect Frank Lloyd Wright and painter Grandma Moses are examples of people who used visual/spatial intelligence in their works.

4. *Body/Kinesthetic intelligence* is the ability to use the body expressively through dance and body language as well as in sports. It also relates to the ability to invent new things. The inventor Thomas Edison and dancer Mikhail Baryshnikov are individuals with strong body/kinesthetic intelligence.

5. *Musical/Rhythmic intelligence* includes capacities to recognize and use rhythm and tone. Composer Wolfgang Amadeus Mozart and singer Barbra Streisand are examples of people with strength in this form of intelligence.

6. *Interpersonal intelligence* involves the capacity to work well with others and to communicate effectively. The most advanced form of this type of intelligence builds on the ability to understand other people's moods, feelings, and motivations. Counselors, teachers, religious leaders, and politicians are among those who usually have high levels of interpersonal intelligence. Mother Teresa and Rev. Billy Graham are examples of individuals whose successes were influenced by strength in this form of intelligence.

7. *Intrapersonal intelligence* is intelligence in the form of self-awareness and requires the application of skills from the other six intelligences to fulfill itself. It involves the ability to be aware of our own inner feelings, thinking processes, and spirituality. People with strong interpersonal intelligence know themselves well and are able to analyze themselves as an outside observer would. The introspective poet Emily Dickinson and Mohandas Gandhi, known in his later life as *Mahatma* ("great soul") because of his philosophy of nonviolent confrontation, are examples of individuals who applied strong intrapersonal intelligence.

8. *Naturalist intelligence* involves having abilities to identify and appropriately use elements of the natural world including flora and fauna and having a natural curiosity about the natural world, its creatures, weather patterns, and natural history. Naturalist intelligence can be observed in farmers, hunters, gardeners, cooks, veterinarians, zookeepers, nature guides, and forest rangers.

Figure 7.2 provides a Multiple Intelligences Capacities Wheel which illustrates specific capacities, or subintelligences, related to Gardner's eight ways of knowing (Lazear 1999). Gardner (1993) suggests that most normal individuals possess the capacity to develop all eight areas of intelligence, but

◆ **FIGURE 7.2** *Multiple Intelligences Capacity Wheel*

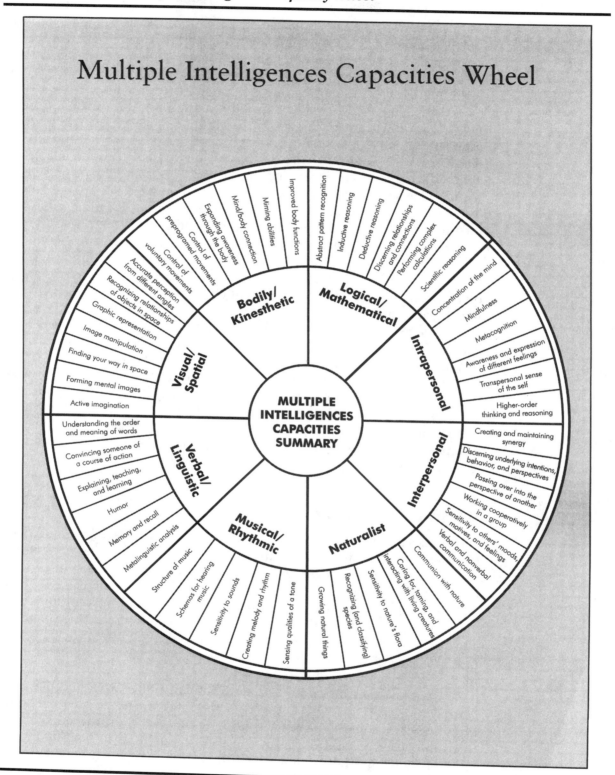

From *Eight Ways of Teaching: The Artistry of Teaching with Multiple Intelligences*, 3rd ed., by David Lazear. © 1991, 1999 by Skylight Training and Publishing, Inc. Reprinted by permission of Skylight Professional Development, www.skylight-edu.com or (800) 348-4474.

are influenced by contextualization and distribution. In other words, development of these intelligences is influenced by the social and cultural environments and by the human and material resources available to each individual. Therefore, it is important that young children have opportunities to develop all eight categories of intelligence. Lazear (1999) provides many suggestions for awakening, amplifying, teaching, and transferring each of the eight intelligences when using this as a framework for teaching.

Campbell (1992) provided a learning centers model for thematic teaching with learning centers focused on the multiple intelligences. This model is especially effective for second- and third-grade teachers whose students are ready for more cognitive challenges in learning centers. It would enable the children to experience success and satisfaction in working in one or more of the intelligences at which they excel. Figure 7.3 on page 177 provides a grid teachers can use to assure that their lesson plans and/or learning centers are incorporating all eight of the multiple intelligences on a weekly basis.

Erickson (1980) describes the years between ages seven and eleven as a time of industry versus inferiority. During this period the child is busy learning and acquiring new skills through school and other activities. He or she quickly comes to view him- or herself as either competent and productive or inferior and unable to do anything well. Because cognitive competence is closely related to a child's feelings of worth and psychosocial development, it is critical that children in the primary grades experience more success than failure in school-related tasks. Wasserman states that "when certain conditions exist in primary classrooms, children are empowered. They grow in their feelings of self-respect, self-worth and intellectual competence—that is they are imbued with a can-do spirit" (1990, xi). How can primary grade teachers foster industry, empowerment, and a "can-do spirit" in children? It is important to consider what primary grade teaching strategies will promote these attitudes of competence at this critical time of learning.

Work and Play in the Primary Classroom

For decades teachers and administrators have drawn an imaginary line so that when children left kindergarten and entered the primary grades play should stop and work should begin. As a first-year kindergarten teacher more than twenty-five years ago, Jan Sherman taught in a school where the only children allowed to use the playground during the school day—except for scheduled physical education classes—were kindergarten children. There were no outdoor recesses scheduled for children at this school. The principal's attitude was that play was acceptable only for kindergarten children as they made the transition to public schools.

It is important for us to consider what constitutes work and play. According to Wasserman (1990), Dewey (1971), and others, play involves having some choice and control over what we do. Work, on the other hand, tends to consist of tasks that others expect or require us to do. The importance of allowing children choice over what they do or when they do something does not end with kindergarten. In fact, throughout life we feel empowered when we have a choice. When asked what they are going to do on a

◆ **FIGURE 7.3** *Planning with Multiple Intelligences*

Eight Ways of Teaching Weekly Checklist

Have I taught for the eight ways of knowing this week? Check yourself by listing the specific strategies, techniques, and tools you have used in classroom lessons this week.

	MONDAY	TUESDAY	WEDNESDAY	THURSDAY	FRIDAY
Verbal/Linguistic					
Logical/Mathematical					
Visual/Spatial					
Bodily/Kinesthetic					
Musical/Rhythmic					
Interpersonal					
Intrapersonal					
Naturalist					

Note: This blackline is provided as a useful tool for teachers to think through their weekly multiple intelligences strategies.

From *Eight Ways of Teaching: The Artistry of Teaching with Multiple Intelligences*, 3rd ed., by David Lazear. © 1991, 1999 by Skylight Training and Publishing, Inc. Reprinted by permission of Skylight Professional Development, www.skylight-edu.com or (800) 348-4474.

day off from work, adults will often respond "play," indicating that there are no specific tasks or schedules that control them for that day. Wasserman asserts that play empowers children because it enables them to experience flexibility, risk-taking, conceptual awareness, and inventiveness.

William Glaser identifies five basic human needs in *Control Theory in the Classroom* (1985). These needs, which guide human behavior, include (1) survival, (2) love and belonging, (3) power, (4) freedom, and (5) fun. Wasserman warns that if children are rarely provided empowerment through choice and others constantly exercise power over them, they will experience difficulty in growing into adults who feel capable and competent in making their own decisions. She writes:

> *When the power to choose is taken away by others who exercise the options on their behalf, children become frustrated, even enraged. Through such adult actions, children learn that they are not to be trusted to decide for themselves. They learn not that they can do, but that they can't do. They learn to doubt themselves. When their drives for power-to continue to be thwarted, children are likely to show increased frustration and anger that reveals itself in acts of aggression. It is no wonder that adults with frustrated power-to needs desire power-over.* (1990, 7–8)

Elkind (1990) and Katz and Chard (1989) also warn of the effects of a curriculum with too much teacher control and direction. The dispositions to take risks, to be internally motivated, and to feel competent and capable may be lost in programs that fail to provide children with opportunities to choose, make decisions, experiment, imagine, and create new things through play—a

◆ *More and more primary classrooms are equipped with materials that allow children to find a balance between work and play.*

primary source of our creativity as human beings. Many important inventions and discoveries have resulted through the curiosity, experimentation, testing and exploration "play" provides. Think of Benjamin Franklin's discovery of electricity while flying a kite. There is not a point on the human life line that separates the major periods of work and play—play is important throughout life. Nor is there an inflexible line that divides learning from work and play—we learn from both kinds of activities. Indeed, some of our most rewarding and productive work may come through "play " that we choose to engage in.

Teachers who recognize the relationship of learning to both work and play and the importance of balancing work and play throughout life are finding ways to empower children through choice and self-directed learning opportunities. More primary-grade classrooms are equipped with the materials, space, and schedules that allow a balance of work and play. To overcome the stigma that play is not a part of learning and to foster the idea that learning is taking place, this part of the primary-grade curriculum may be referred to as, for example, self-directed learning or learning center time. An article entitled "If we call it science, *then* can we let the children play?" (Goldhaber 1994) describes how a teacher's use of investigative play became more acceptable and deserving of attention to administrators, colleagues, and parents when described as "doing science." By carefully naming these scheduled periods of the day or week and by educating others about the importance of open-ended and cognitively challenging play experiences, teachers can incorporate play in the primary curriculum.

A sample of a hand-out that one primary-grade teacher uses to educate parents and colleagues about the learning that takes place during the hour-long self-directed learning (SDL) period scheduled for the last hour of each school day is in Example 7.1. This teacher, like many primary-grade teachers across the country, is using an adaptation of High Scope Preschool's Plan–Do–Review process as a tool in self-directed learning. This is a method that helps keep children responsible for the choices they make during this unstructured time of the day. It is also an excellent record-keeping tool that the teacher can use for student assessment and parent communication or conferences.

Plan–Do–Review, initially developed by High Scope for the Ypslanti Perry Preschool Project and recently modified for the primary grades, is a three-step procedure in which children (1) think about what they plan to do during SDL time; (2) carry out their plan; and (3) review, record, or report their accomplishments (Goffin 1994). The methods used for planning vary from classroom to classroom. Some teachers ask children to orally state their plans as they leave the large group planning session, while others have children sign up on a class planning board or use individual weekly planning sheets. Planning time, while important, should last no longer than five to ten minutes of the hour-long period. The "do" portion lasts about thirty to forty minutes and includes a warning period and time for clean-up. Review, lasting ten to fifteen minutes, can take many forms including having the children write about what they did in a SDL journal, reporting to the entire class, or reporting to a small group or a partner.

◆ **EXAMPLE 7.1**
Self-Directed Learning

Self-Directed Learning is an essential part of our daily schedule. This learning center approach provides an intentional strategy for the active involvement of children, experience-based learning, and individualization in relation to children's developmental abilities, interests, and learning styles. It promotes development of the creative, physical, emotional, social, and cognitive selves of a child.

The Art Center

At the art center your child will use a variety of art processes. The students will develop an eye for color, design, proportion, and an appreciation for a product carefully done as well as enjoyment of the art techniques. We use scissors, glue, paint, paper, fabric, Play-Dough, and other materials at this center. Again your contributions of craft materials can enhance our classroom experiences. Collages, prints, sculptures, mosaics, paintings, and other art forms will be created at this center. Most children love art and we will encourage their choices of materials and processes.

The Sand/Water Center

This center provides sensory experiences that allow for experimentation, exploration and problem solving. Spatial awareness and conservation of volume and matter are developed as students work with these materials. Different utensils and props add new challenges to the child's thought processes. The cooperation needed for sharing space and materials, creating together, and cleaning up afterwards is a life-long skill we want to develop in our students.

Puzzles, Games, Manipulatives

Small muscle development, hand–eye coordination, and social skills are practiced in this center. Children use small pieces to build a larger project, or begin to learn cooperative skills as they await their turn in game situations. Strategies, problem-solving skills and creativity are fostered in this setting. Games and puzzles of varying levels of difficulty are available to allow for success and yet challenge the more capable inventors and gameplayers.

The Reading Center

We read both individually and in groups. We teach phonics and other important reading skills through a Whole Language approach. Our students are taught to use many tools to decode unknown words. They will use phonetic clues, grammar clues, and contextual or meaning clues. Pictures are essential aids for detecting meaning.

Who can resist curling up with a good book, especially when a friend is included?! We want our students to be able to read and then to go the next step of choosing what to read. We will provide books, magazines, and a wide variety of printed materials for ample choice opportunities. Our lofts will offer a special quiet place for some of this reading to occur.

The Listening Center

For children who are just beginning to read, listening to a tape and following along in a book is an invaluable early reading experience. Children truly enjoy hearing stories over and over again. Repetition gives the child a sense of order, accomplishment, and familiarity. Children who are already reading benefit from hearing a story read with expression (a difficult task for many good readers—adults included!) The acquisition of good story language, which includes proper story sequence, grammar, and labeling cannot be overlooked when structuring a reading program for children.

The Construction Center

The construction center offers children the opportunity to work with blocks, racetracks, railways, cars and trucks, and other materials. Building offers a unique process for children to create their own worlds and to work out basic principles of math, physics, and cooperation. There are developmental stages in block building technique, from simple flat roads to towers to complex three-dimensional lattice works and communities, involving balance and sophisticated spatial awareness. Large and small muscle coordination is developed in these activities, as well as problem solving, communication, and artistic skills.

The Creative Dramatics Center

We cannot overemphasize the importance of dramatic play for children at this age level. The students need opportunities to act out what they are doing and learning. We encourage them to show feelings, emotions, and their understanding of story sequence and dramatic elements. Language development, cooperation, problem solving, and working through "complex" life situations can be accomplished in this safe environment. Puppets can also be used to act out stories and real and make-believe situations. It is amazing to stand back and observe student behaviors as they assume new roles.

The Math/Science Center

At the math center we provide many different activities. Sometimes we use basic materials such as geoboards and unifix cubes: sometimes we use theme-related objects. Some of the skills we want children to use are patterning, measuring, weighing, comparing, addition, subtraction, and problem-solving.

Observation skills form the basis of any science program. Finding commonalties and differences in materials from nature helps children make assumptions about the natural world and then test those assumptions. Using magnifying glasses to find interesting patterns or idiosyncrasies is fun and instructional. Sorting and classifying are good beginning science skills that we want our children to acquire. We ask our children to record their observations if possible.

The Theme Center

The theme center is a combination of what we are discussing in PIC (Primary Integrated Curriculum); Whole Language, Self-Directed Learning, and related subjects. The science, social studies, and/or health topics are integrated to provide children with experiences to connect information and make learning meaningful for them. Creative use of materials is encouraged while they explore and discover. Good related literature (both fiction and nonfiction) and collections of hands-on materials will be available for expanded learning opportunities. Child and family contributions are encouraged. Your resources can add to our shared learning for all.

(continued)

◆ **EXAMPLE 7.1**
   Self-Directed Learning (continued)

The Writing Center

Many children will learn to read by writing first, rather than the other way around. At the writing center students write notes, make books, write stories, or come up with their own project using their choice of writing materials. In the early stages, a series of letters which seem unconnected, a label, or a very short sentence is the rule rather than the exception. Each child, at his own pace, will be encouraged to keep writing and soon you will be noticing marked differences. We encourage children to write down their thoughts and do not correct their spelling, handwriting, or organization at this stage. Their ideas are the most important aspect, but we will gently guide them toward well-formed letters, conventional spelling, and composition skills. At this stage the center is more process than product oriented, but watch for notes and signs of their growing interest in this communication process.

Source: Patricia Temple, Bamber Valley Elementary School Rochester, MN. Reprinted with permission.

A sample of a weekly planning sheet used by first-grade children is provided in Figure 7.4 on page 183. Children can use colorcoding or an abbreviation of the day (use the color red or the letter *M* to indicate activities completed on Monday, for example). This teacher assigns "have-tos," tasks each child must complete some time during the week. The children plan when they will complete each "have-to," thereby remaining empowered by choice over how to use their time wisely. Other teachers use the label "I-cares" to indicate that these are centers or activities that the teacher feels are important for each child's cognitive development. Still other teachers make use of a "teacher table" during SDL or center time where children are called for individual or small group instruction or assessment. Caution should be used in the tendency to overstructure self-directed learning or center time, however, so that children's choices and opportunities to explore, invent, and create are not too limited. Note that in Figures 7.5 and 7.6 (pages 184–85) only three out of twelve self-directed learning centers are "have-tos" and that the "have-tos" vary from week to week. Note also that this teacher has made an effort to incorporate the theme being studied (in Figure 7.5 the rain forest and the environment, in Figure 7.6 "I'm proud to be an American") into some, but not all, of the centers.

Figure 7.7 on page 186 is the format this same first-grade teacher uses for the review portion of self-directed learning. For each day of the week, children are provided with a space to write or draw about accomplishments of which they are proud.

Wasserman (1990) offers a different model for the use of play as a means of fostering children's cognitive development in the primary grades. Her

◆ **FIGURE 7.4**   *Planning Sheet for Self-Directed Learning*

Name _____ Date _____

Self-Directed Learning

Monday   Tuesday   Wednesday   Thursday   Friday

Have-to Centers*

Art	Math/Science	Construction
Puzzles/Games	**Sand/Water**	**Creative Drama**
Theme	**Listening**	**Reading**
Writing		

I used my time wisely (Yes or No):

M   T   W   Th   F

◯   ◯   ◯   ◯   ◯

Source: Patricia Temple, Bamber Valley Elementary School Rochester, MN. Reprinted with permission.

instructional model of Play–Debrief–Replay provides opportunities for creative, investigative play in a variety of curricular areas, followed by reflection by the children on their experiences during play. They are then allowed to extend their learning through additional play opportunities, which are provided in areas equipped to foster exploration in science, math, social studies, language arts, and creative arts (music, drama, and arts and crafts). Wasserman's

◆ **FIGURE 7.5** *Sample Thematic Planning Sheet for SDL*

Name ————————————————————— Date ——————————

Self-Directed Learning

| Monday | Tuesday | Wednesday | Thursday | Friday |

Have-to Centers*

Art Junk Sculpture from recycled items (in hall)	**Math/Science*** Gorilla number words Rain forest animal problems	**Construction** Create an invention to save the rain forest or to help our earth
Puzzles/Games Card games Floor puzzles Board games Rain forest games	**Handwriting*** Sentences about Earth Week	**Creative Drama** Tropical rain forest Toucan finger puppets
Theme* Color, cut and glue Rain Forest Animals	**Listening** Spring stories	**Reading** Teacher or parent volunteer Independent choice reading
Writing Rhyming word families	**Book Publishing** Teach or parent volunteer	**Spelling*** Use pre-test practice words

I used my time wisely (Yes or No):

   M   T   W   Th   F

◯   ◯   ◯   ◯   ◯

Source: Patricia Temple, Bamber Valley Elementary School Rochester, MN. Reprinted with permission.

instructional model requires teachers to develop questioning skills and inter-actions that lead children to reflective thinking about their activities. Example 7.2 (pages 187–89) summarizes the interaction skills necessary for debriefing. *Serious Players in the Primary Classroom* (Wasserman 1990) provides suggestions for materials, procedures, and debriefing questions to help the teacher develop a cognitively challenging curriculum based on play. Suggestions made in *Play*

◆ **FIGURE 7.6** *Sample Thematic Planning Sheet for SDL*

Name ——————————————————— Date ——————————

Self-Directed Learning

Monday	Tuesday	Wednesday	Thursday	Friday

Have-to Centers*

Art* USA Cooperative Flag — Stars — Stripes — (in the hall)	**Math/Science** Patterns Dappy shake-up	**Construction** Picture of what you made
Puzzles/Games Card games Plus and minus game Flag puzzle	**Handwriting*** Sentences about the USA	**Creative Drama** Burger King… The all-American fast food restaurant
Theme USA — Presidents — Flag — Statue of Liberty	**Listening*** *Arthur Meets the President*	**Reading** Teacher or parent volunteer
Writing Notes Story Typewriter	**Book Publishing**	**Valentines Party**

I used my time wisely (Yes or No):

M	T	W	Th	F
◯	◯	◯	◯	◯

Source: Patricia Temple, Bamber Valley Elementary School Rochester, MN. Reprinted with permission.

at the Center of the Curriculum (Van Hoorn *et al.* 1993) can also be used to help teachers integrate play into the academic curriculum of the primary grades.

Cognitive development during the primary years is important, foundational, and "primary," or basic, to learning throughout life. In addition, it is strongly related to a child's feelings of competence and self-worth, thus influencing his or her social and emotional development.

◆ **FIGURE 7.7** *Student Response Sheet for Plan–Do–Review*

I am proud of:

Monday

Tuesday

Wednesday

Thursday

Friday

Source: Patricia Temple, Bamber Valley Elementary School Rochester, MN. Reprinted with permission.

Technology and Cognitive Development in the Primary Grades

Developments in the world of technology have given teachers and children resources for learning that were previously not available. This technological explosion can literally allow children to see places all over the world. The curriculum map and technology resources for a second-grade unit on China are shown in Figure 7.8. This is an example of how teachers are utilizing technology to enhance their teaching and enrich the learning of their students. The use of technology can greatly enhance the cognitive development of children in the primary grades.

Over the past decade, much work has been done to identify appropriate and safe use of technology with young children. NAEYC has developed a position statement regarding the appropriate use of technology and the Internet with young children. NAEYC's position statement may be found on their website at www.naeyc.org. Lists of award-winning developmentally appropriate software and websites are available at www.computersandchildren.com. Awards are made annually and are based on criteria to rate the developmental appropriateness of the software or website. This website also provides links to the National Gallery of Art for Kids (www.nga.gov/kids) and the American

◆ **EXAMPLE 7.2**
Debriefing: Using Interactions That Promote Reflection

In teachers' repertoires there are different kinds of responses or interactions. The examples below indicate some of the repertoires that teachers use daily.

Responses that give information:

> *Child:* What is the name of the bird we saw yesterday?
> *Teachers:* Do you mean the woodpecker, Linda?

Responses that direct and demonstrate:

> *Child:* How do you fold this origami pattern?
> *Teachers:* First you fold down the top, like this. Then . . .

Responses that are confrontational and manage behavior:

> *Teachers:* If you do that one more time, John, I'll have to ask you to leave the game.

Responses that are evaluative:

> *Child:* Is my work good?
> *Teachers:* (Possible responses)
> No, Ranae, that's not quite right.
> I think it's the best picture you've ever done.
> You spelled three words wrong.

Responses that provide empathy:

> *Child:* I feel mean. I hate the world.
> *Teachers:* (Possible responses)
> You are upset because your family is moving at the end of school.
> You are angry because the girls wouldn't let you jump rope.

Responses that enable children to think about new ideas, issues, and concepts:

> *Teachers:* (Possible responses)
> Tell me more about what you did.
> When Bob measured it, it was 13 cm wide. When Sue measured it, it was 14 cm wide. How could that be, do you suppose?
> Which would be the better way to go? Why did you choose that way?

Because responses come from teachers, a respected person of authority, they have the potential to hurt or to help. Appropriate responses incorporate guidelines of **attending, empowering, and respecting.**

- I know you were interested in the sea horses, Bill. But I was worried that you would get separated from the rest of the group and become lost.
- Those sea horses were fascinating. I can understand that you wanted to watch them for a long time. I know it's hard for you to come away when you would like to stay longer.

(continued)

◆ **EXAMPLE 7.2**
   Debriefing: Using Interactions That Promote Reflection (continued)

Alternatives that are **disrespectful, inattentive, and disempowering** include:

- We don't have time for that now, Bill.
- Save your questions until we get back to class.
- You've kept the entire group waiting.

Strategies that teachers may use to expand their repertoire of **attending, responding, and empowering** responses include the following:

Responses that paraphrase: Saying back in different words what the child has said:
   Child: Sometimes you find sharks in deep water.
   Teachers: Sharks live in the deeper parts of the ocean.

   Interpreting what the child has said, by using inferences:
   Child: Sometimes you find sharks in deep water.
   Teachers: So sharks are not likely to be found in shallow water. Is that what you mean?

   Interpreting by adding new information to what the child has said:
   Child: Sometimes you find sharks in deep water.
   Teachers: So it might be safer to swim in shallow parts of the ocean and more dangerous to swim where it is deep.

Responses that require analysis: These responses require children to dig more deeply and go beyond their first-hand observations.
   Teachers: Tell me about the ocean.
   Child: It's salty.
   Teachers: The ocean has salt water. (Paraphrase). How did you discover that? (Analysis)
   Child: When I went swimming, I got water in my mouth and it tasted salty.
   Teachers: So tasting water would be one way of telling if it was salty. (Paraphrase)
   Child: Yeah.
   Teachers: I see. (Nonjudgmentally). Thanks for sharing your idea. Are there other things someone can tell me about the water in the ocean?
   Another Child: There are parts that are very, very deep. Sometimes you find sharks in the deep part.
   Teachers: You are saying that sharks may live in the deep part of the ocean.
   Child: Yep.
   Teachers: How would you know that, Noel? (Asking for analysis).
   Child: I saw it on T.V.
   Teachers: The T.V. program gave you information about sharks living in the ocean. (Paraphrasing).

Responses that challenge: These types of responses ask children to
   Generate hypotheses
   Interpret data
   Identify criteria used in decision making
   Apply principles to new situation
   Make predictions
   Explain how a theory can be tested
   Create a new or imaginative idea

Challenging questions shift the focus of the discussion onto new and different levels. Use challenge questions sparingly to prevent the discussion from jumping from one idea to another.

Sample challenge questions include:

Asking for **supporting data**—"Why do you say that?"

Asking **principles be applied to a new situation**—"I wonder if that would work in this situation?

Asking for **predictions**—"What do you think will happen next? What will happen if we do this?"

Asking for **a way to find out**—"How do you think we could find out about this?"

As you use these types of interactions, keep the following in mind:

1. Allow yourself growth time to develop these skills.
2. Don't try to do too much. Pace yourself by attempting only as much as you can handle.
3. Practice and continually examine your use of debriefing skills. These skills grow through hard work and not spontaneously.

Adapted from S. Wasserman (1990). *Serious Play in the Primary Classroom*. New York: Teachers College Press. Printed with permission.

Library Association (www.ala.org) websites. The ALA website provides resources for parents, teens, and kids as well as lists of award-winning books including Caldecott Medal, Newberry Medal, Coretta Scott King, and Laura Ingalls Wilder awards. The links and possibilities for use to enhance the cognitive development of children are endless.

Observing Cognitive Development through Work and Play in the Primary Grades

Complete the following activities to learn more about the cognitive development of children in the primary grades.

◆ **ACTIVITY**
7.10

Your Own Primary Classroom

Before observing in a primary-grade classroom, think back to one of your own primary-grade classrooms. Draw a diagram of it and label the learning areas, materials, and anything else you remember. On the back of the diagram list the subject areas and any important concepts, topics, or themes that you remember studying. Then observe in a primary-grade classroom of the same level. Make a diagram of the same things you remembered from your own classroom. Examine the daily or weekly schedule to determine which subject areas are taught. Look around the room for evidence of important concepts, topics, and themes that are being studied. How does what you observe compare with what you remember about your own classroom?

◆ **FIGURE 7.8**   *Sample Primary Unit Utilizing Technology Resources*

Technology
- Tangram website
- Virtual China website
- Beijing website
- Calligraphy website

Social Studies
- Geography: maps/ environment/climate
- Customs/traditions
- Lifestyle
- Contributions
- Flag
- Celebrations

Language Arts
- Chinese literature
- Folk tales
- Dragon stories
- Chinese words
- Chinese legends

CHINA

Music
- Chinese songs

Science
- Plants and animals
- Endangered animals

Math
- Tangrams
- Word problems
- Study of numbers

Art
- Origami
- Chinese art
- Paper cutting
- Lanterns
- Kites
- Dragons

Physical Education
- Dragon dances
- Chinese games

Related Websites:
- Great Wall of China
  www.enchantedlearning.com/subjects/greatwall/Allabout.html
- Virtual China
  www.kiku.com/electric_samuri/virtual_china/index.html
- CIA World Factbook: China
  www.odci.gov/cia/publications/factbook/geos/ch.html
- Animated Chinese Characters
  www.ocrat.com/chargif/indfram.html
- Chinese Calligraphy
  http://tqjunior.thinkquest.org/3614/
- Get Your Own Chinese Name
  www.mandarintools.com/chinesename.html

Source: Kristen Hass, Katie Lodermeir, Tammy Van Moer, Winona State University Graduate Students. Reprinted with permission.

◆ **ACTIVITY**

7.11

Piagetian Conservation and Classification Tasks

Perform some Piagetian classification and conservation tasks with children in first and third grades. Complete the same three tasks with each child and then write a summary of each child's performance on each task. Prepare activities similar to the following:

1. Provide buttons of assorted sizes, colors, shapes, styles, and compositions. Ask each child to sort the buttons into groups and then to name the groups of buttons according to the classifications he or she used. Analyze the groupings the child names to determine how many attributes are included in each. (For example, two groups of white buttons—one with two-holed and one with four-holed buttons—would indicate that the child is grouping based on two attributes rather than simply grouping all white buttons together, or grouping on one attribute.)

2. Provide a large variety of small, everyday items on a cafeteria tray. Ask each child to pick up two items with something in common and explain why he or she selected them. A child may pick up a pen and pencil, for example, and state that their common characteristic is that they are both writing tools. Another child may pick up the pencil and a ruler and state that they are both wooden. Make a list of all the common characteristics the children identify. This may be performed with individuals or groups of children.

3. Provide six dolls, a pencil, and a circle and a square of paper representing two birthday cakes. Ask the child to divide the cake so each doll gets the same size piece. Use groups of two, three, four, and five dolls to see how well the child is able to perform this task. Compare the ability of first- and third-grade children in solving these problems. Is it easier for the children at either level to divide even numbers than it is to divide odd numbers? Can older children more easily divide the cake into more pieces than the younger children? Is it easier for them to divide the round cakes or the square cakes?

4. Gather seven plastic vases and at least seven stems of silk flowers. Line up the vases and ask a child to pick enough flowers from the pile to be able to put one in each vase. Then hold the flowers as a bouquet. Ask the child if there are more flowers or more vases, or if there are the same number of flowers and vases. Vary the process by providing pennies and telling the child that each flower costs one penny. Ask the child to figure out how many pennies he or she needs to buy all the flowers. Compare the abilities of the children to understand the concept of one-to-one correspondence through these tasks.

Good sources for other Piagetian activities are either of the following books: *The Piaget Handbook: Children in the Age of Discovery, Preschool–Third Grade,* Rosemary Peterson and Victoria Felton-Collins 1986, Teachers College Press, New York; and *Piagetian Activities: A Diagnostic and Developmental Approach,* Richard Copeland 1988, Thinking Publications, Eau Claire, WI.

◆ **ACTIVITY**

7.12

Cognition

Interview two kindergarten or first-grade children and two second- or third-grade children using the following questions suggested by Berns (1994).

1. What makes the stars shine?
2. What causes dreams?
3. What makes it get dark?
4. What makes a car go?
5. What makes a clock tick?
6. What causes clouds?
7. Why do leaves fall in autumn?
8. What does "birthday" mean?
9. What makes an airplane fly?

Analyze each child's responses to compare differences in cognition. Are there still evidences of *egocentrism* (the ability to see and understand things only from his or her own perspective or experience), *participation* (the belief that he or she or others can control nature), or *animism* (the belief that the world of nature is alive or that all things that move are alive)? Write a brief, two- to three-page analysis of what you learned about each child.

◆ **ACTIVITY**

7.13

Teacher's Plan Book

With consent, analyze a teacher's plan book. Determine how each of the eight intelligences is incorporated into lessons for the week. What opportunities are there for visual/spatial learning, musical learning, interpersonal learning, body/kinesthetic intelligence, and so forth? Use Figures 7.2 and 7.3 to guide your analysis. Which intelligences seem to be emphasized through the planned learning experiences? Which need to have more emphasis?

◆ **ACTIVITY**

7.14

Learning Centers

If you are in a student teaching or practicum setting that allows you to plan and implement a curriculum, read *Multiple Intelligence in Action* by Campbell [in *Childhood Education, 68*(2), pp. 97–101] and use it as a model for planning learning centers based around the multiple intelligences. Discuss your plans and results with your classroom and university supervisors. Be sure to include feedback from students as to which learning centers they found most interesting and beneficial.

◆ **ACTIVITY**
7.15

Choices in the Classroom

Observe in a primary-grade classroom for a day and keep track of the choices children are allowed to make during the day. Do they choose with whom they will work? What to do? Where to sit in the lunchroom? What story or book they will read? Also look for other ways in which you could offer children choices if this were your own classroom. Write a brief, one- to two-page report of what you observed and what you would do to increase choices for students in your classroom.

◆ **ACTIVITY**
7.16

Work versus Play

Interview children about their conceptions of the differences between work and play. Ask them to list activities from school and home that involve play and those that involve work.

◆ **ACTIVITY**
7.17

Developmentally Appropriate Software and Websites

Review one award-winning developmental software program or website from the most recent list at the www.computersandchildren.com website. Review the ten developmentally appropriate criteria and scale for websites or software. Would you rate the software or website higher or lower than the reviewers did? Share your findings and a preview of the website or software with your class or a small group.

Social and Emotional Development in the Primary Grades

A variety of factors influences the importance that social and emotional development play during the primary grades. As previously mentioned, success—or lack of it—in school affects a child's feelings of self-worth. In addition, a child is typically becoming less egocentric at this age and has a greater understanding of his or her relationships with others. Because of the increased amount of time spent away from family and with peers in school and other activities, the size and importance of the child's social circle are both increasing.

Black *et al.* (1992) suggest that the child moves from being *egocentric* (focused on the self) to being *sociocentric* (focused on family, friends, and culture group). The recognition of oneself as part of one or more groups is linked to the child's increased ability to classify and focus on a variety of characteristics at the same time. As a result, the primary-grade child becomes more aware of dress, hairstyle, and language of those members of the group that he or she most admires. Piper provides an interesting and humorous example of this.

When she was in kindergarten, Piper failed the vision screening. The school nurse called and recommended that she have a full vision screening by a pediatric optometrist. At the conclusion of an extensive examination, the doctor asked Piper to look at the books in the reception area while he talked with her mother. The doctor reported that Piper nearly had him convinced that she had a severe vision problem until he tried corrective lenses and was unable to find any that worked. As it turns out, Piper wanted glasses because of her admiration for her friend Maria, who was two years older and wore glasses.

Aboud (1988) suggests that during this period children progress from being preoccupied with groups and the differences between one's own group and others to becoming aware of the similarities—as well as the differences—among groups. Thus, the child at this age, for example, is susceptible to ethnic stereotypes until he or she is able to focus on and form relationships with individuals based on their unique personalities rather than on ethnic qualities. This characteristic of primary-grade children points to the need for multicultural and antibias curriculum.

Example 7.3 summarizes fears that Black *et al.* (1992) identify in children at various developmental stages. Note that with increasing cognitive development the child's list of fears—an aspect of emotional development—increases and the nature of those fears changes. Fear of rejection by peers, parents, and teachers is evidence of movement from egocentric to sociocentric thinking.

For children of this age being popular is often related to attractiveness of name, physique, clothing, or personal possessions. Sociometric techniques enable teachers and others to determine who is popular, rejected, neglected, or controversial (Cole *et al.* 1982). Peer group acceptance can be determined

◆ **EXAMPLE 7.3**
Changes in Children's Fears as They Get Older

Infants	*Toddlers*	*4–5*	*6–8*
Loud noises	Heights	Noises	Dark
Loss of support	Separation	Imaginary creatures	Being left alone
	Strangers	Punishment	Scolding
	Sudden surprise; e.g.,	Dogs/Small animals	Physical injury/sickness
	Jack in the Box toy	Storms	Ridicule/failure
		Supernatural	Criticism
		(ghosts/witches)	Being different in clothes/ hairstyles, etc.
			Worries (what could be): nuclear war, hurricane, family safety, death of family member
			Parental/teacher rejection

Source: The young child. Copyright ©1992, by Black, Puckett, and Bell, Delman Publishers. Reprinted with permission.

by asking children to name privately several classmates they like and dislike. Teachers can then use this information to help children develop social competence. Sensitivity and professionalism must be exercised when using this technique. Rather than making it seem as if you are conducting a popularity poll, it would be more appropriate to ask children to list three people with whom they would like to work or play on a particular project and three they would prefer not to have in their group. A class list can be used to tally the number of votes each child receives in response to each category indicating levels of popularity and rejection. Children who are seldom or never named in either category are classified as *neglected*. This means that they are neither *popular* (well liked by many and rejected by few), or *rejected* (liked by few and disliked by many), but are quite invisible and isolated by the group in general. The fourth category, *controversial* children, are those who are liked by many but are also disliked by many. An example of this type of child is one who is liked for his or her good looks and material possessions, but is conceited about those looks and clothing and won't share material possessions, thereby estranging others.

Multi-age classrooms

Peer relations are related to aspects of both social and cognitive development. Just as children in a family can benefit socially and cognitively from having younger or older siblings, children who are grouped with mixed-aged rather than same-aged classmates benefit socially and cognitively (Katz, Evangelou, Hartman 1990). Some of the advantages of mixed or multiage classrooms include the following:

1. Children have the opportunity to experience more than one birth order position. That is, they get to experience being in the youngest, oldest, and middle child position (in cases of three-year groupings).

2. Children experience more of real-life age groupings. Schools tend to be one of the only places we group people consistently by chronological age with little more than a twelve-month time span. Some societal organizations have followed schools in this pattern of groupings (church school classes, for example) while others use age-span groupings of similar but not the exact same age within a calendar year (for example, Cub Scouts and Brownies for younger children, Boy Scouts and Girl Scouts for older children).

3. Children and teachers both benefit from spending more than one year together. Teachers who are able to use what they learn about the child in year one, do a more effective job in planning the child's education during years two and three. At the same time, teachers and second- or third-year classmates work together to orient the new children in the group. There is also enhanced parent–teacher communication, since this relationship extends beyond one year.

4. Both younger and older children benefit from the peer teaching relationship. Younger students can be inspired and guided by older students, while older students experience advanced thinking about concepts as they explain them to younger students.

Many teachers and parents who are accustomed to a grade level system have many questions and concerns regarding multiage groupings in classrooms. Some of these concerns and their responses include the following:

1. How can the curriculum be organized so there is no repetition or gaps in content and skills taught and children are sufficiently challenged? This area of concern stems from traditional curriculum expectations that assumed all first-graders should learn to read and all third-graders should begin to use cursive writing, and from single-grade/single-subject textbooks that have dominated curricula in public schools. Multiage schooling assumes that goals are more longitudinal and looks more at the long-term benefits than at the short-term gains.

2. How can the cognitive and social needs of children be met in multiage classrooms? These concerns are related to assumptions that younger children will hold back the learning of older children and that older children may have negative influences on the behavior and "innocence" of younger children. These same differences may exist in traditional graded classes, where children have differing cognitive abilities and a variety of social experiences and backgrounds.

Pavan (1992) reviewed the results of research that had been done on nongraded or multiage schooling since 1967. Her synthesis of the research provides clear evidence of the benefits of nongraded, multiage, or continuous progress systems of schooling in the following ways:

1. Nongraded grouping of students resulted in 91 percent of students performing better than or as well as graded groups of students on measures of academic achievement.

2. School attitude and mental health studies indicated that 95 percent of students in nongraded settings did as well as or better than students in graded settings. Only 5 percent showed nongradedness to have negative effects on students' self-esteem or attitudes toward schooling.

3. Benefits of nongradedness increase with the length of time that students are provided nongraded school experiences.

4. At-risk students, including boys, African Americans, low socioeconomic level students, and underachievers, benefit both socially and academically from nongraded programs.

Kentucky and Oregon are two states currently using nongraded schooling as a key component of school reform. The Kentucky Education Reform Act of 1990 established a statewide nongraded system for prekindergarten through third grade. A survey conducted by the National Association of Elementary School Principals, published in *Education USA* in April 1990, indicated that two-thirds of the principals surveyed believe that abolishment of grade levels would be advantageous to restructuring elementary schools. Despite the evidence and support that research and educational experts provide, nongraded schooling has many obstacles of tradition to overcome before it is widely accepted.

The effects of gender, ethnicity, and socioeconomic status are other aspects of psychosocial development that increase as children enter the primary grades (Macoby 1990; Asher *et al.* 1982). Left on their own, children tend to spend more time in groups and activities segregated by sex, ethnicity, or socioeconomic status. In other words, girls spend more of their time with girls, boys and girls engage in different types of activities, and children of like ethnic groups and similar socioeconomic levels tend to seek each other out. Teachers must be proactive in examining and facilitating experiences for children to engage in a wide variety of activities with a wide variety of peers.

Observing Psychosocial Development through Work and Play in the Primary Grades

Complete the following activities to learn more about the psychosocial development of children in the primary grades.

◆ **ACTIVITY**

7.18

Children's Self-Recognition

Interview a six-year-old and an eight-year-old child by asking them to describe themselves. Develop questions that will lead them to classify themselves according to a variety of groups to which they belong. The questions may include some of the following: (a) Describe yourself to me; (b) tell me about your family; (c) what activities do you participate in or what groups are you a member of? Analyze the responses to determine if children's recognition of themselves as part of a variety of groups increases with age. You might incorporate drawing or letter-writing techniques as a part of this exercise. (Be sure to clear this activity and the questions you will be asking with your classroom and university supervisors so you do not violate school privacy policies.)

◆ **ACTIVITY**

7.19

Children's Fears

Interview primary-grade children regarding their fears. You might use a story book, such as *There's a Nightmare in My Closet* by Mercer Mayer, to initiate the discussion. Then ask children to develop individual lists of things they are fearful of to be compiled into a class list. Compare the individual lists with the list of Black *et al.* (1992) of fears of six- to eight-year-olds presented in Example 7.3. With the classroom teacher, develop a lesson or unit that would help children to understand and overcome their fears.

◆ **ACTIVITY**

7.20

Sociometric Technique

Work with the teacher to employ a sociometric technique for a second- or third-grade or multiage classroom as described in this chapter and in Chapter 2. Carefully word the questions you ask the children. For example, it would be more appropriate to say, "Name two children from our class you would prefer not to have in your work group" than it would be to say "Name two children you don't like to work with." Also be sure to communicate to the children that their choices are going to be used by the teachers to decide on groups that would work or play well together and should remain private. Use the responses to analyze which children are popular, rejected, neglected, or controversial, using the definitions provided earlier.

◆ **ACTIVITY**
7.21

Friendships

Ask children of different ages to name and describe their best friend(s) outside of school. Do children mention physical characteristics, possessions of their friends, or social aspects of friendship such as common interests, loyalty, sensitivity, understanding, and so forth? Are there differences in the friendship attributes mentioned by younger and older children? By boys and girls? This activity can be tied to a lesson or story on friendship that you present to the class before you ask them to write, draw, or talk about their non-school friends.

◆ **ACTIVITY**
7.22

Multi-age Classroom Observance

Observe in a multiage classroom. Note the similarities and differences between this classroom and a traditional classroom. Interview the classroom teacher regarding changes he or she has had to make in his or her approach to curricula and evaluation. How do the teacher and school ensure the curriculum is not repeated and does not have gaps as a result of the change from grade-level expectations? Inquire about the efforts to educate parents regarding the benefits of having children in this type of classroom setting as well as the response and receptivity of parents to this change. Refer to the concerns and questions about multiage classrooms in this chapter to formulate the questions for your observation before completing it.

◆ **ACTIVITY**
7.23

Paley's Rule

Read about Vivian Paley's implementation of the rule in the title of her book *You Can't Say You Can't Play*. Interview teachers, parents, and children of different ages and grade levels to learn what they think of such a rule in the classroom and whether they think it would work. Analyze the responses and write a two- to three-page paper summarizing the responses of each group.

◆ **ACTIVITY**
7.24

Development in Literature

Read two books by Beverly Cleary: *Beezus and Ramona* and *Ramona Quimby, Age 8*. In *Beezus and Ramona*, Ramona is age four and in nursery school, and her sister Beezus is age nine. Compare and contrast Ramona's and Beezus's development in the two books. Look for common developmental themes in both books and note changes in the two girls—especially Ramona, who is ages four and eight in the books. Consider some of the following as possible themes for your comparisons: physical and motor development; cognitive and language development; egocentrism versus sociocentrism; gender role development; friendships; family relationships and peer relationships; and sibling relationships. Write a two- to three-page paper analyzing three or four of the developmental changes Ramona exemplifies using the format provided below:

1. Provide a brief overview of each book and identify the developmental themes you will be discussing in the paper.
2. State the developmental principle, including pages from this text or other early childhood texts where you found the information.
3. Quote or summarize examples from the Ramona books to either substantiate or refute the developmental principle you are illustrating.
4. Discuss why you think the developmental principle is congruent or incongruent with Cleary's description of Ramona at ages four and eight.
5. Write a brief paragraph giving an overall reaction to the books. What understandings did you gain concerning developmental changes in early childhood as a result of reading these books? How will the reading of these books benefit you as a future early childhood educator?

◆ **ACTIVITY**
7.25

Developmental Needs

Read Table 7.1 on pages 200–03. Use it as a basis to determine how the developmental needs of the children in the classroom(s) you have observed or are participating in are being met. Using this table and what you have learned through your observation or practicum activities, write a brief, two- to three-page summary of the ways you will meet the physical, cognitive, and social-emotional needs of students in your own primary-grade classroom.

◆ **ACTIVITY**
7.26

Event Sampling

Do an event sampling of a social interaction problem you observe in a primary classroom using the example (in Chapter 2) of Simon and Mrs. W. as a model.

◆ **ACTIVITY**
7.27

Teaching Tolerance

Visit the Teaching Tolerance website at www.teachingtolerance.org. You will find resources for teachers, parents and children to help teach and promote tolerance with children while they are very young. You can review articles from the *Teaching Tolerance* magazine available on the website. Preview this website and report to your class how you might use resources from this website to promote tolerance among primary-grade children.

◆ **TABLE 7.1** *Developmental Characteristics of Children Ages 6–9*

Psychomotor Characteristics	Psychomotor Needs	Implications for Instruction
The child is . . .	*The child needs . . .*	*Adults should . . .*
Extremely active; enjoys activity for its own sake but tires easily.	Opportunities to use energy constructively; frequent change of pace.	Alternate active and sedentary activities; plan for physical activity in and outside of classroom; allow children to move around in the room.
Establishing eye–hand coordination; boys may have more difficulty in manipulating small objects.	Variety of manipulative experiences.	Gradually increase work which requires concentration and precision.
Better coordinated; enjoys stunts; may overestimate physical skills.	Activities which are appropriate to skills of coordination; close supervision.	Plan games which are safe but require maximum physical involvement; help awareness of physical limitations.
Still far sighted, eye–hand coordination may lag until a child is about eight years old; may have difficulty focusing on small objects.	To avoid eye strain.	Avoid requiring too much reading or close visual attention at one time; watch for signs of eye fatigue.
Most susceptible to common childhood illnesses.	To learn practices for maintaining health.	Teach the practice of preventing illness as well as good eating habits and recognizing the signs of illness; allow time in daily schedule to work with absentees.
Interested in accomplishment; enjoys responsibility; may hurry through work.	Opportunities to demonstrate industry.	Praise accomplishments; tailor assignments to reachable levels; provide assistance as needed to assure satisfaction from performance; allow enough time to complete assignments; help with proofreading; recopying and perseverance as needed; provide ample activities.
Sensitive to criticism and ridicule; concerned about being good; begins to show self-criticism.	Frequent praise and recognition.	Aid the development of self-confidence by discussing earned successes; give frequent feedback and reassurance; avoid using sarcasm and ridicule; correct privately; help with manners, habits; desire to be right.
Learning to delay gratification by exercising self-control.	Positive reinforcement for exercising control.	Praise patience; discuss goals and goal setting; provide ample choices.

Affective Characteristics	*Affective Needs*	*Implications for Instruction*
The child is . . .	*The child needs . . .*	*Adults should . . .*
Eager to please adults yet tests limits.	Approval and independence.	Provide approval and affection for achievements (in all areas); provide fair and firm limits; allow choices; allow children to experience the consequences of their actions; avoid group punishment; disapprove of behavior, when necessary, not the child.
Becoming more self-assertive; words begin to replace physical aggression, especially in girls.	To learn acceptable ways of getting attention and working with others.	Provide leader and follower experiences; intervene before quarrels become feuds; discuss peaceful means of settling disputes.
Applying the letter of the law by literally interpreting rules, emphasizing fairness, tattles.	Clear limits; simple rules; experiences in playing fairly.	Clarify limits; keep groups small and flexible most of the time; be reasonably sympathetic to complaints; draw a distinction between tattling and information needed to prevent injury; don't accept gross exaggerations.
Wanting to belong to groups, but groups remain flexible; more selective of friends; beginning to select "best" friends.	Successful experiences in making friends.	Use sociograms to identify isolates; discuss ways in which friends are made; guide individuals as needed.
Beginning to play organized, simple games but not always by formal rules; boys and girls begin to have different interests.	Ideas for games; participating in self-selected groups when appropriate.	Provide ideas for games and needed equipment; discuss rules of fair play; ask for agreement to clearly stated rules before play begins; plan activities which are not highly organized and are of short duration.
Interested in competition; boasting is common; varies in ability to play in groups.	Success.	Avoid the use of comparison and competition; encourage competition with self and previous performance.
Generally tolerant of others unless influenced by adults.	Flexible social groupings.	Form groups based on interests; discuss the common needs and desires of all people.
Requiring successful and satisfying learning experiences in order to continue interest.	Experiences to build self-esteem; must view self as a successful learner.	Assign tasks that can be accomplished; personalize expectations and use a variety of materials and strategies to assure success; give simple, clear directions.

(continued)

◆ **TABLE 7.1** *Developmental Characteristics of Children Ages 6–9 (continued)*

Cognitive Characteristics	*Cognitive Needs*	*Implications for Instruction*
The child is . . .	*The child needs . . .*	*Adults should . . .*
Generally extremely eager to learn; curious and less distractible.	Information and labels.	Support built-in motivation by making demands which can be met successfully; minimize distractions.
Becoming more goal directed in learning; more interested in the product.	Experiences in achieving goals.	Structure learning experiences for success and satisfaction; provide only as much guidance as is necessary to assure satisfaction; increase responsibilities of child to successful coping levels; set goals cooperatively and involve group planning.
Synthesizing information by categorizing and classifying experiences; using inductive reasoning.	Opportunities to organize information.	Emphasize both concepts and vocabulary as information is gained and organized; work from smaller examples to larger concepts; provide activities that require thinking.
Demonstrating some abstract thinking (ability to generalize); thinking involves reasoning by analogy to actual experiences.	Opportunities to develop reasoning abilities.	Work from concrete experiences, use analogies in class discussions.
Recalling sequences successfully (numbers, letters, time); reasoning becomes more apparent.	Opportunities to demonstrate capabilities.	Plan learning experiences that apply knowledge in practical, concrete situations.
Learning best through active participation with concrete materials especially if learning new concepts.	Variety of concrete learning experiences.	Provide a variety of concrete materials on a variety of difficulty levels; introduce processes gradually (classification, seriation, hypothesizing.)
Lengthening attention span; resents being disturbed at play or work if interested.	Time for involvement and mastery.	Provide an environment that allows concentration, is without too many sensory stimuli; provide ample time for completion of tasks; plan a flexible schedule and be prepared to change activities.

Cognitive Characteristics	Cognitive Needs	Implications for Instruction
The child is . . .	*The child needs . . .*	*Adults should . . .*
Understanding language ahead of ability to use language; speaks more fluently than writes; learning the power of words; experiments with vulgar speech.	To extend oral and written language skills.	Plan many opportunities requiring use of listening, speaking, reading and writing skills; strengthen and expand vocabularies; accept child, rejecting the use of vulgar language.
Eager to share idea; assertive; likes to talk and answer questions even if information is erroneous.	Opportunities to share ideas.	Encourage sharing between verbal and less verbal children; insist on taking turns when sharing in a group.

Source: Georgia Department of Education. Reprinted with permission

Atypical Development

As children engage in more academic activities during the primary years, several developmental differences that were not evident during the less-structured, nonacademic activities of preschool and kindergarten may be noticeable. "Learning-disabled" is a term used to describe children who experience difficulty in academic settings. Public Law 94-142 defines learning disabilities as difficulties in using written or oral language—including speaking, listening, writing, and thinking skills—or difficulty with mathematical calculations (Federal Register 1977). Learning disabilities are not the result of impaired vision, hearing, or motor skills; mental retardation; emotional disturbance; or economic or environmental deprivation. Because of this definition, many children who are from culturally diverse families or are economically disadvantaged may have difficulty qualifying for the special services they need to succeed in school (Allen 1992).

Many of the characteristics of learning-disabled children, such as constant motion and short attention span, are also characteristics of children with the behavior disorders *attention-deficit disorder (ADD)* and *attention-deficit hyperactivity disorder (ADHD)*. ADD differs from ADHD in the level of motor activity of the child. Children with excessive motor activity who have difficulty remaining still are diagnosed as having ADHD.

While controversy over whether such learning and behavior disorders actually exist (McNellis 1987), behaviors associated with ADD and ADHD can certainly be troublesome to teachers and parents (Allen 1992). Common treatments for ADD and ADHD include use of medications to decrease the child's activity level or putting the child on a special diet that restricts his or her intake of certain foods or foods with additives. Behavior modification programs that reward the child for appropriate behavior can also be helpful as the child is learning new behaviors to replace the bothersome ones. In developing a behavior modification program several things should be kept in mind.

First, for the behavior modification program to work, the "reward" must be something meaningful to the child. It is useful to engage the parents and child in developing the plan so a realistic and appropriate reward can be determined. Second, behavior modification programs work best when the teacher and parents work as partners. Ideally, the program worked out should involve sending home a daily message about how the child performed in school that day. Parents and teachers can work together to set realistic goals for the child so the reward that he or she is working toward is attainable in a relatively short time. It is also helpful to put the parent in charge of keeping track of progress and providing the reward. This alleviates the problem of the teacher having to provide a reward for one child, which may not seem fair to the other children, who are not in need of behavior modification. Finally, it is important that other children in the class understand why a child is on a behavior modification program so they can become partners in helping the child meet his or her goals. In addition, children should be given an explanation of why that child is taking home a note each day.

The following situation is an example of using a behavior modification plan effectively. Sara has difficulty completing her work to the extent that she is suspected of being ADD or ADHD. She has trouble remaining at her seat long enough to complete daily math problems—rarely does she complete her math work. During the first parent–teacher conference, Sara's parents and the teacher develop a behavior modification plan for her. If Sara takes home a completed math assignment three out of five school days, her parents will take her to a movie on Friday night. Each day before leaving school, Sara takes her math paper to her teacher to sign if it has been completed during the time period allotted for math. If this works, Sara's parents and her teacher may increase the expectation to her completing her math problems four days a week; she will then be taken to a movie and out for dinner, and so forth.

◆ **ACTIVITY**

7.28

ADD or ADHD Observation

Observe in a classroom where a child has been labeled ADD, ADHD, or learning disabled. During your observation, watch for the following:

1. How does the teacher respond to this child? Does he or she call on the child more or less often than on other children in the classroom? Does the teacher adapt instruction or the classroom environment to meet the special learning or behavioral needs of this child? For example, is the child seated where he or she will be less distracted? Has a behavior modification plan been developed for this child? Learn as much about the child as you can, but be aware of and respect privacy issues that may limit the teacher's ability to share information with you.

2. How do other children in the classroom respond to this child? Are they tolerant? Helpful?

3. Keep an anecdotal record of your observation of this child to share with your classmates. Remember to be objective and specific in recording both nonverbal and verbal behavior. It would not be helpful to say, for example, that Greg's behavior was disturbing to his classmates. Rather you should record, *Greg was tapping his pencil and kicking the desk in front of him while the other students were copying their spelling lists. The boy in front of him turned and said, "Greg you are bothering me. Please stop kicking my desk. We are supposed to be copying our spelling list."* Share your anecdotal record in class.

Summary

Primary education has always been considered fundamental to life and later learning. Recent information about the ways children learn and how they stay motivated to learn is leading to changes in primary education. Some of these changes include self-directed learning opportunities and multiage classrooms. In addition, there is a greater understanding that both work and play are important to learning during the primary grades. Those classroom practices that view children as active and empowered learners who progress at their own rates of development and pursue their own interests are responsive to this new information.

Peer relationships become increasingly important as the child is about to leave the period of early childhood. Academic success also influences the child's social and emotional development. Teachers of primary-grade children have a tremendous amount of responsibility to provide an environment that is sensitive to each child's physical, cognitive, social, and emotional needs.

REFERENCES

Aboud, F. (1988). *Children and prejudice.* New York: Basil Blackwell, Inc.

Allen, K. E. (1992). *The exceptional child: Mainstreaming in early childhood education.* Albany, NY: Delmar.

Allen, K. E., and L. Marotz (1994). *Developmental profiles: Pre-birth through eight.* Albany, NY: Delmar.

American Association of School Administrators. (1992). *The nongraded primary.* Arlington, VA: Author.

Asher, S., L. Singleton, and A. Taylor (1982). Acceptance versus friendship: A longitudinal study of racial integration. Paper presented at American Educational Research Association, New York.

Berns, K. (1994). *Topical child development.* Albany, NY: Delmar.

Black, J., M. Puckett, and M. Bell (1992). *The young child.* New York, NY: Merrill.

Campbell, B. (1992). Multiple intelligences in action. *Childhood Education, 68*(2), 197–201.

Charlesworth, R. (1992). *Understanding child development.* Albany, NY: Delmar.

Checkley, K. (1997). The first seven . . . and the eighth: A conversation with Howard Gardiner. *Educational Leadership, 55*(1), 8–13.

Cleary, B. (1955). *Beezus and Ramona.* New York: Avon Books.

Cleary, B. (1981). *Ramona Quimby, age 8.* New York: Dell Publishing.

Cole, J. D., K. A. Dodge, and H. Coppotelli (1982). Dimensions and types of social status: A cross-age perspective. *Developmental Psychology 18,* 557–570.

Copeland, R. (1988). *Piagetian activities: A diagnostic and developmental approach.* Eau Claire, WI: Thinking Publications.

Dewey, J. (1971). *The child and the curriculum: The school and society.* Chicago, IL: University of Chicago Press. (Originally published in 1915).

Elkind, D. (1990). Academic pressure—too much too soon: The demise of play. In E. Klugman and S. Smilansky, Eds., *Children's play and learning: Perspectives and policy implications* (pp. 3–17). New York: Teachers College Press.

Erikson, E. (1980). *Identity and the life cycle.* New York: W.W. Norton.

Federal Register, Part 3, December 29 1977.

Gardner, H. (1983). *Frames of mind.* New York: Basic Books.

Gardner, H. (1993). *Multiple intelligences: the theory in practice.* New York: Basic Books.

Glaser, W. (1985). *Control theory in the classroom.* New York: Harper & Row.

Goffin, S. G. (1994). *Curriculum models and early childhood education: Appraising the relationship.* New York: Merrill.

Goldhaber, J. (1994). If we call it science, *then* can we let the children play? *Childhood Education, 71*(1), 24–27.

Katz, L., D. Evangelou, and J. Hartman (1990). *The case for mixed-age groupings in early childhood ed-ucation.* Washington, DC: National Association for the Education of Young Children.

Katz, L. G., and S. Chard (1989). *Engaging children's minds: The project approach.* Norwood, NJ: Ablex.

Lamme, L. L. (1979). Handwriting in early childhood curriculum. *Young Children, 35*(1), 20–27.

Lazear, D. (1999). *Eight Ways of Teaching: The Artistry of Teaching with Multiple Intelligences.* Arlington Heights, IL: Sunlight Professional Development.

Macoby, E. E. (1990). Gender and relationships: A developmental account. *American Psychologist, 45,* 513–520

Mayer, M. (1968). *There's a nightmare in my closet.* New York: Penquin Books.

McNellis, K. L. (1987). In search of attentional deficit. In S. J. Ceci, Ed., *Handbook of cognitive, social, and neurological aspects of learning disabilities,* Vol. 2. Hillsdale, NJ: Lawrence Erlbaum Associates.

Paley, V. G. (1992). *You can't say you can't play.* Cambridge, MA: Harvard University Press.

Pavan, B. N. (1992). The benefits of nongraded schools. *Educational Leadership, 50,* 2, 22–25.

Peterson, R., and V. Felton-Collins (1986). *The Piaget handbook for teachers and parents.* New York: Teachers College Press.

Seifert, K. L., and R. J. Hoffnung (1991). *Child and adolescent development.* Boston, MA: Houghton Mifflin.

Sternberg, R. J. (1986). *Intelligence applied.* San Diego: Harcourt Brace Jovanovich.

Van Hoorn, J., P. Nourot, B. Scales, and K. Alward (1993). *Play at the center of the curriculum.* New York: Macmillan.

Wasserman, S. (1990). *Serious play in the primary classroom: Empowering children through active learning experiences.* New York: Teachers College Press.

VIDEOS ABOUT THE PRIMARY GRADES

Active Learning (1991). High Scope Press, Ypslanti, MI.

Developmentally Appropriate First Grade: A Community of Learners (1993). National Association for the Education of Young Children, Washington, DC.

Using What We Know: Applying Piaget's Theory in Primary Classroooms (1990). Davidson Films, Inc., Davis, CA.

Places to Start: Implementing the Developmental Classroom (1989). Northeast Foundation for Children, Greenfield, MA.

Chapter 8

Working with Families of Young Children

In this chapter you will read information and choose from a menu of activities to help you learn more about:

◆ Diversity in family structures

◆ How to involve parents in their children's education

◆ Family education

◆ Making home visits

◆ The role of parents as volunteers

◆ Home–school communication.

Understanding Diversity in Families

While children spend a significant amount of time in and are influenced by early childhood settings, they typically spend even more time and are influenced more by their family/home setting. Therefore, it is important for teachers to understand diversity of children and families with whom they are working. Barbour and Barbour (2001) identify at least seven different family configurations that are common in the United States today. These include the following:

• *Nuclear families* are defined as those in which parents are first-time married and the children living with them are their biological children. No other children or adults live in the household. According to the U. S. Bureau of Census (1998), only 48% of U. S. families fall into this category. Homes with legally adopted children are also included in this classification. The post-World War II *Leave it to Beaver* family consisting of a two-parent family with a breadwinner father and homemaker mother accounts for only 26% of American Families according to the Census Bureau report.

- *Extended families* are multigenerational families that resemble nuclear families but also include additional family members, usually another adult. The head of household is the wage-earning adult with young children. Extended families are less common in today's industrialized/technological society than they were when we were primarily an agrarian society. They occur most often among minority and single-parent families. Economics coupled with the presence of additional adults to provide care for children are among the advantages that people find for this family configuration.

- *Single-parent families* consist of one parent living with his or her children. This may be a result of out-of-wedlock births, death of a spouse, divorce or separation. Most often these households consist of mothers living with their children. Statistics of this group are difficult to calculate because of cohabitation of adults. Census data from 1998 indicates that approximately 26% of children now live in single-parent families. It has been estimated that, due to the rising divorce rate, more than 50% of children born after 1987 will spend part of their childhood in a single-parent home (Bianchi 1990).

- *Blended or reconstituted families* result when a single-parent, divorced or widowed person marries or remarries or when parents realign their living arrangements without marriage. Studies from the late 1990s indicate that this family structure may soon become the most common in the United States when cohabiting couples with children are included (Edin & Lein 1997; Mason 1998).

- *Adoptive families* often function as nuclear families. Some families may include children that are both biological and adopted. Adopted families may also be headed by a single parent when divorce or death occur or when a single adult chooses to adopt one or more children. Same sex families, with gay or lesbian partners, may also choose to adopt children.

- *Subfamilies* consist of a family grouping residing in another household for economic or protective reasons. The most common situation is when a young unwed mother resides with her parents or other family members. The major difference between an extended family and a subfamily results from the qualification for head-of-household tax status of the single-parent. Two or more family units living in a communal arrangement would also be considered in this family classification.

- *Other family groupings* include children with no organized family living in an institution or boarding institution that serves as a family substitute. Runaway or abandoned children who have found their own informal living arrangement would be another example.

The quality of parenting can vary within each category of family structure, but effective parenting is feasible within all of the above types of families. Other social factors regarding family background that can impact the education of young children include:

- Ethnic and cultural diversity (including language)
- Socioeconomic status
- Families with children with special needs
- Religious orientation

Parental Involvement in Education

"Parents are their children's first and most influential teachers" (U.S. Department of Education 1986, 7). Research findings that were synthesized and published by the U.S. Department of Education show the strong relationship between strong parental involvement and the academic success of their children. The importance of parenting and parent involvement in education cannot be overemphasized.

At birth and throughout infancy, survival is impossible without the nurturance and care given by an adult. Although children become increasingly less dependent on parents or other adults as they grow older, the relationship with their parents—for most children—remains important throughout childhood and life. Although no "until death do us part" vow is exchanged between parents and children, the relationship can be considered to be just that for most. Once a child, always a child. Once a parent, always a parent. Gestwicki (1992) refers to this as the "irrevocability" of parenthood.

Because becoming a parent comes easily to most humans through acts of nature, society has historically not paid much attention to preparing individuals to be parents or to valuing the potential contributions they can make in the education of their own and other children. As a result of the reports by the Department of Education, the important role of the parent has received much greater attention. In addition, the increasing number of infants, toddlers, and preschool-aged children in early childhood programs has meant an increasing need for strong parent–teacher relationships. Gestwicki (1992) points out that teachers of young children must understand the many different roles parents play to understand both the complexities of their lives and the implications those multiple roles have for any relationship with their child's teachers.

Parents as Nurturers

Although other adults may provide some of the nurturance, parents have the primary and ultimate responsibility for the physical and emotional nurturance necessary for the optimal development of each of their children, including the selection of substitute nuturers—caregivers and teachers. This nurturant role begins even before the child is born, as the mother practices good nutritional habits during prenatal development.

Parents as Participants in Adult Relationships

Most parents are extensively involved in marital or nonmarital relationships with the child's other parent before the child is born. The birth of a new child requires adaptation of this relationship. For example, if a couple participates in many social or sport activities together before the birth of the child, this level of participation may have to be modified after the child is born to provide for the child's needs. In any case, the birth of a baby means there is a change in the relationship of the adults, since another, very needy individual is involved and must be considered.

Parents as Individuals

Because Americans highly value the lifelong development of the individual, the birth of a child often causes a change in the individuality of each parent. The impact this has on each parent will vary and may be related to which of Erickson's psychosocial stages the individual is currently in. For example, if parenthood is thrust on an unwed adolescent who is still sorting through issues of self-identity, the prospect of premature parenthood can cause a significant change in direction for the adolescent's identity status. For older adults, becoming a parent might be accompanied by feelings of joy and anticipation as a dream of many years is about to come true. On the other hand, a pregnancy could be viewed as an unplanned career interruption. Caregivers and teachers of young children must be aware of each parent's individual identity in addition to his or her identity as parent of a child in the classroom.

Parents as Workers

The majority of children today live in families in which both parents work part- or full-time (Gestwicki 1992). Many parents have inflexible forty-hour work schedules that prohibit or significantly limit their participation in the educational settings of their children. Therefore, it is very important that teachers find alternative ways or times to involve all parents in their children's school experiences. In addition, it is important that teachers help parents of young children overcome the guilt and worry many of them feel because they are unable to devote more time to their children.

Parents as Consumers

Rising costs of living, including rising costs for child care, place additional stress on parents even when both are working. The cost of child care varies according to the size of the community, region of the country, age of the child, and other factors. Although many parents pay a significant portion of their income for child care, the wages and benefits paid to child-care workers and early childhood teachers remain low as compared to other occupations. Until this inequity is remedied through federal and state funding sources, caregivers and teachers must be sympathetic to the financial pressures that child care places on the budgets of parents, while at the same time continuing to advocate for an increase in their own standard of living.

Parents as Community Members

The increasing numbers of civic clubs, recreational and entertainment activities for adults and children, religious activities, and the like have resulted in additional stresses on the time, energy, and financial resources of parents. Teachers of young children can be responsive to parents as community members by assuring that parent involvement and educational events are optional, well planned, and worthwhile.

Parents as Educators

Parents serve as educators of their children as they transmit the values and knowledge of the society, culture, and community of which they are a part. In addition, parents have the responsibility to select and monitor educational settings and experiences for their children. Early childhood educators can be responsive to this parental role by providing parent education opportunities and by helping parents to understand child development and appropriate educational experiences for young children. For example, teachers can teach parents about the importance of bed time rituals and routines, help them to identify appropriate literature to read to children of different ages, and show them how ordinary household routines such as sock sorting and setting the table can be used to develop math concepts in young children.

It is also important that caregivers and teachers of young children understand the deep emotional impact of parenting. In addition to the irrevocability of parenthood (parenting is a twenty-four-hour-a-day, seven-days-a-week, 365-days-a-year job), early childhood educators must understand that parents experience many emotions, including fatigue, frustration, isolation, guilt, and insecurity in their parenting abilities, in addition to the rewards of joy, love, and pride in their children. To work effectively with young children, the early childhood educator must develop empathy for parents and skills for effective home–school relationships. We will now consider four different aspects of these important relationships: parent/family education, home visits, parent involvement/volunteers and home–school communication.

Parent/Family Education

Many parents learn parenting skills from their own or other parents. As the importance of the parenting role in school has been recognized, however, more provisions have been made for parent education programs. Gestwicki defines the term *parent education* as "specific attempts to offer knowledge and support to parents in hopes of increasing parenting effectiveness" (1992, 264). The prenatal classes provided for expectant parents are one of the earliest parent education opportunities for prospective parents. These classes offer information on proper nutrition and exercise for the expectant mother as well as information that will prepare both parents for the labor and delivery of their child. Often both mother and father participate in these classes so fathers can offer support and encouragement during the pregnancy, labor, and delivery.

Gestwicki (1992) points out the difficulty in this context of the use of the word "education," which has the connotation of the studying of formal facts or a set body of knowledge. Most parent education programs use a much broader concept of education as a dynamic interactive process that involves problem solving and discussion of issues relevant and of interest to the particular group of parents.

Some parent education program models have been developed and used for nearly two decades, including *Parent Effectiveness Training* (Thomas Gordon, 1975), *Systematic Training for Effective Parenting* (Dinkmeyer and McKay, 1982), and *Active Parenting* (Active Parenting Inc., 1982). Although these programs have had a fairly wide appeal among middle-class families, lower-income parents may feel uncomfortable with the democratic processes and group discussion procedures these models are built on (Gestwicki 1992). In addition, these and other parent education programs operate on the assumption of a deficit in parenting skills. Therefore, recent attempts at parent education have recognized the importance of matching parent education programs with parent characteristics as well as the need for egalitarian relationships between parents and leaders of parent education groups. This trend toward active involvement of parents in parent education is based on the following philosophical assumptions:

1. Parents can learn. Parenting behaviors are not always innate and can be improved and enhanced.
2. A body of knowledge on effective parenting exists. Research and studies have been able to point to parental attitudes and behaviors that are related to specific responses of children.
3. Knowledge is not enough for effective parenting. Parent education must also deal with the affective aspect of parenting—feelings and attitudes about power, authority, and so forth.
4. Parents at all socioeconomic and educational levels need to learn about the parenting role.
5. Parents care about their children and want to learn how to be effective parents.
6. Parents learn best when information is relevant and meaningful to them and their children.
7. Parents are excellent sources of information for each other. The experts are not the sole holders of useful information.
8. Parents learn in a variety of ways. Effective parent education programs must offer diverse ways of learning for parents. (Gestwicki 1992)

Parent education efforts may start out as informal gatherings in which participants get to know and trust each other and the leader or facilitator.

Parents can be involved in the planning of parent education sessions through brainstorming sessions or by responding to surveys. Information to be gathered from the survey should include convenient meeting times, interest level in proposed topics, and suggestions for other topics of interest to parents.

Minnesota provides a statewide comprehensive program of parent education opportunities through the Department of Education's Early Childhood Family Education (ECFE) division (Cooke & Engstrom 1992). Program funding for ECFE was based on a grant support concept from 1974 to 1983. In 1984 and 1987 the state legislature adopted statewide funding formulas that guaranteed equalized revenue for ECFE based on a school district's population of children under age five. ECFE programs are designed to meet the needs of families in each Minnesota community through (1) parent discussion groups, (2) play and learning activities for children, (3) parent–child activities, (4) special events for families, (5) home visits, (6) early screening for children's health and developmental problems, (7) information on other community resources for families and young children, and (8) libraries of books, toys, and other learning materials. The mission of ECFE is to strengthen families and support the ability of parents to provide optimal environments for the healthy growth and development of their children.

The positive results of parent and family education in Minnesota have been documented since its beginnings. Parent interviews conducted by Kristensen and Billman (1987) reveal self-reported improvement in self-esteem and parenting skills. One parent reported feeling better about herself as a result of participating in parent education classes because she realized that she had knowledge about being a parent she could share with others. Another interviewee reported that as a result of parent and family education she felt better about herself because she did more things with her child, listened more, and used more positive methods of discipline.

The results of a 1990 survey (Cooke & Engstrom 1992) of 183 parents involved in Minnesota ECFE programs conducted by the Minnesota Department of Education revealed five themes of change as a result of participation in ECFE programs:

1. An increased feeling of support from others, knowing they are "not alone" in their emotions and experiences and that other parents have the same problems and concerns;
2. An increased sense of confidence and self-esteem as a parent;
3. Increased knowledge, awareness, and understanding about children and child development and the parental role in relation to child development;
4. Changed perceptions and expectations for themselves as parents and for their children based on increased knowledge, awareness, and understanding about children and child development and the parental role in relation to child development; and
5. Changes in behavior based on increased feelings of support from others, increased self-confidence, increased knowledge, and changed perceptions and expectations of their children and themselves.

Some of the specific behavior changes reported by parents included:

1. Stopping to observe, listen, and think before acting with their children; moving from spontaneous reactions to situations to forethought before action in situations;
2. Becoming more understanding of a child's perspective, being more in tune with and sensitive to their children's needs and points of view;
3. Giving more time and attention to their children;
4. Giving their children more choices;
5. Encouraging their children to explore and solve problems rather than doing things for them;
6. Recognizing the need to model new behaviors;
7. Talking about and explaining situations more to their children;
8. Using redirection to guide their children's behavior;
9. Removing themselves and/or their children from tense situations for either or both to regain composure; and
10. Involving another adult when needed.

Over three-fourths of the parents also indicated a number of changes in their children as a result of participation in ECFE programs, including: improved social interaction and social skills; an increase in self-confidence and self-esteem; language development and enhanced communication skills; and greater expression of feelings.

A variety of program activities are offered several times during the day, evenings, and weekends. Program sites include schools, apartment buildings, shopping centers, homeless shelters, churches, and other community facilities throughout Minnesota. Programs work with other agencies including public schools and health and human services agencies to obtain needed services for parents and children.

Family Literacy Programs

New federal funding through part B of H.R. 6, The Improving America's Schools Act of 1994, resulted in the establishment of new family literacy programs. The purpose of these programs, according to section 1201, of the Bill is as follows:

"It is the purpose of this part to help break the cycle of poverty and illiteracy by improving the educational opportunities of the Nation's low-income families by integrating early childhood education, adult literacy or adult basic education, and parenting education into a unified family literacy program to be referred to as 'Even Start'. The program shall

(1) be implemented through cooperative projects that build on existing community resources to create a new range of services;
(2) promote the achievement of the National Education Goals; and
(3) assist children and adults from low-income families to achieve challenging State content standards and challenging State student performance standards.

Some of the requirements of programs funded under this act include:

- Provision of a schedule and location of services that allows for joint participation by parents and children.
- Provision of high-quality instructional programs to promote adult literacy and empower parents to support their child's educational growth.
- Operation on a year-round basis including instruction or enrichment during summer months.
- Coordination with programs under other parts of the Act, the Adult Education Act, the Individuals with Disabilities Act, the Job Training Act, Head Start, volunteer literacy programs, and other relevant programs.
- Assurance that the program serves those families most in need.

In some communities, there has also been a need for ESOL instruction (English for Speakers of Other Languages) for those participants whose native language is not English.

In 2001 federal funding for Even Start was increased to $250 million. This should result in establishment of more family literacy programming in the states.

New federal funding has made programs available for family literacy programs. Many of these programs incorporate the same elements of early childhood education opportunities for young children into parent/family education with literacy opportunities for adults. The adult literacy component provides opportunities for increased proficiency in language through English as a Second Language (ESL) training for non–English- or limited-English-speaking parents. While children attend preschool programming, the adults work with adult education and ESL specialists. In addition, parents must attend one parent education session weekly.

◆ **ACTIVITY**

8.1

Parent Education Activities

Contact the local hospital or health clinic to find out what types of parent education programs are provided for expectant parents. Inquire whether you could attend a session. After the session, write a brief, one- to two-page report describing your experience.

◆ **ACTIVITY**

8.2

Minnesota Early Childhood Family Initiatives

Visit the Minnesota Early Childhood and Family Initiatives website at http://clf.stats.mn.us/ecfi. Select the "publications" option on the menu at the bottom of the page. The listing of *A Good Start for Parents & Children* will enable you to watch a 13-minute on-line video about Minnesota's Early Childhood Family Education program for young children and their families. You can also find other on-line resources that may be printed out, including the *Minnesota Early Childhood Indicators of Progress* (2000) and *No Better Time: Starting Early for School Success* (2001).

◆ **ACTIVITY**

8.3

Parent Education

Explore the local community to find out about parent and family education opportunities. Attend a session, if possible. Write a brief, one- to two-page report about the session.

◆ **ACTIVITY**

8.4

Family Education Activities

Work with a small group of your classmates to plan a family activity night. Work with your instructor to identify an early childhood program that will allow your group to work with them to plan the event. The most successful activities are usually simple ones, such as bedtime story with milk and cookies, public library story hour, swimming party at the community pool, outdoor winter party, holiday event, or Oktoberfest.

◆ **ACTIVITY**

8.5

Parent Education Meeting Plan

Work with a small group to plan a parent education meeting that will last for one hour. First select an appropriate topic, such as: establishing bedtime routines, selecting literature for your child, appropriate discipline, selecting educational toys for your child, children and the media, or nutritious snacks. Research adequately before planning the meeting. Develop a time line and an outline for the activities.

◆ **ACTIVITY**

8.6

Family Literacy Websites

Visit the Even Start Website at www.evenstart.org to learn more about the national organization that promotes family literacy. In addition, you can link to many other sites from this site. To access a list of sites that support family literacy, including links to Children's Television Workshop, At-Home Dad Newsletter, and Family.com, follow these instructions:

- From the Evenstart homepage, click on research links;
- From the Research links page, click on parent links.

Print out the list of links and as a class select different sites to review. Summarize and share the type of information available at the site you reviewed.

Home Visits

Visiting a child's home is an effective way for a teacher to form a good relationship with a child and his or her family. Although the role of the home visitor in early childhood programs is a complex one with limited research evidence to support it, home visits offer an opportunity to individualize encounters with families and to meet the needs and characteristics of each (Powell 1990).

Teachers demonstrate respect for families and concern for each child by making home visits. Early childhood educators can use home visits in a number of ways. First, they can serve as an initial introduction to the parents. Second, visits to the family can be a way to find out more about a child or to work out a plan for a child who is having some kind of difficulty in the child care or school setting. Third, in some programs making home visits may be the primary method of delivering services such as respite care for parents of special needs children. In many programs, such as some nursery schools or Head Start, teachers are mandated to make home visits.

Johnston and Mermin (1994) suggest that a twenty- to thirty-minute visit to a child's home before he or she enters an early childhood program can be beneficial to the child, the parents, and the teacher. The child has an opportunity to become familiar with the teacher in a nonthreatening environment and any anxieties about the first few days of school are lessened because he or she already knows at least one person, the teacher. Teachers also get to know each child as an individual. They can obtain information about the child's favorite activities or toys at home that can aid in planning for that child in the classroom. Parents generally appreciate the time taken and the effort made by the teacher to get to know their child. While the teacher spends most of the visit playing or talking with the child, the parents can be asked to fill out a short questionnaire in which they can express their feelings about their child going into a group care or school situation and also give additional information about their child. Teachers may need time to listen to or respond to parents' concerns.

Teachers can also learn about the circumstances in which children are being raised by making home visits. For example, knowing that many of the children in the class live in crowded, urban apartments with few opportunities for learning physical skills may help the teacher plan appropriate gym and playground activities for children. Or children who live in rural areas or have no siblings may need help learning to play together.

Children who are having problems adjusting in an out-of-home setting could also benefit from a home visit. A toddler could be having difficulty separating from parents, a preschooler may be exhibiting aggressive behavior, or a first grader may seem depressed and withdrawn. All of these would be valid reasons for a home visit. For many parents this is a unique opportunity to meet privately and personally with a professional to discuss their child (Kostelnik *et al.* 1993). Often the teacher and parents can work together to create a plan to help the child feel more content or function more appropriately in the group. Sometimes neither teacher nor parents can meet all of a child's needs, in which case the teacher may be able to make a referral. Teachers should be familiar with other community services to recommend to families (Eliason & Jenkins 1990).

In some early childhood programs teachers work primarily in children's homes. For example, most children under age three with physical or mental handicaps are visited in their homes. For children this age the home is considered "the least restrictive environment." Case managers offer support to parents and help them find the kinds of services they seek for their child.

Some Head Start programs are home-based because parents are seen as "the primary factor in a child's development and the home as the central facility" (*Federal Register* 1975). Home-based programs are especially prevalent in rural areas, where transportation to centers might be difficult to arrange. Such programs must offer the same range of services that center-based programs offer, such as nutrition education, health services, early childhood curriculum, social services, and so forth.

Other programs and schools have a home-visiting component, usually made up of a social worker or trained paraprofessionals. Their job is to provide a liaison between the home and the school. They maintain regular contact with the family, interpret for them what the school requires, and offer practical help such as arranging babysitting, a translator, or transportation to school functions. Having home visitors working in conjunction with a program can be beneficial for all, but it is not a substitute for the teachers' home visits.

Johnston and Mermin (1994) offer practical tips for making home visits and explain why it is important for even the busiest teachers with the largest classroom enrollments to make them. For parents who object to home visits they suggest that some neutral place such as a park, coffee shop, or community center be found. Teachers in child-care programs can be given compensatory time or overtime pay for making home visits (Billman 1993). Schools could hire substitutes so teachers would have the flexibility and time to visit each child's family. However, evenings and weekends may be the only time working parents can schedule a visit.

◆ **ACTIVITY**

8.7

Role-Playing a Home Visit

With two to five classmates playing the roles of teacher, child, parents, or siblings, act out an initial home visit to the family home of a child who will be enrolling in your classroom in the next month. Try several scenarios—the child is shy and will not talk, siblings demand your attention, the mother wants to talk about her own problems, or the father would rather watch baseball on TV, for example. Imagine how the teacher should handle these situations.

◆ **ACTIVITY**

8.8

Making Home Visits
(Student Teachers and Advanced Students)

As a class, establish guidelines for home visits. The following suggestions are simply to get you started:

1. Establish well-stated reasons for each visit.
2. Let the parents know why you are coming and what you expect to do on your visit.
3. Try to find a time that suits both you and the parents.
4. Start and end your visit at the times you have agreed on with the family. Try to keep visits to thirty to forty minutes.

5. Be sensitive to families' cultural and language background. Engage an interpreter if necessary.
6. Keep the focus on the child as much as possible; do not be distracted by other family members' problems.
7. Find something else for siblings to do (such as draw a picture or model with clay) while you interact with the child in your class.

Consult with a teacher and choose three children to visit at home. Write a one-page report after each visit, discussing what you learned about each child. This report will be included in the child's folder and can be read by other professionals as well as by his or her parents. If you want to share information from home visits with your classmates remember that confidentiality must be maintained. All references to names and other identifying information must be deleted from discussions.

◆ **ACTIVITY**
8.9

Home Visit
(Student Teacher or Advanced Student)

Accompany an early childhood or special educator as he or she visits the home of a child under the age of three. Find out as much as you can by talking to the teacher before the visit. After your visit, write a one-page report, considering the following questions:

1. What is the relationship between the parent(s) and the teacher like?
2. Were there certain tasks or behaviors the child was expected to perform? How appropriate did you find these for the child's age and condition?
3. What did you learn about the family from observing the physical aspects of their home?
4. What additional information did you learn about the child from listening to the parent(s) and teacher?

Parent Involvement/Volunteers

Parental Support of the Program

Berger (2000) identified six types of typical roles that parents may assume in their child's educational setting. These include:

- Parents as teachers of their own children
- Parents as spectators
- Parents as temporary volunteers
- Parents as volunteer resources
- Parents as employed resources
- Parents as policy makers

Parents may be involved in more than one of these ways. It is important for teachers to build on the strengths of the parents of their students. It is often helpful to survey parents at the beginning of the year to determine their interests in becoming involved in their child's education. (See activity 8.11.)

Parents can be enlisted to assume some ownership of the early childhood program. Involving parents as policy makers, volunteers in the classroom, or assistants on special projects not only strengthens the program, it enables parents to see themselves as effective adults able to have an impact on what happens to their children. A parent serving on a center board or in a parent–teacher organization, helping a teacher prepare a classroom display, accompanying a class trip, or repairing equipment lets the young child see his or her parent in a new light. Young children are delighted to have their parents come to school with them. Parents should be given credit and recognition for any contribution to the program.

Through visits and participation in the center or school parents also learn more about the program their child is in. Often, they become advocates for the program. Satisfied parents are the center's or school's best form of public relations.

Early childhood students and teachers must learn how to involve parents in the care and education of young children. Having a family-friendly enrollment process is the first step, since the family's initial contact with the school can set the tone for any potential interest in involvement. The director or principal must establish procedures and training for all staff to ensure that families are welcome and their needs for information and support are met.

Teachers must forge mutually trusting relationships with each parent. When parents bring their young child to the center or school, it is with the

◆ *The help of parents or other volunteers in general teaching tasks allows the teacher to individualize instruction for young children.*

understanding that teachers will do everything they can to meet the child's education and care needs and will keep parents informed about what is happening with the child while he or she is in their care. Parents must feel that, at the very least, no harm—physical or psychological—will come to their child while he or she is at the center or school. At the same time, teachers must trust that even though parents have complex lives with many employment-related demands on their time and energy, they are trying to be good parents and want what is best for their children.

In programs for young children, parents are increasingly seen as an integral component (Galinsky & Weissbourd 1992). The terms "parent education" and "parent involvement" are being supplanted by the concept of "family-centered care," in which adults' needs, as well as the needs of children, are being met. The center or school becomes a community center that is linked to social service providers. Parents become active participants in designing and delivering services.

While the family-support approach retains much that is good in the parent-involvement model, such as the importance of frequent communication between teachers and parents, it goes farther and emphasizes some of the following principles.

1. Prevention is seen as a key to promoting the health and well-being of the family. Concentrating on the strengths of the family, rather than on its weaknesses, is seen as the way to preserve the parents' self esteem and increase opportunities for growth and change.
2. Parents' knowledge, resources, and history shape who they are as parents.
3. Child-rearing techniques reflect cultural, individual, and community values to which professionals must be sensitive.
4. Family health and well-being are dependent on social support networks.
5. Parents need information about children's developmental needs to fulfill their parenting role adequately.
6. Parents who are supported by schools and other agencies are empowered to become advocates for their own children and for themselves. (Galinsky & Weissbourd 1992).

Teachers can show respect for families in many ways. Never undermining a parent's sense of competence, giving encouragement for the difficult tasks of parenting, scheduling meetings or conferences that meet the needs of busy parents, making the center or school a welcoming place, and setting up peer support groups are some ways to help parents. Inviting and responding to their ideas about program policies, openly listening to them discuss their child, and trying to honestly address their concerns are other ways teachers can promote good teacher–parent relationships. Teachers must also realize that some parents will not welcome any but the most superficial involvement with the center or school staff. The attitudes of both the parents and the teachers are crucial to the formation of a family-centered approach (Kontos & Wells 1986; Galinsky *et al.* 1990).

Valuable methods of involving parents in the educational process of their children can include allowing parents to work directly in their child's classroom on a regular basis; make occasional visits to their child's classroom to participate in special events; observe in their child's classroom; or serve as resources for information or preparing materials.

Providing guidelines for and planning the work of parent volunteers in the classroom can ensure a positive experience for parents, teachers, and children. If parents are working in a classroom, they need guidelines so they know what is expected of them during the time they will be there. Preparing a list of tasks for them to do while they are there will make them feel they are needed and that their time is being well spent.

Berger (2000) points out that parents and other volunteers can perform both teaching and nonteaching tasks or make contributions from home. It is important to establish the comfort level of the parents or volunteers in performing the task and to provide a variety of volunteer activities. Some volunteers may feel comfortable performing several types of tasks while others may have a preference for one kind of task. Specific examples for each type of volunteer tasks might include:

Teaching Tasks

- Tutoring individual children
- Listening to students read or dictate stories
- Reading/telling stories to children
- Assisting with selection of library books
- Playing games, assisting in learning centers, or working with a small group of children
- Speaking on a hobby, travel, or occupation

Nonteaching Tasks

- Reproducing instructional materials
- Clerical tasks of grading, recording, attendance, lunch money, book orders
- Organizing cupboards, files , shelves
- Preparing and/or displaying a bulletin board
- Helping with book publishing, laminating, etc.

At-Home Tasks

- Making telephone calls to recruit field trip supervisors, treats for parties, etc.
- Making/soliciting items for dramatic play, art aprons, etc.
- Making instructional games, etc.
- Writing/typing a newsletter, designing a classroom website, etc.
- Caring for children of another parent or volunteer
- Coordinating volunteers

Nonparental volunteers can also make an important contribution to early childhood education settings. High school or college students, grandparents, senior citizens, and others may have extra time and energy that can benefit both children and teachers. Early childhood educators should communicate to volunteers any expectations they have for the children the volunteers will be working with. A set of general guidelines for parents and volunteers working in the classroom can be developed and posted so expectations for children are clear and consistently communicated. In addition, it can be helpful to develop and post guidelines in different activity areas of the early childhood classroom so volunteers and parents know specific expectations for children using materials in each area. For example, in the block area, posted guidelines might state:

1. Children should wear hard hats when building with blocks.
2. Block structures should be limited to approximately the child's shoulder height.
3. Blocks should be carefully unstacked rather than knocked down and then returned to the shelf.
4. Children may use carpet squares to define their building areas.
5. Gently repeat the rules for children who tend to forget.
6. Redirect children to another activity area if they refuse to follow the rules.

It is important to state the guidelines positively and concisely. The guidelines can serve another purpose by modeling appropriate expectations and communication strategies for parents.

◆ **ACTIVITY**
8.10

Activities for Volunteers

With a small group, brainstorm a list of teaching and nonteaching activities that parents or other volunteers could be involved in.

◆ **ACTIVITY**
8.11

Parent Involvement Survey

Develop a parent survey to determine ways in which parents could be involved in and contribute to the classroom. Use the list of teaching, nonteaching and at-home tasks for volunteers that are provided on page 222 of this chapter to get you started. Be sure to design the survey to include times parents are available and how they may be contacted.

◆ **ACTIVITY**
8.12

Volunteer Guidelines

Develop a set of guidelines for classroom volunteers so clear and consistent expectations are maintained for children by all who work with them. State the guidelines positively and concisely; for example: "Remind children to walk and to use inside voices in the classroom."

◆ ACTIVITY
8.13 *Volunteer Observation*
Observe in an infant or toddler program, preschool setting, kindergarten, or primary grade classroom. Focus on one area of the room and develop a set of volunteer guidelines for that area—the diapering area, playground, art area, or computer area, for example.

Home–School Communication

Communication between the parent and the early childhood setting is vital. Parents of infants, toddlers, and preschoolers are especially eager to know what their child has been doing during the time they are apart. For infants and toddlers, there is a particular need for daily oral or written caregiver–parent communication, since these very young children are unable to communicate for themselves. At the same time, parents must provide caregivers with information concerning any special needs their child might have during the day. For example, if a parent notes that an infant has not been maintaining the same sleeping or eating pattern, it is important to communicate that to the caregiver.

Oral Communication

It is essential for the early childhood caregiver and parents to develop positive oral communication. The following patterns tend to foster such interactions between teachers and parents:

1. Teachers should be available to communicate with parents during drop-off and pick-up times.
2. Parents are more secure and positive when they feel their child is noticed and welcomed.
3. Clear, established policies requiring parents of infants, toddlers, and preschoolers to bring their children into the classroom must be established. A sign-in/-out policy and desk can facilitate this.
4. The caregiver should communicate an interest in the parent as an individual.
5. Alternative times to talk for parents who need to talk with someone or who have concerns that should not be discussed in front of the child are useful.

Many early childhood centers and most public schools hold regularly scheduled conferences one to three times per year. Having successful conferences hinges on careful planning. The following are suggestions for ensuring successful conferences.

1. Remember that parents are the true experts on their child. They can lead you to greater understanding of the child if you approach the conference with that in mind.

2. Preconference preparation is the most important step. This might include some of the following procedures:
   a. Send notices stating purpose, schedule, and place. Offer parents a choice of times, if possible.
   b. Prepare portfolios of student work including samples of written work and art, photos of class projects, audio-recordings of the child reading or giving a brief report, or a videotape of a special project or activity.
   c. Plan a brief agenda or list of topics to be covered during the conference, allowing for input from the parents.
   d. Arrange comfortable, interesting environments for both waiting and the conference (coffee, reading materials, class scrapbook, seating arrangement that places parent and teacher on an equal basis).
   e. Eliminate interruptions by posting the schedule outside the door, maintaining the schedule, and refusing phone calls.

3. During the conference:
   a. Welcome parents by walking to the door and greeting them by name.
   b. Begin and end on a positive note.
   c. Provide an opportunity for parents to share information by asking questions and listening.
   d. Summarize at the end of the conference.
   e. Remind parents when time is up and that other parents are waiting.
   f. Walk parents to the door and thank them for coming.

4. Make note of steps or actions to be taken and timelines set. (For example, teacher will send home weekly notice on child's progress in completion of work. Parents will ask children daily about work completion. Schedule another conference in one month).

5. If a conflict arises during the conference, try to remedy the situation with the parent. If this fails, gently bring the conference to an end and suggest that you meet in the future when you have more time to discuss the issue. Let children of parents with whom there has been a conflict know that everything is the same in your relationship with them through your actions, without directly discussing the conflict with the child.

Occasionally, teachers and parents may have difficulty communicating with one another. When conflict arises, immediate steps must be taken to resolve the conflict for the benefit of all. Kostelnik *et al.* (1993, 441–450) provide "Skills for Working with Parents," helpful tips for forming an effective partnership with parents. Their advice about conflict resolution is to keep it as positive as possible. Compromising whenever possible, always showing respect for parents no matter how negative they are, finding areas of agreement, listening, and reflecting back what the parent is saying are ways to elicit the parents' ideas and feelings. The teacher can then briefly explain his or her own position and what he or she wants the parent to do. If irreconcilable differences remain, another meeting can be set up with a mutually agreed-on third party, who could mediate the situation.

Telecommunication systems are an important oral communication tool. Some early childhood centers and school districts have established electronic voice mail systems to enable parents and teachers to leave each other messages. Teachers may use the voice mail to communicate about the curriculum, remind parents of needed classroom supplies, or relay assignments to students who were absent. In our increasingly complex society, telecommunications can serve to lessen the paper blizzard and save not only time, but a tree or two.

Written Communication

Teachers still need to give parents many types of written messages in addition to the oral communication that occurs. These may include, but are not limited to, the following.

1. Daily written messages. Teachers in infant and toddler groups in many states are required to give parents a daily record for each child, which includes information about eating, bodily functions, sleeping, and developmental milestones (Billman 1993). Parents of older children would also enjoy getting an occasional note from the teacher about something positive their child did that day.

2. A handbook containing the school's or center's policies and a statement of the program's philosophy and program goals.

3. A newsletter outlining upcoming events and information of interest to parents to be sent to parents at regular intervals (see Figure 8.1 on page 227).

4. A calendar of the school, center, or classroom's year, including scheduled events.

5. A bulletin board with notices for parents. This can also be a place parents can leave event-related messages for other parents.

6. Other written messages. Teachers can send notes to specific parents to share information about their child, to report any injuries or illnesses the child experienced, or to set up a conference appointment. Teachers can keep a notebook at the entrance to the room so parents can leave messages for them when they are busy or not there. Relaying information about a fever the child had over the weekend or explaining that the family will be away for the next two weeks would also be helpful information to relay.

◆ **FIGURE 8.1** *Format for a Parent Newsletter*

Kindergarten Post

Issue 1   Kinder Press Inc.   February, 1993

Notes From Mr. J

Announcements & Activities

Suggested Parent/Child Activities

Songs & Fingerplays

Family News

Lost and Found

Recipes

Shorts
(Short Quotations)

Thanks to:

Calling All Parents (Requests)

Times
of
Celebration

Children's Suggested Reading

Adult Reading

Children's Work

Source: Eric Johnson, Winona State University, Rochester, MN. Reprinted with permission.

◆ *Transportation plans for getting young children to and from school safely must be carefully worked out through communication between parents and school officials.*

7. A brief form that parents can fill out once or twice a year can help staff pinpoint any areas that need more thought and work. Evaluative feedback from parents about the program or classroom experiences they and their children have had can be helpful in monitoring and improving services to families. Often this kind of information is also helpful to administrators.

◆ **ACTIVITY**
8.14

Role-Play Parental Interaction

In a small group role-play interacting with parents as they drop off or pick up their children. Demonstrate use of the oral communication patterns suggested in this chapter.

◆ **ACTIVITY**
8.15

Role-Play a Parent Conference

In a small group, role-play parent conferences for a preschool, kindergarten, and primary-grade child. Demonstrate understanding of the steps suggested in this chapter.

◆ **ACTIVITY**
8.16

Role-Play a Conflict

Role-play a parent–teacher interaction that results in conflict. Demonstrate understanding of the suggestions for ending the conversation or conference and resolution of the conflict. Include role-play of your interactions in the classroom with the child on the "day after" the conflict with the parent.

◆ **ACTIVITY**
8.17

Parents' Bulletin Board

Sketch a design for a parent bulletin board. Make a list of ways to easily change the board each month.

◆ **ACTIVITY**
8.18

Create a Newsletter

Design a format for a newsletter that can be used on a regular basis to inform parents about the classroom. (See Figure 8.1 for an example.) Think of other categories of information you would like to include in your outline.

◆ **ACTIVITY**
8.19

Activity Calendar

Work with a partner to design an activity calendar for at-home activities parents can do with their children. Select a particular age group and month to target in designing your calendar.

Parent Meetings/Orientations/ Open Houses

A variety of meetings with parents, children, and early childhood educators can be planned as a means of building closer relationships and greater understanding between the school and home settings. These may include meetings for parents to learn about their child's school or meetings with both parents and children to experience or celebrate school activities. Parent meetings have higher attendance rates when young children are included. "Parents will come to watch their children perform even if they only sing a few songs. If invited, grandparents, close friends, and neighbors will come too" (Billman 1993, 180). Because the majority of young children have working parents, any meeting that involves a meal is usually well attended. Meetings should be kept short and parents should have input into the agenda or can even be responsible for planning the meetings.

Teachers will want to have some time to talk to groups of parents about what will happen in the classroom. An orientation to the teacher's curriculum and philosophy and how it will be carried out should be explained to parents early in the school year. Visiting the classroom also gives parents a basis for talking about school with their child. If teachers need to talk to just the parents, the center or school should arrange alternative activities for the children during this time.

In public school settings, it is often customary to hold parent–child orientation events. At the kindergarten level, this might include a kindergarten round-up that involves registration of children and an informational meeting for parents as well as activities planned for children in the kindergarten class-room. Some kindergarten orientation programs even involve parents and children riding the big yellow school bus together.

At these types of meetings or open houses for all age levels, teachers often present a brief overview of the philosophy of the program and class-room management policies. A sample agenda for a first-grade fall parent in-formation night might include:

1. Who is my child's teacher?
2. What other specialty area teachers work with us?
3. What is our daily/weekly schedule?
4. What trips will we take?
5. What about snacks, birthdays, and other special activities?
6. How will we communicate this year?
7. What are the goals and curricular expectations for first grade?
8. How can parents be involved as volunteers?

Sometimes parents and children come together and participate in class-room activities to help parents understand the kinds of learning activities their child will be experiencing. These events can enhance parental under-standing and foster strong parent–teacher–child relationships.

◆ **ACTIVITY**
8.20

Initial Contact with Parents

With a partner set up a procedure for office and teaching staff for making families welcome at the center or school. This may include, for example, a telephone script for answering parents' requests for information about the program. Also design a procedure for families who come in person to enroll their young children.

◆ **ACTIVITY**
8.21

Parental Evaluation of the Program

In a small group of three or four students prepare a one- or two-page form with which parents can evaluate how the program meets or does not meet their needs or those of their children. Make it easy to fill out, and provide room for written comments.

◆ **ACTIVITY**
8.22

Plan the First Family Meeting

With a partner, plan an evening meeting for the families of children in a preschool or primary classroom. What activities will you include that the whole family can enjoy? What will you tell them about your philosophy and curriculum for this class? Will the children perform? What will you serve as refreshments, if anything? How will parents be involved in planning for this meeting? How long will the meeting last?

◆ **ACTIVITY**

8.23

Plan a Kindergarten Orientation

With a partner, plan a kindergarten round-up or orientation that lasts for one to one-and-a-half hours. Plan a timeline that shows how parents and children will spend the time together and apart. Be specific in your plan. What story will you read to the children? What activities will you provide for them (remember to keep them simple)? Will you provide nametags? Will you develop a theme for the event? How will you integrate the theme into the activities?

◆ **ACTIVITY**

8.24

Parental Thank You

As a class, brainstorm a list of inexpensive ways to thank parents for their contributions to the center or school.

Summary

As the first teachers of their children, parents can be invaluable resources to early childhood educators. While becoming a parent comes "naturally," parenting skills do not. There is now a greater recognition of the importance of good parenting skills during the early childhood years and throughout life.

Boyer (1991) suggests seven steps to ensure that children arrive at public schools ready to learn. The seven steps include:

1. A healthy start
2. Empowered parents
3. Quality preschool
4. A responsive workplace
5. Television as teacher
6. Neighborhoods for learning
7. Connections across the generations.

While "empowered parents" is listed separately, careful thought about the list reveals that parents and families are at the heart of all seven steps. For example, a healthy start depends on prenatal care and good nutrition by the mother as well as clear health and nutrition provisions for the child after birth. Valuing families is at the heart of early childhood education.

REFERENCES

Active Parenting, Inc. (1982) *Active parenting.* Atlanta, GA.

Barbour, C., and Barbour, N. H. (2001). *Families, Schools and Communities: Building Partnerships for Educating Children.* Upper Saddle River, NJ: Prentice Hall.

Berger, E. H. (1987). *Parents as Partners in Education: The school and home working together.* Columbus, OH: Merrill.

Berger, E. H. (2000). *Parents as Partners in Education.* Upper Saddle River, NJ: Merrill/Prentice Hall.

Bianchi, S. M. (1990). America's children: Missed prospects. *Population Bulletin, 45*(1), 7–10.

Billman, J. (1993). *Starting and operating a child care center*. Dubuque, IA: Brown and Benchmark.

Boyer, E. L. (1991). *Ready to learn: A mandate for the nation*. Princeton, NJ: The Carnegie Foundation for the Advancement of Teaching.

Cooke, B., and L. Engstrom (1992). *Changing times, changing families.* St. Paul, MN: Minnesota Department of Education.

Dinkmeyer, D., and G. McKay (1982). *The parents' handbook: STEP*. Circle Pines, MN: American Guidance Service.

Edin, K., and L. Lein (1997). *Making ends meet: How single mothers survive welfare and low wages*. New York: Russell Sage Foundation.

Eliason, C., and L. Jenkins (1990). *A practical guide to early childhood curriculum*. New York: Macmillan.

Evenstart Website (July 2001) @evenstart.org

Federal Register (Monday, June 30 1975). Appendix A—Program Options for Project Head Start.

Galinsky, E., B. Shinn, D. Phillips, C. Howes, and M. Whitebook (1990). *The parent/teacher study*. New York: Families and Work Institute.

Galinsky, E., and B. Weissbourd (1992). Family-centered child care. In B. Spodek and O. Saracho, Eds., *Issues in child care*. New York: Teachers College Press.

Gestwicki, C. (1992). *Home, school and community relations: A guide to working with parents*. Albany, NY: Delmar.

Gordon, T. (1975). *Parent effectiveness training*. New York, NY: Wyden.

Johnston, L., and J. Mermin (1994). Easing children's entry to school: Home visits help. *Young Children, 49*(5), 62–68.

Kontos, S., and W. Wells (1986). Attitudes of caregivers and the day care experiences of families. *Early Childhood Research Quarterly, 1*(1), 47–67.

Kostelnik, M. J., L. C. Stein, A. P. Whiren, and A. K. Soderman (1993). *Guiding children's social development* (2nd ed.). Albany, NY: Delmar.

Kristensen, N., and J. Billman (1987). Supporting parents and young children: Minnesota Early Childhood Family Education Program. *Childhood Education, 63*(4), 276–282.

Mason, M. A. (1998). The modern American stepfamily: Problems and possibilities. In M. A. Mason, A. Skolnick, & S. D. Sugarman (Eds.), *All our families: New Policies for a new century* (pp. 95–116). New York: Oxford University Press.

Powell, D. R. (1990). Home visiting in the early years: Policy and program design decisions. *Young Children, 45*(6), 65–73.

U.S. Bureau of the Census (1998). *Current Population Report: P20-497-1998*. Washington, DC: Author.

U.S. Department of Education. (1986). *What works: Research about teaching and learning*. Washington, DC: U.S. Department of Education.

◆◆ Chapter 9

Curriculum and the Young Child

In this chapter you will read information and choose from a menu of activities to help you learn more about:

◆ The components of curriculum
◆ Different curriculum models
◆ Literacy development
◆ Activities to help you understand different approaches to teaching and learning in early childhood settings

What Is Curriculum?

Observations of young children and participation in their activities serve to inform and shape the curriculum teachers develop. Curriculum for young children includes everything that happens in the early childhood setting. It encompasses all parts of the day, from arrival to departure, and attends to all aspects of the child's development—physical, cognitive, social, and emotional, as well as structured and unstructured activities. Curriculum decisions concern the hours of the program, the ages of the children involved, and group size parameters. Curriculum involves responding to questions such as:

How much time is allotted for play?
When and in what way are snacks offered?
How are health and physical needs met?
How much teacher direction and planning are necessary?
What kinds of materials are safe and beneficial for children of this age?
  How many sets of materials do I need? How and when should children use the materials?
How do I feel about children working and playing together?

How do I ensure that the environment is arranged and maintained so that it is both safe and interesting for children?

What kinds of rules are needed to assure the safety, well-being, and benefit of all children in the program?

What do I think children need to spend their time doing? What do others to whom I must answer (parents, boards, supervisors, etc.) think children should spend their time doing?

The physical and social environments of the classroom are part of the curriculum, as teachers equip and organize the environment to meet the needs of young children and to interact with them both formally and informally. Routines, climate, and expectations teachers set for children interacting with each other are also part of the curriculum.

In previous chapters we discussed the development of young children at various stages of early childhood and curriculum as it specifically related to developmental characteristics of children during those stages (infancy, toddlerhood, the preschool years, kindergarten, and the primary grades years). In this chapter we will more fully consider how to plan curriculum for children at these stages within the period of life that we call early childhood. When considering appropriate curriculum for each specific age period, it is important to engage in a discussion of curriculum models that have helped to shape the early childhood education field and new curriculum models that are being advocated.

Early Childhood Curriculum Models

A curriculum model is defined as a framework for decision making about the educational goals, curriculum content, and methods used in instruction and evaluation that may be replicated or adapted by others (Goffin 1994; Spodek & Saracho 1994). For instance, refer to the example in Chapter 7 of how the High Scope Curriculum Model has been adapted and modified by a first grade teacher in the Plan–Do–Review process used for self-directed learning. In replicating or adapting curriculum models, teachers must ask themselves several important questions:

1. Are my educational goals for children the same as the curriculum model that I am implementing?
2. Does this curriculum model meet the developmental and educational needs of the population of children and families I am working with?
3. Is the content of the curriculum model suitable for the cultural and environmental circumstances of this educational setting? For example, does it make more sense to study polar bears or sea turtles as an example of an endangered species if the educational setting is in Hawaii?
4. Does the curriculum model that I am using represent the best and most current information known about developmental theory and educational theory?

In the preface of Goffin's *Curriculum Models and Early Childhood* (1994), Lilian Katz addresses the dilemma the book presents regarding the adoption of curriculum models that could result in standardizing early childhood curriculum and that might not be responsive to the specific educational setting. Katz proposes that the dilemma might be resolved by teachers adopting general "principles of practice" that still allow for the creativity and innovation of well-trained and experienced professionals. She further suggests that professional organizations such as the National Association for the Education of Young Children (NAEYC) and the Association for Childhood Education International (ACEI) must play an important role in articulating the continuing development and refinement of the general principles of sound early childhood educational practice.

According to Goffin (1994), curriculum models have changed and been influenced by societal expectations for early childhood education at various points in history. Therefore, the five curriculum models that will be briefly discussed here are presented in chronological order of development.

Froebel's Kindergarten Gifts and Occupations

Friedrich Froebel's (1782–1852) methods of kindergarten education, which were transported to the United States from Germany, are recognized as the first early childhood education curriculum model. Although Froebel stressed the importance of play in the young child's learning, his methods of art activities, crafts, games, finger puppet plays, and songs, were called *occupations* and were carefully structured and programmed. Specific occupations included activities of perforating, stitching, drawing, paper twisting, weaving, paper cutting, paper folding, and clay modeling. Froebel also developed specific materials known as *gifts*. The ten gifts Froebel developed are illustrated in Figure 9.1 on page 236. Materials and activities that are adaptations of Froebel's gifts and occupations curriculum model can still be found in many early childhood classrooms today.

◆ **ACTIVITY**

9.1

Froebelian Occupations and Gifts

Observe in a kindergarten classroom. Make a list of the materials and activities that are reminiscent of the Froebelian kindergarten occupations and gifts depicted in Figure 9.1 on page 236.

The Montessori Method

The methods and materials of Maria Montessori (1870–1952) were transported to the United States from Rome early in the 1900s, a time when there was considerable discontent with Froebel's methods (Goffin 1994). Initially

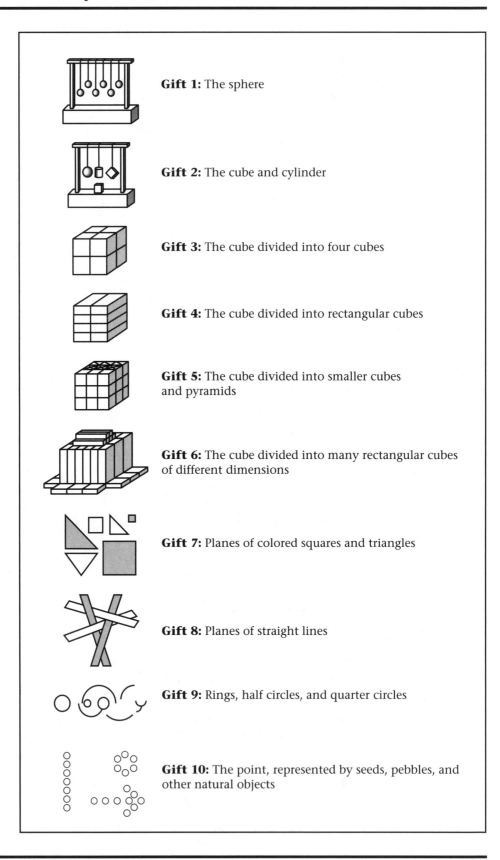

Gift 1: The sphere

Gift 2: The cube and cylinder

Gift 3: The cube divided into four cubes

Gift 4: The cube divided into rectangular cubes

Gift 5: The cube divided into smaller cubes and pyramids

Gift 6: The cube divided into many rectangular cubes of different dimensions

Gift 7: Planes of colored squares and triangles

Gift 8: Planes of straight lines

Gift 9: Rings, half circles, and quarter circles

Gift 10: The point, represented by seeds, pebbles, and other natural objects

Source: *Froebel's Gifts* by Watertown Historical Society. Reprinted with permission.

developed to meet the needs of children who were mentally retarded or economically depressed, Montessori's methods were quickly adopted by those working with "normal" and more affluent children as well. As a result, some of the comprehensive components of this approach, including child nutrition and family support, received less emphasis, and there was a shift of focus in the materials and methods Montessori developed and used. The programmed materials, sequenced lessons, and carefully prepared environment have become the trademarks of Montessori education. Some of Montessori's greatest contributions—understanding how young children learn and the importance of linkages between child, family, and school—have received less emphasis as her work has been interpreted and implemented by others.

The Montessori curriculum for young children is organized around daily living activities, sensorial activities, and academic/conceptual activities. Materials are organized in specific areas of the classroom and children are carefully instructed in how to use and care for them. There is a high regard for order and organization in the Montessori classroom. Daily living activities include pouring, cutting, sweeping, washing, and other activities that teach children self-help skills and skills for caring for their surroundings. Visitors to a Montessori classroom might be surprised to see young children using real knives for cutting or electric irons for ironing. Sensorial activities help children develop and organize their learning through sight, sound, taste, touch, and smell. Activities in this area might include organizing colors from the lightest to the darkest shade or playing with a set of tone bells. Academic/conceptual activities include using sandpaper letters to learn the alphabet in cursive, using songs about and models of land formations and globes to study geography, or using Montessori Golden beads to learn about the decimal system. Materials in this area are designed to be self-correcting.

In many Montessori classrooms you will note the absence of materials to promote fantasy play or creative art. In addition, some Montessori settings limit the use of materials for discovery or imaginative play. For example, if a set of materials includes plastic animals, pictures of the animals, and animal name cards for matching, the child might be expected to use the materials in matching activities only and would be discouraged or prohibited from using the animals for imaginative play or for other purposes. The Montessori teacher might approach the child who was using these materials for such play and ask "How do we do this work?"

From the beginning, Montessori's methods were not embraced by many early childhood professionals who felt that:

1. The methods were too limiting of children's self-expression and creativity;
2. The methods lacked promotion of children's natural initiative and problem-solving capabilities;
3. The methods were insufficient in providing for each young child's social and emotional needs;
4. The teacher played too passive a role, particularly in contrast to the Froebelian method, which emphasized teacher-directed activities; and

5. The dissemination of Montessori materials was limited to one manufacturer who was able to sell the materials at premium prices, and Montessori teacher training was authorized and supervised solely by the Association Montessori Internationale.

Despite these criticisms and concerns, the Montessori method has withstood the test of time and remains an attractive schooling option (Chattin-McNichols 1992). The Montessori approach is currently being offered as an elementary school alternative for parents and children through magnet schools in larger school districts. In a few metropolitan areas that option exists up through the high school years.

◆ **ACTIVITY**
9.2

Montessori Classroom

Observe in a Montessori preschool classroom. Make a list and drawings of some of the materials in each of the designated areas of the classroom and diagram the identified areas of the room. Then visit a non-Montessori preschool to look specifically for materials designed like the Montessori materials you observed. Make a drawing of this preschool room as well. Compare the similarities and differences in the curricula of the two preschool classrooms. Does the non-Montessori classroom seem to embrace the philosophy of one of the other curriculum models described in this chapter? Which one? Give reasons to support your decision. Visit the Montessori Website @ www.montessori.org to enhance your experience with this activity. Click on the *Montessori Schools* button for help in locating Montessori schools in your area. Click on the *Montessori Teacher Education* button for help in finding out about availability of training in your state. Articles about Montessori Education and information about Montessori materials can also be found at this website.

The Bank Street Approach/ Developmental–Interactionist Model

The Bank Street Approach, which got its name from its association with the Bank Street College of Education in New York City, has its roots in the progressive movement of the early 1930s (Goffin 1994; Roopnarine & Johnson 1993). It is grounded in the philosophy of John Dewey and other early educational progressives, who believed that learning must be active exploration and experience-based, and influenced by Sigmund Freud's theoretical claims of the profound formative influence of the early childhood years. Initially, the Bank Street Approach was not a prescribed curriculum of materials and methods but an approach based on direct observation of children and their schooling needs.

The Bank Street Approach is sometimes criticized as being overly concerned with the child's creativity and emotional security. However, the goals of this approach are much broader, and include (1) promoting autonomy and exploration; (2) developing a positive learner self-concept by developing competence; (3) developing communication and self-expression; and (4) establishing impulse control (Essa 1992; Roopnarine & Johnson 1993). The Bank Street Approach emphasizes meaningfulness, continuity, and depth of knowledge rather than achievement of specific academic objectives. It has come to be known as the developmental–interactionist model because it is concerned with the interaction of all areas of a child's development and because it places emphasis on interaction between the environment and the child's development. The child's environment and experiences are considered the foundation of curriculum, which is explored in depth.

The classroom environment and materials under this approach are arranged into conventional interest areas including music, art, reading, science, and dramatic play. Teacher-made and child-made materials are believed most suitable for the unique needs of children in individual classrooms. Examples of child-made materials include collections of items to be counted or sorted and books that children have made. In addition, print materials, including magazines, trade books, text books, reference books, charts summarizing classroom activities, written work, lists of activities, and classroom-generated rules that show children the function of the written word, are critical to the classroom environment. A listening center and writing center provide other opportunities to develop language competence in a useful context. Math materials, in addition to the child-made collections, include many manipulatives for counting, weighing, measuring; number games; puzzles; task cards; and workbooks. The science curriculum relies on materials from nature (plants, rocks, animals) and materials that can be used for experimentation and observation including magnets, magnifying glasses, and such.

The Bank Street Approach relies on competent teachers who are knowledgeable in child development principles and able to interpret the individual needs of children through observations they make of the children in their classrooms. It has remained rooted in its beliefs in an education responsive to the developmental needs of children, but it has also responded to educational change. These changes have included the first production of materials depicting multiethnic children in urban settings and the use of new technologies to support children's learning.

The push for educational evaluation to prove educational effectiveness continues to be difficult for educators using the Bank Street Approach. Because the approach emphasizes long-term goals rather than specific short-term objectives, the results of standardized tests that tend to measure the latter are sometimes used to discredit this approach to education and many of the long-term psychological influences of the school experience are more difficult to observe and document. However, a few studies have been conducted that indicate that children's cognitive gains and motivation to learn are enhanced over the long term through this educational approach. See Activity 9.3 to gain more insight into the Bank Street Approach.

◆ **ACTIVITY**
9.3

Bank Street Website

Visit the Bank Street Website @ www.bnkst.edu to learn more about this approach to early childhood education. Click on the following menu options to expedite your search.

1. From the Bank Street Home Page click on "About Bank Street" in the menu bar to the left.
2. Next click on "A Brief History."
3. Also click on "The Bank Street Approach." After reading this page click on "Our Credo" at the bottom of the page.
4. Within this same section click on "Facts at a Glance."
5. Browse through other parts of this website for a general overview of educational materials and training available through Bank Street.

Write a one–two-page report for your class about what you learned about Bank Street.

The Direct Instruction Approach

During the early years of Head Start programming Carl Bereiter and Siegfried Engelmann developed an approach aimed at helping children from low socioeconomic backgrounds gain skills needed for success in elementary school (Essa 1992; Goffin 1994). Essa points out that Head Start was initially a summerlong program for children preparing to enter kindergarten the following school year. Therefore, emphasis was placed on getting the children academically ready for public school rather than on a "whole child" developmental approach.

The direct instruction approach is based on behavioral principles of cause and effect, stimulus and response, and behavior modification. While often criticized as being too mechanistic and controlling, the behaviorist philosophy is optimistic about the possibility of discovering relationships to explain children's behavior and thereby alter learning. Analysis of behavior enables the educator to facilitate change through behavior modification techniques (Roopnarine & Johnson 1993).

Behaviorist educational approaches focus on teacher-directed activities, with carefully planned lessons, drills, and exercises for practicing important concepts. The Bereiter–Engelmann model offered lessons in three academic areas—language, math, and reading—with precise teacher questions requiring specific student responses. The teacher, for example, might present a lesson on shapes in the following manner:

> *Teacher:* (Pointing to a card with a star on it) Repeat after me. This is a star.
> *Children:* This is a star.

Teacher: What is this?
Children: This is a star.
Teacher: Janelle, what is this?
Janelle: This is a star. . . .
Teacher: (Pointing to a card with a different shape on it) Is this a star?
Children: No, that is not a star.

Teachers use constant reinforcement to motivate children's participation with the use of both positive words of praise and tangible rewards (often food). Other forms of reinforcement for learning include prizes, tokens accumulated and later exchanged for tangible items or special privileges, special certificates, and the like. Critics of this approach point out that overreliance on such external reinforcement takes away the internal (or intrinsic) motivation of children; the satisfaction of successful task completion is considered the optimal type of reinforcement.

In the Bereiter–Engelmann preschool, twenty-minute small-group lessons in each of the three subject areas were interspersed with the large-group activities of snack and music (the latter was also used to teach language skills). There were no materials or periods for free play with peers because that was not considered part of any goal of the program. The assumption was that children had adequate opportunities and materials for play outside the school setting (Essa 1993).

The social tenor of the 1960s influenced the adoption of this direct instruction model in the public-school sector as well. The growth of Head Start promoted the idea that preschool programs were acceptable as the child's first out-of-home educational experience. As a result, many kindergarten classrooms turned toward the more "academic" or instructional approach of the primary grades. Curriculum materials published under the trade name DISTAR provided teachers with sequenced and prepared lessons in the three curriculum areas of language, math, and reading at three levels of difficulty.

Educational practices based on behavioral theory have received a lot of criticism from the early childhood education field in general and from those interested in more holistic (total child) approaches to education in the public schools in particular. However, when used thoughtfully and balanced carefully, many of the techniques and strategies can be beneficial to teachers and students. Neisworth and Buggey (1993) delineate six important behavioral strategies that might be useful to teachers.

1. *Shaping* is used to teach new behaviors. The child is rewarded for simple approximations of the task until the targeted behavior has been accomplished. The teacher observes the child's progress and provides reinforcement for even slight improvement. For example, if a first-grade child has a difficult time staying in his or her seat, the teacher might first reward the child for staying close enough to the chair to be able to touch it when asked. After the child has become successful at this part of the behavior, the teacher might reward the child for remaining seated during part of a story, then through all of a story, and so on.

2. *Chaining,* or sequencing, of behaviors involves determining the steps in a given task and teaching the child the individual steps in the task. The steps in getting dressed, brushing teeth, making a peanut butter sandwich, baking a cake, or clearing the dinner table are examples of everyday adult tasks that require chaining for preschoolers. The child might be required to perform the first or last event in the sequence of the task and gradually be taught the next or previous step.

3. *Modeling* allows children to imitate the behavior or task of an adult or peers. An example of modeling in a kindergarten classroom might involve a statement of positive reinforcement by the teacher, such as "I like the way Allen put the lids back on the paint and washed the paintbrushes after he was finished at the easel today. It shows that he is a responsible student. Thank you, Allen."

4. *Prompting* provides a signal or cue that helps a child perform a task. For example, first-grade teachers might use picture symbols together with unfamiliar words on a language chart. Gradually the teacher uses the prompt less often until the children recognize the word without the prompt.

5. *Behavior rehearsal* involves giving children repeated practice at a task. For example, a kindergarten teacher wanting to teach children to recognize the letters of the alphabet might ask them to sing the alphabet song each day while he or she points to the letters on a chart. A preschool teacher might dramatize using the telephone to teach how to dial 911 for emergencies as a form of behavior rehearsal.

6. *Discrimination training* teaches children how to respond when presented with two or more stimuli. An example of discrimination training is learning to recognize colors: The child is taught to recognize the color red before being asked to discriminate between that color and one or more others.

In the early stages of the developmentally appropriate practice movement by NAEYC in the late 1980s and early 1990s, there was a tendency to oppose and bash direct instruction practices as developmentally inappropriate. Since that time, however, many early childhood educators have recognized the need to select from all early childhood curriculum models those practices that are both age appropriate and individually appropriate to use with the children with whom they are working. For example, a reward system for good behavior that provides daily reinforcement might be inappropriately used if applied in a kindergarten classroom with *all* children *every* day. However, if an individual child in the kindergarten classroom has significant behavior difficulties, the teacher might develop a behavior modification plan for that child alone. Similarly, it might be considered inappropriate to drill the entire preschool class on recognizing the eight basic colors every day (some children may already know them and some may be in the process of learning them, while others don't seem ready to learn them at all). Using discrimination training of color recognition with a small group of preschoolers during a play or art period could help meet the needs of those children who are developmentally ready to learn the names of the colors. As in all aspects of life, it is important to use moderation and good judgment when selecting curriculum models and instructional approaches.

The Cognitively Oriented High Scope Approach

This approach, based on the cognitive development theory of Jean Piaget, was developed under the leadership of David Weikart's High Scope Foundation in Ypslanti, Michigan. It was initially designed for preschool children during the 1960s when there was a societal concern for the welfare of impoverished children. The basic premise of this approach is that children are active learners who are in the process of constructing their knowledge through meaningful experiences. The term *constructivism* has recently come to be a way of describing this educational approach for young children through adults.

Chapter 7 provided significant detail on the Plan–Do–Review process, which the High Scope model employs as a framework for active learning. The curriculum provides a way for teachers to extend the cognitive development of children through key experiences in eight concept areas including: (1) *active learning*, which employs use of all the senses and allows the child to select activities and materials for learning; (2) *using language* through talking, writing ideas (self or the teacher), and playing with language; (3) *representing experiences and ideas* through art, writing, role playing, and use of the senses; (4) *classification* using a variety of materials, which allows the child to learn the attributes of materials and to group materials in a variety of ways; (5) *seriation,* which develops the ability to order, compare, and match objects; (6) *number concepts,* which provide the foundation for mathematical understanding and computation as children count, add, subtract, and arrange objects in

◆ *Active learning allows children a selection of activities and materials.*

one-to-one correspondence; (7) *spatial relationships,* examined as children assemble and take apart puzzles or other materials and explore the environment with their own bodies, and describe the location, position, and distance of objects in their environment; and (8) *time concepts,* which involve understanding units of time (hour, day, month, year) and sequencing of time (yesterday, today, tomorrow; first, next, last).

The role of the teacher in this approach is critical to effective cognitive development (Weikart & Schweinhart 1993). The teacher must master the art of questioning so children's thinking is extended; for example, asking "What happened? How did you do that. Show me how you did that. Why do you think that happened? What do you think would happen if . . ." This questioning style encourages free dialogue between children and adults and models language for children to use with their peers. In addition, it provides a model for the teacher and child to interact as thinkers rather than, as in traditional school roles, the teacher as the holder of the correct answers—active teacher, passive learner.

Adoption and modification of the cognitively oriented approach is currently experiencing popularity and expansion into the primary grades for use as a framework for self-directed learning, as described in Chapter 7. See activity 9.4 to gain more information about the High Scope Approach.

◆ **ACTIVITY**
9.4

High Scope Website

Visit the High Scope website @ www.highscope.org to learn more about this approach to early childhood education. To facilitate your search for important information, follow these steps:

1. At the end of the introductory paragraph on the homepage click on "click here for more information."
2. Click on "About High Scope." Find the answer to what High Scope refers to on this page.
3. For a more comprehensive history of High Scope click on "Dr. David P. Weikart" in one of the paragraphs on the "About High Scope" page.

Prepare a report for your peers that explains how High Scope originated in the 1960s and what activities it continues to support in the twenty-first century.

Early Childhood Curriculum in a New Millennium

The movement toward developmentally appropriate curriculum that began in the late 1980s evolved because of the belief of many early childhood educators that children need to acquire early the in-depth concepts, decision-making skills, negotiation, and creative problem-solving skills they will need to do well in the complex social milieu and world of work of which they will be a part during the twenty-first century (Bredekamp 1987). As a result of the publication of the National Association for the Education of Young Children (NAEYC) guidelines for developmentally appropriate practice in 1987, many programs used the guidelines to improve practice. What resulted were misinterpretation and a trend to adopt the developmentally appropriate label for curriculum and testing materials that did not necessarily uphold the principles of developmentally appropriate practice that NAEYC intended. In 1997, revised guidelines were published in an attempt to clarify and address ideas that are susceptible to misunderstanding. It is the intent of the association to review these guidelines every seven years with new guidelines to be published every ten years (Bredekamp and Copple 1997).

The new NAEYC guidelines provide the following criteria for constructing developmentally appropriate curriculum:

- Developmentally appropriate curriculum provides for all areas of a child's development: physical, emotional, social, linguistic, aesthetic, and cognitive.
- Curriculum includes a broad range of content across subject areas that are socially relevant, intellectually challenging, and personally meaningful to children.
- Curriculum builds on what children already know and are able to do (activating prior knowledge) to consolidate their learning and to foster their acquisition of new concepts and skills.
- Effective curriculum plans frequently integrate across traditional subject areas to help children make meaningful connections and provide opportunities for rich conceptual development; focusing on one subject is also a valid strategy at times.
- Curriculum content has intellectual integrity, reflecting the key concepts and tools of inquiry of recognized disciplines in ways that are accessible and achievable for young children. These tools might include conducting scientific experiments, writing, performing, solving mathematical problems, collecting oral history, etc.
- Curriculum provides opportunities to support children's home culture and language while also developing all children's abilities to participate in the shared culture of the program and the community.
- When used, technology is physically and philosophically integrated in the classroom curriculum and teaching. (NAEYC 1997).

Literacy Development in a New Millennium

During the late 1990s a vigorous debate arose among proponents of whole language instruction and those who favored more traditional, phonics-based instruction for the teaching of reading and writing (Robinson, McKenna, & Wedman, 1996). An either/or mentality of whole language *or* phonics-based instruction prevailed among those involved in the debate. As a result, professional organizations such as the International Reading Association (IRA) and the National Association for the Education of Young Children joined together to form position statements regarding the best way to approach literacy education for young children (NAEYC/IRA 1998). They did this in an effort to assure that the "goals and expectations for young children's achievement in reading and writing should be developmentally appropriate, that is, *challenging but achievable*, with sufficient adult support" (page 31). The organizations developed a continuum of Children's Development in Early Reading and Writing which details five phases and goals for children from preschool through grade three. These five phases are detailed in Figure 9.2, but include the following:

- Phase 1: Awareness and exploration (goals for preschool)
- Phase 2: Experimental reading and writing (goals for kindergarten)
- Phase 3: Early reading and writing (goals for first grade)
- Phase 4: Transitional reading and writing (goals for second grade)
- Phase 5: Independent and productive reading and writing (goals for third grade)

In addition, criticisms of the whole language approach resulted in literacy education for young children that is more sequenced, purposeful and planned rather than a casual or haphazard approach. As a result many early childhood programs such as the National Headstart Association have developed literacy goals for children which include:

- Developing phonemic, print, and numeracy awareness;
- Understanding and using language to communicate for various purposes;
- Understanding and using increasingly complex and varied vocabulary;
- Developing and demonstrating an appreciation of books; and
- In the case of non-English background children, making progress toward acquisition of the English language.

The current approach to literacy instruction incorporates what many refer to as a balanced approach to reading and writing instruction. This balanced approach, according to Fountas and Pinnell (1996), incorporates different types of reading including *guided reading,* during which the teacher works with small groups of children who are at similar reading levels and who use similar reading processes. Fountas and Pinnell describe The Ohio State University Literacy Collaborative Framework as a way that teachers can achieve a balanced approach to literacy instruction. This framework incorporates four types of reading instruction and four types of writing instruction as described below:

1. **Reading Aloud:** The teacher reads aloud to the whole class or small groups of children. The teacher carefully selects a body of children's literature, which incorporates several genres (types of literature) that represent the diversity in our society. Some texts, selected for particular features, may be reread many times.

◆ **FIGURE 9.2** *Learning to Read and Write: Developmentally Appropriate Practices for Young Children, Part 4: Continuum of Children's Development in Early Reading and Writing*

A joint position of the International Reading Association (IRA) and the National Association for the Education of Young Children (NAEYC)

Note: This list is intended to be illustrative, not exhaustive. Children at any grade level will function at a variety of phases along the reading/writing continuum.

Phase 1: Awareness and exploration (goals for preschool)

Children explore their environment and build the foundations for learning to read and write.

Children can
- enjoy listening to and discussing storybooks
- understand that print carries a message
- engage in reading and writing attempts
- identify labels and signs in their environment
- participate in rhyming games
- identify some letters and make some letter-sound matches
- use known letters or approximations of letters to represent written language (especially meaningful words like their name and phrases such as "I love you")

What teachers do
- share books with children, including Big Books, and model reading behaviors
- talk about letters by name and sounds
- establish a literacy-rich environment
- reread favorite stories
- engage children in language games
- promote literacy-related play activities
- encourage children to experiment with writing

What parents and family members can do
- talk with children, engage them in conversation, give names of things, show interest in what a child says
- read and reread stories with predictable text to children
- encourage children to recount experiences and describe ideas and events that are important to them
- visit the library regularly
- provide opportunities for children to draw and print, using markers, crayons, and pencils

Phase 2: Experimental reading and writing (goals for kindergarten)

Children develop basic concepts of print and begin to engage in and experiment with reading and writing.

Kindergartners can
- enjoy being read to and themselves retell simple narrative stories or informational texts
- use descriptive language to explain and explore
- recognize letters and letter-sound matches
- show familiarity with rhyming and beginning sounds
- understand left-to-right and top-to-bottom orientation and familiar concepts of print
- match spoken words with written ones
- begin to write letters of the alphabet and some high-frequency words

What teachers do
- encourage children to talk about reading and writing experiences
- provide many opportunities for children to explore and identify sound-symbol relationships in meaningful contexts
- help children to segment spoken words into individual sounds and blend the sounds into whole words (for example, by slowly writing a word and saying its sound)
- frequently read interesting and conceptually rich stories to children
- provide daily opportunities for children to write
- help children build a sight vocabulary
- create a literacy-rich environment for children to engage independently in reading and writing

What parents and family members can do
- daily read and reread narrative and informational stories to children
- encourage children's attempts at reading and writing

(continued)

◆ **FIGURE 9.2** *Learning to Read and Write (Continued)*

- allow children to participate in activities that involve writing and reading (for example, cooking, making grocery lists)
- play games that involve specific directions (such as "Simon Says")
- have conversations with children during mealtimes and throughout the day

Phase 3: Early reading and writing
(goals for first grade)

Children begin to read simple stories and can write about a topic that is meaningful to them.

First-graders can

- read and retell familiar stories
- use strategies (rereading, predicting, questioning, contextualizing) when comprehension breaks down
- use reading and writing for various purposes on their own initiative
- orally read with reasonable fluency
- use letter-sound associations, word parts, and context to identify new words
- identify an increasing number of words by sight
- sound out and represent all substantial sounds in spelling a word
- write about topics that are personally meaningful
- attempt to use some punctuation and capitalization

What teachers do

- support the development of vocabulary by reading daily to the children, transcribing their language, and selecting materials that expand children's knowledge and language development
- model strategies and provide practice for identifying unknown words
- give children opportunities for independent reading and writing practice
- read, write, and discuss a range of different text types (poems, informational books)
- introduce new words and teach strategies for learning to spell new words
- demonstrate and model strategies to use when comprehension breaks down
- help children build lists of commonly used words from their writing and reading

What parents and family members can do

- talk about favorite storybooks
- read to children and encourage them to read to you
- suggest that children write to friends and relatives
- bring to a parent–teacher conference evidence of what your child can do in writing and reading
- encourage children to share what they have learned about their writing and reading

Phase 4: Transitional reading and writing
(goals for second grade)

Children begin to read more fluently and write various text forms using simple and more complex sentences.

Second-graders can

- read with greater fluency
- use strategies more efficiently (rereading, questioning, and so on) when comprehension breaks down
- use word identification strategies with greater facility to unlock unknown words
- identify an increasing number of words by sight
- write about a range of topics to suit different audiences
- use common letter patterns and critical features to spell words
- punctuate simple sentences correctly and proofread their own work
- spend time reading daily and use reading to research topics

What teachers do

- create a climate that fosters analytic, evaluative, and reflective thinking
- teach children to write in multiple forms (stories, information, poems)
- ensure that children read a range of texts for a variety of purposes
- teach revising, editing, and proofreading skills
- teach strategies for spelling new and difficult words
- model enjoyment of reading

What parents and family members can do

- continue to read to children and encourage them to read to you
- engage children in activities that require reading and writing

- become involved in school activities
- show children your interest in their learning by displaying their written work
- visit the library regularly
- support your child's specific hobby or interest with reading materials and references

Phase 5: Independent and productive reading and writing (goals for third grade)

Children continue to extend and refine their reading and writing to suit varying purposes and audiences.

Third-graders can

- read fluently and enjoy reading
- use a range of strategies when drawing meaning from the text
- use word identification strategies appropriately and automatically when encountering unknown words
- recognize and discuss elements of different text structures
- make critical connections between texts
- write expressively in many different forms (stories, poems, reports)
- use a rich variety of vocabulary and sentences appropriate to text forms
- revise and edit their own writing during and after composing
- spell words correctly in final writing drafts

What teachers do

- provide opportunities daily for children to read, examine, and critically evaluate narrative and expository texts
- continue to create a climate that fosters critical reading and personal response
- teach children to examine ideas in texts
- encourage children to use writing as a tool for thinking and learning
- extend children's knowledge of the correct use of writing conventions
- emphasize the importance of correct spelling in finished written products
- create a climate that engages all children as a community of literacy learners

What parents and family members can do

- continue to support children's learning and interest by visiting the library and bookstores with them
- find ways to highlight children's progress in reading and writing
- stay in regular contact with your child's teachers about activities and progress in reading and writing
- encourage children to use and enjoy print for many purposes (such as recipes, directions, games, and sports)
- build a love of language in all its forms and engage children in conversation

National Association for the Education of Young Children (NAEYC).

2. **Shared Reading:** Using a big book or enlarged text that all children can see, the teacher involves children in reading together following a pointer. The reading may include rereading of big books, poems, songs, interactive writing, and retellings of stories or events.

3. **Guided Reading:** The teacher works with a small group of children who have similar reading processes. New books are selected by the teacher who supports the reading of the children and provides instructional points during and after the reading.

4. **Independent Reading:** Children read on their own or with partners. There is a wide range of materials and some material may be from a special collection at their reading level.

5. **Shared Writing:** Teacher and children work to compose messages and stories. The teacher guides the process and serves as scribe.

6. **Interactive Writing:** Teacher and children compose messages and stories using a "shared pen" technique that places more emphasis on writing mechanics, spelling, etc.
7. **Guided Writing or Writing Workshop:** Children engage in writing in a variety of styles and texts. The teacher guides the process by providing instruction through minilessons and conferences.
8. **Independent Writing:** Children engage in their own writing including stories, retellings, information writing, lists, labeling, etc.

In addition, letter and word study is woven into the framework through the instructional activities and through use of alphabet centers and word walls. The framework also incorporates strategies for home and community involvement and documenting children's progress. Curriculum coherence is accomplished through extensions and themes that incorporate literature as an integral part of the process.

Shared Reading Experiences

This approach to reading aloud, developed by teachers in New Zealand, was inspired by the bedtime story ritual (Holdaway 1979). A good deal of discussion precedes the reading of the story—teachers ask children to predict the plot of the story, discuss who wrote and illustrated the book, who the book is dedicated to, and so on. The teacher then uses the big book to model the reading process as he or she points to the words in the text. For emergent (beginning) readers, it is often helpful to use a book with predictable language (repetitive phrases, rhyming, or patterns of language) so the children can join in the reading of the text as soon as they are familiar with it. Repeated and varied readings of the text (using motions, singing, or dramatizations)

◆ *Shared reading using quality children's literature is part of a balanced approach to literacy development.*

provide the children with opportunities to develop fluency in "reading" the book, and enable them to view themselves as readers. Lessons related to word analysis, phonics, punctuation, or grammar patterns that are repeated in the texts occur after the initial reading of the text. These types of lessons are not eliminated, as many critics of whole language assert. Rather, they are given a different perspective and priority than in traditional reading instruction methods: The phonics and grammar lessons emerge from the literature and themes being studied instead of being a prescribed prereading activity.

Writing Opportunities

Many opportunities are provided for children to engage in writing activities in whole language classrooms, such as:

1. Daily journal writing (or drawing, for emergent writers);
2. Writing activities related to learning centers in the room (writing prescriptions in the dramatic play doctor's office for example);
3. Class or individual book-making opportunities using a variation of the language pattern in the big book being studied;
4. Dialogue journals for upper primary children (journals in which teachers respond to the child's writing);
5. Reader response logs or activities allowing upper primary children the opportunity to write about the book(s) that have been read in class; and
6. Daily class chart letters enabling children to pick up sentence patterns they may begin to use in their own writing (It is Monday. It is library day. It is cold outside.).

Integrated Curriculum

Acquiring literacy skills enables us to acquire information in other subject areas. Relating literacy instruction to science, math, social studies, and the arts gives a "wholeness" to the curriculum and purpose to reading instruction ("We read to learn" rather than "We learn to read"). It is also important to keep all areas of development (physical, cognitive, and social/emotional) in mind when integrating curriculum. Developing a whole language/whole child curriculum that integrates many subject areas and developmental domains is an exciting and rewarding process. While it can be initially time consuming, establishing a model for curriculum planning and "team planning" with other teachers allows for efficient and productive use of planning time in the long run. There are a number of steps involved in integrated curriculum planning. Teachers must:

1. Determine a topic of interest and rationale for the children and teachers involved (why is it important or interesting to study this topic?);
2. Brainstorm all the possibilities for concepts and instruction related to the theme;
3. Organize and categorize (web) curriculum possibilities by developmental areas and subject areas (see Figure 9.3 on page 252);

4. Develop a skills list or outcomes for the theme being studied (see Table 9.1 on page 253);
5. Select and plan activities and lessons from those topics generated as possibilities; discuss with children what things they would like to learn related to the topic and which activities they would find interesting;

◆ **FIGURE 9.3**   *Integrated Curriculum Web*

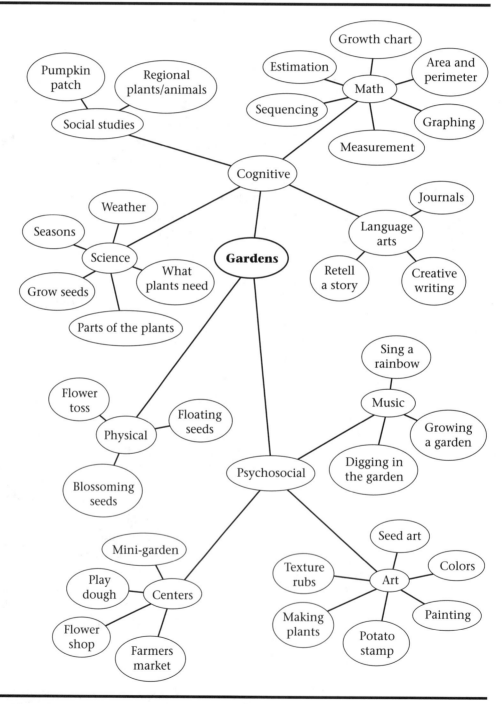

Source: Heather Albertson, Chris Streiff, and Sheryl Sorgenfrie, Winona State University, Rochester MN. Reprinted with permission.

6. Gather and organize resource materials and learning centers (see Example 9.1); when possible, involve children, both to generate ideas for materials they think are important and to access materials that may be in their homes; and

7. Evaluate.

The whole language/whole child unit developed by a team of undergraduate students demonstrates the richness of curriculum that can be developed using this type of process.

◆ **TABLE 9.1**   *Learner Outcomes for Garden Unit*

Theme	Art	Language Arts	Math	Music	Physical Education	PIC
Gardens	The student will use textures when making visual art. The student will know and identify the primary and secondary colors.	The student listens for information (directions, facts, details, main idea, sequence, etc.) The student uses oral language to effectively communicate in formal situations (recall a story).	The student will order objects by consistent criteria. The student will collect data and make a chart independently. The student will become familiar with bar graphs and their uses. The student will add single-digit numbers.	The student will enjoy music through creating, performing, and listening. The student will feel and perform the steady beat in music.	The student will demonstrate non-locomotion movements; curl, twist, stretch, bend. The student will move using an indirect path through space.	The student will identify the primary parts of a plant (leaves, stem, roots). The student will explain that roots, stems, leaves, flowers, fruits, and seeds have specific functions within the life cycle of a plant. The student will recognize what living things need in order to live (food, air, water, a place to live). The student will compare and contrast a forest, a plain, and a desert in terms of what plants need, and what animals need in order to live.

Source: Heather Albertson, Chris Streiff, and Sheryl Sorgenfrie, Winona State University, Rochester, MN. Reprinted with permission.

◆ EXAMPLE 9.1
Resource Materials for Garden Unit

Rationale

There is so much for children to learn by studying gardens. They can learn about the environment and how it affects plant growth. Students are also learning how to take care of their environment. Gardens play a very important part in the world.

- They provide food.
- Some garden plants are used to make clothing and other things.
- Gardens make our surroundings beautiful.
- Some very important medicines are made from plants.

Introduction

Display a variety of seed packets on a table for children to see. Encourage them to tell what they know about seeds and to ask questions. Use the following questions to help move the discussion along:

1. Which of these packets of seeds would you like to plant?
2. Where would be a good place to plant the seeds?
3. How would you take care of the seeds to help them grow?
4. How long do you think it would take these seeds to grow into plants?

Have the students pick out a seed, and plant them in plastic cups with their names on them. They will continually care for, study, and monitor the progress of the plants.

Literary Basket

A literary basket will be available in the room, with the central theme being gardens. The books to be included are:

Heller, R. (1984). *Plants that never ever bloom*. New York: Scholastic Inc.
Henkes, K. (1991). *Chrysanthemum*. New York: Greenwillow Books.
King, E. (1990). *The pumpkin patch*. New York: Dutton Children's Books.
Krauss, R. (1945). *The carrot seed*. New York: Harper & Row Publishers.
Livingston, M.C. (1982). *A circle of seasons*. New York: Holiday House.
Parkes, B., & J. Smith (1986). *The enormous watermelon*. Hong Kong: Rigby, Inc.

Source: Heather Albertson, Chris Streiff, and Sheryl Sorgenfrie, Winona State University, Rochester, MN. Reprinted with permission.

◆ ACTIVITY 9.5

Integrated Curriculum Unit

Working with a team of students in your class, use the seven steps for planning an integrated curriculum and the model provided in the "Gardens" unit to develop your own integrated curriculum unit for a kindergarten or primary classroom. Make sure that you incorporate both a multicultural antibias component and suggestions for modification of activities for special needs children in your unit.

Transformational Curriculum

In the transformational curriculum model proposed by Rosegrant and Bredekamp, the transformations, or changes, are twofold. The curriculum is transformed in response to the developmental needs and interests of the child and the child is transformed as a result of the curriculum. Figure 9.4 provides a graphic of the important components of this model, based on "meaning-centered, integrated, 'mindful' curriculum" (1992, 70) that builds on:

1. Child development knowledge in all domains (whole child focus);
2. Individual developmental continuums of each child in the group that involve realistic development of learning goals that provide a flexible framework for instruction (in both grade level or multiage settings there will be variations in development);
3. Conceptual organizers, the glue that makes the curriculum integrated, meaningful, and relevant; and
4. Disciplines or subject areas that ensure the curriculum has not only intellectual integrity but also depth and breadth.

◆ **FIGURE 9.4** *Transformational Curriculum*

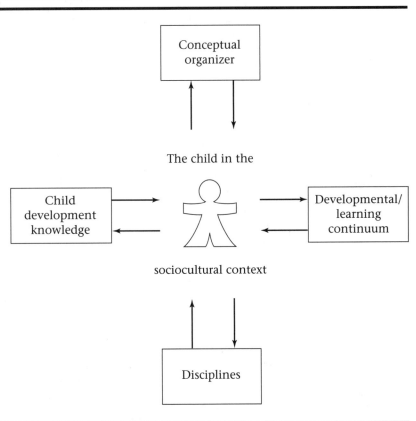

Source: Data from T. Rosegrant and S. Bredekamp, eds., Reaching Potentials: Appropriate Curriculum and Assessment for Young Children, Vol. I (Washington, DC: National Association for the Education of Young Children, 1992), p. 74.

Figure 9.4 illustrates that this curricular framework is child-centered and must take into account the child's sociocultural background. This means that a relevant, meaningful curriculum for inner-city Detroit children might be very different from that of children living in ranching communities of rural New Mexico, for example.

The Project Approach

While the Project Approach was utilized in the Progressive Education Movement in the early 1900s and in the British Infant Schools in the 1960s and 1970s, it has received renewed attention and implementation as a result of several publications and exhibits related to the pre-primary schools of Reggio Emilia, Italy (Helm & Katz 2000).

A project is an extensive study undertaken by an individual child or a group of children that incorporates "writing, measurement, drawing, painting, model making, reading, creating stories, dramatic and fine arts" (Katz & Chard 1993, 209) according to the abilities of the participating children. The project typically involves the following activities: collecting information through observation, interviewing experts about the topic being studied, performing experiments, collecting artifacts, and preparing oral and written reports and displays. Because of their engagement in these types of activities, Helm and Katz (2000) refer to children involved in a project as "Young Investigators."

Katz & Chard (1989) identified four types of learning goals for all levels of education that the project approach helps to facilitate.

1. Knowledge, including the social, physical, and logicomathematical categories identified by Piaget, as well as other ideas and experiences that may be personally relevant to the individual.
2. Skills that are the small observable units of behavior and actions (motor skills such as skipping rope, cognitive skills such as counting to ten or saying the alphabet and social skills such as learning cooperation are included in this category).
3. Dispositions that are enduring habits and ways of responding to situations, and trends or patterns of behavior that are maintained by opportunities to engage in repetition of experiences (kindness, generosity, habits of reading, desire for order, organization, or cleanliness).
4. Feelings that are inner states of emotion and attitudes about self and others.

In selecting a topic for a project, several criteria should be considered: relevancy to the child and usefulness in later life; potential for curricular integration; potential for study of real objects; potential for in-depth study for a week or more; opportunity for problem solving; opportunity for collaboration and cooperation among children; opportunities for construction, investigation, and dramatic play; opportunity for parental involvement; availability of local resources. Another test for appropriate topic selection is to state the topic in question or narrative form rather than as a single word topic. For

◆ *Steps in the Project Approach include the collection of artifacts and preparation of written, oral, or artistic reports.*

example, questions such as "How do gardens grow?" or "Where does food come from?" provide focus for further questions and investigations that can shape the project.

After the topic is selected, the teacher engages the children in a discussion of their personal experiences and knowledge of the topic through talking, writing, or drawing. This enables the teacher to determine special interests of children and to establish a baseline of the children's backgrounds in the topic. In addition, children can be encouraged to raise questions about the topic, which informs the teacher about the gaps of knowledge or misconceptions that children have related to the topic. These questions can form the basis for gaining new information through field trips and interviews with people who have experience related to the topic. Children take notes, make drawings, and so forth. In the classroom, children recall details of the new information they learned through discussion, drawing, writing, and representing in other ways. The use of printed material is considered important but secondary to the information collected "in the field." The last phase of the project results in presenting or summarizing what has been learned.

Katz and Chard (1989) suggest the following groupings of topics for possible study:

1. *Personal lives of children:* homes, babies, families, food, school bus, TV shows, toys, games.
2. *Community:* people, hospital, shops, construction sites, transportation services, waterworks, fish market.
3. *Local events and current events:* Annual carnival, county fair, election day, Independence Day, visit by a famous person.
4. *Places:* neighborhoods, roads, directions, landmarks, rivers, hills, local monument.
5. *Time:* clocks, seasons, calendar, festivals, holidays, historical objects or events.
6. *Natural phenomena:* weather, water, wind, air, plants, animals, rocks.
7. *Concepts:* opposites, patterns, colors.
8. *General knowledge:* deserts, ships, inventions, space, travel, rivers.
9. *Miscellaneous:* hats, black holes, puppets, math week, book week.

The Reggio Emilia early childhood schools, described in the next section, have served as a model for the project approach and emergent curriculum approach, discussed later in this chapter (Gandini 1993).

The Reggio Emilia Approach

Reggio Emilia is a town of about 130,000 inhabitants in northern Italy. Since the end of World War II, a unique approach to the education of young children has evolved there. In Italy, publicly funded municipal and national programs have been in place for young children since the 1970s. About 90% of children three to six years of age attend some kind of school. In Reggio Emilia, where about half of the children attend the municipally funded schools, the efforts of parents and teachers in developing quality early childhood programs were greatly influence by the late Loris Malaguzzi. (Hendrick 1997).

Over the past two decades, fascination with the approach has resulted in a European and North American tour of an Reggio Emilia exhibit called "The Hundred Languages of Children" as well as hundreds of visitors from Europe, the United States, Australia, and East Asia. The exhibit hallmarks the learning of children through the art, writing, and documentation of their in-depth study and work. Reggio Emilia educators have been readers of the works of Dewey, Piaget, and Vygotsky, but at the same time are students of the current research about child development and early childhood education in the United States. Their philosophy is grounded in their own interpretation, ideas, and hypotheses about teaching and learning.

The basic principles of the Reggio Emilia approach are interwoven as a cohesive philosophy (Hendrick 1997). Each principle is dynamically interrelated to the others and includes:

- *The image of the child,* with a belief that children have preparedness, potential, curiosity, interest in social interactions, construction of their learning, and ability to negotiate their environment. Teachers therefore work to be aware of children's potentials and plan the work and environment with regard to children's experiences and responses.

- *Children's relationships and interactions within a system* are recognized as including parents, other children, teachers, the school, community, and wider society environments. Schools are viewed as systems where these relationships are interconnected, reciprocal, activated, and supported.

- *The three subjects of education include children, parents, and teachers,* and the well-being of children is connected with that of parents and teachers. By recognizing that children have the right to the best education that society can offer, parents are assured the right to be involved in the education of their children and teacher's rights for professional development are guaranteed.

- *The role of parents* is highly valued and evident through the advisory committees running each school and the expectation for parent participation in a variety of ways. Parents are active in the learning experiences of their own children and help ensure the welfare of all children in the school.

- *The role of space,* particularly as noted in the infant-toddler schools, conveys the message of the potential for space to play a role in instruction. The environments at these schools are designed to be very beautiful and personal. Much thought is given to color, shape, furnishing, and arrangement of objects and plants. The use of natural light and mirrors helps to highlight and illuminate the work of children. Spaces are created to encourage communication through message boxes and children's work is displayed everywhere you look including places outside the classroom such as stairways and bathrooms.

- *The value of relationships and interaction of children in small groups* can be observed in the organization of space that allows children to be with a few or many teachers and children as well as find space to be alone. Homogeneous age groups of 2–5 children are encouraged by teachers in an effort for children to communicate, negotiate, plan, and make decisions regarding their learning.

- *The role of time and importance of continuity* is not governed by a clock or calendar. The full-day schedule allows teachers to use the child's personal rhythm and sense of time in planning and carrying out activities. Teacher and children (3–6 year olds) stay together for 3 years, but change environments each year to meet the changing developmental needs and interests of the children.

- *Teachers as partners* refers to the role of the teacher as a continual learner and researcher regarding the learning of children. This is accomplished through the process of observing children at work, discussing their observations with other adults, and making flexible plans and preparations for children's learning with the support of a pedagogical coordinator (*pedigogista*).

- *Cooperation and collaboration* is emphasized at all levels of the schools through the pairing of teachers in each classroom without designation of a head teacher. The team of *pedagogisti* also supports cooperative relationships among parents, teachers, community members, and city administrators. Each *pedagosista* is assigned to support three or four schools in the city.

- *The interdependence of cooperation and organization* is recognized through the minimum of six hours per week that are scheduled for meetings with colleagues and parents, preparation, and inservice training. Everything from teachers' schedules to the dietary needs of children is discussed and organized with great care. All are committed to this level of organization and cooperation because it is believed to be necessary in order to offer the best possible experiences for children.

- *The many languages of children* are developed through work with an *atelierista* (a teacher trained in the visual arts) and by children and teachers working together in a special studio called an *atelier* (workshop). Mini-*ateliers* are set up in each classroom so that projects can be worked on throughout the school day. The use of media is considered to be a necessary way for children to express the cognitive and symbolic expression involved in the learning process.

- *The power of documentation* is displayed through transcriptions of children's comments and discussions, photos of them working on their projects, etc. The teachers and *atelierista* carefully arrange the documentation in order for parents and teachers to better understand children and the process of learning.

- *The emergence of curriculum* refers to the flexibility in project goals and outcomes, which results through the continuous dialogue among teachers and children. Teachers have general goals and express ideas about what direction and activity or project might take as they make appropriate preparations for the work of children. Then after observing the children at work, they make additional choices and decisions about how to best support the children in their learning and exploration.

- *Projects* are the primary framework for learning in the Reggio Emilia schools. Ideas for projects grow out of the experiences of children and their conversations with teachers as they construct knowledge together. Projects or themes for work grow out of these conversations. For example, as a result of a field trip to a city park, children were engaged in an in-depth project on lions after observing a statue of a lion in the park.

◆ **ACTIVITY**
9.6

Reggio Emilia Websites

To learn more about implementation of the Reggio Emilia approach in Italy and the United States, conduct an Internet search using the descriptors **"Reggio Emilia Preschools."** This will lead you to dozens of websites with information about Reggio Emilia, including some written in Italian. Bookmark some of these websites and make a presentation to your class. Make sure you include information about "The One Hundred Languages of Children" exhibit.

Emergent Curriculum

Jones and Nimmo describe emergent curriculum as "responsive to particular people in a particular place, at a particular time" (1994). It requires adults to trust in the power of play and the power of children's choices, and teachers to be professionals who shape and guide those choices into a curriculum that is meaningful and cognitively challenging for children.

Emergent curriculum has a life of its own. It differs from the traditional thematic approach, which makes use of predetermined themes for a designated time period—the teacher may plan the curriculum for the entire year using a different theme for each five- to ten-day period. Emergent, or organic, curriculum, on the other hand, makes use of themes that are important and relevant to the children. The direction each theme takes is based on careful observation of the interest level and questions that children have about the topic. People who are unfamiliar with the concept of emergent curriculum may assume from this definition that the curriculum emerges only from the children. There are many more aspects and sources to emergent curriculum, however. Example 9.2 describes some of those sources.

Jones and Nimmo contrast emergent curriculum with curriculum that is canned, embalmed, or accidental/unidentified. *Canned* curriculum is teacher-proof and comes from the school district, state, or a publishing company. It is designed by experts who propose to know "all that children need to know." However, it is limited because it is not responsive to the individual teacher, children, the "culture of the group," or the context of the setting. *Embalmed* curriculum originates with the teacher who has developed the curriculum after years of experience; it has become stagnant or unchanging for the most part because the teacher has run out of energy or motivation. *Accidental/unidentified* curriculum just happens. Teachers do not put in the time or energy to purposefully plan to make classroom activities meaningful to children or themselves. These teachers are just putting in their time.

◆ EXAMPLE 9.2
Sources of Emergent Curriculum

Children's Interests

Children whose own interests are acknowledged and supported don't need to be motivated to learn: their own excitement will keep them learning. Different children have different interests: how many of them can be built into the emerging curriculum?

Teacher's Interests

Teachers are people with interests of their own which are worth sharing with children. By doing some things *they* like, they can model knowledge and enthusiasm—even adults keep learning—and stay interested in teaching.

Developmental Tasks

At each developmental stage, there are tasks to be mastered: crawling, walking, talking, pouring, cutting, skipping—the list goes on and on. Appropriate curriculum provides many opportunities for children to choose activities providing spontaneous skill practice. Similarly, appropriate curriculum is responsive to the social-emotional issues which characteristically surface powerfully at different stages: autonomy, power, strength, and friendship among them.

Things in the Physical Environment

Children's experience of place is unique to the place they are in. The man-made things in their physical environment are typically standardized and predictable: thus unit blocks facilitate orderly building. The natural things are unstandardized and unpredictable—each plant and animal is different—and reflect the local climate and terrain. Children need experience with both.

People in the Social Environment

Children are interested in all sorts of people, who they are and what they do. Parents and cooks and big brothers and librarians and custodians and bus drivers and neighbors are right there to learn about and relate to.

Curriculum Resource Materials

Teacher need not reinvent the wheel. Libraries, exhibits at conferences, school resource centers are full of curriculum ideas ready to use. Use them and *adapt them* to your own setting, your teaching style, and your children's interests.

Serendipity: Unexpected Events

When the unexpected happens in the classroom, the community, the natural world, teachers have choices. They can try to ignore it, or join in briefly, or invent ways of incorporating it into their plans, short- or long-term. It's important to become skilled in on-the-spot decision making.

Living Together: Conflict Resolution, Caregiving, and Routines

Cooperation, expression of feelings, conflict resolution, and all the daily tasks of living together are potential curriculum for young children. Physical care, self-help skills, eating and resting and washing and dressing are the everyday life experiences that nurture the growth of young children. Caregiving and the resolution of interpersonal issues are not interruptions to the curriculum, they are basic curriculum.

Values Held in the School and Community, Family, and Culture

It is important to be accountable to their expectations and to *evaluate* programs in that framework. It is not necessary to teach directly from expectations; learning activities should be developmentally appropriate and adapted to the situation. It is important to define the curriculum planning process clearly so that you know when you are actively engaged in it.

Reprinted by permission from E. Jones and J. Nimmo, *Emergent Curriculum* (Washington, DC: National Association for the Education of Young Children, 1994), p. 127. ©1994 by NAEYC.

The year-end comments of Betty, a teacher involved in the case study that forms the basis for Jones and Nimmo's book on emergent curriculum, summarizes the concept of emergent curriculum:

Maybe we should just look at this conversation as one more example of the curriculum questions that never get resolved and will always be there for each group of teachers to struggle with: What's the right balance between spontaneity and planning? How much subject matter knowledge does a teacher of young children need, and are you a better teacher if you are full of answers or full of questions? How much should adults scaffold children's learning and when should children just be left alone to explore at their own rate? It's the continuing dialectic process again: it never stops. And so learning isn't a destination, it's a journey. To learn is to be alive, discovering new possibilities we hadn't thought of before. (1994, 138–139)

◆ **ACTIVITY**

9.7

Observe Two Classrooms

Use the continuums in Figure 9.5 on pages 264–65 as an observation tool for observations of two classrooms at the same grade level. If possible, observe in two different school districts which would likely follow a different philosophy and curriculum. Use a different color or symbol to code your observations for each classroom. Some of the items may not be observable and will require interviewing the teacher. Work with your classmates to determine which items are observable and to develop appropriate questions for non-observable items. After your observations, use the information on the continuums to share what you observe with a small group of your classmates, remembering to keep your comments objective, professional and non-judgmental.

Multiethnic, Multicultural, Anti-bias Curriculum

King *et al.* (1994) assert that curricula built on developmental theories of the past had little regard for the diversity in groups of children. Recently, however, there has been increased awareness and attention paid to gender, social class, and ethnic diversity in the development of appropriate curricula for young children (McCracken 1993; Ramirez & Ramirez 1994; York 1991; Zarillo 1994).

The ideal way to implement a multiethnic, multicultural, or anti-bias curriculum is to integrate it into the everyday curriculum of the classroom, rather than teach specific units or add-ons to units that relate to diversity. "Looking at curriculum through an anti-bias lens affects everything a teacher does" (Derman-Sparks 1989, 8). According to Derman-Sparks, an anti-bias curriculum incorporates the strong aspects of multicultural curriculum but tries to avoid a "suitcase" or tourist approach, in which children "visit" a country or

◆ **FIGURE 9.5** *A Continuum for Observing Developmentally Appropriate Practices*

PHILOSOPHY

Outside experts are _____ Teacher is trusted to _____ Teacher is trusted to _____ Children are trusted
trusted to provide recognize needs and recognize needs; to recognize own
curriculum for each plan course of study. children help to plan needs and plan
level of skills course of action. own study.

Teacher has control of student _____ Teacher is a facilitator, provider _____ Teacher is a questioner and
learning. of appropriate activities. guide in discovery, an equal
partner in a democratic
classroom.

Learning is equated with _____ The learner is active, a discoverer _____ The learner constructs own
mastering skills that are of knowledge. knowledge as a result of inter-
predetermined by the action with the environment.
curriculum.

Social interaction has less _____ There is provision for social _____ Social skills are emphasized and
importance than "time interaction during specified viewed as a life issue.
on task." times.

Build curriculum first, _____ Use interests of children _____ Use needs and interests _____ Children actively
then fit children into to make set curriculum of children to participate in
curriculum. more meaningful. build curriculum. building curriculum,
based on their
interests and needs.

Play is viewed as an _____ Play is used with _____ Play is viewed as_____ Play is viewed as
outlet; is restricted to directed objects to necessary to social essential means
time after work is done. support the learning and emotional growth. through which
process. learning takes place.

INSTRUCTIONAL STRATEGIES

Teacher directed _____ Teacher plans, but _____ Children have equal _____ Children select
and planned. children's interests are input in planning areas of interest and
included in planning. (i.e. through webbing) recognize skills they
need to acquire.

Skills-based, time specified for_____ Goals-based; thematic units may be _____ Interest-driven study with skills
each content area. used in an interdisciplinary approach. addressed as needed.

Begin with parts (discrete skills) and build_____ Begin with whole concept; break into parts as
toward whole (concept) skills acquisition is needed.

Predominately whole group_____ Whole group and small group_____ Small group and individual
instruction. instruction. instruction/conferencing as
well as whole group instruction.

Library books may be read at_____ Library books are used to _____ Reading instruction is based on
specified times or when work supplement the basal readers. children's literature and
is finished. children's own writing.

Competition among children is _____ Teacher looks for ways to _____ Competition with oneself is
used to motivate. Extrinsic rewards minimize competition, foster focus so that rewards become
(i.e., stickers and prizes) are given. cooperation. intrinsic. Learning is its own
reward.

THE ENVIRONMENT

Desks are for individual _____ use, may be arranged in rows or a U-shape. Social interaction is minimized by room arrangement.	Desks are clustered, _____ learning centers are located around perimeter of room.	Room is arranged in _____ learning centers, with teacher-selected materials and tasks, shared furniture.	Teacher/students organize environment to facilitate social interaction and student-initiated activities.
Teacher's desk is focal point. _____	Teacher's desk moves to less _____ conspicuous area.		Teacher's desk may give way to flexible area to be used for student conferencing, parent conferencing, record keeping. Area might be equipped with file cabinet, comfortable chairs and shelves for professional resources.
Room remains much the same _____ throughout the year; may be changed for variety.	Children may help teacher plan_____ room changes during the year.		Room arrangement and traffic patterns reflect the diverse developmental needs of children.
Basal textbooks, paper/_____ pencil tasks are pre-dominately used. Distribution is controlled by the teacher.	Concrete materials available; ____ distribution controlled by the teacher.	Concrete materials used_____ as needed, desired by children to assist in problem-solving.	Children use concrete materials to assist in problem-solving and to create problems for solving.
Room is prepared with commercial _____ or teacher-made displays for children's arrival.	Teacher has some bulletin boards _____ prepared; reserves space for children's own work.		Wall space may be empty when children arrive; children help plan spaces and displays of their work.

CLASSROOM MANAGEMENT

Discipline is controlled and _____ monitored by teacher.	Children begin to assume some _____ responsibility for their own behavior.		Children practice self-discipline. Rules are established by the class and are followed by all. Children help/teach each other.
No choices provided. Everyone_____ is required to complete specified activities.	Few choices provided, often _____ after work is completed.		Many choices provided. Children not only choose center but also the activity for that center.
Conflict is settled by the teacher. _____			Conflict resolution skills are learned and practiced by the children.

From *Developmentally Appropriate Practice: A Guide to Change*. Reprinted with permission of the Maine Department of Education and Cultural Services.

culture, its foods, holidays, and customs before packing the "suitcase" of materials away for the year. In addition, care must be taken so that the multicultural activities do not misrepresent, trivialize, or stereotype the cultures being studied. For example, if children studying Native American culture only make headbands, play in teepees, make Native American pottery, and read stories about Native American life in the nineteenth century, they may come away from the "unit of study" with either the stereotype that all Native Americans lived with the same lifestyle in the past or the misconception that this is the way Native Americans live today.

Anti-bias curriculum is more inclusive because it expands beyond cultural diversity by also considering differences in gender, age, and physical ability. According to Derman-Sparks (1992), the four major goals and developmental expectations of multicultural anti-bias curriculum for young children to foster include (1) construction of a knowledgeable, confident self-identity; (2) comfortable, empathetic interaction with diversity among people; (3) critical thinking about bias; and (4) ability to stand up for him- or herself and for others in the face of bias.

Teachers must take into consideration appropriate ways to meet these goals according to the ages and developmental stages of the children in the groups they are working with. In addition, teachers must consider the context and the cultural backgrounds of the children in the classroom, which may consist of (1) ethnically diverse children, (2) only white European American children, or (3) all children of color—all African American or all Native American, for example (Derman-Sparks 1992). Curriculum development must be responsive to the developmental levels, ethnic backgrounds, and other experiences of the children as well as to the backgrounds of the teachers, parents, and community of each school. The use of multiethnic literature, skin tone art materials, photographic displays of diverse ways of living in contemporary society, and persona dolls technique (developed by Kay Taus of the Anti-Bias Task Force), are just a few of the ways that teachers are finding to implement multicultural anti-bias curricula.

◆ **ACTIVITY**

9.8

Classroom Practices Inventory

Use the following *Classroom Practices Inventory* developed by Charlesworth *et al.* (1991, 1992) and modified by the Minnesota Association of Early Childhood Teacher Educators (1994) during your observations or practicums in a kindergarten or a multiage primary classroom. Use the rating scale provided to think about each of the statements related to classroom practices and curriculum. You may also use the numerals 2 or 4 to indicate a midpoint decision. Use these as a basis for discussing differences in early childhood curriculum with other classmates or seminar participants. Remember to consider this a learning experience by keeping your comments confidential and professional. Based on your understanding of the curriculum models described in this chapter, use the following code to label each of the statements on the *Classroom Practices Inventory:*

PA = Project Approach
DI = Direct Instruction
MAC = Multicultural Anti-bias Curriculum
HS = High Scope

Classroom Practices Inventory

1	3	5
Not at all like this classroom	Somewhat like this classroom	Very much like this classroom

Fill in the blanks below with the number rating based on the scale above.

_____ Teachers tell the children exactly what they will do and when. The teachers expect the children to follow their plans.

_____ Teachers encourage children to stand up for themselves and for others in the face of bias.

_____ Teachers use activities such as block building, measuring ingredients for cooking, woodworking, and drawing to help children learn concepts in math, science, and social studies.

_____ Teachers try to get children involved in activities by stimulating children's natural curiosity and interest.

_____ Teachers use redirection and encouragement as guidance or discipline techniques.

_____ Teachers create opportunities for children to develop emotional empathy to know that bias hurts.

_____ Teachers show affection in individually and culturally appropriate ways.

_____ The sound of the environment is marked by conversation, laughter, and spontaneous interaction.

_____ Children have planned lessons in writing with pencils, duplicating teacher models, tracing, or the correct use of scissors.

_____ Art projects involve copying an adult model, coloring predrawn forms, finishing a project the teacher has started, or following other adult directions.

_____ Children use a variety of art media, including easel, finger paints, and clay, in ways of their own choosing.

_____ Teachers encourage children to deal with their emotions in culturally appropriate ways.

_____ Large group teacher-directed instruction is used most of the time. Children are doing the same things at the same time.

_____ Children use workbooks, ditto sheets, flash cards, and other learning materials.

_____ Teachers ask questions that encourage children to give more than one right answer.

_____ The sound of the environment is characterized by enforced quiet.

_____ Reading and writing instruction emphasize direct teaching of letter recognition, reciting the alphabet, coloring within the lines, and instruction in the correct formation of letters.

_____ Teachers expect children to respond correctly with one right answer. Memorization and drills are emphasized.

_____ Separate times or periods are set aside to learn material in specific content areas such as math, science, and social studies.

_____ Children have daily opportunities to use pegboards, puzzles, building blocks, markers, scissors, or other similar materials in ways that the children choose.

_____ Teachers rely on results of standardized tests to make program decisions.

_____ When teachers try to get children involved in activities, they do so by requiring their participation, giving rewards, and disapproving of failure to participate.

_____ Children are physically active in the classroom, choosing from activities the teacher has set up and spontaneously initiating many of their own activities.

_____ Children are involved in concrete, three-dimensional learning activities, with materials closely related to children's daily life experiences.

_____ Teachers discourage children's use of words to solve problems.

_____ All children are expected to meet the same learning outcomes at the same time.

_____ Teachers expect children to sit down, watch, be quiet, and listen, or do paper-and-pencil tasks for long periods of time.

_____ Children are encouraged to identify unfair and untrue images, comments, and behaviors directed at their own or another's identity.

_____ Children select their own activities from a variety of learning areas the teacher prepares such as dramatic play, blocks, science, math, games and puzzles, recordings, art, and music.

_____ Children work individually or in small, child-chosen groups most of the time. Different children are constantly doing different things.

_____ Multicultural, nonsexist materials and activities are *not* available.

_____ Teachers concentrate on similarities among people and ignore differences.

_____ Teachers use competition, comparison, and criticism as teaching or discipline techniques.

_____ The classroom environment encourages children to listen to, read, and dictate stories, notice print in use in the classroom, engage in dramatic play, and experiment with writing by drawing, copying, and inventing their own spelling.

Marlene Thompson, a kindergarten teacher at Rogers Elementary School in Rogers, Minnesota, has been working on the development of an anti-bias curriculum project for a graduate-level staff development course on developmentally appropriate practices (Sherman and Thompson 1994). Marlene recognized the need to introduce the children in her classroom to people of color because of the limited ethnic and cultural diversity of the region in which they live. In addition, the school where she teaches had selected a multicultural theme, "Be a World Citizen," for the year, and Marlene wanted to ensure that her multicultural teaching approach was integrated and relevant to the rest of the curriculum to avoid the "tourist" approach.

Marlene set goals for her project in August after the first two class sessions had been held. She based her goal-setting on the knowledge she had gained from *Anti-Bias Curriculum: Tools for Empowering Children* (Derman-Sparks 1989). During the last class meeting, in January 1994, Marlene shared the success she has had in implementing her goals in her kindergarten with other primary-level teachers in the class. Marlene's process of goal setting and implementation of the goals can best be understood by reading excerpts from the journal she turned in for her project.

◆ **EXAMPLE 9.3**
Marlene's Story

8-5-93

The first part of this paper will outline my plans for implementing anti-bias strategies. This is written in the summer when I have large blocks of time for reflecting and organizing my efforts. The second part will be written as a response after these activities have been implemented.

Strategies to implement during the 1993–94 school year:

1. Make my classroom more diverse. Display more photographs of people of color during their everyday lives. Goal—one-half of images should present diversity.

2. Purchase art supplies—skin tone crayons, paper, and paint.

3. Include discussion of our anti-bias activities in weekly newsletter that goes home to parents.

4. Make a collage of eye shapes and colors. Graph eye colors in our classroom.

5. Make a book, "We All Look Special," using photographs and student descriptions of how they look.

6. Have students bring in pictures of family members. Talk about ways we look or don't look like other family members.

7. Use black and brown colors as desirable alternatives in the art center (paint, paper, and play-doh).

8. Get paint chips and sort by students' skin, eye, or hair color.

9. Read books that depict people of color in present day life in real-life situations that would be interesting to kindergarten students. I have researched a beginning list, which is attached.

(continued)

10. My biggest concern is implementing these strategies in an integrated fashion that will connect to these students' interests and needs. To do this, I plan to integrate many of the activities around the theme of self-concept, which is a major social studies focus in our kindergarten. As they learn about themselves and each other, I hope to introduce and weave cultural diversity into the ongoing curriculum. To do this, I hope to use the persona doll technique as described in the text. However, we have no funds to purchase dolls, so I have written an Innovative Classroom Practices Grant at our district level. If that is not funded, I will substitute multicultural puppets which I do have available. As I don't have enough knowledge yet to write my own stories, I am going to choose published books as a beginning point for my dolls' stories. Then, as we learn about other cultures through our schoolwide project, we can add stories and/or information about our dolls' lives. I want to start small so we can be successful. This will be our starting cast of dolls:

   - Jamie (White European boy from *Pumpkin Pumpkin* by J. Titherington). He will be introduced during our study of fall.
   - Rosa (Hispanic girl from *Something Special for Me* by Vera B. Williams). She will be introduced during our study of self-concept and our birthdays.
   - Ling Sung (Asian boy from *Cleversticks* by Bernard Ashley). He will be introduced during our study of self-concept and a discussion of our individual strengths.
   - Peter (Black American boy from *The Snowy Day* by Ezra Jack Keats). He will be introduced during our study of winter.
   - Jaimaica (Black American girl from *Jamaica's Find* by Juanita Havill). She will be introduced during our study of self-concept and friends.
   - Misty Dawn (American Indian from *Misty Dawn*, published by St. Paul Public Schools). She will be introduced during our study of self-concept and our family.

   The main emphasis I have planned will be to learn about racial differences and similarities. My hope is that the dolls or puppets will give the students new ideas and information and also provide a meaningful framework for discussions to solve any discriminatory behavior that occurs.

11. Finally, I would like to use the dolls to provide a connection for the students when we are exposed to cultural events and presentations during the school year. As we learn about foods around the world, we can make fry bread that Misty Dawn makes with her grandma, or breakfast tortillas (a favorite food of Rosa's), etc. Hopefully, this will make the experiences more real for these five- and six-year-olds.

12-8-93 entry

As school started, I began to organize and teach the strategies I had planned during the summer. As I will be working on implementation all year, what I describe is only what has been achieved so far.

Our school had decided to have an alternative Halloween party this year and focus on our schoolwide multicultural theme. So in kindergarten we celebrated with a color parade. Our theme was "Kindergarteners Like All Colors." We painted paper bag vests and stapled paper strip hats for our costumes. We included blacks and browns and tans along with all the other colors. We were an impressive sight. This activity served as an introduction to our study of self-concept and likenesses and differences.

I have worked on activities 1–9 during our unit on self-concept and how we are alike and different. Instead of paint chips to depict skin colors, however, I purchased construction paper. This worked much better. It is difficult for kindergarten children to match skin colors, but the bigger pieces made comparison easier. Also when they had chosen their skin color, we used it to make construction paper faces. We made a bulletin board of faces, and the variety of skin colors chosen led to a great discussion of how much skin colors can vary.

The persona dolls became the largest area of focus for our anti-bias study. My principal liked the proposal and made the decision to allocate funds for the project. So I ordered a set of 10 dolls, a boy and a girl of each: African American, Asian, Hispanic, Native American, and European American. Then I looked again for books which would match the physical appearance of the dolls I received. The dolls were introduced as new classroom friends who brought a story to share about themselves. These are the characters we have so far:

Peter:
- African American with a baby sister (Susie) and a mom and a dad
- books—*The Snowy Day* and *Peter's Chair* by Ezra Jack Keats
- has a dog named Willie
- lives in the city where there is snow
- celebrates Kwanza

Nicola:
- Asian American with a big sister (Angel) and a mom and dad
- adopted and goes to kindergarten
- book—*Families Are Different* by Nina Pellegrini
- has a dog named Buster

Ling Sung:
- Asian with a baby sister and a mom and dad
- book—*Cleversticks* by Bernard Ashley
- goes to school and tries to find what he does best (using chopsticks)

Misty Dawn:
- Native American with three brothers (Hayna, Kuna, and Dusty)
- has a mom and a dad and a dog named Radar
- book—*Misty Dawn* by St. Paul School District
- goes to kindergarten in St. Paul
- 6 years old
- makes fry bread with her grandmother

Olivia:
- African American with a mom and a dad
- book—*Rachel Elizabeth Parker, Kindergarten Showoff* by Ann Martin
- has a cat named Rosie and a friend named Rachel
- goes to kindergarten
- celebrates Kwanza

(continued)

◆ **EXAMPLE 9.3**
Marlene's Story (continued)

Gilberto:
- Hispanic
- book—*Gilberto and the Wind* by Marie Hall Ets
- plays with a friend—the wind

These are the "friends" we have introduced so far. I had to make some adjustments because some of the dolls did not look like the characters I had originally planned. These dolls have been great so far, and as usual the children have extended my original ideas greatly. After we introduce the dolls, they become our new friends in the library center. They are treated as additional students in the classroom. The students read to them, play school with them, and make up games to involve them. One of the most popular is "Duck, Duck, Gray Duck." The boys play with them just as much as the girls. They notice when a friend is absent (they visit other kindergarten classrooms) and are patiently waiting to be introduced to the last four friends.

We used the dolls when we talked about physical likenesses and differences, partly because we don't have much diversity in our classroom, but also because it is less threatening to look at differences in dolls than in classmates. I know this through my own parenting experience. In first grade I remember vividly my Korean daughter telling me that they had talked about colors of hair at school, and she was so embarrassed that the teacher pointed out she was the only one with black hair.

We have also started to use the dolls as connections for other events that happen in our schools. When the superintendent shared his slides from Central America, we talked about Gilberto and noted that his grandparents lived in Central America. When the media specialist did a presentation about Kwanza, we included the fact that Olivia and Peter celebrated Kwanza too. Hopefully this will provide more meaning to the students. When we do our multicultural unit on food in April, we can learn about one food which each of our friends enjoy. Hopefully this will prevent over generalizing which can sometimes lead to new stereotypes (such as all Asians eat with chopsticks; Ling Sung does, but Nicola doesn't, etc.). We continue to emphasize that differences are good. It continues to be a fun and exciting experience. And our theme will continue to be: "We're the same. We're different. That's what makes the world such fun. Many kinds of people, not just one!" (Kates 1992).

Marlene's story of growth and success is a reflection of many other primary grade teachers who are trying to incorporate anti-bias concepts into the curriculum in appropriate and meaningful ways. First-grade teachers in Rochester, Minnesota, who have used persona dolls in multicultural and handicap awareness curricula report that children begin writing about their dolls in their journals and ask to take them home for overnight visits. In the past several years, excellent resources have been published to help teachers develop strategies and locate materials that are multicultural, gender-fair, and handicap-aware. Some of those useful resources are described below.

Anti-bias Curriculum: Tools for Empowering Young Children (1989) by Louise Derman-Sparks and the ABC Task Force (National Association for Young Children, 1509 16th Street, Washington, DC; 1-800-424-2460). This book provides both underlying principles and methodology for implementing an anti-bias curriculum, which advocates social change so that the ultimate goal of developing every child to his or her greatest potential can be achieved. An excellent thirty-minute video that gives an overview of what it means to teach with an anti-bias curriculum approach is also available (Pacific Oaks Bookstore, 5 Westmoreland Pl., Pasadena, CA 91103; 818-397-1330).

Including All of Us: An Early Childhood Curriculum About Disability (1984) by Froschl, Colon, Rubin, and Sprung of Project Inclusive (distributed by Gryphon House, Inc., 3706 Otis Street, Mt. Ranier, MD 20712). This book, originally designed with children ages three to five in mind, can also be useful to teachers in the early elementary grades as it provides suggestions of activities, approaches, and resources to expand children's experiences to include "nonstereotyped images and role models of people of color and people with disabilities." Many of the activities and strategies suggested in the guide involve the use of "new friend" dolls.

Multiethnic Children's Literature (1994) by Gonzalo Ramirez, Jr., and Jan Lee Ramirez (Delmar Publishers Inc., 3 Columbia Circle, Box 15015, Albany, NY 12212-5015) is a resource for educators "who wish to bring quality multiethnic literature to our children." The book provides grade-level suggestions of literature for and about the four major nonwhite populations in America—Latinos, African Americans, Asian Americans, and Native Americans. Information about the history of multiethnic children's literature, guidelines for selecting appropriate multiethnic literature, and suggested activities to use with multiethnic literature are also provided in this useful text.

Developing Roots and Wings: Affirming Culture in Early Childhood Programs (1991) by Stacey York (distributed by Gryphon House, Inc., 3706 Otis Street, Mt. Rainier, MD 20712) offers suggestions to early childhood educators for providing classroom environments and activities that are responsive and sensitive to culture, gender, and handicaps. A trainer's guide (published in 1992) can be used by teachers to explore and expand their understanding of multicultural education.

Valuing Diversity: The Primary Years (1993) by Janet Brown McCracken (NAEYC, 1509 16th Street, Washington, DC 20036; 1-800-424-2460) was written specifically for primary-grade teachers. This brief but thoughtful book provides essential information teachers need for providing classroom environments, materials, and strategies that integrate and value human diversity.

Books about African Americans

Amazing Grace, Mary Hoffman, 1991, Scholastic.
Black Snowman, Phil Mendez, 1989, Scholastic.
Bigmama's, Donald Crews, 1992, Greenwillow.
Bright Eyes, Brown Skin, C. Hudson and B. Ford, 1992, Scholastic.
Cherries and Cherry Pits, Vera B. Williams, 1986, Greenwillow.
Corduroy, Don Freeman, 1968, Viking.
Jamaica Tag Along, Juanita Havill, 1989, Houghton-Mifflin.
Jamaica's Find, Juanita Havill, 1986, Greenwillow.
Mary Had a Little Lamb, Sarah Josepha Hale, 1990, Scholastic.
A New Dress for Maya, Malorie Blackman, 1992, Gareth Stevens Children's Books.
Peter's Chair, Ezra Jack Keats, 1967, Harper & Row.
Rachel Elizabeth Parker, Kindergarten, Show-off, Ann Martin, 1992, Scholastic.
The Snowy Day, Ezra Jack Keats, 1963, Viking.
Ten, Nine, Eight, Molly Bang, 1983, Greenwillow.
Wild Wild Sunflower Child Anna, Nancy Carlstrom, 1991, Scholastic.

Books about Asians

Cleversticks, Bernard Ashley, 1991, Crown Publishers.
Families Are Different, Nina Pellegrini, 1991, Scholastic.
Lion Dancer by Ernie Wan's Chinese New Year, Kate Waters and Madeline Slovenz-Low, 1990, Scholastic.
Rise and Shine, Mariko-chan! 1992, Scholastic.
Umbrella, Tara Yashima, 1958, Viking Press.

Books about Hispanics

A Chair for My Mother, Vera B. Williams, 1982, Greenwillow.
Gilberto and the Wind, Marie Hall Ets, 1963, Viking.
Music, Music for Everyone, Vera B. Williams, 1984, Greenwillow.
Something Special for Me, Vera B. Williams, 1983, Greenwillow.

Books about Native Americans or Alaskan Eskimos

Eskimo Boy—Life in an Inupiaq Eskimo Village, Russ Kendall, 1992, Scholastic.
Mama, Do You Love Me?, Barbara M. Joosse, 1991, Scholastic.
Misty Dawn, Grant # G007901081, St. Paul Public Schools.
On Mother's Lap, Ann Herbert Scott, 1993, Scholastic.
Powwow, Linda Coombs, 1992, Modern Curriculum Press.

Books about People of All Colors

Bread Bread Bread, Ann Morris, 1989, Lothrop, Lee and Shepard Books.
Everybody Cooks Rice, Norah Dooley, 1991, Carolrhoda.

Friends, Rachel Isadora, 1990, Greenwillow.
Hats Hats Hats, Ann Morris, 1989, Lothrop, Lee and Shepard Books.
Here Are My Hands, Bill Martin, Jr., and John Archambault, 1985, Henry Holt.
I Am Freedom's Child, Bill Martin, Jr., 1987, DLM Teaching Resources.
People, Peter Spier, 1980, Doubleday.
Potluck, Anne Shelby, 1991, Scott Foresman.
We Are All Alike . . . We Are All Different, Cheltenham Elementary School Kindergarten 1991, Scholastic.

Curriculum for and about Young Children with Special Needs

The federal government enacted Public Law 94–142 in 1975 and Public Law 99–457 in 1986 requiring that free, appropriate public education and services be provided for all children with disabilities or developmental delays from birth. As a result of these laws more children have been "mainstreamed," "integrated," or "included" in early childhood programs. Teachers working with these children need to learn skills to adjust, adapt, or modify the curriculum for children who may have hearing, visual, physical, or mental impairments or be developmentally delayed.

Programs that embrace a developmentally appropriate philosophy will not find it difficult to make adaptations for children with special needs because they are already providing curricula and activities that recognize the developmental variations of children. Morris and Schulz (1989) offer general guidelines for adapting activities for children with various special needs in *Creative Play Activities for Children with Disabilities*. When working with children who are deaf or hearing impaired, it is important to compensate for the child's inability to hear some or all sounds. The teacher must (1) make sure that hearing aids are maintained and working properly; (2) use visual and physical cues through facial expressions and touching the child and objects being talked about; (3) seek the child's attention before speaking; (4) speak distinctly and at the child's eye level; (5) use open-ended questions (tell me about what you are drawing) and allow the child adequate time to respond.

Suggestions that Morris and Schulz make for working with children who are blind or visually impaired are for the teacher to (1) structure activities and provide materials that allow the child to explore through touch, sound, taste, and smell; (2) help children to identify voices and common sounds and to locate objects by playing sound games; and (3) use specific rather than general points of reference (Teddy is standing by the window, rather than Teddy is over there).

Morris and Schulz suggest that teachers discuss the special needs of physically impaired children with a physical and an occupational therapist. Many questions need to be addressed when working with children with limited mobility. (1) What positions allow maximum mobility with appropriate support? (2) What is the best way to help the child change positions? (3) What special materials, adaptive equipment, or modifications of materials are needed? (4) What types of activities will provide the child with the types of movement that he or she needs?

Morris and Schulz (1989), Deiner (1993), and Dolinar *et al.* (1994) provide texts with excellent suggestions for modifying everyday classroom activities so that differently abled children are able to participate in the same activities with slight variations. For example, Morris and Schulz (1989) suggest how to modify play activities involving the senses, movement, waterplay, arts and crafts, music, and so forth for the hearing-impaired, visually impaired, or motor-impaired child. Deiner (1993) provides suggestions for increasing or decreasing the level of difficulty of activities related to specific curriculum areas including language arts, math, science, computers, motor development, social studies, health, and the creative arts. Dolinar *et al.* (1994) offer curriculum suggestions related to themes and ways to modify each thematic unit for children with special needs. For example, when studying a thematic unit on animals, children with visual impairments can be given animal models to hold while stories about animals are being read so they can feel the features of the animals. They also offer useful suggestions such as providing some clothing with velcro fasteners in the dramatic play area as a way to modify the learning environment for children who are physically impaired.

Froschl *et al.* (1984) offer suggestions for teaching children about disabilities through the use of "new friend" dolls, which are used to introduce children to the concepts of hearing impairment, visual impairment, and motor impairment. This aspect of curriculum development is important for children in classrooms without special needs children as well as in preparing children for the inclusion of special needs children in the classroom. It is important to expand children's cognitive, social, and emotional development through their understanding, appreciation, and respect for human differences and disabilities. Suggestions for stories and activities to help young children understand that some things are the same and some are different for children with visual, hearing, or motor impairments are provided. Simple activities such as learning about Braille by making a Braille chart or use of a six-cup muffin tin and cotton balls, which can be manipulated to make letters of the Braille alphabet, are explained. For example, the Braille letter *X* is formed by placing cotton balls in the two top and two bottom cups of the muffin tin. The letter *S* is formed by placing cotton balls in the top right, middle left, and bottom left cups of the muffin tin.

In providing curriculum for and about young children with special needs, care must be taken to talk about special needs in a "natural" way. It is important that discussion take place about the special needs of a child who will be working in the group so the group is sensitive and responsive to that child. To the greatest extent possible, special needs children should participate in activities with the group. Special educators and educational assistants can play an important role in helping the classroom teacher modify activities for the special needs child.

◆ **ACTIVITY**

9.9

Special Needs Observation

Observe for a half day in a preschool, kindergarten, or primary-grade classroom that includes a special needs child. "Shadow" the special needs child (follow him or her for the entire morning, even during times when he or she is out of the classroom for special services). Write a one- to two-page report describing what it would feel like to participate in that classroom as a child with a particular special need. Also discuss the special adaptations that have been made in the environment and in instruction to facilitate that child's participation in a "least restrictive" manner.

Decision, Decisions, Decisions!

The role of today's teacher could be described as that of a decision maker and tightrope walker. Teachers, including those working with young children, must make decisions while maintaining an educational balance and considering the needs of both the group of children and individual children in building the curriculum, and responding to the expectations of parents, administrators, community, and society in general. In truth, no single curriculum model can meet the needs of every teacher in every infant program, preschool, kindergarten or primary classroom.

Elkind (1990) has described teaching as both a science and an art. The scientific aspect of teaching comes from the teacher's understanding of child development and the structure of curriculum. Much of that information comes from observing children, classrooms, and experienced teachers as you have been asked to do throughout this book. Because our understanding of child development and effective education is informed by ongoing research, curriculum must be considered fluid rather than fixed. What was relevant and appropriate in the 1970s may not be relevant or appropriate in the 2000's, based on new information. Who among us would settle for a doctor who was using all of his or her methodology from thirty years ago while disregarding new information related to the field of medicine? As professionals we must keep abreast of the new information about child development and educational theory as we incorporate that knowledge into the curriculum we develop for young children.

The artistic aspect of teaching comes from each teacher's personality, experiences, and talents (Elkind 1990). This might include incorporation of vocal talents, knowledge of sculpture, or sharing of artifacts from travel experiences. Teachers and prospective teachers have a responsibility to continue to foster both their scientific and artistic skills for effective curriculum development.

In addition, teachers must respond to the curricular expectations of others who share the responsibility of educating the young child, including parents, school boards, boards of directors, the community, and state departments of education. Being responsive to all these constituencies and being true to oneself can be challenging. In the end the teacher is faced with the task of making many decisions that must reflect the scientific knowledge he or she possesses about education for the young child, expectations from others in the educational arena, and his or her own artistic style and capabilities to make curriculum exciting, challenging, and meaningful to children in the classroom.

Summary

The academic curriculum for young children is rich in history and variety. Curriculum models continue to be reflected and developed in current programs for young children today. Both increased knowledge of child development principles and effective educational practice have served to improve the early childhood curriculum. The concept of developmentally appropriate practice incorporates principles from many of the curriculum models described in this chapter, including the whole language, project, Bank Street, and High Scope approaches. Developmentally appropriate practice includes a wide range of strategies. Early childhood educators must view the change process toward developmentally appropriate practices as movement along a continuum, as are the practices developed by the Maine Department of Educational and Cultural Services (refer back to Figure 9.5). While many behaviorist or direct instruction practices are rejected by advocates of developmentally appropriate practice, some strategies can be useful for instruction and behavior management when used thoughtfully and in moderation.

Today's early childhood educator is more responsive to cultural diversity and the special needs of young children when planning a curriculum. The early childhood professional has a career-long responsibility to continue to learn how to best provide for the education and care of children from birth through age eight.

REFERENCES

Ashley, B. (1991). *Cleversticks*. New York: Crown Publishers.

Bredekamp, S. (1987) *Developmentally appropriate practice in early childhood programs serving children from birth through age 8*. Washington, DC: National Association for the Education of Young Children.

Bredekamp, S., and C. Copple (1997). *Developmentally appropriate practice in early childhood programs* (rev. ed.). Washington, DC: National Association for the Education of Young Children.

Charlesworth, R., C. H. Hart, and D. C. Burts (1991). Kindergarten teachers' beliefs and practices. *Early Child Development and Care*. 70 17–35.

Charlesworth, R., C. H. Hart, D. C. Burts, R. Thomasson, J. Mosley, and P. Fleege (1992). *A school system's profile of kindergarten teachers beliefs and practices*. (Unpublished manuscript).

Chattin-McNichols, J. (1992). *The Montessori controversy*. Albany, NY: Delmar

Cook, R. E., A. Tessier, and M. D. Klein (1992). *Adapting early childhood curricula for children with special needs*. New York, NY: Merrill.

Deiner, P. L. (1993). *Resources for teaching children with diverse abilities.* Orlando, FL: Harcourt Brace Jovanovich.

Derman-Sparks, L. (1989). *Anti-bias curriculum: Tools for empowering children.* Washington, DC: National Association for the Education of Young Children.

Derman-Sparks, L. (1992). Reaching potentials through antibias, multicultural curriculum. In S. Bredekamp, and T. Rosegrant, Eds., *Reaching potentials: Appropriate curriculum and assessment for young children.* Washington, DC: National Association for the Education of Young Children.

Dolinar, K., C. Boser, and E. Holm (1994). *Learning through play: Curriculum and activities for the inclusive classroom.* Albany, NY: Delmar.

Elkind, D. (1990). *Using what we know: Applying Piaget's theory in primary classrooms.* Davis, CA: Davidson Films, Inc.

Essa, E. (1992). *Introduction to early childhood education.* Albany, NY: Delmar.

Ets, M. H. (1963). *Gilberto and the wind.* New York: Viking.

Fountas, I. C., and G. S. Pinnell (1996). *Guided reading: Good first teaching for all children.* Portsmouth, NH: Heinemann.

Froschl, M., L. Colon, E. Rubin, and B. Sprung (1984). *Including all of us: An early childhood curriculum about disability.* New York, NY: Educational Equity Concepts, Inc.

Gandini, L. (1993). Fundamentals of the Reggio Emilia approach to early childhood education. *Young Children, 49*(1), 4–8.

Glazer, S. M., and E. M. Burke (1994). *An integrated approach to early literacy.* Boston, MA: Allyn & Bacon.

Goffin, S. G. (1994). *Curriculum models and early childhood: Appraising the relationship.* New York: Merrill Macmillan.

Havill, J. (1986). *Jamaica's find.* New York: Greenwillow.

Helm, J. H., and L. Katz (2001). *Young investigators: The project approach in the early years.* Washington, DC: National Association for the Education of Young Children.

Hendrick, J. (Ed.) (1997). *First steps toward teaching the Reggio way.* Upper Saddle River, NJ: Prentice Hall.

Holdaway, D. (1979). *The foundations of literacy.* Sydney, Australia: Ashton Scholastic.

Jones, E., and J. Nimmo (1994). *Emergent curriculum.* Washington, DC: National Association for the Education of Young Children.

Kates, B. J. (1992). *We're different, we're the same.* New York: Random House.

Katz, L., and S. Chard (1989). *Engaging children's minds: The project approach.* Norwood, NJ: Ablex.

Katz, L., and S. Chard (1993). *The project approach.* In J. L. Roopnarine, and J. E. Johnson, Eds., *Approaches to Early Childhood Education.* New York, NY: Macmillan.

Keats, E. J. (1962). *The snowy day.* New York: Viking.

Keats, E. J. (1967). *Peter's chair.* New York: Harper & Row.

King, E. W., M. Chipman, and M. Cruz-Jansen (1994). *Educating young children in a diverse society.* Boston, MA: Allyn & Bacon.

Maine Department of Education and Cultural Services. *Developmentally appropriate practice: A guide to change.*

Martin, A. (1992). *Rachel Elizabeth Parker, kindergarten show-off.* New York: Scholastic.

McCracken, J. B. (1993). *Valuing diversity: The primary years.* Washington, DC: National Association for the Education of Young Children.

Minnesota Association of Early Childhood Teacher Educators (1994). *Classroom Practices Inventory.* (Unpublished research instrument). Mankato, MN: Mankato State University

Morris, L. R., and L. Schulz (1989). *Creative play activities for children with disabilities: A resource book for teachers and parents.* Champaign, IL: Human Kinetics.

National Association for the Education of Young Children and International Reading Association. (1998). Learning to read and write: Developmentally appropriate practices for young children. *Young Children, 53*(4), 30–46.

Neisworth, J. T., and T. Buggey (1993). Behavior analysis and principles in early childhood education. In J. L. Roopnarine, and J. E. Johnson, Eds., *Approaches to early childhood education.* New York: Macmillan.

Neuman, S. B., and K. A. Roskos (1993). *Language and literacy learning in the early years: An integrated approach.* Orlando, FL: Holt, Rinehart and Winston.

Pellegrini, N. (1991). *Families are different.* New York: Scholastic.

Ramirez, G., and J. L. Ramirez (1994). *Multiethnic children's literature.* Albany, NY: Delmar.

Robinson, R. D., M. C. McKenna, and J. M. Wedman (1996). *Issues and trends in literacy education.* Needham, MA: Allyn & Bacon.

Roopnarine, J. L., and J. E. Johnson (1993). *Approaches to early childhood education.* New York: Macmillan.

Rosegrant, T., and S. Bredekamp (1992). Planning and implementing transformational curriculum. In S. Bredekamp and T. Rosegrant Eds., *Reaching potentials: Appropriate curriculum and assessment for young children.* Washington, DC: National Association for the Education of Young Children.

Sherman, J., and M. Thompson (1994). Reflections on diversity: Implementing anti-bias curriculum in the primary grades. *Insights into open education.* Grand Forks, ND: University of North Dakota, Center for Teaching and Learning.

Spodek, B., and O. N. Saracho (1994). Right from the start: Teaching children ages three to eight. Boston, MA: Allyn & Bacon.

St. Paul Public Schools. (1982). *Misty dawn.* St. Paul, MN: Multicultural Resource Center, St. Paul Public Schools.

Titherington, J. (1990). *Pumpkin pumpkin.* New York: Scholastic.

Watertown Historical Society. (1988). *Froebel's gifts.* Watertown WI: Watertown Historical Society.

Weikart, D. P., and L. J. Schweinhart (1993). The High Scope curriculum for early childhood care and education. In J. L. Roopnarine, and J. E. Johnson, Eds., *Approaches to early childhood education.* New York: Macmillan.

Williams, V. B. (1983). *Something special for me.* New York: Greenwillow.

York, S. (1991). *Roots and wings: Affirming culture in early childhood.* St. Paul, MN: Redleaf.

Zarillo, J. (1994). *Multicultural literature, multicultural teaching.* Orlando, FL: Harcourt Brace Jovanovich.

A Time-Sampling
Technique for Evaluating
Infant/Toddler Programs

The quality of an infant and toddler day care program depends, by and large, on the quality of the interactions that take place within that environment. The physical setting plays an important role in promoting positive interactions, as do administrative policies such as group size, child–staff ratio, and training requirements for staff. However, it is the quality of interactions which will, in the final analysis, distinguish the setting which promotes the well-being and healthy psychological development of the children. Very young children need an emotionally safe and secure environment. They need adults who are loving, responsive, and empathetic. They need adults who converse with them, and who can turn everyday living into everyday learning opportunities for the children. Babies and toddlers in group care need adults who help them learn to live with other children, while at the same time respecting their individuality.

All infant and toddler group programs should have some systematic means of assessing the quality of their program. The assessment guide described in the following pages focuses on the quality of interactions that occur primarily between the caregivers and the infants. It is based on the assumption that, in a quality setting, certain types of interactions and events should be occurring frequently, and others should rarely occur. Certainly every center has "good days" and "bad days," and all caregivers at times respond to children in a less than ideal manner. However, if the following assessment guide is used systematically over a period of time, it will be possible to gain some insight into the general climate of the classroom and the proportion of positive to undesirable interactions.

Taken from *Evaluating Programs* by Rena Shimoni, Denise MacLean, and Cathy MacWilliam (1990, 42–46). Reprinted with permission of Human Sciences Press, Inc.

This assessment guide is recommended for students who wish to utilize an objective method of observing and evaluating infant and toddler programs. It is also recommended that day care staff use this as a self-evaluation tool as a basis for discussion and training.

This assessment guide is based on a technique called "time sampling." The observer places himself or herself in a position where he or she has a good vantage point covering the entire room. At steady time intervals (say, every hour), the room is observed for a period of two minutes. Immediately following this, the observer notes on the checklist whether or not the events/actions occurred.

Several samples of a center are required in order to obtain a reliable picture of the proportion of positive to negative events.

Below is a description of both the positive and negative events/actions that the observer will note.

Positive Items

1. *Caregiver Expresses Affection and/or Positive Regard for the Child.* Positive regard is displayed by hugging, kissing, genuine praise, or indicating verbally or otherwise that the child is special. Children need to feel liked and to be nurtured for their own self-esteem, self-worth, and overall emotional well-being.

2. *Caregiver Responds to and Expands on Child's Vocalization or Words, or Body Language.* When a prelinguistic infant babbles, coos, or makes a gesture, the caregiver should respond as if the child is speaking. With a linguistic child, the caregiver responds by repeating and expanding upon the utterance (e.g., child: "Dog"; caregiver: "Yes, a dog. A big, brown dog".) By being responsive to a child's vocalizations, the caregiver is indicating that the child is an important individual, which in turn encourages the development of language. Talking to or at a child (i.e., giving directions, commands, etc.) does not count for this item.

3. *Caregiver Uses Tone of Voice, Facial Expression, and Body Language in a Way That Noticeably Expresses Her or His Emotional State.* When the caregiver is expressing happiness, laughter, sadness or enthusiasm, she or he is facilitating communicative understanding in children and provides a more stimulating environment.

4. *Caregiver Expresses Empathy to Child.* The caregiver, in this way, acknowledges how the child is feeling, that she or he understands the child, and that "it's okay" to express emotions. An empathic response to a child who has fallen and is crying could be "Ouch! I know that your knee must really hurt."

5. *Caregiver Turns Routine Experience (An Everyday Occurrence) into a Learning Experience.* The caregiver is utilizing valuable interaction time to expand on a child's knowledge of his or her surroundings. For example, while

rinsing out a cloth, the caregiver might take the opportunity to teach how to turn a faucet on and off.

6. *Caregiver Is Involved with One Child But Remains Responsive to Other Children.* In group care, it is important to ensure that all children are included and that all needs are met. Being involved with one child gives that child one-to-one time, and being responsive to the other children is letting them know that they are still important and the caregiver is there for them.

7. *While Caregiver Is Busy with Task Not Related to Caregiving, He or She Still Remains Responsive to Children.* Example of nonchild tasks are cleaning, filing, and arranging the room, which are unrelated to the children's present activities. The caregiver should be aware of and able to interact even while doing a nonchild task, not merely keeping an eye on them.

8. *Caregiver Makes Use of Teachable Moments.* This means that a caregiver spontaneously focuses a child's attention on an object, event, or person and elaborates. It is not planned as part of a structured activity. The caregiver verbally labels, describes, or shows how something works to the child (e.g., "Look at the light. You can turn it on and off. Would you like to try?").

9. *Caregiver Assists Children in Getting Along with Each Other.* Facilitating peer relations is essential for social skill development. This may be accomplished by the use of distraction to avoid conflict, providing enough toys to avoid conflict, establishing clear limits, etc. Arranging and planning the environment will minimize the need to intervene when children are at play.

10. *Caregiver Is at a Distance from Child But Still Involved.* When a caregiver is at a distance from a child but still involved—maybe verbally commenting, smiling at, or showing something to a child—she or he is displaying awareness of what the child is doing and readiness to assist the child if necessary.

11. *Caregiver Is at Eye Level with Children While Interacting.* The caregiver is able to establish eye contact with the child(ren) and is more easily heard and understood, and the children will not feel that they are being talked down to.

12. *At Least One Child Is Engaged in Exploring a Nontoy Object.* A nontoy object is any object which has not been manufactured for the sole purpose of being a child's toy (e.g., pots and pans, wooden spoons, boxes). This encourages the child to be more creative and constructive with objects available in the environment.

13. *Most of the Children (All But One or Two) Look Happy and/or Content.* This should speak for itself! Everyone would like to see children happy, and the best indication that a program is suiting the needs of the children is a room full of happy and/or contented children.

Negative Items

1. *Child Is Crying and Fussing.* Although it is quite normal for children to cry or fuss sometimes, if this occurs in more than 15 percent of the observations, it may suggest a need for changes in the program or the responsiveness of the caregiver.

2. *Caregiver Physically or Verbally Prohibits Child from Doing Something.* The room arrangement and activities should be planned in such a way as to minimize prohibitions (e.g., "Don't run," "Don't touch"). Every child must have a safe environment to allow for freedom of choice and movement. As well, the social environment should not prohibit children from expressing emotions (i.e., "Don't cry").

3. *Child Is Placed in a Physically Restrictive Device (e.g., Walker, Highchair, Crib, Jolly Jumper) and Is Unattended and/or Unobserved for One Minute or Longer.* When a nonambulatory or an ambulatory child is placed in a restrictive device, she or he is solely at the mercy of the caregiver. The child is unable to remove herself or himself from the device at will; therefore, the child loses control and choice within her or his environment.

4. *Children Are Not Occupied and Are Waiting for Something to Happen.* Transitional times (i.e., lunch, naptime, going outside) are when children most often have to do some waiting. To expect a child to be patient and wait without being occupied in some way causes children to become frustrated and irritable. Recognizing transitional times and planning accordingly (i.e., songs and stories) will minimize the waiting.

5. *Caregivers Are Involved in Conversation among Themselves That Is Unrelated to Immediate Tasks.* When caregivers are conversing with each other, they are in fact ignoring and unaware of the children if the topic of conversation is unrelated to the immediate tasks. Communication between caregivers is essential, but it does not need to be lengthy or completely exclude the children. In addition, if planning is done properly beforehand the necessity to ask each other questions will decrease (caregivers should not discuss children in front of children).

6. *One or More Children Seem Bored, Uninvolved, and/or Aimless.* Although children need time to rest, integrate and absorb experiences, and daydream, too much time spent uninvolved could mean that the child is bored and may need some direction or a more stimulating, challenging, and interesting activity.

7. *Routine Care Task Is Done with Little or No Interaction.* When the caregiver treats the caregiving tasks (e.g., diapering, feeding, putting child to bed) as chores and the child is related to as an object rather than as a person, valuable one-to-one interaction time is lost and the caregiving is disrespectful.

8. *Caregiver Behaves Negatively (Sarcasm, Teasing, Belittling, Threatening, Yelling) Toward the Children.* Respecting children is the foundation of qual-

ity care. Sarcasm, teasing, belittling, threatening, and yelling at the children are disrespectful behaviors which are hurtful to the children. In addition, as children learn so much from the examples adults provide, these behaviors should not occur.

This adaptation of the Belsky and Walker scale is intended for program evaluations and training for practitioners rather than for strictly research purposes. However, measures should be taken to ensure systematic and objective use of this scale. The procedure recommended below may be varied to meet the time and staff limitations of the various centers employing this scale as long as whatever schedule of observation has been decided on remains consistent. That is, if it is decided to do a time sampling of two minutes every thirty minutes, for the entirety of the evaluation the time intervals should remain at thirty minutes.

Before using any observation tool, it is very important to be very familiar with it and to have memorized almost all the items. Read and reread the scale, and discuss with colleagues what kinds of observations would constitute positive and negative scores.

As a note of caution, when evaluating a room, the observer must rate only what is observed during the two-minute period, not what is believed or known to be the normal occurrence. For example, if the observer is observing in a room that is familiar to the observer and "knows" that the caregiver frequently expresses empathy, the observer can only check this item positively if it is observed during the two-minute observation period.

If possible, it is advisable to complete the evaluations in pairs. In this way, if two evaluators' results differ significantly, then clearly the items on the checklist must be studied and clarified before the room is reevaluated. If it is not possible to work in pairs throughout the entire evaluation, it is strongly recommended that initially the evaluators pair up and the scale be used in a pretest situation until there is an agreement on how what is observed should be scored on the checklist.

For example, two observers may have observed a caregiver changing a diaper. The caregiver placed a rattle in the child's hand and said, "That will keep you busy while I am changing your diaper" and proceeded to change him with no further verbal interactions. One observer gives a negative score for #7: Routine task done with little or no interaction. The second observer does not. The observers must then compare and justify their own scores. In this way, they will eventually agree on what kinds of behavior constitute a positive or negative score. Aside from clarifying the points on the observation scale, this process of dialogue can be an extremely valuable learning tool for staff.

Procedure

1. Decide on the time intervals between the two-minute observations. (Recommended timing of observation is two minutes, at twenty-minute intervals over a period of a day, to be repeated over at least three days).
2. Select the room to observe.

3. Observe intently for two minutes.
4. Leave the room immediately and mark with a check mark all the items observed during the two-minute observation.
5. Repeat the procedure every twenty minutes for a period of at least three hours according to the prearranged schedule.
6. Calculate the scores. The manner in which the scores are calculated will depend on how the information gleaned from the observation is to be used.

If, for example, the primary goal of the evaluation was for staff training, it will be necessary to calculate the number of times each positive and negative item was displayed during the observation period. In this way, staff will be able to see what positive behaviors were not observed frequently, and what negative behaviors were observed too frequently. For example, one negative behavior that staff tend to use frequently without being aware of is #2: caregiver physically or verbally prohibits a child from doing something. Often, after seeing the results of the evaluation, caregivers will monitor their own behaviors and attempt to reduce them. Similarly, if over the entire period of observation some of the positive behaviors are infrequently seen (e.g., #11: caregiver is at eye level with children while interacting), caregivers can make a conscious attempt to get down to eye level more and monitor the number of times this behavior occurs. Therefore, if you are trying to isolate the staff behaviors that need to be increased or decreased, an item-by-item score should be recorded.

In order to have some overall evaluation of the quality of interaction, scores may be calculated in percentages. That is, over the course of the evaluation process, there may be 60 time samplings. The frequency of positive and negative items may be calculated individually (e.g., #13 child happy, scored 30 check marks; therefore, 30–60 (time samplings) = 50 percent of the time).

The percentages of negative and positive items are totaled, and the respective totals are divided by the number of possible items to be seen (i.e, 13 positive, 8 negative). The end results are the percentages of time that positive and negative interactions occur over the course of a day.

If the negative interactions were observed 25 percent or more of the time, there is cause for concern. Likewise, the positive interactions should be observed 75 percent of the time. A lower score of positive items indicates the need for caregivers to make a conscious effort to increase positive interactions.

◆ **EXAMPLE A.1**
Evaluating Infant/Toddler Programs: Positive Items

Playroom _____   Date _____

Score Sheet

Positive Items	Time of Observation										
1. Caregiver expresses affection or positive regard.											
2. Caregiver responds to and expands upon gestures, sounds and words of infants.											
3. Caregiver uses tone of voice, gestures in an expressive manner.											
4. Caregiver expresses empathy.											
5. Caregiver turns routines into learning opportunities.											
6. Caregiver involved with one child yet responsive to other children.											
7. Caregiver involved in nonchild task yet remains responsive to children.											
8. Caregiver makes use of teachable moments.											
9. Caregiver assists children in getting along with each other.											
10. Caregiver distant from child but still involved.											
11. Caregiver at eye level with children while interacting.											
12. Child engaged in exploring a nontoy object.											
13. Most of children look happy.											

◆ **EXAMPLE A.2**
 Evaluating Infant/Toddler Programs: Negative Items

Playroom _____   Date _____

Score Sheet

Negative Items	*Time of Observation*									
1. Child crying and fussing.										
2. Caregiver physically, verbally prohibits child from doing something.										
3. Child placed in restrictive device and is left unattended and/or unobserved for one minute (or longer).										
4. Children unoccupied and waiting for something to happen.										
5. Caregiver involved in conversation amongst themselves that is unrelated to immediate task.										
6. One or more children bored, uninvolved and/or aimless.										
7. Routine care task done with little or no interaction.										
8. Caregiver behaves negatively toward children.										

Appendix B

Playground Improvement Rating Scale

Program _____

Number of Children _____   Date _____

Ages of Children _____   Rater _____

Number of Staff _____

Score each item: **3**—outdoor play area meets this goal very well

2—outdoor play area needs to be improved to meet this goal

1—little or no evidence that outdoor play area meets this goal

(Examples of items to look for are listed in parentheses.)

Activities and Equipment
Range of Activities

____ 1. The equipment provides appropriate and stimulating levels of difficulty for all the age groups served (infants, toddlers, preschool children, school-age children).

____ 2. A variety of equipment is provided to stimulate different types of physical activity (balls, balance beams, wheel toys, swings, climbing equipment, jump ropes, ladders, planks).

____ 3. Some of the equipment and materials invite cooperative play (outdoor blocks, rocking boat, dramatic play props).

____ 4. Creative materials are readily available for children (clay, carpentry, paints, water, and sand).

From "Playground Improvement Rating Scale," *Young Children,* March, 1985, pp. 7–8. Copyright ©1985 by the National Association for the Education of Young children. Reprinted by permission.

_____ 5. Some of the equipment is flexible so that it can be combined in different ways by the children with adult help if necessary (planks, climbing boxes, ladders).

_____ 6. The climbing equipment incorporates a variety of spatial relationships (through tunnels, up or down ramps, over or under platforms).

_____ 7. There is a suitable place for gardening (window box, tubs with soil, garden plot).

_____ 8. There are enough options for the children to choose from without unreasonable competition or waiting.

Safety and Health

_____ 9. The equipment is substantially constructed (anchored climbing structures and swing frames).

_____ 10. Cushioning is provided under swings and climbing apparatus (loose sand or tanbark at least 1 foot deep within a containing edgeboard, rubber padding).

_____ 11. Swing seats are made of pliable materials.

_____ 12. Swings are separated from areas where children run or ride wheel toys.

_____ 13. Protective railings prevent children from falling from high equipment.

_____ 14. Equipment is well maintained (no protruding nails, splinters, flaking paint, broken parts, frayed ropes).

_____ 15. The play area is routinely checked and maintained (trash picked up, grass mowed, good drainage).

_____ 16. The health hazards from animal contamination are minimized (sand box covers, fences, children wash hands after playing outdoors)

Organization of Play Area

_____ 17. The play area is well defined (fence that cannot be climbed)

_____ 18. There are clear pathways and enough space between areas so that traffic flows well and equipment does not obstruct the movement of children.

_____ 19. Space and equipment are organized so that children are readily visible and easily supervised by teachers.

_____ 20. Different types of activity areas are separated (tricycle paths separate from swings, sand box separate from climbing area).

_____ 21. Open space is available for active play.

_____ 22. Some space encourages quiet, thoughtful play (grassy area near trees, sandbox away from traffic).

____ 23. Blocks and props can be set up outdoors for dramatic play.

____ 24. Art activities can be set up outdoors.

____ 25. The area is easily accessible from the classroom.

____ 26. The area is readily accessible to the restrooms.

____ 27. A drinking fountain is available.

____ 28. Accessible and sufficient storage is provided.

____ 29. A portion of the play area is covered for use in wet weather.

____ 30. An adequate area is sunny in cold weather.

____ 31. An adequate area of shade is provided in hot weather.

Variety of Play Surfaces

____ 32. A hard surface is available to ride wheel toys, play group games, or dance.

____ 33. Soil, sand, and water are available for digging and mud play.

____ 34. A grassy or carpeted area is provided.

____ 35. Good drainage keeps all surfaces usable.

Surrounding Environment

____ 36. The fence creates an effective screen for the playground by blocking out unpleasant or by admitting pleasant aspects of the surrounding environment. It protects children from intrusion by passers-by.

____ 37. The setting visible from the play area is pleasant.

____ 38. The location is relatively quiet (little noise from railroads, traffic, factories).

Supervision and Use of Play Area

____ 39. A sufficient number of adults supervise the children during outdoor play.

____ 40. Responsibility for specific areas is assigned to staff to assure that the entire playground is well supervised.

____ 41. Teachers focus their attention on and interact with the children to enhance learning and maintain safety (adults do not talk together at length or sit passively when supervising children).

____ 42. Children are guided to use the equipment appropriately (climb on ladders instead of tables).

____ 43. The daily schedule includes morning and afternoon active play periods for all age groups, either outdoors or in suitably equipped indoor areas.

____ 44. The schedule for use of the play area minimizes overlap of age groups to avoid conflicts, overcrowding, and undue competition for materials.

_____ 45. Special activities are planned for and set up in the outdoor area daily (games, painting).

_____ 46. Teachers add to or rearrange the large equipment at least every six months (spools, crates, tunnels).

_____ 47. Teachers encourage and assist children in rearranging small flexible equipment (ladders, planks, boxes).

_____ 48. Most of the children are constructively involved with the equipment and activities in the playground.

_____ 49. Children help clean up the area and put away equipment.

_____ **Total Score**

 **Appendix C**

Ways to Increase Positive Social Interaction among Children

Dramatic Play Centering on the Home

Approaches Likely to Induce Positive Social Action

- Be prepared to suggest ongoing ideas from time to time when play appears likely to lag or fall apart. ("Hmmm—do I smell vegetable soup?")
- Provide both male and female items in order to welcome both sexes and provide opportunities to try out other-sex roles. These might include shaving equipment, tools, wedding dresses, or boots.
- Stimulate variety in the play by varying the equipment. Offer market supplies, hospital things, or the large blocks and boards.
- Vary the location. Move equipment to a new area—perhaps outside or into a large bathroom for water play.
- Include items that attract children particularly, such as water, several large empty boxes, or guinea pigs.
- Foster cultural respect by offering multiethnic equipment, such as wooden bowls from Africa, a bedspread made of Guatemalan material, or dolls of various ethnic backgrounds, and speak casually, but respectfully, of such things as our "Mexican chair," our "Zambian bowl," and so forth.
- Offer more than one piece of the same large equipment, such as two baby buggies or two suitcases.

From *Total Learning: Developmental Curriculum for the Young Child* by Joanne Hendrick (1994). Reprinted with the permission of the Macmillan College Publishing Company. Copyright ©1994 by Macmillan College Publishing Company, Inc.

- Split the housekeeping equipment into two households, and encourage the children to improvise additional needed items.
- Set up an office or a market in conjunction with the housekeeping area.
- To encourage role playing, offer items large enough for the children to get into themselves, such as a regular high chair and a child-size bed.
- Increase the reality-information base of the play by having a baby visit, going to a real market, or actually visiting places where parents work to see what their mothers and fathers do there.
- Offer a simple cooking experience, such as making peanut butter sandwiches in the housekeeping corner.
- Encourage more than one age to play together. This is fairly easy to do in housekeeping because of the variety of family roles that are available.
- Encourage the children to solve problems together. How could they turn the house into a camper? What could they use for bananas?
- Pay attention to the children's requests and ideas. This helps them feel valued and important and encourages children to listen to each other.
- When necessary, help new arrivals enter the group successfully by suggesting how they could help, what they could be, or what they might say to the children who are already playing there.
- Put all the regular equipment away and encourage the children to develop their own house, using blocks, boards, and accessories.

Approaches Likely to Induce Negative Social Action

- Make the play area too small and congested so that the children get in each other's way much of the time.
- Allow clothing or other equipment to accumulate on the floor so that the children stumble over it, mistreat it, or can't find what they need.
- Offer only female-type items, with the result that the boys feel subtly excluded. This makes attacks by the boys more likely.
- Don't set up the homemaking area before the children arrive. Leave it as it was the day before.
- Provide no physical barriers, so that children who are passing through intrude either intentionally or unintentionally.
- Keep equipment skimpy so that children have to wait too long for a chance to use it.
- Allow equipment to become broken or dirty. This tells the children that this play area and what happens there aren't really important and that you don't care about them.

Outdoor Large Muscle Play

Positive Social Action

- Whenever possible, select equipment that invites or requires more than one child's cooperative use for best success, such as double rocking boats, a hammock, large parachute activities, jump ropes, wagons, and horizontally hung tire swings.

- Offer several of one kind of thing, not only to reduce bickering but also to induce social play. Several bouncy horses together facilitate social congeniality, for example.

- Provide plentiful equipment for dramatic play. In particular, a good assortment of blocks, ladders, sawhorses, and boards encourages the children to build things together. Smaller equipment, such as ropes, hats, and horses, also encourage this kind of social play.

- Think of the sandbox as providing an interesting social play center (particularly for younger children), and provide things to do together, such as a fleet of little cars or a good supply of pans and sturdy spoons and shovels.

- Stay alert and aware of what is going on to provide input and control in time when it is needed.

- Occasionally encourage more physically proficient children to teach less skilled children how to do something.

- Encourage children to help each other—push each other on the swing, for example.

- Develop play spaces so that complex and super play units are offered rather than simple ones.

- Offer outdoor sand, mud, and water play whenever possible. This encourages peaceful social interaction for lengthy periods of time.

- Offer large-group projects that involve doing something together, such as painting a large refrigerator box to make something to play in, or gardening. This isn't exactly play, but it's so much fun it feels like play to the children.

Negative Social Action

- Provide no focus for the play—let the children mostly just run around.

- Keep the children indoors so long that they are pent up and desperate for physical activity when they do get out.

- Sit idly by.

- Offer the same kind of large-muscle activities every day. This lack of variety breeds boredom and fighting.

- Store equipment in inaccessible places so that it's difficult to get out and hence will not be frequently used.
- Suggest competitive activities—who can run fastest, get there first, and so forth. This breeds ill feeling and hurt feelings.
- Encourage games with many rules. This baffles the younger children, increases frustration and reduces spontaneity and creativity.
- Permit the older, more powerful children to monopolize the equipment.

Appendix D

Websites Related to Early Childhood Education

Administration for Children and Families
370 L'Enfant Promenade SW
Washington, DC 20447
www.acf.dhhs.gov

American Academy of Pediatrics
141 Northwest Point Blvd.
Elks Grove Village, IL 60007-1098
www.aap.org/visit/contact.htm

American Montessori Society (AMS)
281 Park Avenue South, 6th Floor
New York, NY 10010-6102
(212) 358-1250
www.amshq.org/index.html

American Speech, Language and Hearing Association
10801 Rockville Pike
Rockville, MD 20852
Answer line: (888) 321-ASHA
Action Center: (800) 498-2071
www.professional.asha.org

Association for Childhood Education International (ACEI)
17904 Georgia Ave., Suite 215
Olney, MD 20832-2277
(800) 423-3563
www.acei.org

Association Montessori Internationale
410 Alexander Street
Rochester, NY 14607-1028
(716) 461-5920
www.ami.edu

Center for Disease Control
1600 Clifton Road
Atlanta, GA 30333
(404) 639-3311
(800) 311-3435
www.cdc.gov

Children's Defense Fund
25 E Street NW
Washington, DC 20001
(202) 628-8787
www.childrensdefense.org
e-mail: cdfinfo@childrensdefense.org

Council for Exceptional Children (CEC)
Division of Early Childhood (DEC)
1920 Association Drive
Reston, VA 22091-1589
(888) CEC-SPED
www.cec.sped.org
e-mail: service@cec.sped.org

High Scope Educational Research Foundation
600 N. River Street
Ypsilanti, MI 48198-2898
(734) 485-2000
www.highscope.org
e-mail: info@highscope.org

International Reading Association
800 Barksdale Rd., P.O. Box 8139
Newark, DE 19714-8139
(302) 731-1600
www.reading.org

National Association of Child Care Professionals
207 W. Main St., Suite 1
Christiansburg, VA 24073
(800) 537-1118
www.naccp.org
e-mail: admin@naccp.org

National Association for the Education of Young Children (NAEYC)
1509 16 th Street NW
Washington, DC 20036
(292) 232-8777 or (800) 424-2460
www.naeyc.org
e-mail: naeyc@naeyc.org

National Black Child Development Institute (NBCDI)
1023 15th St. NW, Suite 600
Washington, DC 20005-5493
(202) 387-1280
www.nbcdi.org
e-mail: moreinfo@nbcdi.org

National Head Start Association
1651 Prince St.
Alexandria, VA 22314
(703) 739-0875 or (703) 739-0878
www.nhsa.org

National Network for Child Care
North Carolina State University
P.O. Box 7606, 200 Ricks Hall
Raleigh, NC 27695-7606
(919) 515-8488
www.nncc.org

Zero to Three: National Center for Infants, Toddlers, and Families
2000 M Street, NW, Suite 200
Washington, D.C. 20036
(202) 638-1144
Oto3@zerotothree.org

◆ Index

Abandoned children, 208
ABC Inventory, 37
Abnormalities, genetic, 50–52. *See also* Atypical development; Special needs
Academic/conceptual activities, 237
Academic skills in kindergarten, 155
Acceptance, 195
Accidental/unidentified curriculum, 261
Accuracy, 142
Active learning, 243
Active Parenting (Active Parenting, Inc.), 212
Adcock, D., 114
Addiction, 57
Adoptive families, 208
African-Americans, books about, 274
Aftercare (birthing), 53
Age, school readiness and, 156, 159–160
Aggressive children, 114, 151
AIDS virus, 57
Ainsworth Strange Situation Test, 64
Alaskan Eskimos, books about, 274
Alerts, developmental, 153. *See also* Atypical development; Delays, developmental; Special needs
Alternate-day kindergarten, 158
American Academy of Pediatrics, 67
American Federation of Teachers (AFT), 11
American Heritage Dictionary, 167
America's Kindergartners, 156
Anecdotal recording methods, 22–24
Anti-bias curriculum, 123–124, 263–275

Anti-Bias Curriculum: Tools for Empowering Children (Derman-Sparks), 269, 273
Art projects, 118–119
Asians, books about, 274
Assessment, 2, 9–10, 37–38
Association for Childhood Education International (ACEI), 235
Associative play, 151
At-home observations, 84–87, 216–219
At-risk children, 56–58, 157
Attachment, 62, 79–80, 112
Attention-deficit disorder (ADD), 203–204
Attention-deficit hyperactivity disorder (ADHD), 203–204
Attention span, 122, 156, 203–204
Atypical development, 152–154, 203–205
Audio recording methods, 20–21
Autonomy, 78–79, 95, 239
Avoidant infants, 62

Babinski reflex, 56
Bank Street curriculum, 238–240
Bayley Motor Scales, 59
Behavior
  egocentric *versus* sociocentric, 193–194
  of kindergarten children, 155–156
  modification of, 204–205
  observation of, 1–4
  of preschool children, 122–123
  problem, 25–26, 113
  reflexive, 55
  symbolic, 77
  of toddlers, 82–83
Behaviorist educational approaches, 240–241
Behavior rehearsal, 242
Bereiter, Carl, 240

Birthing, 52–54
Blended families, 208
Blindness, 50, 69
Blink reflex, eye, 56
Blow, Susan, 154
Body/kinesthetic intelligence, 174
Brain development, of infants, 59–60
Bredekamp, S., 88, 107, 255–256
Breech births, 52

Cadiz, S. M., 116
Caldwell Preschool Inventory, 38
Campbell, B., 175
Canadian Child Care Federation, 57
Canned curriculum, 261
Capitalization, 144
Caregivers. *See* Infants; Toddlers
Carter, M., 79
Case studies, 37–39
Cassell Developmental Schedules, 38
Centration, 77
Cephalocaudal development, 58–59
Cerebral palsy, 56, 69
Cervix, dilation of, 53
Cesarean deliveries, 52
Chaining, 242
Chard, S., 256
Checklists, 34–36
Child care. *See* Out-of-home care
Child-child interactions, 112
Child Observation Record (High Scope Educational Research Foundation), 33
Children's privacy, 7
Child studies, 1, 39–42
Classroom
  management of, 6
  multiage, 195–196
  practices inventory for, 266–268
Clinton, William J., 65

Cognitive development
  of infants, 60–61
  of kindergarten children,
    138–140
  of preschool children, 106–110,
    112
  of primary grade children,
    171–176
  of toddlers, 76–77
Cognitively oriented High Scope
  curriculum, 243–244
Cohort effects, 40
Color, people of, 274–275.
    See also Cultural differences
Comments, supervisory, 19
Communications with families,
  224–229
Competition, 122
Componential intelligence, 172
Comprehension, 142
Comprehensive Identification
  Process, 37
Concrete operations (Piaget),
  138–139, 172
Conferences with parents,
  224–226
Confidentiality, 7, 114
Conflict, 113–114, 151
Contextual intelligence, 172
Control Theory in the Classroom
  (Glaser), 178
Controversial children, 195
Cooperative play, 151
Cooperative Preschool Inventory,
  37
Copple, C., 88, 107
Creative expression of preschool
  children, 118–119
*Creative Play Activities for Children
  with Disabilities* (Morris &
  Schultz), 275–276
Cretinism, 50
Critical comments, 19
Cross-sectional studies, 40
Cryer, D., 79–80, 89
Cultural differences
  curriculum and, 263–275
  in families, 207–209
  out-of-home care and, 69–70,
    89
  preschool children and,
    123–124
Curriculum, 5, 232–280
  anti-bias, 123–124, 263–275
  Bank Street approach to,
    238–240
  cognitively oriented High
    Scope approach to, 243–244

decisions on, 277–278
Direct Instruction approach to,
  240–243
emergent, 261–263
Froebel's kindergarten model
  of, 235–236
in infant programs, 65
literacy development in,
  245–254
Montessori method of, 235–238
project approach to, 256–261
special needs and, 275–277
teacher control of, 178–179
transformational, 255–256
*Curriculum Models and Early
  Childhood* (Goffin), 235
Cystic fibrosis, 50

Daily-living skills, 69, 237
Day care. *See* Out-of-home care
Deafness, 50
Delays, developmental, 56–57,
  275. *See also* Special needs
Delivery of babies, 53
Denver Developmental Screening
  Test, 37
Denver II (assessment), 38, 85
Derman-Sparks, L., 269, 273
*Developing Roots and Wings:
  Affirming Culture in Early
  Childhood Programs* (York),
  273
Development, 5
  alerts on, 153
  delays of, 56–57, 275. *See also*
    Special needs
  of infants, 58–63
  norms of, 39–42
Developmental Indicators for the
  Assessment of Learning, 37
*Developmentally Appropriate
  Practice in Early Childhood
  Programs* (Bredekamp &
  Copple), 88, 107
Developmentally appropriate
  practices, 264–265
*Development Characteristics of
  Children, Ages 4-6* (Georgia
  Department of Education),
  132–136
Dewey, John, 238
Diabetes, 50
Diaries of observations, 16–20
"Difficult" children, 113
Dilation and effacement, 53
Dinkmeyer, D., 212
Direct Instruction curriculum,
  240–243

Discipline, 89, 122
Discrimination training, 242
Diversity, 207–209. *See also*
  Cultural differences
Down syndrome, 50
Dramatic play, 22, 120, 293–294
Drug addiction, 57

Early Childhood Family Educa-
  tion (Minnesota Department
  of Education), 213–214
Early Childhood Longitudinal
  Study-K (ECLS-K), 155
Eckerman, C., 80
"Educarers," 81
Education of teachers. *See*
  Teachers
Education USA (1990), 196
Egocentric behavior, 193
Elkind, D., 116–117
Embalmed curriculum, 261
Embryos, 50
Emergent curriculum, 261–263
Emotional development. *See*
  Socioemotional development
Engelmann, Siegfried, 240
Engleman's Basic Concept
  Inventory, 38
English for Speakers of Other
  Languages (ESOL), 215
Entry age, school, 159–160
Environment
  of infant programs, 65–67
  in toddler programs, 89–91
Epilepsy, 50
Erickson, E., 151, 176
Erikson, E. H., 79
Ethnic differences. *See* Cultural
  differences
Evaluating programs, 281–288
Even Start, 100, 214–215
Event sampling, 25–28
Event tally, 5
Experiential intelligence, 172
Experiential learning, 243
Experimental research designs, 41
Extended families, 208
Eye blink reflex, 56
Eyer, D. W., 82

Factual comments, 19
Families, 157, 207–232
  communications with, 224–229
  diversity in, 207–209
  educational involvement of,
    209–211
  home visits to, 216–219
  literacy programs for, 214–216

meetings with, 229–231
parental skills in, 211–214
as program volunteers,
219–224
Family day-care homes, 87–88
Fears of children, 78, 194–195
Feedback, 122
Femininity, 114
Fertilization, 50
Field experiences, 10–13
Fine motor development, 76
Floor Time: Tuning in to Each Child
(Greenspan), 117–118
Fluency, 142
Follow-Through funds, 2
Frames of Mind: The Theory of
Multiple Intelligences
(Gardner), 172–176
Frank, Lawrence, 39–40
Freud, Sigmund, 238
Friendships, 114, 151–152
Froebel, Friedrich, 154, 235–236
Functional writing, 144

Gardner, Howard, 172–176
Genetic abnormalities, 50–52
Georgia Department of
Education, 132–136
Gesell, Arnold, 39–40
Gifts, Froebel's kindergarten
model of, 235–236
Glaser, William, 178
Goffin, S. G., 235
Gonzalez-Mena, J., 82
Gopnik, A., 60–61
Gordon, Thomas, 212
Government-subsidized child
care, 100
Greenman, J., 90
Greenspan, Stanley, 117–118
Gross motor development, 76
Group dramatic play, 120
Guided reading, 246–249
Guided writing, 250

Hall, G. Stanley, 39–40
Hand dominance, 132
Hand-eye coordination, 76
Handicapped children. *See* Special
needs
Handwashing, 89
Harm, T., 91
Hattiesburg, Mississippi, Public
School District, 35
Head Start, 2, 100, 218, 240, 246
Health
eye checks and, 169
of families, 221

infant out-of-home care and,
67–68
of kindergarten children,
155–156
of preschool children, 105–106
Hemophilia, 50
High Scope Educational Research
Foundation, 33, 179, 186,
243–244
Hispanics, books about, 274
Homes
observations in, 84–87
play centered on, 293–294
visits to, 216–219
Hyperactivity, 156, 203–204

Illinois Test of Psycholinguistic
Abilities, 38
Improving America's Schools Act
of 1994, 214
Impulse control, 239
Impulsive children, 114
Including All of Us: An Early
Childhood Curriculum About
Disability (Project Inclusive),
273
Independence in toddlers, 79
Independent reading, 249
Independent writing, 250
Individualized Education Program
(IEP), 39
Individualized Family Service Plan
(IFSP), 39, 125
"Industry *versus* inferiority"
conflict, 151, 176
Infant and Toddler Spot
Observation Scale, 65
Infants, 49–74
at-risk, 56–58
birth of, 52–54
brain development of, 59–60
cognitive development of, 60–61
evaluating programs for,
281–288
language development of, 61–62
newborn, 54–56
out-of-home care of, 63–71
physical development of, 58–59
prenatal effects on, 50–52
socioemotional development
of, 62–63
Infant/Toddler Environment Rating
Scale, 88–89
Infectious diseases, 67
Informational writing, 143
Insecurely attached infants, 64
Insurance, liability, 11
Integrated curriculum, 251–254

Intellectual development of
preschool children, 106–110,
112
Intelligence, 172–176
Interactional synchrony, 55, 62
Interactions, 24–25, 187–189
Interactive writing, 250
International Reading Association
(IRA), 245–246
Interpersonal intelligence, 174
Interviewing, 25
Intrapersonal intelligence, 174
Inventory, practices, 266–268

Jewish Family and Children's
Service Agency of Boston, 57
Johnson, Lyndon B., 2
Jones, E., 261
Journals, 16–20, 41
Justificatory comments, 19

Katz, L., 256
Kentucky Education Reform Act
of 1990, 196
Kindergarten, full-day *vs.* half-
day, 158
Kindergarten Checklist
(Hattiesburg, Mississippi,
Public School District), 35
Kindergarten children, 131–166
atypical development of,
152–154
cognitive development of,
138–140
curriculum model for, 235
description of, 155–157
history of kindergarten and, 154
literacy development of,
140–150
physical development of,
132–138
preschool as preparation for,
126
programs for, 157–164
socioemotional development
of, 150–152
Kuhl, P. K., 60–61

Labor (birthing), 53
Language development
High Scope curriculum and,
243
of infants, 61–62
of kindergarten children,
139–140, 144
of preschool children, 110–112
special needs and, 69
of toddlers, 77–78, 94

Large muscle play, 295–296
Learning, 180–186, 243
Learning-disabled children, 203
Lesch-Nyhan syndrome, 50
Liability insurance, 11
Likert scale, 32–33
Literacy development, 214–216,
    245–254
    guided reading in, 246–249
    integrated curriculum in,
        251–254
    of kindergarten children,
        140–150
    shared reading in, 250–251
    writing in, 247–251
Literature, 144
Logical/mathematical intelli-
    gence, 172
Logs of observations, 16–20
Longitudinal studies, 40
Lovell, P., 91

Mainstreaming, 275. *See also*
    Special needs
Management, classroom, 6
McCracken, Janet Brown, 273
McKay, G., 212
Medical regulations, 13
Meetings with families, 229–231
Memory, 77
Mental retardation, 50. *See also*
    Special needs
Methods of observation, 7–9
Metropolitan Readiness Tests,
    37–38
Minnesota Association for
    Early Childhood Teacher
    Education, 266
*Minnesota Early Childhood
    Indicators of Progress,* 100
Mixed age classrooms, 195–196
Modeling, 242
Montessori method, 235–238
Moro reflex, 56
Morris, L. R., 275–276
Mother-child attachment, 79–80,
    112
Motor development
    in infants, 58–59
    of preschool children, 100–105
    special needs and, 69
    in toddlers, 76
Multiage classrooms, 195–196
Multicultural curriculum,
    263–275
Multicultural issues, 70. *See also*
    Cultural differences

Multiethnic Children's Literature
    (Ramirez & Ramirez), 273
Multiple intelligences, 172–176
Music, 118–119
Musical/rhythmic intelligence,
    174
Mutism, selective, 152–153

Narrative writing, 143
National Association for the
    Education of Young Children
    (NAEYC), 9–10, 12, 186–187,
    235, 242, 245–246
National Association of
    Elementary School
    Principals, 196
National Board of Professional
    Teaching Standards, 45
National Council for the
    Accreditation of Teacher
    Education (NCATE), 11
National Council of Child Health
    and Human Development,
    64
National Education Association
    (NEA), 11
National Headstart Association,
    246
National Network for Child Care,
    75, 83
Native Americans, books about,
    274
Naturalist intelligence, 174
Neglected children, 195
Neglected classification, 25
Neonatal intensive care units,
    56
Newborns, 54–56
Newsletters, 224–226
New Standards Literacy
    Committee, 140
Nimmo, J., 261
Nonintrusive assessment, 2
Nonparental volunteers, 222
Norms, 39–42, 58–59
Nuclear families, 207
Number concepts, 243–244
Nutrition programs, 106

Observation, 1–10
    in assessment, 9–10
    children's privacy and, 7
    in day-care settings, 88–96
    definition of, 1–4
    in family day-care homes,
        87–88
    in homes, 84–87

methods of, 7–9. *See also*
    Recording methods
purpose of, 4–6
Occupations, Froebel's
    kindergarten model of,
    235–236
Ohio State University Literacy
    Collaborative, 246
Open houses for families,
    229–231
Optimum periods, 60
Oral language, 139–140
Orientations for families, 229–231
Outdoor play, 294–296
Out-of-home care
    controversy about, 64
    with cultural differences, 69–70
    environment for, 65–67
    government-subsidized, 100
    health problems and, 67–68
    for infants to 16 months old,
        65
    special needs and, 68–69
    staff training for, 70–71
    toddlers and, 87–96

Pairing children, 114
Paley, V. G., 114, 151
Palmar grasp reflex, 55
Parental leave policies, 65
Parental skills, 211–214
Parent Effectiveness Training
    (Gordon), 212
Parent-teacher relations, 89, 123,
    204–205. *See also* Families
Participation, 10–13
Pavan, B. N., 196
Peabody, Elizabeth Palmer, 154
Peabody Picture Vocabulary Test,
    38
Peer group acceptance, 195
People of color, books about,
    274–275
Performance assessment system,
    42–43
Permission requirements, 7–9
Perry Preschool Project, 40
Phenylketonuria (PKU), 50
Phillipsen, L., 89
Physical development
    of infants, 58–59
    of kindergarten children,
        132–138
    of preschool children, 100–105
    of primary grade children,
        168–171
    of toddlers, 76, 91

Physical environment
    of infant programs, 65–67
    in primary classrooms, 176–186
    in toddler programs, 89–91
Piaget, Jean, 77
    cognitive curricula and, 243
    conservation and classification
        tasks of, 191
    infant cognitive development
        and, 60–61
    intellectual development and,
        106–107
    on kindergarten children,
        138–139
Placenta, birth of, 53
Plan-Do-Review process, High
    Scope, 179, 186, 243–244
Planned variation models, 2
Play
    dramatic, 22, 293–294
    of kindergarten children,
        151–152
    outdoor, 294–296
    of preschool children, 113,
        120–121
    pretend, 93–94
    of primary grade children,
        176–186
    spatial arrangements for,
        89–91, 289–292
    of toddlers, 80–81
Playground Improvement Rating
    Scale, 91, 289–292
Play in the Lives of Children (Rogers
    & Sawyers), 120
Popular children, 195
Popular classification, 25
Portfolio process, 10
Portfolios of observations, 42–46
Practices, developmentally
    appropriate, 264–265
Practices inventory, classroom,
    266–268
Practicum, 11–13
Prejudice, 123–124
Pre-labor, 53
Premature infants, 56
Prenatal effects on infants, 50–52,
    211–212
Preoperational stage (Piaget),
    77
Preschool children, 99–130
    behavior of, 122–123
    creative expression of, 118–119
    cultural differences and,
        123–124
    health and safety of, 105–106

intellectual development of,
    106–110
kindergarten transition of, 126
language development of,
    110–112
motor development of,
    100–105
play of, 120–121
socioemotional development
    of, 112–118
with special needs, 125
teacher education for, 126–127
Pretend play, 93
Prevention, 221
Primary grade children, 167–206
    atypical development of,
        203–205
    cognitive development of,
        171–176
    developmental characteristics
        of, 200–203
    physical development of,
        168–171
    socioemotional development
        of, 193–200
    technology and, 186–193
    work and play of, 176–186
Print-sound code, 141–142
Privacy, 7, 114
Problem behaviors, 25–26
Progress, 5
Progressive Education Movement,
    256
Project approach, 118–119,
    256–261
Project Inclusive, 273
Prompting, 242
Prosocial behavior, 122
Proximodistal development, 59
Prudential comments, 19
Psychosis, childhood, 50
Public Law 94-142, 125, 203, 275
Public Law 99-457, 125
Punctuation, 144

Quasi-experimental studies, 41

Racial differences. *See* Cultural
    differences
Ramirez, Gonzalo, 273
Ramirez, Jan Lee, 273
Random sampling, 26
Rating scales, 32–33
Readiness for school, 156
Reading, 141–143, 246–251
Reciprocal shaping, 55
Reconstituted families, 208

Recording methods, 15–48
    anecdotal, 22–24
    audio, 20–21
    case studies as, 37–39
    checklists as, 34–36
    child studies as, 39–42
    event sampling as, 25–28
    journals and logs as, 16–20
    portfolios as, 42–46
    rating scales in, 32–33
    running record as, 28–32
    sociometric techniques for,
        24–25
    video, 21–23
Reflection, 187–189
Reflective diaries of observations,
    16–20
Reflexive behavior, 55
Reggio Emilia, Italy, curriculum,
    258–261
Reinforcement, 241
Rejected children, 195
Rejected classification, 25
Report card, kindergarten,
    146–148
Report writing, 143
Resistant infants, 62
Respect for families, 221
Retention, kindergarten, 160
Reversal of operations, 77
Rogers, C. S., 120
Rooting reflex, 55
Rosegrant, T., 255–256
Rule violations, 122
Runaway children, 208
Running records, 28–32

Safety and health, 105–106
Sanctuary, child-care center as,
    116
Sawyers, J. K., 120
Scales, rating, 32–33
School readiness, 156
Schultz, L., 275–276
Schurz, Margaret Meyer, 154
Screening instruments, 37–38
Securely attached infants, 62
Segal, M., 114
Selective mutism, 152–153
Self-concept, 78, 112, 239
Self-directed learning, 180–186
Self-discipline, 122
Sensorial activities, 237
Sensorimotor development, 77,
    91
Sequencing, 242
Sequential studies, 40–41

Seriation, 243
Sex chromosome disorders, 50
Sexual identity, 114, 157
Shaping, 55, 241
Shared reading, 250–251
Shared writing, 249
Sickle cell anemia, 50
Single-parent families, 208
Smiles, 55, 62
Social environment of infant
    programs, 65–67
Social interaction, 24–25,
    293–296
Social referencing, 78
Social reform efforts, 1
Sociocentric behavior, 193–194
Socioemotional development
    of infants, 62–63
    of kindergarten children,
        150–152
    of preschool children, 112–118
    of primary grade children,
        193–200
    of toddlers, 78–80, 95
Sociometric techniques, 24–25
Southern Association of Children
    Under Six (SACUS), 9
Spatial arrangements, 89–91
Spatial relationships, 244
Special needs
    curriculum and, 236–237,
        275–277
    out-of-home care and, 68–69
    preschool children with, 125
Speech. *See* Language
    development
Spelling, 144
Staff development, 6, 70–71,
    126–127. *See also* Teachers
*Stages of Sensori-Motor Cognitive
    Development* (Piaget), 61, 77
Stanford-Binet Intelligence Scale,
    38
Startle reflex, 56
Stepping reflex, 56
Sternberg, Robert, 172
Stimulation, 60
Stress Test for Children (Elkind),
    116–117
Student teachers. *See* Teachers
Subfamilies, 208
Substitute families, 208

Sucking reflex, 55
Sudden Infant Death syndrome
    (SIDS), 56
Supervisory comments, 19
Surveying, 25
Symbolic behavior, 77
Symbolic thought patterns, 139
Synchrony, interactional, 55
*Systematic Training for Effective
    Parenting* (Dinkmeyer &
    McKay), 212

Tay-Sachs syndrome, 50
Teachers
    field training of, 10–13
    infant care and, 70–71
    of kindergarten children,
        160–164
    for preschool children,
        120–121, 126–127
    relations with parents, 89, 123,
        204–205. *See also* Families
    for toddlers, 81–82
Technology in primary classroom,
    186–193
Temper tantrums, 78, 83
Thalassemias, 50
Time concepts, 244
Time-sampling evaluation
    technique, 281–288
Toddlers, 75–98
    at-home observation of, 84–87
    behavior of, 82–83
    child-care observation of,
        88–96
    cognitive development of,
        76–77
    evaluating programs for,
        281–288
    family day-care observation of,
        87–88
    language development of,
        77–78
    parent-teacher relations and,
        83–84
    physical development of, 76
    play of, 80–81
    socioemotional development
        of, 78–80
    teacher preparation for, 81–82
Toileting, 12
Tonic neck reflex, 56

Toxic substances, exposure to, 50
Training
    discrimination, 242
    in infant care, 70–71
Transformational curriculum,
    255–256
Triacrchic model of intelligence,
    172
Trial and error learning, 76
Turn-taking, 62

U.S. Department of Education,
    155
U.S. Department of Labor, 99–100
Unidentified curriculum, 261

*Valuing Diversity: The Primary
    Years* (McCracken), 273
Verbal/linguistic intelligence, 174
Viability of fetus, 50
Videotaping, 6, 21–23
Violations of rules, 122
Visual/spatial intelligence, 174
Vocabulary, 78, 143, 144
Volunteers, program, 219–224
Vygotsky, Lev, 106–107

War on Poverty, 2
Webbing, 5
Websites on early childhood
    education, 297–298
Wechsler Preschool and Primary
    Scale of Intelligence, 38
Weikart, David, 243
Welfare, 100
Wide-stance toddling
    locomotion, 76
Women's Bureau of U. S.
    Department of Labor, 99–100
Work in primary classrooms,
    176–186
Work Sampling System, 42–43
Writing
    kindergarten children and,
        141
    in literacy development,
        247–251
    preschool children and, 111

York, Stacey, 273
You Can't Say You Can't Play
    (Paley), 114, 151